YALE UNIVERSITY PRESS
PELICAN HISTORY OF ART

FOUNDING EDITOR: NIKOLAUS PEVSNER

WOLFGANG LOTZ

ARCHITECTURE IN ITALY
1500–1600

WITH AN INTRODUCTION BY DEBORAH HOWARD

Wolfgang Lotz

Architecture in Italy 1500–1600

Introduction by Deborah Howard

Yale University Press
New Haven and London

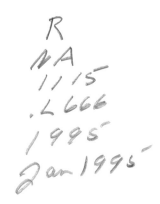

This book was previously published as Part Two of *Architecture in Italy 1400–1600* by Penguin Books Ltd, 1974

This edition first published by Yale University Press, 1995

10 9 8 7 6 5 4 3 2 1

Set in Linotron Ehrhardt by Best-Set Typesetter Ltd, Hong Kong and printed in Hong Kong through World Print Ltd

Translated by Mary Hottinger

Designed by Kate Gallimore

Library of Congress Cataloging-in-Publication Data

Lotz, Wolfgang, 1912–1981
    Architecture in Italy, 1500–1600 / Wolfgang Lotz: revised by Deborah Howard.
        p. cm. – (Pelican history of art)
    Includes bibliographical references and index.
    ISBN 0-300-06468-3 (cloth). – ISBN 0-300-06469-1 (paper).
    1. Architecture, Renaissance-Italy. 2. Mannerism (Architecture)-Italy. 3. Architecture-Italy. I. Howard, Deborah. II. Title. III. Series.
    NA1115.L666 1995
    720' – 945'09031 – dc20   95-9124
                                                    CIP

Title-page: Antonio da Sangallo the Elder: Montepulciano, Madonna di S. Biagio, begun 1518

To the Memory of
Piero Tomei
and
Costantino Baroni

Contents

Introduction

by Deborah Howard

LOTZ'S TEXT: ITS ACHIEVEMENT AND SIGNIFICANCE

THE NEW EDITION

This book was first published in 1974 as the second half of *Architecture in Italy 1400–1600*, the volume written by Wolfgang Lotz in collaboration with Ludwig H. Heydenreich, the latter contributing the account of the earlier century. The book was commissioned by Sir Nikolaus Pevsner as part of the ambitious series, *The Pelican History of Art*, but has long been out of print. Apart from Peter Murray's two introductory surveys, *The Architecture of the Italian Renaissance* and *Renaissance Architecture*, no other straightforward, factual account of this period of Italian architecture is currently available in any language.[1] The usefulness and stature of the present book was immediately recognized; as one reviewer remarked, 'With its lucid organization and ample coverage the book has established itself already as far and away the best treatment of the subject in any language.'[2]

It could, indeed, be argued that no-one today could write such a book. When Heydenreich and Lotz were preparing their text, it was still technically possible for them to read every article or book that appeared on the subject, whereas the proliferation of scholarship since that time has made it a hopeless task for any one scholar to be an authority on the whole of Italy for the entire sixteenth century. It is for this reason that the present edition has been prepared with some apprehension, and a few remarks should be made at the outset to explain how the challenge has been faced.

It soon became clear that a full up-dating of the text would be an impractical task, without totally compromising the integrity of Lotz's original. This difficulty is immediately apparent in Lotz's opening chapter on Bramante, in which the Tempietto is regarded as the architect's first Roman work. This assumption is based on the inscription dated 1502 in the crypt. There is, however, no secure evidence that this date refers to any part of the structure above the crypt, and this writer agrees with Bruschi that the Tempietto itself is of a later date.[3] Such a conclusion would, however, require a complete rewriting of Lotz's text, because of the pivotal role of the Tempietto in his account of the architect's Roman career. In any case, the question remains controversial – Hubertus Günther, for instance, has even claimed a date before 1502.[4] To complicate matters further, Bramante's Palazzo Caprini, known as the 'House of Raphael', is thought by Frommel to date from the start of Bramante's Roman career.[5]

Faced with such problems it has been decided to retain the original text unchanged as far as possible, correcting only obvious misprints and those minor factual errors which, we believe, the author would himself have regretted. No guarantee can be given that every such mistake has been detected, because of the wide scope of the book. In cases where it is felt that recent scholarship renders Lotz's version

of events seriously misleading, this is indicated by asterisked endnotes for the guidance of unsuspecting readers (p. 190). The revision has been based on Mary Hottinger's translation rather than on the German original, because the English version was prepared in close collaboration with the authors. Lotz's own command of English allowed him to ensure that his meaning was accurately represented, and the translation is admirably clear and fluent.

Because of the profusion of new work, it would not have been practical to attempt a complete bibliography of all literature on the subject since the publication of Heydenreich and Lotz's volume in the early seventies. While bibliographical completeness was inevitably a futile quest, the selection of certain articles alone would have been invidious. For this reason the supplementary bibliography is restricted to books alone, omitting all articles, book reviews and unpublished dissertations, however significant.[6]

WOLFGANG LOTZ (1912–1981)

Born in Heilbronn, Germany, Wolfgang Lotz studied Law at Freiburg and the History of Art at Munich.[7] His Ph.D. thesis on Vignola's architecture was prepared under the guidance of Ludwig Heydenreich, and he gained his doctorate at Hamburg in 1937. He spent the next five years at the Kunsthistorisches Institut in Florence, until he was called up to serve in the German Army. He was briefly taken prisoner in 1945, and in the following year became deputy director of the Zentralinstitut für Kunstgeschichte in Munich, under his former professor Ludwig Heydenreich. In 1952 he moved to the United States, succeeding Richard Krautheimer as professor at Vassar College, and later in 1959 inheriting Krautheimer's chair at the Institute of Fine Arts at New York University. From 1962 until his retirement in 1980 Lotz was director of the Biblioteca Hertziana (Max-Planck Institut) in Rome, where he expanded the institution to establish its role as a major international focus of research in Italian art and architecture, and a magnificent resource for scholars of all nationalities.

Lotz's cosmopolitan career put him in an ideal position to undertake a work of synthesis such as the present volume. He was able to draw on the full range of new work emanating from Germany, Italy and the English-speaking world, as well as older publications, and to reconcile the contrasting approaches of each culture in an entirely personal way. He was impatient with the philosophical approach of pre-war German art-history, but gained a scholarly rigour and precision from his Germanic origins. From his years in Italy he derived a close familiarity with the buildings he describes so eloquently in this book, and he exchanged ideas freely with Italian scholars as well as foreigners.

Most of Lotz's published work appeared in the form of scholarly articles and book reviews, even though some of his major articles, such as 'Die ovalen Kirchenräume des Cinquecento' (*Römisches Jahrbuch für Kunstgeschichte*, VII, 1955, pp. 7–99), were in effect book-length monographs.[8] Generous with his time, as with his ideas, he was easily distracted because, as James Ackerman perceptively observed, 'he had inexhaustible strategies for finding pleasure in people and places.'[9] The contribution to *Architecture in Italy 1400–1600* was Lotz's only major book, but we are fortunate that in 1975 he agreed to the publication of a selection of his best articles, translated into English, with a full bibliography of his writings, in the volume entitled *Studies in Italian Renaissance Architecture* (MIT Press, Cambridge, Mass. and London, 1977). The creative side of Lotz's personality emerges more clearly from these shorter articles, unconstrained by the specific demands of the *Pelican History of Art* series.

LOTZ AS AN HISTORIAN

Any work of historical synthesis requires the imposition of a pattern on the material, in order to make the vast mass of information digestible and to organize it coherently. Faced with this task, rigorous scholars such as Lotz and Heydenreich aspired to express an unbiased, objective truth. In our post-structuralist age, when objectivity seems a hopeless and even irrelevant ambition, it is easy to find fault with this goal. Nevertheless, it was consistent with the thinking of Pevsner himself, as with other architectural contributors to the *Pelican History of Art* series such as Sir John Summerson, that a coherent line of stylistic development could and should be traced, based on the artistic authority of certain key figures and their buildings.[10] The monolithic coherence of modernist theory encouraged the tracing of similarly dominant strategies in the architecture of the past.[11] Just as Pevsner claimed a single stylistic genealogy from Pugin to Modernism,[12] so, too, Summerson recounted the unfolding of British architecture in terms of its grasp of the doctrine of the classical orders.

Lotz himself would not have consciously formulated such a discourse, but his writings suggest that he, too, was influenced by this prevalent attitude towards style. For a start, the legacy of Vasari was a powerful one. According to the familiar layout of the *Vite*, Italian Renaissance art and architecture evolved in three, century-long periods, the third of which, Vasari's period of 'maturity', forms the subject of Lotz's account. Like Vasari, Lotz sees Bramante's Roman period as the source of inspiration for the generations that followed. According to the Vasarian model, this new Roman style, rooted in the authority of antiquity, then spread centrifugally around Italy, as other provincial centres learned the discipline of the orders. This book offers a similar view:

> The new style did not at first take hold in Florence and the north of Italy; it was introduced there by Bramante's and Raphael's pupils. Obviously, this style must be regarded as Bramante's personal achievement. (p. 23)

Lotz's years at the Hertziana naturally endowed him with a Roman perspective, but he made serious and valuable attempts to come to terms with other regional centres. Despite this, however, the centre of gravity remains firmly fixed in Rome. In Mantua, Lotz claims (on p. 82), 'Giulio Romano's late work is not free of a touch of provincialism.' The whole of southern Italy is missing altogether, and the accounts of northern centres such as Milan and Venice are extremely sketchy.

Moreover, as in the case of Vasari's *Vite*, it is the major architects who dominate the narrative. In their organizational scheme, Heydenreich and Lotz evolved an ingenious compromise between chapters focusing on individual artists and those based on regional centres. The regional chapters, however, tend to be repositories for lesser figures, rather than attempting to define the artistic unity of a geographical entity such as a princely state. Despite the book's focus on the architect, one of those most admired in his own time, Girolamo Genga, the author of the important Villa Imperiale near Pesaro, is missing altogether, though included in Vasari's *Vite*, presumably because he did not fit neatly into any regional chapter. Architects such as Scamozzi, whose careers came too late for Vasari's scrutiny, are given only slight attention by Lotz (except in the bibliography). Even Palladio, certainly the most enduringly influential architect of the whole period in international terms, is treated with tantalizing brevity, despite the fact that Lotz himself was the first non-Italian president of the organizing committee of the Centro Internazionale di Studi di Architettura 'Andrea Palladio' in Vicenza. Furthermore, Palladio's role in the book is to take up the Roman bâtons of Falconetto, Sanmicheli and Sansovino, at the expense of his stature as a scholar of antiquity or his sensitivity to the traditions of his own geographical region (p. 148).

The book focuses primarily on *built* architecture, rather than on ideas and theories. Utopian or unrealized schemes are rarely discussed, because the text is closely related to the selection of photographic images. The main exception is the list of proposals for St Peter's by Bramante's followers on pp. 24–5, which is a baffling one, in that it is virtually impossible to identify all the schemes in the list with known drawings or models. Despite this difficulty, it has been decided to leave the list in the text, in deference to Lotz's original.[13]

LOTZ AS A THEORIST

Lotz's method is pragmatic, flexible and empirical. He approaches each building in terms of the available evidence about it, rather than first constructing theories and seeking to demonstrate them through historical examples. He retains considerable detachment from Wittkower's influential *Architectural Principles in the Age of Humanism*, showing little interest in abstract principles and philosophical speculation, and he is cautious even about Wittkower's emphasis on the centralized church in the Renaissance. His approach is far closer to that of his admired colleague Richard Krautheimer, who recognized the long-established significance of centralized structures from late antiquity onwards for specific functions such as funerary, Marian and votive churches.[14] Lotz shrewdly observes that: 'However often round churches may appear in sketchbooks and paintings, actual centrally planned buildings are very rare' (p. 148).

Theoretical texts of the Renaissance seem to have excited

little enthusiasm from Lotz. The illustrated Vitruvius editions of Fra Giocondo (1511) and Cesariano (1521) are mentioned only in passing. Serlio's treatise is regarded with some exasperation, and even the account of Palladio's *Quattro libri* is brief and factual. Lotz's own theory of the orders seems to be based on Vignola's canonical *Regole* of 1562, and he approaches the use of the orders throughout the century according to quasi-Vignolan criteria. For instance, Bramante's Vatican Logge are described as following 'the usual sequence – Doric, Ionic, Corinthian' (p. 17), whereas the orders were not laid out in that order in any theoretical tract until the publication of Serlio's Fourth Book in 1537. No previous tradition rendered this 'the usual sequence', with the exception of the Colosseum. Similarly, in the discussion of Bramante's Palazzo Caprini, Lotz remarks that the Doric order is 'generally confined to the ground floor' (p. 23), whereas at this date the Doric order had rarely been used at all since antiquity.

Any departure from Vignolan correctness was seen by Lotz as heretical. Thus, the complexity and amibiguity of Sanmicheli's Palazzo Bevilacqua is said in the book to reveal 'the same "heresy" as can be seen in Peruzzi' (p. 69). The 'breach of the rule' in the three superimposed Corinthian orders of Sanmicheli's Palazzo Grimani in Verona is excused on account of the building's 'distinction and splendour' (p. 71). Yet Lotz seems unaware of the imposing Venetian precedents for superimposing Corinthian orders, such as Codussi's masterful Palazzo Loredan (now Vendramin-Calergi) and the Scuola Grande di San Rocco. Regarding Sansovino's Library in Venice, Lotz remarked that: 'For the first time in Venice, the classical orders were correctly applied' (p. 85). Yet this 'correctness' was not a pre-existing concept, but one that was expounded contemporaneously in Serlio's Fourth Book, published in 1537, the very year that the Library was begun. In other words, readers of Lotz's text today should be aware that the theoretical framework of architecture was unfolding gradually over the course of the century, and cannot be regarded as a consistent epistemological construct throughout the Cinquecento.

LOTZ'S CONCEPT OF STYLE

Since Lotz's work was conceived, style has come to be regarded increasingly as a mere descriptive framework rather than as an active creative force or even a mental set. Yet for Lotz, style was the essence of the artistic unity that united the buildings of Cinquecento Italy and differentiated them from other periods and places. He saw his task in the book to analyze this style and trace its development. Style is the privilege of 'high' art, and is propagated by the greatest artists of the age. It is transmitted by the influence of one architect upon another, a process which Lotz's remarkable visual memory enabled him to formulate supremely well. His article on Sansovino's Roman legacy, for example, has been of fundamental importance to later scholars, and the same sensitivity to precedence informs the whole text of the present book. By contrast, vernacular and traditional solutions rarely excite his interest.

Lotz uses the concept of the classical style and its various interpretations both as an organizational tool, to give a thread

to his narrative, and as a descriptive aid. The Bramantesque idiom acts as a filter through which he views other interpreters of the style: 'It is remarkable', he observes of Giulio Romano's house in Mantua, 'that Giulio has refrained in the piano nobile from using engaged columns and pilasters' (p. 81). Michelangelo's Porta Pia in Rome, one of the artist's last works, is so remote from Lotz's stylistic criteria that he admits finding it 'difficult' to analyze (p. 104). His own sympathies lie with orderly designs, and he is impatient with lack of discipline, even in the case of the Palazzo Borromeo in Pavia, the work of an architect – Pellegrini – whom he admired for his 'expert knowledge of architecture' and 'great organizational capacity' (p. 140).

Lotz's youthful research on Vignola seems to have left him with an intuitive sympathy for canonical, if inventive, classicism, whereas he remained uncomfortable with what he defined as 'mannerist' attitudes:

Peruzzi explored architectural ideas developed for St Peter's in theoretical studies without any idea of realizing them. This is the expression of an unmistakably mannerist attitude; a final and binding solution is evaded rather than sought, and intricacy seems more attractive than simplicity. In comparison, Bramante's effort to achieve simplicity, to create immediate comprehensibility in the forms and clarity in the relationships, stands out as a characteristic of the classical style. (p. 25)

As if to register this discomfort, Mannerism is rarely mentioned in the book.[15] Lotz even describes Giulio Romano's work without recourse to the concept, while recognizing what most would call mannerist traits in his work:

Both Giulio and Peruzzi show their knowledge of the canon of the orders but often employ quite heretical forms in the same building. Contemporaries admired as fertility of invention the surprise and shock imparted by this style, and its contradiction in terms (p. 76).

Later, Lotz contrasts Giulio's playful solecisms with the more deeply disturbing effect of Michelangelo's Laurenziana staircase:

His [Giulio's] bizarre ideas are meant to nonplus the observer in the same way as "black humour" does. But for Michelangelo the forces working in the stones are a parable of the tragedy of human life (p. 94).

LOTZ AS A CRITIC

The intertwining of history and criticism is still the principal challenge facing the art-historian today. For many scholars of Lotz's generation the task of elevating the discipline to a respectable academic subject seemed to demand the elimination of personal aesthetic responses. This tendency was perhaps more marked in the Anglo-American tradition, where the legacy of dilettantism still lurked, than among German scholars, for whom art history had an older-established academic respectability and scholarly basis.[16] Lotz was able to unite the rigour of German scholarship with the free expression of his own visual observations, a rare combination that allows this book to serve its indispensable role as an educated and eye-opening *cicerone*.

A strong visual emphasis pervades the whole book. The fact that its selection of photographic images has since rendered certain viewpoints and lighting effects canonical is a measure of the success of the book, rather than a defect in its conception. The emphasis on the interior, both in the writing and in the choice of illustrations, brings a most welcome third dimension to a subject that is too often treated two-dimensionally. For Lotz, space is an active, tangible entity, articulated by, but not represented in, walls, windows, vaults and columns. He is sensitive throughout to the effect of the buildings on the spectator, to the extent that there seems to be no need to explain who this viewer is intended to be. The spectator is Lotz himself, and hence also the reader to whom he conveys his responses. He does not engage with the intricate questions of defining the audience that beset the critical theories of today. He assumes a universal, timeless spectator.

Inevitably, some degree of subjectivity characterizes this procedure. For example, the emphasis on Bramantesque purity of form in Lotz's account makes architectural traditions that depend on colour and decorative richness seem provincial and retarded. 'The North Italian predilection for small-scale ornament and coloured incrustation', he claims, 'was an obstacle to the monumental style of Rome.' Here Lotz seems to hint at a modernist predilection for pure form that was shared by many sensitive critics of his generation. Yet this preference did not endear Palladio's art to him, and he seems almost to apologize for the attention given to that architect in the literature: 'It [Palladio's work] is curiously abstract', he observes; 'it can be visualized independently of its environment, and therefore lends itself to imitation. Many of his works conform to the present trend to smooth surfaces, right angles, and plain cubic forms' (p. 147). In other words, Lotz distrusts Palladio's popularity, though it was based on the very qualities that he seems to admire in so many other masters.

This introduction has focused on certain critical biases in the writing, but on the whole Lotz rarely allows these to intrude, merely describing and attempting to explain the salient features of each design. The use of occasional value-laden terms such as 'admirable' helps to convey his enthusiasm and to enliven the descriptive writing. The reader will not always share his sympathies: the present writer, for instance, is perplexed by his preference for Palladio's façade of San Francesco della Vigna over that of San Giorgio Maggiore. Yet Lotz's own visual exploration of the buildings he describes reveals his enjoyment of the subject as a whole.

LOTZ'S INFLUENCE

Given the limitations of length and format imposed by the *Pelican History of Art* series, it is remarkable how many of the subsequent developments in the study of Italian Renaissance architecture are foreshadowed in this volume. Lotz's awareness of questions of patronage pervades the whole volume, although he tends to offer more comment on these issues in the context of Papal Rome, where such observations are generated by his own familiarity and interest, than elsewhere. Nevertheless he never allows the creative personality of the architect to appear to be dominated by the character of his patronage. The patron is there to offer opportunities, rather than to control the artist's *Kunstwolle*. Lotz's treatment of the Counter-Reformation comes late in the book, and major political events such as the Sack of Rome attract little attention. On the other hand, Lotz's sensitivity to the full range of ecclesiastical commissions has already been mentioned. Few writers of his generation shared his concern for the specific functional requirements of individual churches. One could cite, for instance, his accounts of Pellegrini's San Sebastiano in Milan and Palladio's Redentore in Venice, both of which were votive churches built in response to the great plague of 1575–6.

Lotz was a pioneer in the field of urban history and in the Renaissance conception of civic space. This is most fully developed in his articles, but is apparent even in this book, for instance in his discussion of the urban projects of Popes Julius II and Leo X, and of Michelangelo's Campidoglio in Rome. The profusion of scholarly work on Italian Renaissance towns since that time is a fitting testimony to his inspiration. His sensitivity to interior space, by contrast, has found few echoes, except, perhaps, in the critical writing of Arnaldo Bruschi.

Finally, it is important, here, to acknowledge Lotz's fundamental and revealing work in the field of architectural drawing. Although he has little space in the present book to explore individual drawings, he consistently tries to account for design choices in the built architecture that he examines. In a series of important articles in the 1950s and 60s he focused on the opportunities offered to draughtsmen by the science of perspective, and on its ultimate rejection by Renaissance architects.[17] These essays helped to direct the attention of architectural historians back to the design process, inspiring a succession of scholarly studies of Renaissance architectural drawings.

STUDIES IN CINQUECENTO ARCHITECTURE SINCE 1973

GEOGRAPHICAL SCOPE

The bibliographical addendum at the end of this new edition will guide readers to specific works that can be used to update Lotz's narrative. Even at a glance, the list suggests certain dominant preoccupations in recent scholarship.[18] For example, the profusion of titles relating to Venice and the Veneto, as well as to Palladio in particular, indicates a fertile field of investigation. Although this to some extent reflects the present writer's own interest, the number of works cited in this area also helps to redress an imbalance in the scope of Lotz's original work. The enterprising activities of the Centro Internazionale di Studi di Architettura 'Andrea Palladio' are under-represented in the new bibliography because of the list's restriction to books alone, but the volumes of the Centro's *Bollettino* and, more recently, the *Annali di architettura* are rich in new research.[19] That Lotz himself was aware of the stature of such schemes as Sansovino's renewal of Piazza San Marco is evident from his articles;[20] yet in this book he blandly alludes to the 'classicism which is so characteristic of Venice and the terraferma' (p. 64) without any serious attempt to define or explain it. Regional studies devoted to areas to the south of Rome, too, allow us to address a gaping lacuna in Lotz's account, already mentioned earlier. The influence of Cesare De Seta has been crucial here, not only through his own writings on Naples, but also with the series of volumes on individual cities, *La città nella storia d'Italia*, many of them southern titles, published under his direction since 1980.

Regional studies have brought consequences, both positive and negative, to the study of this period. They have allowed a closer attention to vernacular solutions and to local materials, and have acted to some extent as a counter-balance to the dominance of style already observed in the work of Lotz and his peers (as well as to the concentration on Rome). Whereas style is seen as developing through time and transgressing regional boundaries, local tradition is synchronic rather than diachronic. At the same time, regional specialization has encouraged fragmentation and an intensification of Italian *campanilismo*. Only the greatest intellects of our time, such as Manfredo Tafuri, have invested their scholarly energies in more than one region of Italy.[21]

The biennial colloquia held at the Centre des Études Supérieures de la Renaissance at Tours offer a new dimension to the study of Italian sixteenth-century architecture, but their impact beyond the circle of participants themselves is hard to assess. The importance of these colloquia lies in the fact that they have enabled Italian architecture to be viewed in the context of developments elsewhere in Europe, even if, in the arrangement of the papers, the implication remains that Italy, and Rome in particular, is still seen as the fountainhead.[22] Perhaps only David Thomson's book *Renaissance Architecture: Critics, Patrons, Luxury* (Manchester, 1993) has dared to challenge this traditional standpoint.

TYPOLOGY

While post-modernist dissatisfaction with the Modern Movement and its claims to universality has fostered a growing interest in regional tradition, we can observe a nascent realization that the understanding of typologies, too, depends on a study of traditional solutions. Lotz's interest in the function of specific churches has already been mentioned, but even today there is still a reluctance to engage with medieval rather than classical precedent. Accessible general studies such as Braunfels's *Monasteries of Western Europe* should enable any student of the Renaissance to gain a sense of the individual traditions of specific religious orders, but only the Jesuits (who had no medieval history) have been studied in depth in the context of this period.[23]

Among typological studies there are a few areas in which notable advances have been made. In particular, the study of the art of fortification has yielded such seminal works as Simon Pepper's and Nicholas Adams's study of Sienese military architecture, and the proceedings of the 1982 Vicenza seminar on fortifications in the Veneto edited by Daniela Lamberini.[24] Similarly, with regard to Venice, the study of the Scuole Grande, made possible by Brian Pullan's pioneering historical investigation, has been transformed, thanks to work by Philip Sohm, Manfredo Tafuri and others.[25]

Books on villas have continued to proliferate, ranging from the Marxist analysis of Bentmann and Müller to Ackerman's examination of sixteenth-century villa literature.[26] Our knowledge of villa patronage has been enhanced by the studies of David Coffin and Howard Burns, among others;[27] and garden design has been brought into the forefront of the discourse through the works of Coffin, Lazzaro and Azzi Visentini.[28] These studies have acted as a much-needed counter-balance to the abstract preoccupation with harmonic proportion generated by Wittkower's *Architectural Principles*,[29] but because of the wealth and elevated status of most villa patrons this trend has also intensified the concentration on élite architecture. Surprisingly, in view of prevalent codes of political correctness, we still know little about women in villa life – even the remarkable involvement of the Duchess of Urbino in the building of the Villa Imperiale at Pesaro has attracted scant attention.[30]

Whereas the delights of villa architecture continue to fascinate scholars (and rightly so, in view of the huge influence of the villa on later architecture across Europe – and beyond), palaces are still a relatively neglected field in Cinquecento studies. The outstanding exception is Christoph Frommel's magisterial three volume study of Roman palaces. *Der römische Palastbau der Hochrenaissance*.[31] This is based on a detailed and painstaking examination of documentary and graphic sources, and is unrivalled for its accuracy and its judicious analysis of the evidence; it will be the fundamental reference work for many generations. Frommel's approach is unashamedly positivist and Vasarian, and his own, unspoken critical perspective is based on the degree of influence exerted by the most seminal designs, such as Bramante's 'House of Raphael'. There has so far been little attempt to interpret sixteenth-century palace architecture in a more social framework (on the lines, for instance, of Patricia Waddy's *Seventeenth-century Roman Palaces* (Cambridge, Mass. and London, 1990)); but notable advances have been made in, for example, the publication of Cortesi's text on the ideal cardinal's palace, Peter Thornton's examination of interiors and furnishings, and the volume of the Tours colloquium proceedings entitled *Architecture et vie sociale à la Renaissance*.[32]

PATRONAGE

Parallel to the gradual accumulation of typological studies in the past two decades has been the attention given to architectural patronage. It is now assumed that any serious monograph devoted to a single architect will explore architect-patron relationships, and patrons even receive monographs in their own right.[33] Such a major cultural leader as the Venetian Andrea Gritti (Doge from 1523 to 1538) was still so little known in the early seventies that he earned no mention from Lotz, yet today he is recognized as playing a crucial role in all the arts in Venice, including music, literature and painting as well as architecture.[34] By contrast, a recent biography of Julius II, disappointingly devotes little attention to his remarkable record as a patron of the arts.[35] Meanwhile, since the time of the early Marxist-inspired patronage studies, the limitations of the deterministic approach to understanding architecture have become more apparent. The architect-patron relationship may now be more usefully seen as a creative dialogue than as an instrument of guidance, and even control.

We have already noticed the reluctance of Renaissance scholars to examine medieval precedent. By contrast, we now have a far better understanding of the Renaissance's knowledge of antiquity than existed twenty years ago. Fundamental work has been carried out by Hubertus Günther, Howard Burns and Arnold Nesselrath on Renaissance drawings from the antique, and on the ways in which sixteenth-century ideals influenced draughtsmen's interpretation of the ruins.[36] Careful archaeological research has formed the basis for the computerised 'Census of Antique Works of Art and Architecture known to the Renaissance', based at the Bibliotheca Hertziana in Rome and the Warburg Institute in London, while the volume by Bober and Rubinstein on *Renaissance Artists and Antique Sculpture* offers some of the same material in book form.

THEORY

Meanwhile theoretical studies have transformed our understanding of the use of the classical orders in the sixteenth century. John Onians's courageous book, *Bearers of Meaning* (Princeton, 1988), polemically revisionist in approach, acted as a timely reminder that the orders were not suddenly resuscitated in Renaissance Italy but remained an element in architectural language throughout the Middle Ages. Inevitably, in a book of such wide scope, reviewers have disputed points of detail, and Onians's approach remains a controversial one; but the book's importance in bringing long accepted dogma into the arena of scholarly debate cannot be disputed. His reassessment of Serlio, in particular, seems to this writer to be of fundamental value to the field. The roles of both Vitruvius and Serlio can now be seen as both more profound and more complex than had hitherto been realized, thanks also to the pioneering studies of Rosenfeld, Fiore and Tafuri, among others.[37] Again in this case, two volumes emanating from the Tours symposia, *Les traités* and *L'emploi des ordres*, are rich sources of new observations.[38]

DRAWINGS

The importance of Lotz's own work on architectural drawing has already been mentioned, and the detailed study of drawings remains an important focus of study. The subject is skewed to some extent by the patchy nature of surviving collections of drawings, those by Palladio and the Sangallo family being by far the most numerous. Nonetheless it is still possible to unearth unknown drawings by architects whose graphic *œuvre* has been almost entirely lost.[39] Christoph Frommel and others are currently engaged in the publication of a catalogue of the surviving drawings of Antonio da Sangallo the Younger, of which the first volume has already appeared.[40] Howard Burns's detailed knowledge of the drawings of Palladio is still accessible only in isolated articles, but his writings demonstrate forcefully the value of drawings in penetrating the design process of the individual architect.[41]

TECHNOLOGY

The background and training of architectural historians plays a significant part in determining the direction of scholarship. Whereas most German, English and American scholars are trained as art historians, the Italians who specialize in the subject usually come from an architectural background (although one could, of course, cite exceptions to this generalization). It is therefore unsurprising that most of the serious study of technical and conservation issues is carried out by Italian researchers, usually in connection with the practical investigation of buildings to be recorded or restored. Some of these researches have yielded extremely interesting results: for example, recent restorations of works by Raphael and his contemporaries in Rome.[42] The lesson that close examination of the fabric can transform our view of familiar buildings is a salutory one. The usual view of the sixteenth century as a period in which theory and ideas were more important than technical virtuosity needs careful reassessment.[43]

METHODOLOGY

Despite such areas of relative neglect, scholars today are faced with a profusion of published secondary material, which becomes even more daunting when the mass of literature relating to the broader cultural context is added. Moreover, architecture has been brought into the arena of public debate, not least through the organization of ambitious exhibitions, especially in Italy. Conferences have encouraged the exchange of ideas, but have also given credence to a wider range of standpoints. Both exhibition catalogues and conference proceedings are often presented as multi-faceted, open-ended anthologies, rather than as consistently argued themes.

The tendency in the study of Italian Renaissance architecture towards dispersal into discrete regional units has already been mentioned. The past two decades, however, have also seen a growing pluralism in approach and methodology in the study of the history of art. For many scholars Marxist aesthetics and Anglo-German positivism no longer seem adequate frameworks for analyzing the complexities that are emerging from new research. Documents and graphic evidence can no longer be taken at face value, but must be carefully deconstructed; architecture can be examined as a semiotic system, as a mediation between utopian theory and reality, or as a phenomenological construct; or it can be dissolved into a series of 'readings' depending on the 'gaze' of the individual viewer.[44]

While the bulk of recent scholarship in the field of sixteenth-century Italian architecture remains methodologically cautious and specialized, ambitious attempts have been made to challenge clichéed assumptions – one could cite, for instance, the penetrating analysis of classicism by Tzonis and Lefaivre, or Hersey's more speculative interpretation of the orders, as well as Onians's book already mentioned earlier.[45] Yet, significantly, none of these works relates specifically to the Cinquecento. There are no equivalents in this period to the radical, theoretical writings of Mark Jarzombek, Charles Burroughs, or Christine Smith on fifteenth-century themes.[46] While such approaches can sometimes encourage a dense and jargon-ridden style and a disturbingly non-visual approach, nonetheless they raise fundamental issues which deserve serious debate.

Advances in other disciplines offer promising avenues for architectural exploration. Particularly apposite is recent anthropological work on the role of tradition, ritual theory, and the use of public and private space.[47] Ways of perceiving and representing space, a potent instrument of political control and dramatic effect, are still chiefly the preserve of cartographers and geographers (or of historians of Quattrocento painting).[48] The gulf between vernacular and 'high' architecture is rarely bridged – a notable contribution in this line is Ennio Concina's illuminating work, *Venezia nell'età moderna* (Venice, 1989). Temporary and festive architecture merits more research within the context of architectural activity as a whole.[49] Women's studies have so far hardly encroached on the field at all, and the opening up of the subject to non-European culture is still in its infancy – here, too Concina has done pioneering work.[50] As already mentioned, technology and the role of science in the design process remain under-researched areas.

Finally, the field has much to learn from the growing body of scholarship devoted to print culture. This was the age of 'Renaissance self-fashioning', to adopt Stephen Greenblatt's now familiar term. As Greenblatt remarked, 'in the sixteenth century there appears to be an increased self-consciousness about the fashioning of human identity as a manipulable, artful process'.[51] Greenblatt's observation was made in the context of the study of English literature, but the concepts may with some validity be applied to Italy too. The authority of the printed architectural treatise has become a commonplace, but how this epistemological spectrum interacted with the design process is not yet well defined, except in terms of the simple matching of motifs. Who read treatises, and how were their ideas applied? What was the role of the manuscript treatise after the arrival of printing? Did the ideas in treatises precede or follow built architecture? To what extent can one envisage the existence of a self-sufficient culture of idealized and purely theoretical ideology with little relationship to activity on the building site? And how far did printing provide a public relations service, to reinforce innovation and make it acceptable and comprehensible to the public?

CONCLUSION

The reality of this fragmentation in the study of Cinquecento architecture is evident from the growing number of books that are now anthologies of articles by numerous authors, rather than single-author works. It is becoming increasingly difficult for any one author to claim mastery of the whole field, and even the recent catalogue of the Venice exhibition, *The Renaissance from Brunelleschi to Michelangelo*, does not convey a single idea (the ostensible theme of 'representation' is only faintly sketched), so much as a range of possible interpretations.[52] The mass of material at our disposal, and the research facilities offered by new developments in information technology, can provide us with unlimited raw material, but few scholars have the knowledge or the intellectual agility to rise to this challenge. The legacy of the late Manfredo Tafuri remains an inspiring one. His ability to see architecture as part of 'deep' culture, without in any sense diminishing the achievements of the great masters, depended on his own familiarity with the *dramatis personae*, and above all on his profound understanding of their ideas. Few can hope to rival his rare combination of vision and wisdom.

A potential for confusion and disintegration is apparent; and it is in this hazardous and challenging context that the clarity and confidence of Lotz's account retains its value. The book serves as a rock on which scholars will continue to find a firm footing in a sea of opportunity, rimmed by ever-expanding horizons. His personal distaste for idiosyncracy and pluralism is evident from his concluding words:

> In the world created by God, Hell is the opposite of 'right being'; in the world of the architect, the 'bizzarrie' are the opposite of rule and order.

Foreword to the first edition

The volume is dedicated to the memory of two architectural historians whose studies, published more than thirty years ago, have remained exemplary, both for the methods applied and the factual content. Costantino Baroni (1905–56) built the sound foundation from which research on Lombard architecture of the Renaissance has since proceeded. Piero Tomei (1913–42) in his *L'Architettura del Quattrocento a Roma*, a brilliant synthesis of historical data and visual observations, gave critical definition to the Renaissance of Rome as Caput Mundi.

The period this book deals with is among the richest in the history of Italian architecture. A volume in the present series cannot but offer a selection which necessarily reflects personal preferences and limitations. The reader will inevitably miss buildings and architects that have intentionally or by oversight been omitted.

The preparation and writing of the volume took an unusually long span of time. Considerable parts of the text, especially Part One, were written some time ago. Thus more recent publications could only be incorporated in the Notes and the Bibliography; this holds true – to give only a few examples – for such important contributions as those of Howard Saalman to Brunelleschi, summed up in his edition of Manetti's Vita of the artist, or for the many valuable studies on Florentine palace architecture by Büttner, Bulst, Goldthwaite, and others. The outstanding publication of Count Leonello Ginori on Florentine palazzi appeared only when this book was in the press, as also the new critical edition of Filarete's Treatise on Architecture by Anna Maria Finoli and Liliana Grassi.

The volume could not have been written without the friendly assistance received from the directors and staffs of a great number of libraries, archives, museums, and other institutions. Besides their 'home institutes', the Zentralinstitut für Kunstgeschichte in Munich, the Kunsthistorische Institut in Florence, and the Bibliotheca Hertziana in Rome, the authors are particularly indebted to the Gabinetto dei Disegni of the Uffizi, the Castello Sforzesco in Milan, the Staatliche Graphische Sammlung in Munich, the Avery Library of Columbia University, the Institute of Fine Arts of New York University, the Metropolitan Museum of Art, and the Vatican Library.

Large parts of the text were written while the authors were Temporary Members of the Institute for Advanced Study. They are deeply grateful to the directors of the Institute and to their friend Millard Meiss for having been able to work at Princeton *procul negotiis ordinariis*.

Among the numerous colleagues and friends to whom the authors are indebted for beneficial advice and suggestions are James S. Ackerman, Renato Cevese, John Coolidge, Christoph L. Frommel, Howard Hibbard, Richard Krautheimer, Milton Lewine, Giuseppe Marchini, Henry A. Millon, Loren Partridge, Kathleen Garris Posner, Ugo Procacci, Marco Rosci, Piero Sanpaolesi, Klaus Schwager, John Shearman, Craig Hugh Smyth, Christof Thoenes, the late Rudolf Wittkower, and Franz Graf Wolff Metternich.

The difficult task of translating the German text into English was accomplished by Mrs Mary Hottinger. The authors feel that the queries and objections put to them by Mrs Hottinger frequently helped to clarify and even to correct their work.

Kathleen Garris Posner and Richard J. Tuttle took upon themselves the self-denying task of reading the galleys of Part Two. Their remarks resulted in many substantial improvements. Miss Sheila Gibson who prepared the line drawings as well as the co-editor, Mrs Judy Nairn, and Miss Susan Stow of the publisher's London office had an essential part in giving the book its final shape. Finally, the authors have to thank Sir Nikolaus Pevsner: they are fully and most gratefully aware that only because of his patience, encouragement, and wisdom could they reach their goal.

July 1972   Ludwig H. Heydenreich
                                              Wolfgang Lotz

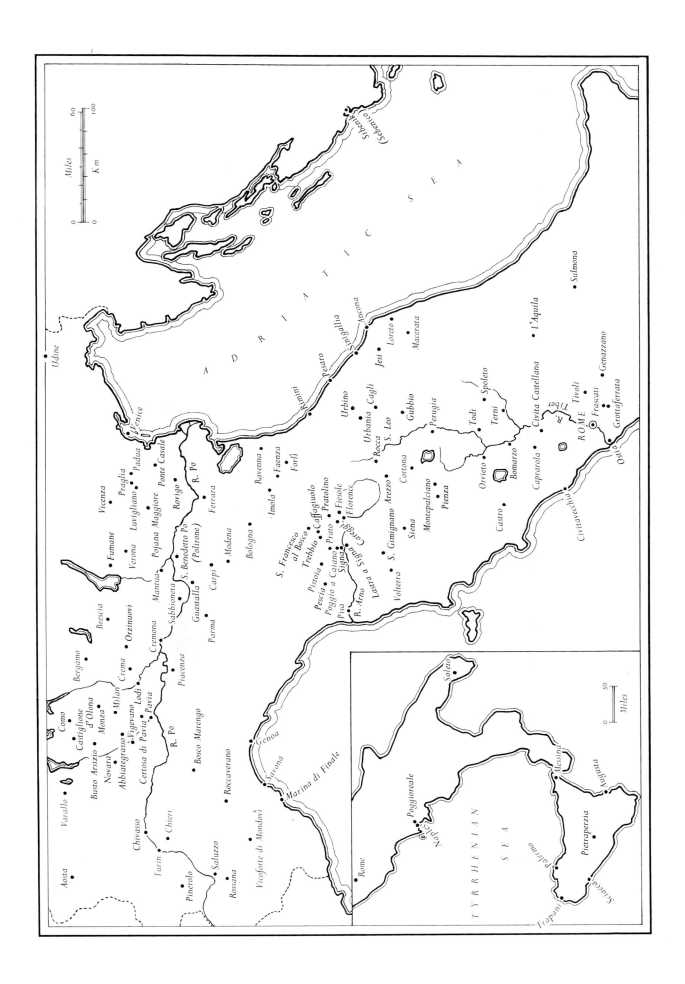

Wolfgang Lotz

Architecture in Italy 1500–1600

CHAPTER I

Classical Architecture in Rome: Bramante

'Bramante was the first to bring to light good and beautiful architecture which from the time of the ancients to his day had been forgotten.' With this remark Palladio justifies the inclusion of Bramante's Tempietto in Book IV of his Treatise on Architecture, which, with this sole exception, dealt with ancient temples only. The Tempietto of S. Pietro in Montorio, Rome, is the first classical building to have been erected in the city. Bramante himself worked later on schemes which were not only far bigger, but were also more important for future developments. But the rebuilding of St Peter's and the Belvedere Court of the Vatican were only completed several generations later; to identify Bramante's hand in them would mean a laborious work of discrimination between many superimposed strata. The same might be said of Raphael, who succeeded Bramante in the work on St Peter's; his buildings too, with a single exception, have suffered drastic alterations. Thus it is not by chance that Palladio includes a reproduction of the Tempietto as the only illustration of the new style; after 1550, when he was working on his treatise, most of the buildings representative of the new style had been so much altered that only the Tempietto was there to give an immediate insight into Bramante's work.

Yet there can be no doubt about the influence of Bramante and Raphael on Italian Cinquecento architecture. Their pupils, particularly Baldassare Peruzzi, Giulio Romano, Sansovino, Sanmicheli, and the Sangallo family, established and gave standing throughout Italy to the classical style, which had made its first appearance in Rome. It is fairly easy to define Bramante's and Raphael's influence, but when it comes to forming a judgement of the works which gave the new style its imprint, we have to rely largely on indirect sources, such as drawings made when work was in progress, account books and contemporary descriptions, buildings by pupils and disciples, and the illustrations in the various architectural treatises. This is especially true of the treatise of Sebastiano Serlio of Bologna, which contains in Book III, first published in 1540, in addition to the Tempietto, reproductions of Bramante's designs for St Peter's and the Vatican Court. Serlio's source was Baldassare Peruzzi, who worked on these buildings under Bramante and Raphael.[1] Any attempt to gain some idea of the work of Raphael and Bramante from this complex material must always make allowances for later corrections.[2]

Bramante's personality made a deep impression on his contemporaries. In his 'School of Athens', Raphael depicted his teacher in the guise of Euclid demonstrating the principles of geometry. Another pupil, Cesariano, relates: 'My teacher, Bramante, was an artist of the first order. He was also familiar with the work of the Italian poets. Though he

could not write, he had a wonderful memory and spoke with ease and eloquence. Originally court architect to Duke Ludovico Sforza, he later restored many papal buildings, especially under Julius II. And so he became the pre-eminent architect, rebuilder, and recreator of the basilica of St Peter.'[3]

THE TEMPIETTO OF S. PIETRO IN MONTORIO*

Bramante's Tempietto of S. Pietro in Montorio [1, 2], a peripteral rotunda, was a foundation of the King of Spain dated 1502 in the crypt, and erected on the traditional site of the martyrdom of St Peter. The rotunda in itself was not an entirely new conception: round buildings had existed in the Quattrocento.[4] But the Tempietto is the first Renaissance building in which the cella is surrounded in the ancient manner by a colonnade bearing an architrave. As in the ancient models, the intercolumnar intervals are equal all the way round; thus the arrangement of the columns gives no indication of where the altar stands inside the cella. There is yet another breach with Quattrocento tradition: the interior is too small for the visitor to feel that its actual purpose was to create a space. The interior diameter of the cella is only about 4.5 m. (14 feet 6 in.). About half the pavement is occupied by the altar and the altar steps, so that there is little room for any congregation beyond the officiating priest and the altar-servers. While the centrally planned buildings of the previous period were primarily conceived as enclosed spaces for the celebration of the rites of the Church, the liturgical fitness of the Tempietto is quite subsidiary; the real 'content' of the building is its exterior. The Tempietto is there to be seen, not used; it is a monument in the traditional sense, not a church. That is probably the idea that underlies Serlio's curious remark that the building is 'not big, but was erected solely in memory of St Peter the Apostle'.[5]

For the new conception of the Christian memorial building exemplified in the Tempietto, the architectural types of the preceding period could not be used, but the circular colonnade on its raised plinth had been preserved in two ancient specimens in Rome and Tivoli.[6] Thus there is in Bramante's work a new interpretation of the architectural problem involved and a new, quite unprejudiced comprehension of ancient architecture. The Tempietto may be regarded as a memorial monument, whose cella-shaped interior houses the altar.

Beyond its general design, the Tempietto also follows ancient models in its vaulting; the dome, hemispherical in section, is executed in cemented masonry.[7] But while in the rotundas of antiquity the dome springs straight from the main order, Bramante has inserted a drum-shaped intermediate storey, the height of which is about equal to the radius of the hemisphere. Thus, as in the Pantheon, a logical and living relationship is established between the circle of the ground-plan, the height of the cylinder bearing the

1. Donato Bramante: Rome, S. Pietro in Montorio, Tempietto, crypt dated 1502

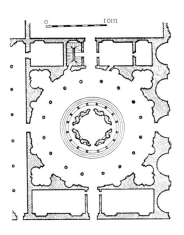

dome, and the hemisphere of the dome itself. At the same time the entablature of the colonnade is prevented from cutting into the exterior view of the dome.

According to Serlio, Bramante's plan was not executed in full. The Tempietto was not to have stood, as it stands today, in a square courtyard; it was to have been surrounded by a circular cloister of sixteen columns. Serlio states that the diameter of the columns in this cloister was to be one and a half times that of the columns in the colonnade, and the height was to have been in the same ratio. Thus, for the spectator standing in this cloister, the view of the Tempietto would have been framed in its columns and entablature, and he would almost certainly have taken the columns in the colonnade as equal in height to those of the cloister. In that way the Tempietto would have gained in monumentality; it would have looked higher and wider, and the surrounding courtyard more spacious.

In spite of the regularity of the design, the Tempietto is calculated for yet other effects of perspective. When the door is open, the spectator standing in front of the building sees the altar, with the crucifixion of St Peter in the predella, enframed in the entrance to the cella. The relief of the crucifixion is at his eye-level.[8] This picture brings home the iconographic significance of the building. If the original plan reproduced by Serlio had been carried out, the colonnade would have appeared in the frame of the cloister, and the altar with its representation of St Peter's martyrdom, i.e. the event in memory and on the site of which the monument was erected, would have appeared as a picture within the picture. From the entrance to the courtyard, both pictures would have been taken in at one glance.

In its formal idiom and structure, as well as in its design as a memorial chapel, the Tempietto is closer to the essential nature of ancient architecture than any religious building of the Quattrocento. Bramante had far outstripped the compromises between medieval Christian tradition and antique form admitted by the fifteenth century. His training at Urbino and his study of architectural theory, especially in the work of Alberti, led him to the vernacular of his works in Lombardy; the classical language of his late style, developed when he was nearly sixty and expressed in the Tempietto, was the product of a very conscious coming to terms with the ancient architecture of Rome.

Yet this late style is not a complete break with Bramante's Lombard style. In spite of all its formal innovations, the conception of the Tempietto is closely akin to the sham perspective of the choir in S. Maria presso S. Satiro. In the Roman work, the exterior and interior views were united in a single picture; the product is a three-dimensional structure, not a feigned architecture in flat relief, and is the consequence of the totally different architectural problems involved. In Rome, as in Milan, the spectator is assigned one definite standpoint, which is the only one to present the right view. In both cases the structure must be seen as a motionless picture, not as a space in which the spectator moves. Both buildings look as if they had been composed in the visual pyramid defined by Alberti. In the Tempietto, the consequences of this kind of composition stand out more clearly, since the smallness of the building would have allowed only one spectator to occupy the 'correct' viewpoint.

2. (*above*) Donato Bramante: Rome, S. Pietro in Montorio, Tempietto, crypt dated 1502, plan (after Serlio) and section (after the Codex Coner)

3. (*left*) Donato Bramante: Rome, S. Maria della Pace, cloister, 1500

4. (*right*) Giuliano da Sangallo: Project for the loggia of the Pope's tuba players, 1505. Florence, Uffizi (A 203)

THE CLOISTER OF S. MARIA DELLA PACE

In 1500, soon after his arrival in Rome, Bramante designed the cloister of S. Maria della Pace [3].[9] A comparison with the cloister of S. Ambrogio in Milan shows a growing assimilation of ancient forms; the result was to be the Tempietto. In Milan, the lower arcades stand on columns, in Rome on piers, yet the Roman system of pier, pilaster, and arch is very similar to that of the upper storey in Milan. In Rome, alternating pillars and columns support the architrave of the upper tier, the pillars standing on the axis, the columns over the keystones of the lower storey. A preliminary stage of the doubling of the number of arcades in the upper storey can be seen in the courtyard of S. Ambrogio and the sacristy of S. Maria presso S. Satiro. On the other hand, the plain architrave and the sequence of the orders – Corinthian over Ionic – already point to the classical style of the Tempietto.*

The cloister is a point of transition in Bramante's *œuvre*; in the development of urban architecture in Rome, coming after the Cancelleria, it could not but present an innovation of capital importance. This was the first time since the courtyard of the great Palazzo Venezia that the structural technique and forms of antiquity were employed on a modern project.

BUILDINGS FOR JULIUS II

Julius II, who was elevated to the throne of St Peter in 1503, had spent the ten years preceding his elevation away from Rome. The buildings erected under him in Rome and at Savona, his native city, were designed by Giuliano da Sangallo. After his patron's elevation to the pontificate, Sangallo was justified in expecting new and more important commissions; in 1504 he left Florence for Rome, where

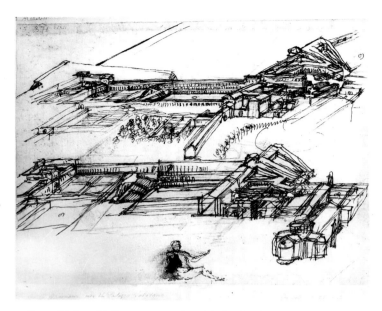

5. Rome, Vatican, bird's-eye perspective with the Cortile del Belvedere, by Sallustio Peruzzi, *c.* 1570. Florence, Uffizi (A 28)

Bramante's Tempietto and the cloister of S. Maria della Pace had been built during the Cardinal's exile. About 1500 there was nothing in Florence to compare with them. When Vasari says that the brothers Giuliano and Antonio da Sangallo represented Tuscan architecture better than any other architects, and applied the Doric order more correctly than Vitruvius, he lays his finger on both the merits and the weaknesses of their style. No architect preserved more faithfully the heritage of Brunelleschi and Alberti than Giuliano da Sangallo, and none of his contemporaries drew the monuments of antiquity with greater application and precision than he. Yet Sangallo's design for the loggia of the Pope's tuba-players [4], made in 1505, shows how completely he lacked the deeper understanding of antiquity which had enabled Bramante to create a synthesis pointing beyond the Quattrocento. The drawing could be taken for a reproduction of an ancient triumphal arch if the decorative detail and the inscription were not there to show the purpose of the design. It was never executed; in 1507 Sangallo returned to Florence. It was not he but Bramante who designed the great buildings for the new Pope.

Under Julius II the Papal State, the Patrimonium Petri, became the supreme state in Italy; for the first time for centuries the papal throne ranked as a great European power. The new conception of the status and task of St Peter's successor is also manifest in the works of art which Pope Julius II left behind him. With the ceiling of the Sistine Chapel, the new St Peter's, the Vatican Palace, and the Pope's tomb, Rome, for the first time since Late Roman times, became the centre of Western art. Even the generation in which these works were created realized that they bore witness to a new claim to universality by the papacy. As Guicciardini points out, the very name which the Pope chose on his elevation was an expression of that claim. Julius felt himself to be as much a successor of St Peter as an heir of the Caesars, and as a building patron too he did everything in his power to reinstate Rome as *Caput Mundi*.

THE BELVEDERE COURT OF THE VATICAN

The first of Julius's great projects was the Belvedere Court of the Vatican [5–11], begun with Bramante as architect-in-chief; the first payments made to him are dated 1505.[10] The structure bridged the dip between the old papal palace next to St Peter's and the originally separate villa which Innocent VIII had built between 1485 and 1487 on the northern slope of the Vatican hill. Julius II had the ground rising towards the villa terraced, connected the terraces by a system of steps, and bounded them on both sides by multi-storey loggia corridors. By one of Julius's portrait medals we can see that he himself felt the dimensions of the project to be outstanding; the reverse bears a view of the new courtyard, which is described as '1000 feet in length and 80 in height'.[11]

The purpose of the building was also unusual. The papal collection of ancient sculpture, to which the Laocoön had recently been added, was deposited in a square courtyard between the old villa, i.e. the actual Belvedere, and the north side of the new cortile. The two upper terraces of the latter were to serve as a garden; the lower courtyard, occupying about half of the area, was to be used for tournaments and pageants. The narrow side of this lower courtyard forms the north front of the old palace with the Pope's private apartment, Alexander VI's Appartamento Borgia, and above it Raphael's Stanze, painted under Julius II. The Stanze are on exactly the same level as the upper terrace of the court, which is 1000 feet distant. This terrace came to an end in a one-storey façade facing the old villa, with a semicircular recess in the middle [11]. The staircase leading from the terrace to the exedra no longer exists. The steps were shaped in concentric circles, the outermost circle circumscribing both the lowest and the uppermost steps. Given the limited space, neither the steps nor the platform they led to had any practical purpose; their function was primarily aesthetic. The exedra was the final note in the artistic crescendo of terraces and stairs which the courtyard presented when seen from the opposite narrow side. This is what Serlio means when he says of the exedra that it 'was built in the form of a theatre'. In the same way as in the Tempietto the viewpoint of the spectator of this 'theatre' can be precisely situated; from Raphael's Stanze a general view can be obtained of the whole site, which rises in terraces from the lower court to the exedra. The design has one thing in common with that of the Tempietto, namely that this viewpoint, which also offered the best view of the pageants in the lower court, was situated outside the court, so that the view was framed by a window. In the Tempietto, however, the eyes rest on a solid building, while in the Belvedere they rest on the open space of the courtyard.

There is irrefutable proof in the sources that the conception of the Belvedere Court originated with Bramante. In this building he applied the principle of perspective composition to a work of architecture comprising landscape and architecture, hill and valley, garden and fountain, and fused the whole into a picture. There were Quattrocento predecessors for some of the features of the composition.[12] But the true model for the Belvedere Court is to be found in antiquity. The descriptions by Tacitus and Suetonius of

6. Rome, Vatican, Cortile del Belvedere, 1505 ff., air view, looking north

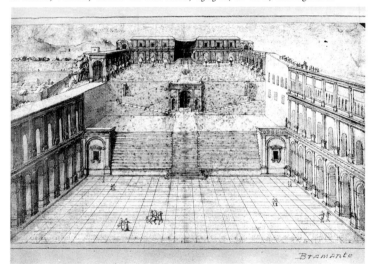

7. Rome, Vatican, Cortile del Belvedere, perspective view from the Stanze, looking north, by Sallustio Peruzzi(?), c. 1560. Private Collection

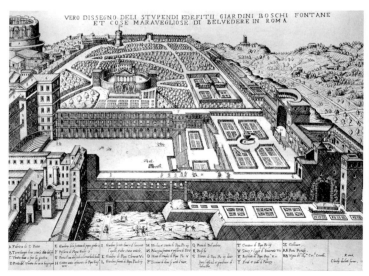

8. Rome, Vatican, Cortile del Belvedere, bird's-eye perspective, looking west, 1579

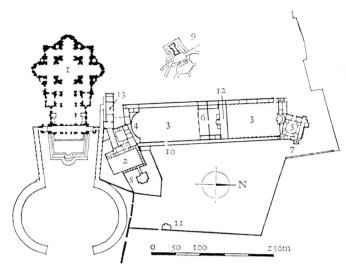

9. Rome, Vatican, Cortile del Belvedere and adjoining structures, plan

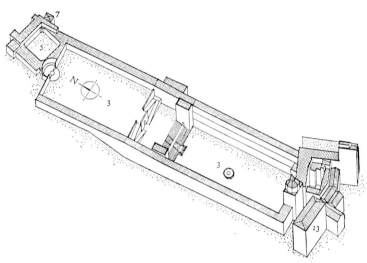

10. Donato Bramante: Rome, Vatican, Cortile del Belvedere, 1505 ff., reconstruction

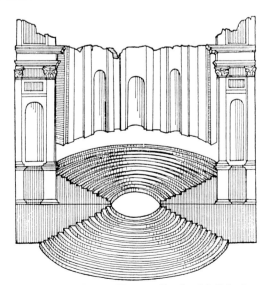

11. Donato Bramante: Rome, Vatican, Cortile del Belvedere, 1505 ff., exedra (after Serlio)

KEY

1. St Peter's
2. Cortile di S. Damaso with Loggia
3. Cortile del Belvedere
4. Exedra of Pius IV
5. Statue Court
6. Library of Sixtus V
7. Bramante's circular staircase
8. Place of Sixtus V
9. Casino of Pius IV
10. Porta Julia
11. S. Anna dei Palafrenieri
12. Braccio Nuovo
13. Sistine Chapel

Nero's Golden House, the remains of the Temple of Fortuna at Palestrina, the long oblong of the hippodrome in the imperial palace on the Palatine, and Hadrian's villa at Tivoli have so many elements in common with the Belvedere Court that there can hardly be any doubt of its true meaning. The papal residence on the Mons Vaticanus, as the hill is called in the inscription on Julius II's medal, was, as a whole, to rival the imperial palaces on the hills of Rome. The inscription reflects perfectly the other political and artistic ambitions of the Pope.

The court itself was never given the form that Bramante had in mind. For fifty years building went on in all essentials according to the original design, but about 1580 Sixtus V finally abandoned Bramante's idea by building a connecting wing across the court to house the Vatican library. Yet no Roman building had a greater influence on the secular architecture which followed than the Belvedere Court. It largely determined the idea of the relationship between architecture and landscape which developed in the sixteenth century. The continuation and alteration of the building compelled all the leading architects of Rome, from Raphael to Domenico Fontana, to come to terms with Bramante's ideas and formal language. There are countless working drawings, vedute, and engravings which have preserved the varying forms of the whole structure. From the time of Julius II it has been one of the wonders of the world.

In the building itself, the only part to have retained its original form is the east portal leading into the lower court [12]. In its combination of neat brickwork, rusticated travertine, and monumental inscriptions in capital letters, the Porta Julia too can rival antiquity. It is not by chance that the inscription is so placed that the letters PONT. MAX. appear immediately above the porch itself, for the Pope shared the office of Pontifex Maximus with the emperors of antiquity. The formal repertory of the porch was drawn upon again and again in the sixteenth century, but its force of expression and monumentality were never equalled.

The three-storey logge on the long side of the lower courtyard, of which Julius II had only begun the eastern one, have been altered out of all recognition, while the intermediary terraces are largely concealed by later additions. The original execution of the upper court has been preserved in the drawings of one of Bramante's pupils [13]. The single-storey logge of the upper court, although later walled up and topped by a second storey, retain the original alternation of wide arcades and narrow bays which are set with two Corinthian pilasters [14].[13] Details such as the window surrounds and flattened rustication date from about 1560; the tall pedestals of the pilasters and the projecting entablatures over the pilasters, on the other hand, have remained in their original form.

12. Donato Bramante: Rome, Vatican, Cortile del Belvedere, 1505 ff., entrance leading to the lower court

13. Donato Bramante: Rome, Vatican, Cortile del Belvedere, perspective view of the upper court (detail), c. 1520, from the Codex Coner. London, Sir John Soane's Museum

14. Donato Bramante: Rome, Vatican, Cortile del Belvedere

THE LOGGE

One item in Julius II's programme for the Vatican was the four-storey façade begun by Bramante, which was set in front of the old papal palace to the east, i.e. facing the city. It can be seen today in the west wing of the Cortile di S. Damaso, but has been deprived of its original function as the main façade, as it was recorded by Heemskerck, among others [15]. The lower range was concealed towards the city and St Peter's by walls, and is therefore treated as a plinth; the second and third ranges consist of piers and arcades, the topmost storey of columns with an entablature.[14] The orders follow the usual sequence – Doric, Ionic, Corinthian. For the first time in the Renaissance the city front of a palace is treated as a system of free-standing supports and logge, and not as a wall. Here again Bramante shows more consistency and insight in the employment of the Roman system of supports and orders than his predecessors. The famous decoration of the interior in stucco and fresco by Raphael and his pupils was only completed under Julius's successor, but it is in perfect keeping with Julius's intentions. The interior of the logge, decorated with subjects from the Old and New Testaments, was intended to rival, as a Christian *domus aurea*, the *domus aurea* of Nero, which had been recently discovered. Its façade was meant to dominate the view of the city.

NEW ST PETER'S

Julius's building programme was to find its crowning achievement in the new St Peter's. As Alberti had already reported, the basilica Constantinian was dilapidated and in need of restoration, but Julius's predecessors had shrunk from interfering with the old building. Neither the choir outside the old apse begun by Rossellino for Nicholas V, nor the foundations of the transept laid after the same plan, impinged on the old building. Even the first pier of the new building, the foundation stone of which was laid in the presence of Julius II on 18 April 1506, stands outside the old apse; it joins up with the masonry of the Rossellino choir, but the Pope made it quite clear that he meant to demolish Constantine's church. As early as January 1506 he had communicated to Henry VIII and the lords spiritual and temporal of England his decision 'to renovate the very dilapidated church of St Peter the Apostle in Rome from its foundations up and to provide it in seemly fashion with chapels and other necessary rooms'.[15] Since the means of the Curia were insufficient, the recipients of the letters were asked for contributions.

Vasari's and Condivi's biographies of Michelangelo gave it to be understood that the Pope's plans grew out of the discussion of his tomb, to be planned by Michelangelo.* The first site envisaged for it was the Rossellino choir; in the course of the discussions the Pope resolved to rebuild the church and selected Bramante's plans from those submitted [16A]. Both Vasari and Condivi relate this at second hand; both strive to cast the brightest light on their hero, Michelangelo. Their version must therefore be accepted with some reserve, though we have no other sources for the course events took.

The exact plan on which work was begun is equally obscure. It was certainly the work of Bramante, who

15. Rome, Vatican Palace with the Logge from Piazza S. Pietro, drawing by Marten van Heemskerck. Vienna, Albertina

16. Rome, St Peter's, projects: (A) Bramante, 1506 ff.; (B) Peruzzi, *c.* 1502; (C) Antonio da Sangallo the Younger, 1539 ff.; (D) Michelangelo, 1546 ff.

17. Donato Bramante: Project for St Peter's, medal by Caradosso, 1506

remained, till his death in 1514, *architetto della fabrica di S. Pietro*. The earliest reproduction of his plan is on the reverse of a portrait medal of Julius II which was probably struck when the foundation stone was laid [17]. This showed, above the Mons Vaticanus, the exterior view of a domed building whose plan must be imagined as a Greek cross. On the ground floor, apses projected from the arms of the cross; in the corners of the cross there are minor domes, while there are towers on both sides of the façade. Whether the remarkable stress on the horizontals and the sobriety of the ornament are due to the medallist or to Bramante it is almost impossible to say. On the other hand, there is every reason to believe that the representation of the main dome accurately renders Bramante's intentions.

A second source for Bramante's ideas is a parchment plan in the Uffizi [18]. It belonged to Vasari, and on the back of it there is a note by Antonio da Sangallo the Younger, who began to work on St Peter's in 1510 and became superintendent of the fabrica in 1520; according to this note, this is a plan 'by Bramante that was not executed'. This is the only known drawing for which there is reliable evidence that it is by Bramante's hand. It tallies with the medal in the general form of the crossing, the transepts, minor domes, and campanili. But as the sheet shows only half of the Greek cross, it cannot be determined, as it can in the medal, whether the other half duplicated the one shown, or has to be imagined in some other form. Neither the plan nor the medal includes the parts of Rossellino's choir at the west of old St Peter's, which were still standing when the foundation stone was laid.[16]

Julius II died in 1513, Bramante in 1514. By that time, after the partial demolition of the nave of old St Peter's, the great crossing arches and the arm of the cross which joined the western pier of the new building had been vaulted, but the other parts were hardly begun. For the vault of the west

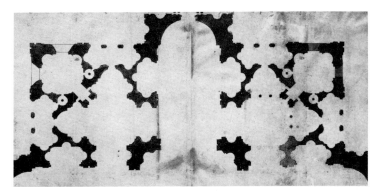

18. Donato Bramante: Project for St Peter's, plan. Florence, Uffizi (A 1)

choir, Rossellino's still-standing walls were used; to the outside they were faced with Doric pilasters, while the piers of the crossing had Corinthian pilasters. A plan in the Soane Museum in London reproduces this stage of the work [19]. In addition to the reproduction of the west choir, it differs in two respects from the parchment plan: the piers of the crossing have been strengthened and the western minor domes abandoned. Sangallo's statement that the parchment plan reproduces a design that was never executed is therefore proved correct. The plan in London further proves that the parts of the building standing about 1514, which varied greatly in height, were not to be continued as a purely centrally planned building; the pair of piers drawn to the east of the crossing can only be interpreted as the beginning of a nave.

As Serlio tells us, Bramante left the building unfinished, and 'there were already cracks in the four arches and piers'. In view of this condition, which is confirmed by other

20. (*right*) Donato Bramante: Project for St Peter's, 1506 ff., dome, plan and section (after Serlio)

19. (*below*) Donato Bramante: Rome, St Peter's, plan, *c.* 1514, from the Codex Coner. London, Sir John Soane's Museum

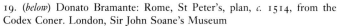

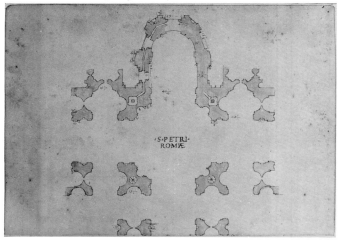

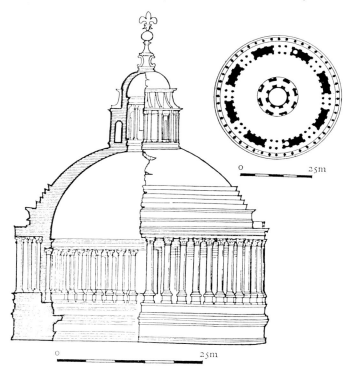

sources, we can understand why Serlio described the dome which was to be erected above these piers as 'bold rather than well considered'. All the same, he reproduces the design for the dome in plan and elevation, since 'it was a great revelation to architects' [20].[17] The exterior and the outline of the dome tally with the hemisphere on a colonnaded drum which appears on the medal of 1506.

For the construction and size of a dome of this kind there was only one model in the western world: the Pantheon. This is also recalled by the steps at the foot of the dome. In all probability Bramante intended to vault his dome with cemented masonry, like the Tempietto; the single-shell hemisphere which Serlio reproduces could only have been constructed in that way. The account books show that the Roman method was actually applied to the arches between the piers at the crossing. The complex curve of the double-shell construction at Florence, which Giuliano da Sangallo still employed at Loreto, could not be brought into line with Bramante's endeavours to achieve simplicity of spatial form and exterior view. For that reason he decided on the single-shell method from the outset; the reversion to the Pantheon was far more than an archaeological reminiscence. If Serlio, with all his admiration for the greatness and beauty of the design, is still doubtful whether it could be executed, he is probably only expressing the general feeling of his contemporaries. He explains tactfully that Bramante's calculations in statics were utopian. 'As the elevation shows,' he goes on, 'the great mass and weight of the dome was to rest on four soaring piers; any prudent architect would do well to place a mass of this kind on the ground, and not so high up.' The hemisphere of the Pantheon dome is supported by a solid cylinder; hence, in Serlio's sense, it literally stands 'on the ground'.

Later, Bramante's piers were reinforced again, while the shape and structure of the dome was radically altered; the idea of single-shell vaulting, and with it the execution in cemented masonry, had to be abandoned. Nor was the system of subsidiary arches and exterior walls to brace the thrust of the dome adequate to the purpose.

Nevertheless, the artistic qualities of Bramante's design were so overwhelming that not one of his successors at St Peter's could quite elude its influence. The dome of today, finished in 1590, rests, in spite of all variations, on the piers and crossing arches of the first stage of building. Their width of about 24.5 m. (75 feet) and height of about 49 m. (150 feet) determined the diameter of the dome as we see it – about 42 m. (128 feet) – as well as the height and width of the present nave. Bramante's measurements were not laid down without reason; his dome spans the width of the middle and inner aisles in old St Peter's, his crossing arches its nave. Thus the main dimensions of the basilica of Constantine have been preserved in the St Peter's we know.

Bramante's dome, which is almost twice as wide as the nave, continues a development which leads from the medieval domes of Florence and Siena to the church of Loreto and Pavia Cathedral; the crossings of these churches occupy the full width of nave and aisles. But while their domes are domical vaults, i.e. are formed of pointed segments, Bramante's project goes back in its form and structure to traditions of the Florentine Quattrocento; for instance, in

S. Spirito round arches and pendentives bear a hemisphere. In plan, the dome of S. Spirito appears as a circle inscribed in the square of the crossing; thus its diameter equals the width of the nave. But Bramante unites the circular type of S. Spirito with the wide span of the medieval type. Under the dome, he chamfers the piers of the crossing, so that the corners of the square in which the circle of the dome is inscribed are formed by the centres and not by the corners of the piers. At the same time Bramante was trying to achieve a rational relationship between the height and the width of the dome. The height of the arches of the crossing is double their span, the total height to the crown of the lantern would have been double that of the arches, and thus the ratio between the span and height of the arches and the total height of the dome would have been $1:2:4$.[18]

In the execution, the piers of the dome were not only reinforced, as a reference to the parchment plan will show; they were also articulated differently [21]. Between the double pilasters of the intrados new niches were inserted, while on the exterior surfaces of the piers, the niches are three times as broad and deep as they appear in the parchment plan. If we try to visualize the elevation of the parchment plan, the pilasters would act primarily as an articulation

21. Rome, St Peter's, interior looking west, with Bramante's piers, vaulted choir, and altar shrine, the drum of the dome designed by Michelangelo, c. 1570. Hamburg, Kunsthalle (21311)

of the wall *surface*. In the execution, however, their structural function was stressed; it is not the total pier but the pilasters which seem to be bearing the weight of the crossing. That is why the wall between the pilasters was hollowed out, as far as possible, in niches. We may assume that the unusually great projection of the capitals and cornices goes back to the alteration in the design.

A characteristically Bramantesque feature was the stepped base of the Corinthian order about 3 m. (10 feet) high [21], which was covered up later when the floor level was raised.[19] This gigantic platform would have raised the order of pilasters far above the spectator's eye-level when he was standing in the church; he would actually have looked up into the structure from below, and be permanently separated from the perpendicular wall by the enormous projection of the steps, i.e. by a distance prescribed by the architect. As in the Tempietto and the Belvedere Court, the spectator was not to feel that he was standing in the building, but that he was looking into it; the Roman orders, the arches, and the dome are primarily conceived as a spatial picture, or as a series of spatial pictures. Their effect in their static or structural function was secondary.

The projects for St Peter's made after Bramante's death show that it was not clear whether the parts already begun were to be completed as a basilica or on a centralized plan. Bramante's interest must have been entirely concentrated on the dome commanding the exterior and interior views. The instructions given to his pupils and successors in drawings and models, as we know from Serlio's illustrations, were concerned only with these views, while the rest of the building took second place for the time being.

The dome was to rise above the tomb of St Peter and crown the Mons Vaticanus. By order of Julius II, nothing was changed at the tomb itself or in the emplacement of the high altar above the confessio. But however the remaining parts of the church of the Apostle may have been planned, it was very different from old St Peter's. Beyond its significance as a place of liturgy, new St Peter's was to be a monument, a funerary monument in the tradition of the ancient mausolea and early Christian martyria.[20]

Bramante's design combined a number of older ideas. Centrally planned buildings on a Greek cross plan with a high dome over the crossing and smaller subsidiary domes figure in Leonardo da Vinci's drawings. As we have seen, Bramante combined Brunelleschi's pendentive and hemispherical form with the type of dome in which the diameter exceeds that of the nave. The giant order of the piers at the crossing had a predecessor in S. Andrea at Mantua. Another Albertian feature is the high plinth of the base which 'forces' a perspective view. Further, Alberti and Francesco di Giorgio Martini after him had provided the theoretical arguments for the use of circular forms in church architecture, and, indeed, Bramante's hemispherical dome was to be erected over a circular plan. Bramante also followed Alberti's suggestions in the use of coffers for the decoration of the shell of the dome and the arches of the crossing.

But the influence of Bramante's design cannot be explained if we see it merely as the sum of Quattrocento experience. The formal repertory of the building, pilasters and niches, arches and domes, was not new, but Bramante was the first

to invest these forms with the monumentality they were to have from that time on. There was no work of architecture in antiquity or the Quattrocento from which this repertory could be derived in its entirety, but Bramante had become familiar with the clarity of proportional relations, the simplicity of great spatial organizations in the Pantheon and the Basilica of Maxentius, and it was in these ancient buildings that posts and lintels expressed the forces at work in the mass of the building with the same power and clarity as in Bramante's crossing.

The revival of the antique which Serlio and Palladio extol as Bramante's achievement must not be understood as a revival by imitation. The dignity of St Peter's as the mortuary church of the Apostle from whom the Popes derived their authority demanded supreme dignity in its architectural forms. From the time of Dante, Petrarch, and Alberti, the Roman ruins were, in Italian eyes, the acme of beauty and dignity. 'Roma quanta fuit ipsa ruina docet' was Serlio's motto. Bramante fused the expressive force of ancient architecture with the tradition of the Christian liturgical and memorial building, and the result was a form which remained the ideal of church building till the age of classicism. Benvenuto Cellini wrote of Bramante: 'He began the great church of St Peter entirely in the beautiful manner of the ancients. He had the power to do so because he was an artist, and because he was able to see and to understand the beautiful buildings of antiquity that still remain to us, though they are in ruins.'[21]

THE CHOIR OF S. MARIA DEL POPOLO

Besides the Tempietto, the only sacred building by Bramante that has been preserved unaltered is the choir of S. Maria del Popolo, which was also commissioned by Julius II [22]. To the square chancel, for whose walls the Pope had commissioned monuments for two cardinals, Bramante added an oblong bay and an apse. The architectural forms – the Tuscan cornice, the shell-vaulted apse, the coffering of the tunnel-vault over the chancel bay – could not be plainer, but just because of that Bramante's principle of design comes out most clearly. The spectator looks into the apse through the triple recession of the jambs, and this 'picture' is framed in its turn by the attached pilasters and the arch of the chancel bay. Unlike those of the Pantheon, the coffers of the vault are oblong, not square; they too guide the eye to the apse. The same purpose is served by the peculiar kind of lighting through slits in the wall and the lowest coffer of the vault. Actually, the spectator is not expected to enter the apse; seen from the altar, i.e. from a distant viewpoint, it unites in a single picture the monuments and Pinturicchio's frescoes in the chancel vault.

Many details recall the choir of St Peter's, which was vaulted by Bramante at the same time. There too the apse was shaped like a shell, and the unadorned windows over the main cornice and the coffers of the vault appear.

22. Donato Bramante: Rome, S. Maria del Popolo, choir and apse, *c.* 1508

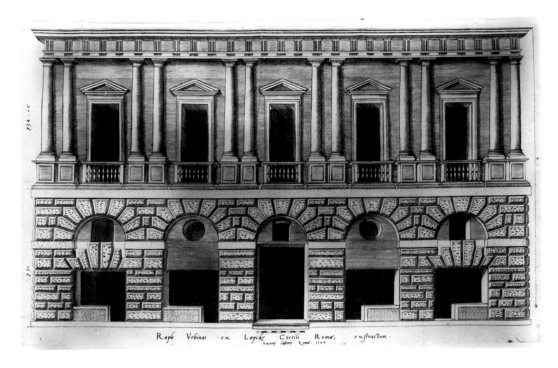

Raph· Vrbinas · ex · Lapide · Coctili · Romæ, · exstructum·

THE PALAZZO CAPRINI (RAPHAEL'S HOUSE)

Bramante's other churches in Rome, the centrally planned S. Biagio alla Pagnotta and SS. Celso e Giuliano, have been demolished, and can only be reconstructed from later drawings. His Palazzo di Giustizia never got past its beginnings; its site is on the via Giulia, which was laid out by Julius II and which is the first straight street to pierce the huddle of houses of medieval Rome. A palazzo built by Bramante for the Caprini family and in 1517 acquired by Raphael has also been pulled down. Its façade, which can be seen in an engraving [23] and several drawings of the sixteenth century, was as important for the development of the palazzo as St Peter's was for religious architecture.[22] For the first time, the ancient Roman order appears as a half-column on the wall, which thus becomes the background of a relief. The distinction between structural articulation and space-filling background was made still more obvious by the coupling of the half-columns, the projection of the architrave, and the forceful jut of the balconies under the windows. The same clear distinction came out in the rusticated ground floor between bearing blocks and plain, space-filling wall. The main entrance was a tall rectangle, the lower openings above the shop doors to its left and right were horizontal oblongs; in the piano nobile the emphasis on the central bay was omitted, as it is in a Roman temple façade. The Doric order in the piano nobile, generally confined to the ground floor, shows that in this case the ground floor was regarded merely as a plinth. The rustication too must be understood in the same way; the seemingly roughhewn blocks, the 'unfinished' door lintels and keystones, support the 'perfected work of art',[23] the artist-architect's 'order' with its columns, plain walls, and articulated entablature. In this way the arrangement of shops and workshops on the ground floor of urban dwellings, which had been traditional since ancient times, was given a meaning in the whole architectural pattern. Even the baseness of the material used for the rustication appears to be significant in this context; it is not roughly hewn freestone, but a type of stucco coating of the brick front, which was, according to Vasari, an invention of Bramante himself.

THE SANTA CASA OF LORETO

Another example of Bramante's use of the ancient orders can be seen in the marble incrustation of the Santa Casa of Loreto, commissioned by Julius II and begun in 1509 [24].[24] As in the Belvedere Court, the articulation is of the triumphal arch type. The coupled half-columns, with their bases and entablature, stand like a structural scaffolding in front of the recessed strata of the wall with its reliefs and portals. Thus, in the same way as in Raphael's house, a distinction is made between supporting and filling elements. In accordance with Serlio's theories, the Santa Casa of the Virgin is given the Corinthian order.[25]

SUMMARY

No other Renaissance architect exercised so widespread and immediate an influence as Bramante. Even during his lifetime, the lead in architecture passed from Florence to Rome, and chiefly because of his work. As early as the first third of the sixteenth century, the new style made its appearance not only in Florence, Padua, and Venice, but in Spain, France, and Germany.[26] This new style has been called High Renaissance, and has been taken to be a continuous development from the Early Renaissance. That view, however, becomes problematical in the light of Bramante's work. True, his late Roman buildings have certain features in common with his work in Lombardy, but it is only the works executed after 1500, i.e. after his arrival in Rome – the Tempietto, the Belvedere Court, the plans for St Peter's, the Palazzo Caprini, and the Santa Casa – that show the new assimilation of antiquity which determined the new classical style. That style, therefore, can hardly be conceived as the result of an uninterrupted and general process of development.

The new style did not at first take hold in Florence and the north of Italy; it was introduced there by Bramante's and Raphael's pupils. Obviously, this style must be regarded as Bramante's personal achievement.

THE DESIGNS FOR ST PETER'S AFTER BRAMANTE'S DEATH

In 1513, soon after his elevation, Leo X called Giuliano da Sangallo, then aged seventy, and Fra Giocondo, then nearing eighty, and appointed them collaborators with Bramante in the Fabbrica di S. Pietro.[27] We can hardly imagine that the Pope thought of dismissing Bramante from his post. Fra Giocondo had previously laid the foundations of a Seine bridge in Paris; thus he was probably called in as an expert on statics, since the piers of Bramante had been built on unstable ground. Sangallo's appointment must be taken as a similar move. In any case, building had progressed slowly since 1511. In the last years of Julius II's reign, the building grants had been reduced, and at times were entirely stopped owing to the expenses for the Pope's campaigns. On 1 August 1514, three months after Bramante's death, Raphael became architect-in-chief of St Peter's.[28] Fra Giocondo died in 1515; in the same year Sangallo left in order to design the façade of S. Lorenzo in Florence. Giuliano's nephew, Antonio da Sangallo the Younger, was appointed Raphael's assistant. Baldassare Peruzzi of Siena was also working on the building from 1520 at the latest.

Bramante's successors were faced with a difficult task. The shifting of the foundations and the cracks in the piers were a matter of general knowledge; in a general way too the public felt that the scheme was too ambitious, or even impracticable.[29] Since there was no definite plan which would have served as a guide to the continuation of the work, the new Pope had to consider how one could be established. Raphael's first official work was to make a model in wood. Further, an unusually large number of drawings has survived from this stage of building, and their attribution

25. Baldassare Peruzzi: Project for St Peter's, bird's-eye perspective. Florence, Uffizi (A 2)

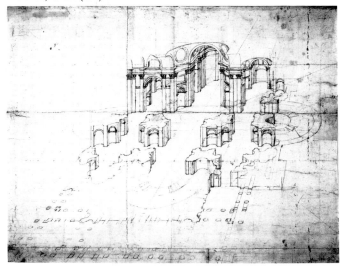

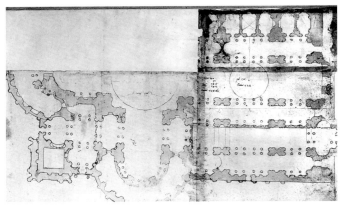

26. (*above*) Baldassare Peruzzi: Project for St Peter's, plan. Florence, Uffizi (A 14)

27. (*below*) Raphael (copy): Project for St Peter's, elevation and section. Washington, Paul Mellon Collection

and dating has ever since been one of the most fascinating and difficult problems in art history [25–31].[30] The number of these sheets, and the variations between them, reflect the bewilderment which reigned among the architects after Bramante's death, and also the conflicts between generations and trends which confronted each other after 1514.

What is common to all these plans is Bramante's piers for the dome, whether it is the centre of a centrally planned building or the crossing of a basilica. The point at issue was the kind of building – a Greek or a Latin cross – and the shape of the arms. Four solutions were put forward for the latter:

(a) Plain apses between the subsidiary domes as shown in the parchment plan, but the west choir begun by Rossellino and completed by Bramante to be retained.

(b) Ambulatories to be carried round the apses of the transepts, but Rossellino's choir to remain in its original form without an ambulatory.

(c) The Rossellino choir, like the transepts, to be provided with an ambulatory, but the latter not to be opened towards the interior by an arrangement of columns and piers.

(d) All the arms of the cross to have identical ambulatories, which would entail the demolition and rebuilding of the west choir.[31]

Apart from the shape of the arms of the cross, the purely central designs are mainly distinguished by their exteriors. The following variants occur:

(a) Square plan with slightly projecting towers at the corners.

(b) The towers and the apses provided with ambulatories to stand out boldly.

(c) The apses of the arms of the cross, but not the towers, to project from the square of the ground plan.[32]

The largest number of variants is to be found in the plans for the nave:

(a) The nave and the inner aisles of old St Peter's to remain as the nave of the new building.

(b) A new, double-aisled, seven-bay nave; tunnel-vault on plain, square piers.

(c) Double-aisled nave of seven bays, the supports with niches on the model of the piers of the dome.

(d) Double-aisled nave, five bays.

(e) Triple aisles, five bays with a simplified form of pier.

(f) Single aisles, five bays, chapels instead of outer aisles.

(g) Single aisles, five bays, with the nave groin-vaulted after the manner of the Basilica of Maxentius.

(h) Single aisles, three bays; a dome over the middle bay of the nave, and tunnel-vaults with penetrations in the first and third bays, i.e. a nave on the triumphal arch principle.[33]

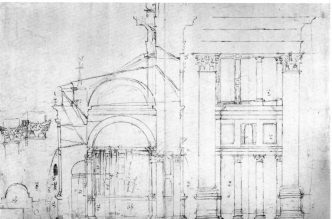

The façades of the basilican plans have a portico as wide as the nave with all the aisles, with or without flanking towers; some of the plans provide for a deep vestibule. The exterior view of the purely central design recalls that of the foundation medal.

This list, which could be increased by several variants, is certainly not very entertaining. It reflects not only the bewilderment of Bramante's successors, but also the more theoretical than practical frame of mind of the architects at work. Peruzzi and Giuliano da Sangallo made perpetually new combinations of all the variants mentioned. Moreover Peruzzi explored architectural ideas developed for St Peter's in theoretical studies without any idea of realizing them. This is the expression of an unmistakably mannerist attitude; a final and binding solution is evaded rather than sought, and intricacy seems more attractive than simplicity. In comparison, Bramante's effort to achieve simplicity, to create immediate comprehensibility in the forms and clarity in the relationships, stands out as a characteristic of the classical style.

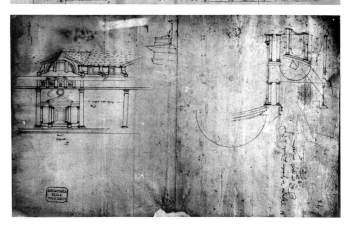

28. Raphael (copy): Project for St Peter's, plan, and Antonio da Sangallo (copy): Project for St Peter's, plan. Washington, Paul Mellon Collection

29. Raphael: Project for St Peter's, section of ambulatory and elevation of transept, drawing by Antonio da Sangallo the Younger. Florence, Uffizi (A 54)

30. Raphael: Project for St Peter's, exterior of ambulatory and cross-section of transept and ambulatory, French copy after Antonio da Sangallo the Younger. Munich, Bayerische Staatsbibliothek (cod. icon. 195)

31. Antonio da Sangallo the Younger: Project for St Peter's, plan. Vienna, Albertina (790 verso)

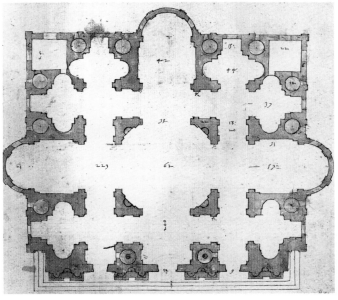

CHAPTER 2

Classical Architecture in Rome: Raphael

Serlio's statement that Bramante had left no finished model for St Peter's at his death is confirmed by Leo X's papal writ of 1514 appointing Raphael as architect-in-chief of the works.[1] According to this writ, it was Bramante who had proposed Raphael as his successor, since his work as a painter was famous. He had also, according to Bramante's praise, given proof of architectural talent and he had already designed the model for St Peter's. We may assume from this way of putting the matter that Raphael had, up to that time, not, in fact, performed as an architect, and that Bramante's judgement was based on Raphael's painting and on casual conversations between the two.[2]

In 1514, Raphael had completed in the Vatican the Stanze della Segnatura and d'Eliodoro. They are a milestone in the history of architectural painting, since the interiors represented in the frescoes appear, in quite unprecedented fashion, to be part of a far greater spatial context, which is left to the spectator's imagination. Looking at the 'School of Athens', for instance, we are given no hint of the height or width of the wall in which the statues of Apollo and Minerva stand; to obtain an idea of its size, the spectator would, as it were, have to step into the picture and look about him. While the full extent of the spaces represented by Quattrocento artists can be grasped at first sight, the width, height, and depth of Raphael's spaces are merely the sum of the impressions of a spectator changing his viewpoint several times – in imagination at least.

THE CHIGI CHAPEL IN S. MARIA DEL POPOLO

This new conception of space is also a feature of the only religious building by Raphael which has been preserved in its original state, the Chigi Chapel in S. Maria del Popolo [32–5].[3] The chapel is entered through an arch in the aisle, and in the interior of the chapel three blind arches respond to this arch. This system of arches supports a dome on pendentives. In its proportions and details the whole looks like a reduced reproduction of the crossing of Bramante's St Peter's. As in St Peter's, the diameter of the dome is greater than the entrance arch; that is why the spectator can only obtain a full view of the space when he has entered the chapel and looked about him, for it is only then that the view into the dome opens. Its mosaics are an integral part of the total composition.[4]

Like Bramante's choir, the Chigi Chapel was added to S. Maria del Popolo as an annex. Like the Tempietto, it is roofed by a dome. As we have observed, the interiors of Bramante's churches must be seen from a distance; it is only then that the full effect of their monumentality can be felt. All the spectator needs – even with the Tempietto – is a single glance; this will take in all that really matters. But in the Chigi Chapel, he has to look in several directions, as can be realized by the placing of statues in the four niches in the piers of the dome. The spectator has to stand *in* the space, not just *facing* the space.

Two important innovations make the distinction perfectly clear. Raphael has abandoned the tall bases of Bramante's piers in St Peter's and of the pilasters in the cella of the Tempietto. Further, while the walls and dome of the Tempietto are bare of ornament, and can therefore only be taken in as a stereoscopic picture in relief, Raphael himself designed mosaics for the dome of the Chigi Chapel with figures floating on a blue ground and the Almighty in the centre. Of the statues in the niches at least one was made after Raphael's design.

Thus the visitor to the Chigi Chapel stands on the same level as the base of the pilasters. The decoration of the wall between the pilasters shows that it is not conceived as a part of the architecture; on the contrary, compared with Bramante's walls it looks almost transparent. In the feigned openwork of the dome, the constellations and the Creator are seen through the interstices of the architectural framework. In Bramante's interiors, walls and orders form one indivisible whole; in Raphael's, the wall between the orders is, as far as possible, dissolved. The architecture of the building is to be understood as a scaffolding of structural members.

PALAZZI

According to Vasari, Raphael planned the palazzo of the papal notary Giovanbattista Branconio dall'Aquila, which was demolished in the seventeenth century to make room for Bernini's colonnades in front of St Peter's.[5] Like that of the Palazzo Caprini, the façade was of five bays. But in the Palazzo dall'Aquila, the ground floor, which was to be let out in shops, was not rusticated, but articulated by an engaged Tuscan order and blind arches [36]. On the upper floor, Raphael broke with the tradition which had descended from the Palazzo Rucellai by way of the Cancelleria to the Palazzo Caprini, and abandoned the classical order. The windows of the piano nobile were surrounded by boldly moulded aedicules with alternating pediments. Thus the weighty, jutting forms of the upper floor responded to the open arches of the lower. Between the aedicules, round-headed niches were recessed in the wall; thus the convex engaged columns of the ground floor were in contrast with the concave forms on the main floor. Similar contrasts can be seen in the piano nobile itself: rising pediments and hanging swags, the looser forms of the stucco ornament beside the architecturally stable forms of the aedicules, the projections of the column and the recess of the niche. If we look back to the strict system of Bramante's palazzo, with its clear differentiation between supporting and space-filling elements, the façade

32. Raphael: Rome, S. Maria del Popolo, Chigi Chapel, begun *c*. 1513, cupola

33. Raphael: Rome, S. Maria del Popolo, Chigi Chapel, begun c. 1513

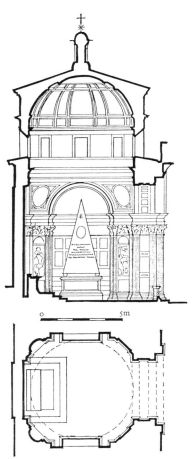

34. Raphael: Rome, S. Maria del Popolo, Chigi Chapel, begun c. 1513, section and plan

of the Palazzo dall'Aquila cannot but appear restless and illogical. Yet even there, definite principles have been consistently applied. The classical order only appears where there is a true relationship between load and support, i.e. where the wall is actually pierced by openings, namely on the ground floor and in the window aedicules of the piano nobile. Bramante's double order was a fiction in so far as the

35. Raphael: Rome, S. Maria del Popolo, Chigi Chapel, detail of entablature

classical system of post and lintel was merely a screen in front of a solid wall. The design of the Palazzo dall'Aquila treats the wall of the upper storey entirely as relief, in accordance with its structural function. That is why there is no articulation of the angles, which Bramante had faced with three-quarter columns.

The Palazzo Vidoni-Caffarelli, although Raphaelesque in style, was probably not designed by Raphael himself.* The original façade was of seven bays; the lengthening and the top storey belong to a later stage of building [37].[6] In this case the ground floor is treated as a rusticated plinth; the coupled Tuscan columns of the piano nobile also recall Bramante. But apart from the lintels, the joints in the rustication are entirely horizontal; the coupled columns stand on a common base, and there are no pediments over the windows. Throughout the façade, the horizontals are emphasized, but for that very reason, the coupled order takes on greater importance as the only vertical feature. Unlike Bramante's palazzo, the Palazzo Vidoni minimizes the axial relationship between the two storeys; the predominantly horizontal ground floor and the predominantly vertical upper floor appear unconnected, while the harmony of Bramante's façade lies in the coordination of five vertical units.

Raphael's late paintings abandon the calm and harmonious monumentality of classical art and show the new anticlassical style. The patron of the Palazzo Branconio

36. (*above*) Raphael: Rome, Palazzo Branconio dall' Aquila, begun 1515–17, view of half of façade by Marten van Heemskerck. Berlin, Staatliche Museen Preussischer Kulturbesitz, Kupferstichkabinett (vol. 1, 55 verso)

38. (*below right*) Raphael: Project for the Villa Madama, Rome, before 1520

37. (*below*) Rome, Palazzo Vidoni-Caffarelli, *c.* 1524, façade

dall'Aquila was the executor of Raphael's will. Vasari's attribution therefore seems very credible, the more so as its façade was one of the first examples of this new style in architecture. On the other hand, the Palazzo Vidoni – the only Roman palazzo of that phase of style to have survived – harks back to the pattern established by Bramante, although its architect failed to achieve the forcefulness of Bramante's design.

THE VILLA MADAMA

In the last years of his life, Raphael was working on plans for the villa of Cardinal Giulio de' Medici, later Pope Clement VII, on Monte Mario.[7] The superintendence of the works was entrusted to Antonio da Sangallo the Younger, who had also been an assistant of Raphael at St Peter's since 1516. A plan of his shows the state of the design about 1520 [38]. The centre of the villa was to be a large round courtyard. In addition to the living rooms, the villa was to have a theatre, stabling for two hundred horses, a huge hippodrome, and spreading gardens with ornamental waters. From the south, i.e. from the valley between the Vatican and Monte Mario, a great open stairway was to lead up to the main entrance of the villa. That programme could only be compared at the time with that of the Belvedere Court in the Vatican, which it was obviously intended to rival.

After the elevation of Clement VII, the Curia hardly had the means to continue the work on the Belvedere Court; thus the group of buildings on Monte Mario remained unfinished. The finished part was burnt down in the Sack of Rome. After a minimum of restoration, the villa passed in 1536 into the hands of Margaret of Parma, the daughter of Charles V, and it is from her that it takes its name, Villa Madama. What we see today is the product of a modern restoration; the only surviving parts of the original building [39] are the stump of the rotunda, five rooms and a loggia of three bays, and parts of the garden.

One factor which is essential to the comprehension of the villa is its situation on the slope of the hill [40]. The idea of terraces had already been applied in the Belvedere Court, but while in that case parts of older buildings had to be included in the plans, there were no restrictions on the choice of a site for the Villa Madama. The site ultimately chosen prevented any clear distinction between the building and the surrounding landscape; the fusion of architectural and natural forms must have been intentional from the beginning. That is why the principle of symmetry, which was the rule in Quattrocento villas and the Belvedere Court, was

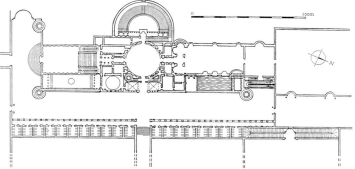

abandoned. True, the buildings surrounding the cortile are laid out on the axes of a cross, but each remains a perfectly independent structure adapted to the terrain, and actually designed with a view to its particular site. Thus the theatre was to be built into the slope of the hill and to be screened off towards the court by the *skene* or backdrop; i.e. it was not to form part of a whole scenic perspective, as in the Belvedere Court. There was no viewpoint from which the villa could be taken in as a whole. The hippodrome, the loggia, and the garden terraces, the theatre, and even the vestibule at the head of the stairs, were planned in such a way that they could be used simultaneously or singly; the spectator could only grasp the plan as a whole by visiting its parts in succession.

In the Villa Madama we find the same emphasis on interior views as in Raphael's Chigi Chapel, the same abandonment of a structural system governing the whole as in the Palazzo Branconio dall'Aquila. In the cortile, large and small orders stand side by side [41]; the garden loggia pilasters are Tuscan in the interior, Ionic outside. The two terrace fronts which have survived are modelled on different systems.

Yet the importance of the villa is not entirely due to the novel use of the terrain and the new relationship between the parts. No previous building had reproduced so exactly the function and form of ancient Roman models. Raphael's own description leaves no doubt that his design consciously conformed to the scheme he found in Pliny's letters. The theatre in Sangallo's drawing is an archaeologically correct specimen of the Roman type. It would have provided an adequate setting for the performance of the humanistic comedies written for the court of Leo X, which, in form and content, rival those of Terence and Plautus. The revival of the architectural types of antiquity goes hand in hand with that of Roman literature.

Further, there is no post-Roman building which reproduces so perfectly the atmosphere of a Roman interior as the garden loggia of the Villa Madama [42]. The immediate model was the stucco and fresco decoration of the Golden House and the Baths of Titus, which had been rediscovered about 1500. In them, as in the loggia, structure blends with ornament in one indissoluble whole. The dome over the central bay, the groin-vaults over the side bays, the extension of the side bays into apses, the system of wall piers and wall niches – there were precise models for all these details in the ruins from the age of Nero and the Flavians. And it was those buildings that Raphael, in a letter to Leo X, called the supreme achievement of the art of antiquity.[8] In the same letter, he says of Bramante's buildings that they came very close to antique architecture without ever having its wealth of *ornamenti*; the significance of that remark becomes evident in the Villa Madama. What Raphael meant was not ornament alone, but the ancient work of art as a whole; what he aimed at in his loggia was to restore the ancient unity of architecture, painting, and sculpture. Lavish though it is, structure and ornament are perfectly balanced there, each part clarifies, determines, and supplements the other, every point of view leads to another, equally significant vista.

The terrace gardens, in spite of centuries of neglect, still communicate something of that fusion of landscape and architecture which was characteristic of the whole villa. The waters from the three springs on the hillside collect in three niches hollowed out of the retaining wall of the main terrace. The type of fountain, composed of fragments of Roman sculpture, was often repeated in the Cinquecento. From those fountains the water is conducted to a large basin on the lower terrace which forms a fish-pond used also for watering horses. The grouping of the arches and niches of the retaining wall follows the pattern of a triumphal arch.

39. (*below*) Raphael: Rome, Villa Madama, begun *c.* 1516, plan before restoration

40. (*right*) Raphael: Rome, Villa Madama, begun *c.* 1516, from the north-east (before modern additions)

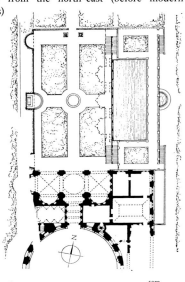

41. Raphael: Rome, Villa Madama, begun *c.* 1516, round courtyard

ST PETER'S

An unlucky star presided over Raphael's work on St Peter's. Leo X was far less interested in the new building than his predecessor. The ambitions of the Medici Pope were concentrated above all on the façade of his family church of S. Lorenzo in Florence and the rebuilding of the Florentines' church of S. Giovanni in Rome. Thus work on St Peter's proceeded slowly, as it had done in the last years of Julius II's life. Yet the pontificate of Leo X was of great importance for the building; it was then that a method was found for the work on St Peter's which was to remain essentially the same till the building was completed. While in Bramante's time planning and superintendence were united in one person, in 1516 the office of coadjutor was founded to carry responsibility for the planning and execution of the working drawings. Antonio da Sangallo the Younger, who held the office from 1516 to 1520, was promoted architect-in-chief after Raphael's death.[9]

Bramante's method probably adhered entirely to the conventions of the Quattrocento, as described, for instance, by Alberti. The project was, as a general rule, laid down in a model; after the plan had been marked out *in situ*, the project was discussed in detail with the masons and stone-cutters, and in certain cases full-size patterns were made for mouldings, capitals, and similar details. In the early part of the sixteenth century the method of work changed, since, besides the model and plan, increasing use was made of elevations for planning and execution. There are reasons why the parchment plan of St Peter's is the only hand-drawn plan that can be attributed with certainty to Bramante, while a surprisingly large number of drawings has been preserved from Raphael's term of office. Raphael, who prepared his paintings in systematic and accurate drawings, must have realized that the planning of the building which he took over from Bramante could not be mastered with a model and a plan alone [28]. Nor could the complex relationship between the piers of the dome, the transepts, and the nave, the dovetailing of old and new, be reproduced in perspective section, a process which Leonardo da Vinci, and still more the Bramante circle, had developed in order to reproduce

the spatial configuration. The linear perspective calculated for a single viewpoint necessarily entails distortions of size and spatial relations. That was the reason why Raphael had to seek for a rendering in which the masons could read off all the structural members in their right proportions, though on a smaller scale.

These new methods were the orthographical projection and the vertical, i.e. nonperspective, elevation. Its first correct definition is to be found in the memorandum already mentioned which Raphael addressed to Leo X in 1519.[10] Raphael begins by pointing out that the architect does not draw in the same way as the painter. What the architect needs is a representation which will permit him 'to master all the dimensions of a building and to see all its parts without distortion'. Three views, Raphael continues, are necessary to a complete representation, namely a ground plan, an elevation, and a section with orthogonal projection. This is the only way to allow all the parts of a building to be correctly presented.

This memorandum is significant not only for the history of architecture. Raphael formulates in it with perfect clarity that total abandonment of Bramante's perspective configuration of space which we have already seen in the Chigi Chapel. What became important was not a single view of a building, but all its aspects; no member must be deprived of its significance, and interior and exterior views must be drawn separately. The designing architect no longer needed to give verbal explanations to familiarize the master-masons with the details of his plan; a trained assistant in the office was now in a position to prepare the working drawings after the original designs and to superintend their execution.[11]

The problems which awaited solution after Bramante's death, and the divergent proposals for the continuation of the building, have already been mentioned. Even before the ratification of his appointment, Raphael was commissioned to prepare a new general design with a corresponding model. The model has been lost; in all probability it reproduced the plan which Serlio gives as Raphael's design.[12] The same plan appears in a rather more exact form in the Mellon sketchbook made by a member of the office; it also contains the corresponding section and front elevation [27, 28].[13]

At the beginning of his text to Raphael's plan, Serlio points out that several parts of Bramante's model were incomplete, and that Raphael, in designing his plan, made use of those left behind by Bramante. Serlio then goes on to discuss the purely central plan by Baldassare Peruzzi [16B], again stating that it incorporates what Bramante had left behind. A comparison between these illustrations and texts shows that Raphael's basilican plan is the first complete reproduction of a plan for St Peter's to have come down to us which we know was intended for execution. Raphael was superintendent of the works from 1514 to 1520. The plan, section, and elevation in the Mellon sketchbook, copied

by a pupil, tally exactly with the three views called for in Raphael's memorandum.

This plan stands out from all its competitiors by its matter-of-fact clarity. An aisled nave of five bays is set in front of Bramante's domed space. This gives the building a longitudinal axis, while the actual façade is a broad, two-storeyed portico. Bramante's system of pilasters is employed for the piers of the nave and aisles, and, with corresponding variations, for the interior articulation of the aisle chapels; thus all the supports are of the same basic form. On the side of the nave and aisles they are faced with double pilasters, under the archivolts with niches. The height of the nave was fixed by Bramante's arches at the crossing; its breadth was to be reduced from 23 to about 19.3 m. (69 to about 58 feet 6 in.) by the reinforcement of the piers.[14] The system of minor domes was restored, though it had been decided about 1514 to remove the two western ones at least.[15]

Beside the nave, the most important feature of the design was the ambulatories round the transepts. These one-storey passages appear in most of the plans made after Bramante's death. It is uncertain whether they had already been introduced by Bramante or came in only under his successors. In itself the motif was statical in nature. We know that the foundation of the piers proved inadequate soon after the elevation of Leo X. But there must also have been some anxiety as to whether Bramante's transepts would resist the thrust of the dome. For that reason it was decided to set the outer walls, which were exposed to the thrust, nearer to the piers of the dome than was originally intended. The ambulatories made it possible to reduce the interval between the crossing and the apses, and at the same time to double the exterior walls of the apse itself. The thrust of the dome could be conveyed over the vaults of the transepts to the lower, tunnel-vaulted ring of the ambulatories, and from them to the outer walls.

The elevation of the arms of the cross is given in Sangallo's drawings [29, 30].[16] The giant order of the crossing is continued in the piers of the transepts; the columns between the piers form a minor order. Above their architrave there was to be a kind of triforium of blind arcades, and a group of three windows was to be inserted in the clerestory. The ambulatories, like the choir of S. Maria del Popolo, were to be lit by slanting shafts in the outer wall.

Exterior views of the ambulatories show a Doric order with engaged columns and aedicules; the insignia of Leo X appear on the metopes. According to the elevation shown in the Mellon sketchbook there were to be Doric columns on the ground floor of the towers and the lower ranges of the front [27]. The giant order of four engaged Corinthian columns and the gigantic pediment which screened the Benediction Loggia in the centre of the façade are a complete innovation.

There is something odd about the way in which Bramante's designs have been transposed and developed in this project. His system of pilasters on their tall plinths was, like the dome, retained without alteration, but a wealth of smaller members was added to the giant order. The exterior now has a richly articulated Doric system with a powerful relief effect. The clear and simple relation between the interior and exterior views, which Bramante had aimed at, is abandoned. The walls enclosing the arms of the cross are no

42. Raphael: Rome, Villa Madama, begun c.1516, interior of the loggia

longer the outer wall, but are separated from it by a new stratum of space – the ambulatories round the transepts and choir, the chapels in the aisles. Thus the interior assumes an autonomy which it did not have in Bramante's plan, nor does the composition of the exterior give any hint of the system governing the interior. Here, once again, we encounter the principle of the independence of the individual views or members of a building which we have already encountered in the Villa Madama and the Palazzo Branconio dall'Aquila.

Raphael had no intention of altering Bramante's dome or the shape and structure of the vaulting. The single-shell vault without a timber roof which appears in the Mellon sketchbook could only be executed in cemented masonry, and even the steps leading to the crown of the nave and transept tunnel-vaults would have had to be cast. Thus in the use of Roman forms and methods the projects agree; yet Raphael went a step further. The exterior view of his church was to be completely dominated by the ancient system of posts and lintels. Both in the ambulatories and the façade, free-standing or engaged columns are surmounted by a Doric architrave; the façade, like that of a classical temple, consists of columns and a pediment. Further, this arrangement is an obvious correction of the system of S. Andrea in Mantua; in the Mellon section of St Peter's the giant order of the façade corresponds exactly to that of the nave, so that the apex of the pediment is at the same height as the apex of the vault, while at Mantua the height of the interior structure does not tally with that of the exterior. Moreover, the classical order is not applied to the wall as a flat ornament, as it is at Mantua; it has become free, and looks like a structural scaffolding of the building.

With its nave, its tall towers, and its colossal front, this project surpassed that of the first phase of building both in scale and grandeur. Considering the financial distress of the Curia under Leo X, it was still more utopian than the centrally planned church begun by Bramante for Julius II. Yet Raphael's design, ratifying Bramante's final scheme, was a return to the traditional T-shaped design of old St Peter's. Raphael's new St Peter's would, like the old church, have been a processional way from the portico of the façade to the Apostle's tomb under the crossing. By deciding on the basilican plan, Bramante's project was relieved of that utopian factor which is inherent in any purely central plan for the solution of liturgical problems. St Peter's is more than the burial place of the Apostle; it is one of the seven churches which every pilgrim to Rome must visit. Moreover at least since the fifteenth century it has functioned as a cathedral, since the Vatican is the official residence of the Pope. The Roman pilgrimage churches, like most Western cathedrals, are basilican in plan. Late in the fifteenth century this form had also been chosen for the church of Loreto, which contains the Santa Casa and is related to St Peter's in many of its functions. Raphael's combination of a dome with a nave

stresses the function of St Peter's as a church, while the centrally planned building designed by Bramante was to have been a triumphal monument to the Apostle and his successor, the reigning Pope.

*

Antonio da Sangallo, who succeeded Raphael at St Peter's in 1520, set forth the defects of Raphael's project in a famous memorandum.[17] The design, he says, provided for only *one* large chapel in addition to the small chapels in the aisles, and that was the west apse. The piers in the nave were heavier than those in the crossing, and the engaged Doric columns on the exterior were too tall in proportion to their circumference; in the interior the relationship between the tall pedestals of the piers and the niches in them was unsatisfactory. The lighting of the nave was inadequate; the space behind the west apse provided no real solution, since it was not connected with the interior of the apse.

What is most enlightening in this memorandum lies less in the details than in the fact that Sangallo accepts the general shape of Raphael's design and also abides by the connection between the nave and the dome.[18] His colleague Baldassare Peruzzi, on the other hand, made a design, which has been handed down by Serlio, proposing a return to the original idea of the purely central plan, with four minor domes, turrets, and the arms of the cross all of the same shape [16B]. Serlio says of this plan that the church was to have had four entrances in the apses of the arms of the cross, with the altar standing in the middle. In later designs Peruzzi too decided on the basilican plan and tried to find a solution in which the vaulting and lighting system of the Roman baths would be retained in the nave.

The building of St Peter's progressed very slowly during Raphael's term of office. Yet the designs created in this period had a determining influence on the development of the new style. It is worthy of note that Antonio da Sangallo the Younger, however critical his judgement of Raphael's design may have been, adopted Raphael's idiom in his own work. As will be seen later, the new style was by no means the only one practised at the time. It only appears in the work of architects who were active in Rome in the twenties of the sixteenth century, and had seen, or even collaborated in, Raphael's new interpretation of Bramante's ideas.

The immediate consequence of the Sack of Rome of 1527 in Rome itself was an artistic vacuum. Like St Peter's, every building enterprise of note came to a standstill, and new buildings were not to be thought of. It was only under the pontificate of Paul III (1534–49) that a new florescence occurred. But the Roman buildings of the forties and still more of the fifties have a stamp which clearly distinguishes them from the classic style of Bramante and Raphael. The development of style in the thirties and forties was determined by Florence and northern Italy.

CHAPTER 3

Other Early Sixteenth-Century Buildings in Rome and Central Italy

ROME

PALAZZI

The pontificates of Julius II and Leo X were of particular importance for the general aspect of Rome. These were the years in which Rome caught up with Florence, where during the great extension of the city in the fourteenth century broad, straight streets leading from the centre to the new city walls had been laid out.[1] The new Borgo Alessandrino had already been erected between the Vatican and Castel S. Angelo under Alexander VI; Julius II had two more streets laid out parallel to the Tiber, on the west bank the via Lungara, which connects the Vatican with the old Trastevere quarter, and on the city side the via Giulia, named after the Pope – the torso of the Palazzo di Giustizia begun by Bramante stands in this street [43]. Leo X then constructed the via Leonina (now called Ripetta) connecting the Ponte S. Angelo with the Porta del Popolo, the northern entrance to the city. The centre of this system was the Castel S. Angelo and the bridge it dominated. The Campo Marzio, enclosed by the great curve of the Tiber, became more and more the centre of the city. The new cardinals' palazzi built there were more habitable than their rather more fortress-like predecessors of the fifteenth century, such as the Palazzo Venezia or the Cancelleria; they are also more urban, since their fronts are aligned with the street frontages. Among this group are the Palazzi Corneto (now Giraud-Torlonia), della Valle, Sora-Fieschi, and Giovanni de' Medici (now Lante).

In the patrician palazzi, too, the aesthetic effect of the façade and the cortile became more important than their defensive strength. Thus the Savelli had their ancient family fortress, the ruins of the Theatre of Marcellus, restored as a palazzo by Peruzzi. New buildings, such as the Palazzo Vidoni-Caffarelli, or Peruzzi's Palazzo Massimi, are not different in type from the cardinals' residences.

Hand in hand with this urbanization of the palazzi of cardinals and the aristocracy there went a rise in the architectural ambitions of the ordinary citizens' dwellings and business premises. The houses of the humanists and bankers working at the Curia rivalled the palazzi of the nobility. The best example of a humanist's house of the time is the recently restored palazzo which the consistorial advocate Melchiorre Baldassini had built for himself to Antonio da Sangallo the Younger's design about 1516–19 [44, 45]. Even for Vasari the house was 'the most comfortable dwelling in Rome, and the first in which the stairs, the cortile with its loggias, the entrances and fireplaces are designed with the greatest charm'.[2]

The Palazzo Baldassini shows marked differences from the preceding type, which is illustrated by the palazzi Caprini, dall'Aquila, and Caffarelli [23, 36, 37]. In these, the five- or seven-bay façade has two main storeys, the ground floor houses the botteghe which were let as shops or workshops, while on the piano nobile there were the private apartments and state rooms of the owners. The intermediate storeys, the mezzanine over the botteghe and the second mezzanine over the piano nobile, can hardly be seen in the façade; the windows were made as small as possible and subordinated to the scheme of the two main storeys.

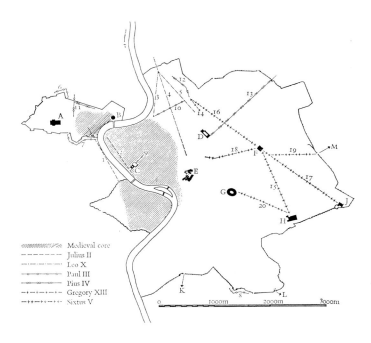

Medieval core
------- Julius II
—·—·—·— Leo X
—◦—◦—◦— Paul III
—◦◦—◦◦— Pius IV
—+—+—+— Gregory XIII
—++—++— Sixtus V

0   1000m   2000m   3000m

43. Plan of Rome with streets planned in the sixteenth century (Gerhard Krämer)

1. Via Lungara	A. St Peter's
2. Via Giulia	B. Castel S. Angelo
3. Via Ripetta	C. Palazzo Farnese
4. Via del Corso (Via Flaminia)	D. Quirinal Palace
5. Via Babuino (Via Paolina)	E. Campidoglio and S. Maria in
6. Fortifications around Belvedere	Aracoeli
7. Fortification Porta S. Spirito-Porta Cavalleggeri	F. S. Maria Maggiore
8. Fortification near Porta Ardeatina	G. Colosseum
9. Piazza Farnese and Via dei Baullari	H. S. Giovanni in Laterano and Lateran Palace
10. Via Condotti	J. S. Croce in Gerusalemme
11. Borgo Angelico	K. Porta S. Paolo and road to S. Paolo fuori le Mura
12. Passeggiata di Villa Medici	L. Porta S. Sebastiano and road to S. Sebastiano fuori le Mura
13. Via Venti Settembre (Strada Pia)	M. Porta S. Lorenzo and road to S. Lorenzo fuori le Mura
14. Via Gregoriana	
15. Via Merulana	
16. Via Sistina	
17. Via Santa Croce di Gerusalemme	
18. Via Panisperna	
19. Street linking S. Maria Maggiore and Porta S. Lorenzo	
20. Street linking S. Giovanni in Laterano and the Colosseum	

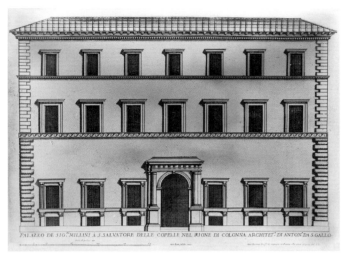

44. Antonio da Sangallo the Younger: Rome, Palazzo Palma-Baldassini, *c.* 1516–19, façade, engraving by Falda

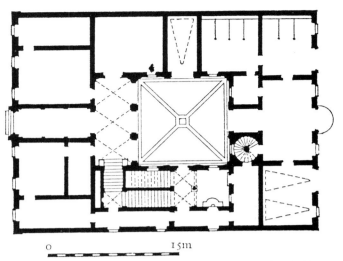

45. Antonio da Sangallo the Younger: Rome, Palazzo Palma-Baldassini, *c.* 1516–19, plan

An idea of the classic palazzo courtyards can be obtained today from the Palazzo Caffarelli; the ground floor consists of three arcades on each side, which are supported by massive, plain piers.[3] In such cases the late Quattrocento had generally employed columns; in more ostentatious buildings such as the Cancelleria, the arcades were carried right round the cortile, while smaller buildings have a two-storeyed loggia only against the front range. It may be that the shape of the supports, and the regular arcading on all sides and its restriction to the ground floor in the cortile of the Palazzo Caffarelli represented an innovation. About 1520 it became customary to face the pillars with pilasters towards the courtyard; the model was probably Bramante's Belvedere Court. An early example of this new type is the Palazzo Baldassini; on the entrance side the cortile has a two-storeyed loggia, with three arches; the pilasters facing the piers on the ground floor are Tuscan, on the piano nobile Ionic.

The most splendid design for a cortile in the classic phase has only been preserved in a drawing. It is Bramante's plan for the Palazzo di Giustizia with its square courtyard, each side consisting of five arcades.[4] Towards the court, the pillars were to be faced with engaged columns after the model of the Theatre of Marcellus. Antonio da Sangallo the Younger gave the pillars of the Palazzo Farnese, begun in 1517, the same form; the later history of this cortile, which was given its final form by Michelangelo, will be discussed further on.

The façade of the Palazzo Baldassini is also an innovation. Instead of the botteghe on the ground floor there are barred windows, their sills resting on brackets [45]. On the piano nobile Sangallo abandoned the articulation by engaged columns and aedicules which is so characteristic of Bramante's and Raphael's palazzi; an ornamental band serves both as the cornice of the ground floor and the window-sill of the piano nobile, while the balconies in front of the windows, customary till then, have been eliminated. The main accent of the façade lies on the portal with the engaged Doric columns and their entablature. The vertical is stressed only by the rusticated travertine quoins; the windows are mere openings in the plain brick surface.

The botteghe on the ground floor disappeared for the most part from the Roman palazzo after the Sack of Rome; obviously they had come to seem undignified. The ground-floor rooms now open on to the cortile and are used by the retainers and clients of the patron. It was possible to reduce the lower mezzanine, which had till then provided room for the indispensable storerooms and workshops of the botteghe, or, as in the Palazzo Baldassini, eliminate it altogether. The second floor, on the other hand, became more important. At the same time, more space was left for staircases and greater attention paid to lighting and comfort. This development can be followed very closely in the buildings of the second quarter of the century; it introduces a type which, in its general appearance, recalls the Florentine palazzi of the Quattrocento rather than the Roman palazzi of the early Cinquecento. The most splendid example of the type is the Palazzo Farnese, begun by Cardinal Alessandro Farnese and

46. Rome, Palazzo Alberini-Cicciaporci, under construction in 1515, façade, engraving by Lafreri(?)

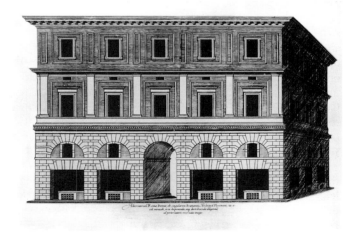

47. Rome, S. Maria di Loreto, begun 1507, looking north

enlarged after his elevation to the papacy in 1534. Sangallo's new façade is a maturer, more ornate version of the façade of the Palazzo Baldassini.

Even in our own day the Campo Marzio is the most densely populated part of Rome. Few of the buildings have preserved their original appearance. The correction of the street and river systems in the nineteenth century, with all the demolitions and renovations it entailed, made further inroads into the old buildings still standing. There has, however, been preserved in the Palazzo Alberini-Cicciaporci one of the banking houses after which the via de'Banchi was named; it led from the Ponte S. Angelo to the former papal mint. In 1515 the builder, Giulio Alberini, let the palazzo, then under construction, to the Florentine bankers Bernardo da Verrazzano and Buonaccorso Ruccellai, though pledging himself to complete the building 'well and decently, and according to the design'.[5]

The old attribution of the Palazzo Alberini to Bramante or Giulio Romano must be abandoned because of its date of building; it cannot be given to Raphael because of its style.[6]* On the other hand, these names are enough to give a hint of the high standing and artistic lineage of the architect. The façade differs from those built by Bramante and Raphael primarily by the remarkably shallow relief of its articulation [46]. The flat rustication of the ground floor and the pilaster strips of the piano nobile look like engraved ornament; an absolutely unprecedented flat framework appears in the upper storey. A plain band separates the botteghe from the openings in the mezzanine, and the rusticated basement is topped by the same jutting cornice as that in the Palazzo Caprini. Another remarkable feature is the material, namely roughcast brickwork in both upper storeys; freestone is used only for cornices and quoins. The rustication of the lowest storey consists, like that of the Palazzo Caprini, of stucco.[7]

The arch of the portal is of the same height and width as the blind arches which frame the botteghe and mezzanine; it leads into a tunnel-vaulted vestibule of exactly the same height as the arcade of the cortile. This relationship between façade and cortile is new. Both in the Palazzo Caprini and

the Palazzo Caffarelli the mezzanines were carried across the portals, so that the entrances leading into the cortile were no higher than the botteghe. Since there is no mezzanine over the portal in the Palazzo Alberini, the central bay is strongly accentuated; at the same time it was possible to establish a consonance between the portal and the cortile. This was the first step to the development which led, not much later, to the complete elimination of the botteghe and mezzanine in the Palazzo Baldassini.

CHURCHES

Church building in Rome in the early sixteenth century was governed, as it was throughout Italy, by the centralized plan.[8] Not only Bramante's Tempietto and his two demolished churches, SS. Celso e Giuliano and S. Biagio della Pagnotta, both situated near the Banchi, but five other centrally planned churches were begun in the city before the Sack of Rome: under Julius II S. Eligio degli Orefici, the church of the goldsmiths, and S. Maria di Loreto in the Forum of Trajan, both vaulted much later; under Leo X the church of the Florentines, S. Giovanni dei Fiorentini, and that of S. Maria in Porta Paradisi, now part of the hospital of S. Giacomo degli Incurabili; and, over a circular plan, the church of S. Salvatore by S. Luigi dei Francesi, begun during the same period by a French architect commissioned by François I, which, however, did not progress beyond its first beginnings.[9] In fact none of these churches has been preserved in its original state.

The domes of S. Maria di Loreto[10] and S. Maria in Porta Paradisi[11] rise from octagonal bases, i.e. they are domical vaults; in both, the transition from the square substructure to the octagon is effected by deep niches in the corner of the square.[12] This type of dome structure is characteristic of the turn of the century. It can be compared with that of the domes of S. Maria della Pace in Rome, the sacristy of S. Spirito in Florence, and the church of the Santa Casa at Loreto, which just preceded it. The exteriors of both the Roman churches are provided with remarkably slender, flat pilasters [47]; in their proportions and the shape of the

48. Cola da Caprarola and others: Todi, S. Maria della Consolazione, begun 1508, plan

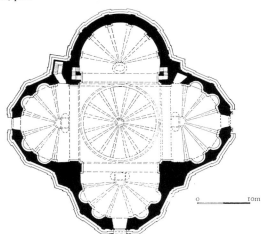

capitals they recall the contemporary façade of S. Maria dell'Anima, which also has the same fine brickwork.[13]

The architect of S. Eligio degli Orefici, doubtless influenced by Bramante's designs for St Peter's, adopted for his dome the hemisphere on pendentives.[14]* The plan, a Greek cross with very short arms, was an innovation, and not only in Rome; it became the model for many family chapels of the late Cinquecento. The shape of the dome, which was not built till about 1530, is exactly the same as that of the Chigi Chapel. The church, however, has been altered out of all recognition.

The predominance of the centralized plan is the expression of the religious building as a free-standing monument which was characteristic of the turn of the century and found its classic form in Bramante's Tempietto. The preference for programmes which admitted a centralized plan is unmistakable. Even in the drawings of ancient buildings the interest of the time was concentrated on the rotunda. The ideal of the free-standing Christian 'temple' could hardly be transposed into reality within the bounds of the city of Rome. One reason for the centrally planned buildings of the early Cinquecento being drastically altered or entirely demolished is that, by the end of the century, the centralized plan was regarded as pagan and unsuited to the Christian church.

CENTRAL ITALY

S. MARIA DELLA CONSOLAZIONE AT TODI

The pilgrimage church of S. Maria della Consolazione at Todi [48–50], begun in 1508, two years after the foundation stone of new St Peter's had been laid, has always been regarded as a simplified version of Bramante's plan for St Peter's. The church stands a little below the town on a terrace which commands an incomparable view of the Umbrian landscape. Crowned as it is with a dome and dominating the scene, offering the same aspect on all sides, consisting in plan and elevation of simple, geometrical forms – the square, the circle, and the semicircle – nowhere was the ideal of the centralized plan as Alberti had first defined it realized in purer form than in this church, and there is no other centrally planned Renaissance church which so harmoniously unites its liturgical function as a place of pilgrimage and worship, its political function as a monumental foundation of the community, and its standing as a work of art.[15]

In the contracts of 1508–9, which allocated the preliminary works, the executant architect is named as Cola da Caprarola. The only information we have about him is that he worked previously on papal buildings in Latium. The church was many years in building; the vaulting was not begun till 1568, and the dome was not closed till 1606.[16]

The plan of the Consolazione is a square with apses on all four sides. Only the apse containing the miraculous image is

49 and 50. Cola da Caprarola and others: Todi, S. Maria della Consolazione, begun 1508. Exterior (*left*) and interior (*right*)

semicircular; the other three are polygonal, both inside and outside, and all have portals. Whether the purely centralized plan was intended from the beginning, it is as impossible to say as with Bramante's St Peter's. The contract of 1509 provides only for three apses, and explicitly avoids any commitment for the plan of the fourth side. This remarkable indecision may be indirect confirmation of the fact that the plans for St Peter's were not settled either at the time; nor does a binding model seem to have existed at Todi, at any rate in 1509.

As a pilgrimage church housing a miraculous image, the Consolazione is of the same type as S. Maria delle Carceri at Prato, built some twenty years before. That the square plan with apses, and not the Greek cross, as at Prato, was decided on is certainly due to the influence of the plans for St Peter's, even if at Todi a nave was envisaged instead of the fourth apse. Yet the simplicity and clarity of the exterior view recall the Tuscan centralized compositions of the late Quattrocento rather than Bramante's far more complex system as it is represented on the medal and in the parchment plan. Towers and subsidiary domes were not used at Todi; the staircases and the sacristy are accommodated in the corners of the square and are invisible from the outside. Except for the three entrances, all four sides of the church

51. Antonio da Sangallo the Elder: Montepulciano, Madonna di S. Biagio, begun 1518, exterior

are articulated in the same way, and the elevation and structure are clear at the first glance. The thrust of the dome is carried over the vaulting of the apses to the exterior walls. The real weight of the dome rests on the arches of the crossing; this is brought out in the colossal piers of the crossing in the interior, and on the exterior by the corners of the square projecting between the apses.

Many details – for instance the flat pilasters, the shape of the windows and capitals on the exterior, the reeded capitals in the interior, the repeated projection of the entablature over the pilasters – are most closely akin to S. Maria del Calcinaio at Cortona, a church which Cola da Caprarola certainly knew. The giant pilasters of the crossing may already show the influence of the articulation of the piers of Bramante's dome.

The ornament of the vaulting ribs and transverse arches is

52. Antonio da Sangallo the Elder: Montepulciano, Madonna di S. Biagio, begun 1518, interior

in the style of the end of the century. The tall drum of the dome with its coupled pilasters cannot reproduce the original plans; it already presupposes the Roman domes of the later Cinquecento.

THE MADONNA DI S. BIAGIO AT MONTEPULCIANO

Ten years after the Consolazione, the Madonna di S. Biagio was begun at Montepulciano [51–53]. It occupies a very similar site, and the history of its foundation is also in many ways similar to that of Todi. It is therefore probable that the design was ultimately determined by the peculiarity of the site. In Rome, the same years saw the beginning of the Villa Madama, which also stands on an open hillside. All these buildings stand witness to a new relationship between architecture and landscape: they are intended to be seen

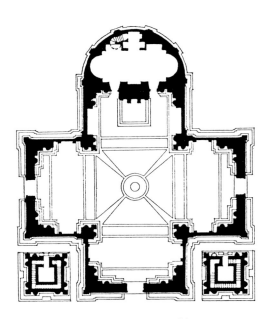

53. Antonio da Sangallo the Elder: Montepulciano, Madonna di S. Biagio, begun 1518, plan

against a background of nature. At the same time the building imparts to the site a new and enhanced significance.

The architect of the Madonna di S. Biagio was Antonio da Sangallo the Elder, the brother of the builder of S. Maria delle Carceri at Prato. Antonio had collaborated with Cola da Caprarola on the fortress of Civita Castellana in 1494; the authorities of Florence, his native city, had employed him for the most part on fortifications. In 1517 he had submitted a model for the logge of the Piazza SS. Annunziata in Florence, though it is uncertain whether the idea of repeating Brunelleschi's Ospedale façade on the opposite side of the square originated with the architect or the building committee. This piazza holds an important place in the history of town planning; the total picture of the uniformly articulated façades becomes more important than the individual building. Sangallo's loggia remains so faithful to Brunelleschi's forms that only the details betray that it was built a century later.[17]

The church of the Madonna di S. Biagio was built so quickly that Clement VII was able to consecrate it in 1529. Antonio da Sangallo, who died in 1534, probably began the vaulting of the dome, the first of the great Cinquecento domes to be completed.[18] Baccio d'Agnolo, the Florentine architect, designed the lantern in 1544; his son Giuliano di Baccio continued the campanile, whose top storey, added in 1564, is most likely not that of the original plan. A second campanile never got beyond the ground floor.

The plan of the church, a Greek cross, recalls the Madonna delle Carceri, built nearly thirty years before; so do the portals and the windows and pediments of the exterior. As at Prato, the square of the crossing appears above the arms of the cross as the base of the dome, but the dome itself already shows the 'Roman' type, i.e. the cylindrical drum faced with pilasters both in the interior and exterior, and the hemispherical shape. There is an echo too of the plans for St Peter's in the double towers of the façade, and in the peculiar placing of the sacristy in an oblong space

enclosed by a semicircle behind the high altar,[19] which, seen from the outside, looks like a one-storeyed choir. Thus, unlike the arrangement at Todi, one side of the church is distinguished as the front, and the opposite arm of the cross as chancel; this gives the church an unmistakable orientation. That is, of course, true only of the exterior; in the interior, apart from the portals and the altar, all the arms of the cross are of the same shape. The sacristy does not figure in the spatial picture.

The vaulting system is the same as at Prato: a dome on pendentives over the crossing, tunnel-vaults over the arms of the cross. The system of the walls supporting the tunnel vaults is quite unprecedented. As the plan shows, the weight of the vault is concentrated on the corners of the building. The corners of the crossing project into the interior like free-standing pillars. Instead of the flat pilasters of Prato and Todi, there are deeply modelled Doric pilasters and engaged columns crowned by a jutting entablature. This scheme runs consistently round all four walls. The relief of the order is given greater force by the fact that the walls beside the piers of the crossing are treated as deep altar niches, so that the function of the wall as a boundary of space can hardly be felt.

The walls enclosing the interior of the Consolazione look two-dimensional; the pilasters are so flat that they resemble an engraved device of verticals and horizontals. At Montepulciano, the pilasters and engaged columns project from the wall in three dimensions, and the order regains its ancient function of support. That, however, only holds good of the interior; as the absence of engaged columns and the low relief of the pilasters show, the exterior is conceived as a membrane-like shell supporting nothing, and, as at Todi, acts as pure surface. This comes out most clearly in the framework of the attic. The system of the crossing piers in the interior only reappears in the tower; there too the weight is imagined as resting on the corners, and the distinction is made between supporting members and filling wall. In the upper storeys, which have less weight to bear, the relief of the order is of course reduced and the intermediate panels widened.

The Madonna di S. Biagio was begun in 1518. Whatever reminiscences of the centralized composition of Prato, Cortona, and Todi it may awaken, the new features just mentioned cannot derive from those sources. Details such as the towers of the façade and the sacristy behind the altar reveal unmistakably a knowledge of Raphael's plans for St Peter's, and in Raphael's buildings, e.g. in the Chigi Chapel, the distinction is made between the order as support and the wall as filling, as in the interior of S. Biagio. For the articulation of the towers Sangallo adopted practically verbatim the exterior elevation of Raphael's transepts of St Peter's. Much of the magnificent effect of the interior comes from the use of the Doric order on a low plinth, and this again looks back to Raphael, and not to Bramante.

THE PALAZZO PANDOLFINI IN FLORENCE

There were other members of the Sangallo family who felt the influence of Raphael or were working for him at the time. Antonio the Younger, the nephew of the architect of Montepulciano, had become Raphael's assistant in the

54. Raphael and others:
Florence, Palazzo Pandolfini,
begun *c.* 1518

office of St Peter's in 1516. His cousin, Gianfrancesco da Sangallo, began the Palazzo Pandolfini in Florence before 1520, after a design by Raphael.[20] This building plays a special part in the history of Florentine palazzo façades [54]; it is a fusion of the Florentine type, represented by such buildings as the palazzi Medici and Strozzi, with the Roman type developed by Bramante and Raphael in the early decades of the Cinquecento. The great Florentine palazzi of the late Quattrocento have three main storeys, rusticated throughout, the windows being framed merely by the voussoirs of the round arches. The Palazzo Pandolfini, on the other hand, has two storeys, like Raphael's Roman palazzi, and their windows have aedicules, i.e. they are given pediments on columns.[21] The great breadth is also of Florentine provenance; except for the Cancelleria, no Roman façade ever had as many as nine bays, as was originally planned for the Palazzo Pandolfini. The absence of shops on the ground floor is a Florentine feature too.

In the same way as in the previous palazzi, the round arch of the entrance does not rise above the ground-floor windows. Its shape and size are an innovation. It is only here that rustication is employed; it projects from the smooth surface of the wall. The keystones above the top of the entrance are so tall that they reach the cornice, and the horizontal blocks on both sides of the round arch are almost as wide as the opening itself. True, the portal in this way certainly remains organically bound to the façade, yet the central bay of the façade is effectively distinguished from the others. Moreover, since the balustrade over the portal is broader than those to left and right, the middle window in the piano nobile too was to have been wider than the others. In that way the central bay in both storeys would have been strongly stressed, an innovation of great consequence which went beyond the Palazzo Caffarelli, and for which there was only one preliminary stage in Rome, namely in the Palazzo Cicciaporci.

55. Giuliano da Sangallo: Project for the façade of S. Lorenzo, Florence, 1516. Florence, Uffizi (A 276)

56. Cola dall'Amatrice: L'Aquila, S. Bernardino, façade, begun 1525

Finally, the designs for the façade for S. Lorenzo in Florence, made by the aged Giuliano da Sangallo in the last year of his life, also show the influence of Raphael [55]. These drawings, dated 1516, are closely akin in style to the church of Montepulciano, designed by Sangallo's brother. The most Raphaelesque idea is to set in front of the façade an order of coupled Doric columns as a kind of portico, with its balustrade crowned with an entablature.[22] There was no predecessor for the proportions and details of this order, either in previous Florentine buildings or in Giuliano's earlier designs. The source of this new and highly monumental style is to be sought in Rome.

A Doric double order which is the almost exact counterpart of Giuliano's design is to be found far away from

57. Naples, S. Giovanni a Carbonara, Cappella Caracciolo, begun c. 1515

Florence in the ground floor of the façade of S. Bernardino at L'Aquila in the Abruzzi [56], a work, dated 1527, by Cola dall'Amatrice, who was also active as a painter.[23] The alternating pediments over the portals and the niches are reminiscent of the drawings for S. Lorenzo. By this time the tall pedestals under the columns in the façade of S. Bernardino were of course antiquated; they make one feel that the architect was only familiar with developments in Rome up to about 1515, but not with the Chigi Chapel and Raphael's later designs. For the upper storey, with only his own imagination to guide him, Cola tried, with no great success, to work the new, classical apparatus of form into the medieval scheme for church façades customary in the Abruzzi.

Another building dating from the same time which shows the new classical repertory of form is the mortuary chapel of the Caracciolo di Vico family in S. Giovanni a Carbonara in Naples [57].[24] This domed family mausoleum resembles the Chigi Chapel in form and function. Yet it is illuminating to note how differently the Neapolitan architect handles his theme. The walls are entirely encrusted with marble, and the tombs and the altar are housed in apse-like niches between which the walls are faced with coupled Doric half-columns on tall pedestals. The spatial effect resembles that of Bramante's Tempietto rather than that of the Chigi Chapel; the treatment of the wall is not far removed from that of the encasement of the Casa Santa of Loreto. The architect must have been familiar with Bramante's buildings, for there is an echo of him in the peculiar disposition of the portal of the chapel, which is cut into the chancel wall at a splay, and gives the visitor a precisely calculated prospect of the altar.

CHAPTER 4

Baldassare Peruzzi and Antonio da Sangallo the Younger

BALDASSARE PERUZZI

Like Bramante and Raphael, Baldassare Peruzzi (1481–1536) was originally a painter. Serlio writes that Peruzzi, as he was making perspective drawings of columns and other members of architecture, was so enraptured by the proportions of the columns that in the end he 'confined himself to architecture and excelled all others in that field'.[1] This may be an invention, but the close connection between architecture and perspective representation implied in it is one of the fundamental features of Peruzzi's art. His *œuvre*, like that of Bramante, shows quite clearly the inseparable bond between perspective and architecture in the building practice of the early Cinquecento.

When he came from Siena to Rome about 1505, Peruzzi was probably familiar with the ideas of Francesco di Giorgio Martini.[2] There is an echo of the latter's work in Peruzzi's predilection for drawing as a means of artistic expression, in his bias towards theory, and in the versatility of his interests. In addition to ancient and medieval plans, his sketches contain fortifications, road plans of Tuscany, and designs for stage scenery.

Peruzzi's first building in Rome was the villa which his fellow-Sienese Agostino Chigi built between 1509 and 1511. It stands on the Lungara, the bank of the Tiber between the Vatican and Trastevere which was at that time being built up. The Farnesina of today stands beside Bramante's works as the most important building of the first decade of the century; it is also the first suburban villa of the Cinquecento.[3] It is typical for Peruzzi in that it neither continues nor inaugurates a tradition. It is distinguished from the villas of the late Quattrocento – Poggio a Caiano, Poggioreale, and Innocent VIII's Belvedere – by the fact that two sides of its exterior appear to be a two-storeyed palazzo. The articulation of these 'urban façades' with Doric pilasters and oblong windows was an innovation in Rome; the Cancelleria and the buildings derived from it still have round-headed windows on the ground floor and the main storey. A notable difference from the Cancelleria is that there is no rhythmic pilaster grouping and no marble incrustation. The garden front of the Farnesina [58], a five-bay loggia flanked by projecting wings, is one of the earliest examples of that U-shaped plan which survived, especially in France, as the *cour d'honneur*. The fourth front, which looks out on the Tiber, is like the urban fronts with the exception of the loggia of the ground floor.

Like the façades, the plan is asymmetrical [59]. Half the ground floor is occupied by the two loggias, which meet at right angles; this was to open the view on to the garden and the river. They contained the famous frescoes by Raphael and his pupils: in the garden loggia the Cycle of Psyche [61], in the loggia overlooking the river the mythological horoscope of the patron and the Triumph of Galatea.[4] Unlike the Villa Madama, built ten years later, in which stucco plays an important part, the decoration of the Villa Farnesina is almost entirely painted, as it is in Raphael's Stanze, which belong practically to the same period. Along with the Stanze, the Farnesina frescoes are the most important examples of that architectural painting in perspective which, according to Alberti, gives the painter his supremacy over the architect.[5] It is perhaps not by chance that Peruzzi the painter executed with his own hand the decoration of his patron's state apartment in the piano nobile. The mere name of the room – Sala delle Colonne – shows how completely it is dominated by its architectural painting [60]; the actual subjects of the frescoes are the gods of Olympus. The perspective illusion is calculated for a viewpoint not far from the entrance. On both short walls heavy piers faced with pilasters alternate with wide-set columns, and the visitor is made to feel that he is looking out on to balconies and over the Roman landscape from the spaces between the columns. There is no socle zone; piers and columns seem to stand direct on the floor, so that the spectator sees only supporting members and an illusory open space. There is not, as there is even in Raphael's Stanze, a continuous pedestal. In the Chigi Chapel in S. Maria del Popolo, built soon after the Villa Farnesina for the same client, Raphael gives the pilasters similar low bases. In both cases the effect is the same; the spectator no longer 'looks into' or 'up to' the building, as he would with a picture, but stands in the midst of the supporting structure.

In the history of perspective painting, the Sala delle Colonne occupies a curious position of transition. The fixing of the viewpoint is still entirely in the tradition of Bramante. Yet Peruzzi goes beyond Bramante in that his perspective cannot really be taken in at one glance; it is in relation to all four walls of the room, and while the illusionist enlargement of the actual space might be regarded as a secular counterpart to the choir of S. Maria presso S. Satiro, Peruzzi goes a step farther by representing the open space beyond the walls. Stylistically the painted architecture clings to Bramante's forms; the treatment of the Tuscan order follows line for line the rules of the Tempietto, and we may also assume that there was a Bramante source for the pilaster-faced piers.

Yet for all the precision and elegance of its details, the real charm of the Villa Farnesina resides in its astonishingly well-planned composition as a whole: the leisurely sequence of the rooms, the comfortable staircase, the two open loggias of the ground floor, in which painting seems to have transcended architecture, as it has in the closed Sala delle Colonne. It would be doing the architecture of the Farnesina less than justice to regard it as painter's architecture, or merely as a foil to the frescoes. The Renaissance has no other building to show which achieves such perfection in the unity of architecture and painting which had been the ideal of Italian art since Giotto's Arena Chapel. In all probability Vasari was also speaking of the unity of the arts when he called the Farnesina 'non murato ma veramente nato' – not built, but born. This ideal was within the scope of the Farnesina, a comparatively small building; in the far more monumental project of St Peter's, the same artist hardly got beyond thinking up plans.

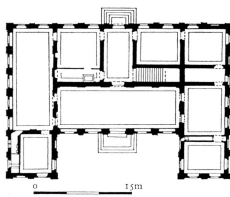

58. (*left*) Baldassare Peruzzi: Rome, Villa Farnesina, 1509–11

59. (*above*) Baldassare Peruzzi: Rome, Villa Farnesina, 1509–11, plan of ground floor

Peruzzi's fame as an architect is overshadowed by that of Bramante and Raphael, since a great deal of his work consisted of perishable decoration for stage scenery or pageants. The importance of Peruzzi's work in stage 'prospects' for Cinquecento architecture can hardly be overrated. For instance, he probably took a leading part in one of the most famous enterprises of the kind, the wooden 'theatre' on the Capitol in Rome which Leo X erected in 1513 on the occasion of the admission of his nephews Giuliano and Lorenzo de' Medici to the Roman patriciate.[6]

This rectangular theatre was covered by a costly cloth representing the sky; its façade was in the form of a Roman triumphal arch whose sculpture was imitated in grisaille. Behind the steps of the auditorium, which provided seating for over a thousand people, there rose walls more than 15 m. (50 feet) high, on which huge pictures were hung between golden pilasters; above the pilasters there was a frieze of vine-scrolls, sea-gods, and the emblems of the Medici. The programme of the occasion is characteristic of the temper of the age: on the first day a solemn High Mass was celebrated before a great altar on the stage; and on the second Plautus's *Poenulus* was performed on the same stage. 'But the most

60. (*left*) Baldassare Peruzzi: Rome, Villa Farnesina, Sala delle Colonne, *c*. 1512

61. (*right*) Baldassare Peruzzi: Rome, Villa Farnesina, 1509–11, Loggia di Psyche, vault frescoes by Raphael begun 1517–18

62. Baldassare Peruzzi: 'Scena tragica'. Stockholm, Nationalmuseum

astonishing thing was the 'prospettiva', namely the scenery of the commedia; for many kinds of buildings, various loggias, strange porticoes and windows were represented with supreme art and fantasy.'[7] There is no doubt that a stage setting like that described by Vasari also served as the background to the High Mass.

A few of Peruzzi's drawings for this kind of stage setting have been preserved [62]; they show an oblong piazza faced with that repertory of 'modern' and 'antique' buildings, loggias, obelisks, temples, or amphitheatres which was to remain characteristic of stage scenery till the eighteenth century, and was also used by Poussin for his mythological fables. Serlio's treatise on architecture contains precise directions for stage settings of the kind. 'Splendid and royal' buildings were prescribed for the setting of the *scena tragica* and 'buildings of the common order' for the *scena comica*. The front of the stage with the steps was to be carried out in wooden relief; the actual prospect consists of two canvases, one for the buildings whose façades stretched along the sides, and another for the scenic prospect in the middle. It is clear from this that the actors played their parts *in front of* the prospect and there were no wings.[8]

When Antonio da Sangallo the Younger became superintendent of the *fabrica* of St Peter's in 1520, after the death of Raphael, Peruzzi was given the office of *coadjutore* which Sangallo had held up to that time. He must have played an important part in the discussions about the continuation of the building. Many drawings, whose chronology is controversial, throw light on his ideas and suggestions. The building itself progressed very little during this time. Neither Sangallo nor Peruzzi had Bramante's genius for inspiring others; they did not succeed in evolving a definite plan out of the many and often divergent suggestions put forward, nor in convincing the Pope that such a plan was feasible. Yet this irresolute kind of speculating on every conceivable solution at this stage of the planning must have been felt, especially by Peruzzi, as

a welcome stimulus. Many of his projects go far beyond the bounds set by the situation; they arise from a peculiar conception of architecture as a 'science'. Speculative 'experiments' are developed from special circumstances, in the same way as in a university lecture room. Thus beside the purely central composition which has come down to us through Serlio, there was the basilican plan in the Uffizi drawing no. 14, with its three alternatives for the aisles and five variants for the side chapels [26].

The same fundamental bias to speculation also appears in Peruzzi's curious interest in the method of architectural drawing. It is in part due to him that the rendering process of the modern architectural drawing was developed during his activity in the *fabrica*. His drawing Uffizi no. 2, the perspective section of a project combining plan and elevation on one sheet, has always been famous [25]; this plan tallies substantially with the plan reproduced by Serlio. The art of its composition makes a drawing of this kind, quite apart from its immediate purpose, a work of art *sui generis*. The draughtsman is as much concerned with the problem of architectural drawing as with the actual erection of the building itself. Further, the sheet shows very vividly that Peruzzi's interest was concentrated on the interior; even where he could have drawn the exterior – for instance on the apse of the transept – he preferred the plan of the ambulatory, i.e. an interior form. Peruzzi's interest in the spatial picture means a departure from that conception of the centralized composition as a monument which underlies Bramante's designs for St Peter's. The organic unity of interior and exterior, the total visibility which is the distinguishing characteristic of Bramante's Tempietto too, in spite of all its perspective calculations, was now a thing of the past. It is certainly not by chance that practically all the designs for St Peter's made in the twenties and thirties of the century deal with the plan and the interior view.

After the Sack of Rome, Peruzzi fled to his native city of

Siena. True, he was reinstated in his office of coadjutor in 1530, but he only returned to Rome for good in 1535, a year before his death.[9] Thus he seems to have had little influence on the subsequent history of St Peter's. At Siena, where he was given the distinguished office of City Architect, he was mainly engaged on fortifications, including the fortifications near the Porta Laterina and the Porta S. Viene. At the same time he built the Palazzo Pollini and the Villa Belcaro, now greatly altered.

An outstanding characteristic of Peruzzi was his power of discovering novel solutions for unusual problems. This talent enabled him to meet the wishes of the building authorities of S. Petronio at Bologna, and to submit, beside a 'Gothic' scheme with flamboyant tracery [63], a design in classical form.[10] It gave him the idea of proposing a church on an elliptical plan for the acute-angled site of the Roman hospital of S. Giacomo degli Incurabili,[11] a heresy in the eyes of those theoreticians of the Cinquecento who, as disciples of Alberti, acknowledged only the circle or the regular polygon as ideal forms. This predilection of Peruzzi's for difficult or eccentric problems also comes out in the designs for the remodelling of the great dome of Siena Cathedral on its six

63. Baldassare Peruzzi: Project for S. Petronio, Bologna, 1522. Bologna, Museo di S. Petronio

piers and of the Gothic church of S. Domenico at Siena. To call these designs utopian is to do them less than justice; they display an interest in the methods of architectural planning which has broken away from the intellectual theories of Alberti and from the meticulous rules in Vitruvius's treatise.

The Palazzo Massimo delle Colonne [64], Peruzzi's last work in Rome, was begun in 1532 to replace a palazzo belonging to the same family which had been damaged in the Sack of Rome.[12] A preliminary design by Peruzzi in the Uffizi shows the scheme of the adjoining streets, which was altered in the nineteenth century. The building stood on the via Papale, which was about 4.5 m. (12 feet) wide and was the route of the papal processions. A street of the same width led up to the façade. In the old palazzo there was a 'loggia in front of the great hall'; thus the idea of planning the ground floor of the new building as a loggia may have originated with the client, who wanted the characteristic feature of the family palazzo renewed. According to Peruzzi's design, the middle of the loggia was to be in line with the central axis of the street leading to the façade, not with that of the façade. The function of the façade in the context of the street was more important to the architect than its symmetry.

While the preliminary design preserves as far as possible the lines of the original walls and makes no alteration in the old cortile [65A], less consideration to existing parts of the building was shown in the execution; even the cortile was altered. The changes in plan went hand in hand with a regulation and slight enlargement of the site. In this way a more convenient place was found for the staircase, and the façade was widened in both directions. Oddly enough, some land was added from the plot adjoining the left-hand boundary, so that a door had to be broken into the old wall; the wall appears still unaltered in the preliminary design. Apses were added on the short sides of the loggia; perhaps they can be explained as an attempt to create the 'vestibulum' of the ancient authors after the pattern of the Early Christian narthex. Above all, however, the façade was given the curve which made it famous [64].

The result of this change of plan was a gain not so much in space as in clarity of the composition, in artistic unity. Although the façade with its loggia and the cortile are not in line, each is symmetrical in itself. The overlapping of the façade on to the neighbouring site makes the palazzo look more sumptuous than it really is. The convex loggia projects beyond the frontage of the neighbouring houses, so that the palazzo dominates the view of the street on both sides. Its function as the focus of the street which opens in front of it is also stressed. A comparison of the design and the finished building makes one feel that the change of plan was dictated by artistic, not practical considerations.

The elevation of the façade is surprising in its contrast between the free-standing columns of the loggia and the flat walls of the three upper storeys. The interior separation of the storeys comes out clearly in the façade. Ever since Alberti's Palazzo Rucellai, one of the four floors had been treated as a subordinate part of one of the three orders: but Peruzzi must have felt how illogical it was to transfer the system of the Roman orders to a palazzo façade. He certainly uses the column on the ground floor, where it supports a

64. Baldassare Peruzzi: Rome, Palazzo Massimo delle Colonne, begun 1532, façade

65A. Baldassare Peruzzi: Rome, Palazzo Massimo delle Colonne, project. Florence, Uffizi (A 368)

65B. Baldassare Peruzzi: Rome, Palazzo Massimo delle Colonne, begun 1532, plan of ground floor: as executed

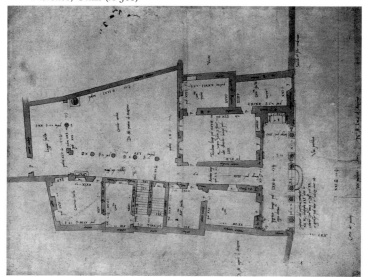

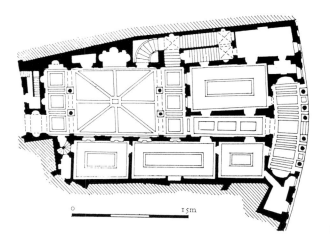

66. Baldassare Peruzzi: Rome, Palazzo Massimo delle Colonne, begun 1532, portico

67. Baldassare Peruzzi: Rome, Palazzo Massimo delle Colonne, begun 1532, courtyard

'genuine' architrave, but in the upper storeys he even abandons the aedicules which Bramante and Raphael had employed as window surrounds, and returns to simpler Quattrocento forms. How far he conceived the façade as a surface can be seen not only in the flattened, practically engraved joints of the rustication, but in the windows of the third floor; their surrounds look like leather, drawn out from within and applied to the wall like strapwork.

In this palazzo the ideal of a rebirth of antiquity has been replaced by a different conception of architectural beauty. The effect of the façade does not come from its harmonious balance, but from its wealth of contrasts. The architrave of the ground floor rests on columns in the middle, on pilasters at the sides; the spacious loggia is flanked by solid walls; the heavy balconies of the windows in the piano nobile bear down on the inter-columnar spaces; above the deep shadow of the architrave of the Doric order there rises the shadowless wall of the upper floors, whose flat rustication contrasts with the lavish decoration in the interior of the loggia [66].

The relationship between the façade and the cortile must be understood in the same way. The entrance to the palazzo leads through a corridor which runs from the *centre* of the façade to the *side* of the courtyard [67]. The façade has four, the courtyard three storeys. The Doric order appears in single columns in the courtyard, in coupled columns on the

façade. In the former it carries a tunnel-vault, in the latter the ceiling is flat.

We have already noticed the breach with the classical canon of form in Raphael's Palazzo Branconio dall'Aquila. But while Raphael interprets the classical vocabulary of form in a new and undogmatic fashion, Peruzzi, in the Palazzo Massimo, combines the highly classical ornament of the loggia with the entirely unclassical windows of the upper storeys. The elimination of the classical canon here makes way for the introduction of older motifs, for instance the window surrounds of the piano nobile and the plain crowning cornice. Thus a consistent line of development leads from Peruzzi's earlier façade of the Farnesina to the late Palazzo Massimo, while the classical style, as it appears in certain details of Peruzzi's work and especially in his designs for pageants, is an intermezzo.

We can see how little interest Peruzzi took in the revival of the Vitruvian canon of columns by what Cellini tells us he said of Vitruvius: 'Vitruvius was neither a painter nor a sculptor; that is why he had no eye for what really makes the beauty of architecture.'[13] Nor has Peruzzi's architecture laid the foundation of rules or types: its charm resides in his faculty of finding inventive solutions for single architectural problems. His sketches are notable for their almost playful fantasy.

ANTONIO DA SANGALLO THE YOUNGER

Antonio da Sangallo the Younger (1484–1546) differed entirely, in both his origins and his artistic personality, from his near-contemporary Peruzzi, who was his colleague at St Peter's.[14] He was a Florentine, Peruzzi a Sienese, Sangallo must have been familiar with building technique from an early age through his mother's brothers, Antonio the Elder and Giuliano; thus he came to architecture from the craft of building, and not, like Peruzzi, from painting. In the account books of St Peter's he first appears as the carpenter who set up the centerings for the arches of Bramante's great dome. Owing to their unusual height and novel function – they were the negative forms for the concrete work – they required a good deal of technical skill. With them, Sangallo founded his reputation and probably his considerable fortune. In 1512, the *carpentario*, then aged about thirty, acquired a house in Rome, while Peruzzi's friends, as late as 1527, had to appeal to the municipal council of Siena for a pension for the famous but impoverished master. In 1516 Sangallo was appointed assistant to Raphael at the office of St Peter's.[15] Raphael, who must have appreciated the practical common sense of his Florentine assistant, probably familiarized him with the problems of planning and drawing. Thus the *carpentario* became an *architetto*, and began to take an interest in architectural theory. His book-plate in the 1513 edition of Vitruvius by Fra Giocondo is dated 1520.[16]

Sangallo, by that time the foremost building expert, and a compatriot of the reigning Pope, entered on Raphael's heritage at St Peter's in 1520. He remained architect-in-chief till his death in 1546. He also continued Raphael's Villa Madama, which had been begun under Cardinal Giulio de' Medici.

It was not as easy for Sangallo to make his way in other places as it had been in the *fabrica* of St Peter's. In the competition for S. Giovanni dei Fiorentini in Rome, announced by Leo X in 1518, he was ousted by his compatriot Sansovino. As late as 1527 he was defeated by Sanmicheli in the competition for the high altar in the cathedral of Orvieto. After the Sack of Rome, when many of his contemporaries fled, Sangallo remained. In the later years of Clement VII's pontificate, and especially under Paul III, all the important building projects of the Curia were entrusted to him.

While the design submitted by Raphael in the competition for S. Giovanni dei Fiorentini has been lost, drawings of those entered by Sansovino, Sangallo, and Peruzzi have been preserved.[17] It seems that all the competitors first thought of a central composition, a 'monument' which should dominate the bank of the Tiber visibly from all sides, with the Borgo and the Castel S. Angelo opposite, and which, as the church of the Florentines, should proclaim the glory of the Medici Pope; about 1520, a centrally planned church must have seemed a matter of course. One of Sangallo's schemes for the plan, preserved in the drawing Uffizi 199, was published, with the corresponding elevation, in an engraving made by Antonio's pupil Labacco [68]. It was a circular, domed space surrounded by sixteen round chapels and an exterior wall, also circular. This rotunda, as Labacco's elevation shows, was to have a pedimented façade of four coupled columns. It

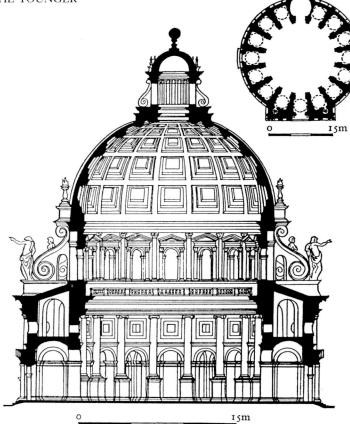

68. Antonio da Sangallo the Younger: Project for S. Giovanni dei Fiorentini, Rome, *c.* 1520, section and plan (after Labacco)

has been seen that during the continuation of work on St Peter's after Bramante's death, Raphael had abandoned the purely centralized composition as it appeared at Todi and Montepulciano. In his design for S. Giovanni, Sangallo, like his uncle, keeps to the central plan, but the stress on the façade itself testifies to the influence of Raphael's design for St Peter's, which Sangallo follows very closely in the details [27–30]. The shape of the dome and the lantern repeats Raphael's design almost literally, though it lacks the stepped rings round the springing of the dome. This difference is not merely one of form; Bramante's stepped rings were to diminish the sideways spread of the dome, and, as in the Pantheon, concentrate its weight on its base-ring. Sangallo's idea was to convey the thrust by means of huge volutes on to the walls between the chapels. It was only logical that these volutes should carry statues like the buttresses of Gothic cathedrals.

In that way a curious paradox came about. The engineer who constructed the centerings in Bramante's St Peter's abandoned Bramante's manner of construction ten years later in his own design for a dome, though in the details he followed Bramante's and Raphael's forms almost slavishly. Was Sangallo drawing his own conclusions from the experiences which had been made during the reinforcement of Bramante's piers? Or is the ring of low chapels a reminiscence of Brunelleschi's S. Maria degli Angeli? There is another explanation which seems more plausible: that Sangallo was trying to transfer the basilican system of the ambulatories of St Peter's as exactly as possible to a purely central plan. He copied the façade and exterior almost literally from the design for St Peter's, which was the ultimate authority, as he did the contour of the dome; at the same time he tried to improve Bramante's construction by reviving the medieval technique of carrying the weight of the dome on to buttresses in the outer wall instead of making it rest on free-standing piers.

After Sangallo had prepared a wooden model for Sansovino's design for S. Giovanni, which had won the prize, he also supervised the work on the foundations, which dragged on so long, owing to the sandy soil of the site, that not even the foundation walls were finished when Leo X died in 1523. These foundations were used many years later for the uninteresting nave of the present church.

During the pontificate of Clement VII, Sangallo was mainly employed on the fortifications of the Papal State, which the Pope realized was the first thing to be taken in hand after the catastrophe of the Sack of Rome. When the Pope, in 1534, created his cousin Alessandro first Duke of Florence, Sangallo was commissioned to design the Fortezza da Basso, a large pentagonal building attached to the medieval city walls, fortified towards both the country and the city. It was intended for a garrison which should ensure the supremacy of the Medici.[18]

Antonio had already been active in 1508 as Bramante's assistant in the construction of the Pope's naval fortress of Civitavecchia. This stronghold still has the rectangular plan with round corner towers which was the favourite design of the later Quattrocento. In the twenties and thirties of the Cinquecento, polygonal bastions replaced the round towers, since the far heavier shells of the new artillery rebounded more readily from them than from the massive round walls of the old system. The Fortezza da Basso shows the new type fully developed, and Antonio had contributed fundamental ideas to its structure. The vaults of the bastions were calculated from the outset for the emplacement of the new heavy artillery, which was now posted on, and no longer in, the towers. This innovation already appeared in Bramante's fortress of Civitavecchia.

In Florence, and later on at Perugia, Sangallo was commissioned to build free-standing strongholds to ensure the authority of the sovereign over the cities. The medieval gates and towers of Rome, Ancona, and Loreto had to be adapted to new developments in artillery. Here too Antonio always made use of the polygonal bastion, while Peruzzi, in his forts at Siena, which were built to serve the same purpose, experimented with complex and novel combinations of curved and angled walls.

In his first palazzi, Antonio employed the formal vocabulary of Bramante and Raphael, as he did in his design for S.

69. Antonio da Sangallo the Younger: Rome, Zecca, façade, c. 1530

70. Antonio da Sangallo the Younger: Project for the mint of the dukedom of Castro. Florence, Uffizi (A 297)

Giovanni dei Fiorentini. The three-bay façade of the Zecca, the papal mint, in Rome, with the triumphal arch motif articulating its piano nobile, was probably erected about 1530 [69]. Leaving the Baroque alterations out of account, the articulation is revealed as a near-faithful copy of Bramante's walls in the Upper Belvedere Court, with the exception of the framed tondi between the coupled pilasters. The rusticated plinth on which this piano nobile rests seems, in spite of its vertical oblong windows, too low for a ground floor and too high for a mere plinth. The idea of connecting the very high pedestals of the pilasters of the piano nobile by a cornice of their own was not very happy either.

In a design for the mint of the Farnese dukedom of Castro, Antonio later modified the motif [70]: the great blind arch of the piano nobile is reduced to a lower, round-headed opening which corresponds to the square-headed windows between the coupled pilasters, while the four pilasters stand on a continuous band. The modelling of the walls is much shallower throughout, and the forms are less exuberant. The design may stand as an example of the somewhat prosaic dignity which is characteristic of Sangallo's later work. The farther the style is removed from its sources, the more it loses freshness and power, and a fundamentally puritan bias comes out more obviously.

*

The elevation of Paul III in 1534 gave fresh impetus to the building activities of the Curia. Once again the Pope was mainly concerned with fortifications. In the Papal State, the fortresses of Ancona and Loreto were reinforced, a new fortress was built at Perugia, and the fortifications of Piacenza, the capital of the new Farnese duchy, were brought up to date. But during the pontificate of Paul III the Sala Regia and the Cappella Paolina in the Vatican Palace were built too, and work went on vigorously on the Belvedere Court, after a collapse in Bramante's east wing had nearly cost the Pope his life. The old ground-floor piers were reinforced, and alterations carried out on the upper storeys.

The superintendent of all these works was Antonio da Sangallo. A letter of 1536 from Paul III lays down his duties.[19] In the same way as under the preceding popes he was appointed life-superintendent of the Fabrica of St Peter's and of all other building enterprises projected or in progress in the Papal State. His total annual salary was seven hundred and twenty ducats, of which the office of St Peter's was to bear three hundred. Two years before the Pope had raised Peruzzi's salary for St Peter's to three hundred ducats a year, so that the two architects now received the same salary. Peruzzi returned from Siena to Rome in 1535, but died in the following January. After his death, Sangallo's authority was unassailable; he alone could say that he had worked in the Fabrica with Bramante and Raphael.

ST PETER'S

After the Sack of Rome work on St Peter's came practically to a standstill. In the first years of Paul III's pontificate, apart from necessary works of maintenance, nothing was built but a wall between the area of the new dome and the surviving parts of Constantine's nave. From 1529 to 1540 the costs for the building amounted to 17,620 ducats,[20] of which 7,000 went for the salaries of the two architects. As late as 1536 Sangallo had to complain to the Pope about the dilatoriness of the payment.[21] In order to fill the building coffers, the Pope resorted to the same measures as his predecessors: he confirmed and increased the indulgences of Julius II and Leo X. At the same time he founded a confraternity for the promotion of building. In 1536 he approached the King of France and the German Emperor, and in 1540 the King of Poland, for subsidies. In his letter to the latter he declared that the church was less splendid now than Constantine's old basilica. The troubles of the times were responsible for the cessation of work on the building.[22] Marten van Heemskerck preserved, in his famous vedute, the view of St Peter's at the time [71]. The picturesque group of the Early Christian nave, Nicholas V's choir, and the arches of Bramante's dome looked more like a ruin than a new building.

The Pope's efforts were successful. Between 1540 and 1546, 162,000 ducats could be spent on the building,[23] nearly half of which came from Spain. Thus part of the gold of the Incas, which the Conquistadores brought home from the new continent, was built into St Peter's. In particular, this money was used for two costly measures which played a fundamental part in the further history of the building. The first was that in 1539, as always at the beginning of a new stage of building, a model was commissioned, and was executed by Antonio Labacco after Sangallo's design [72, 73, 16C]. It is both the first and the largest of the models for St Peter's to have been preserved; the costs came to over 5,000 ducats, and the model was over four years in the making.[24] This model no more determined the ultimate design of the church than its predecessors, yet, after twenty years of irresolution and experiment, it formulated once again a plan which the Pope approved and which was binding on all the authorities of the Curia.

The raising of the floor of the new church by about 3.20 m. (12 feet 6 in.) above the pavement of the old basilica was a far more costly process and played a far more important part in the progress of the building.[25] The reasons for an operation which, considering the size of the building, was a very serious matter, are to be sought in aesthetic rather than in structural considerations. It did little to reinforce the piers; the layout of the chapels in the crypt (Grotte Vaticane) of today, which was rendered possible by the raising of the pavement, was made at a later date. Yet with the suppression of Bramante's tall podium under the pilasters there came a development in St Peter's which had been foreshadowed twenty years before in Raphael's Chigi Chapel and Peruzzi's Villa Farnesina. Piers, columns, and pilasters were now to be conceived primarily as a structural scaffolding; their function as articulation of the enclosing walls was neglected. The structure is more important than the spatial impression. About the same time Serlio formulated the new ideal of beauty in his Fourth Book: 'Columns whose bases rest on the floor of the building are far more beautiful than those which stand on a pedestal.'

The raising of the floor also led to a change in the great piers of the dome. The wide round-headed niches on the outer sides, which are to be seen in all plans of the first stage

71. Old and New St Peter's, drawing by Marten van Heemskerck, *c.* 1534. Berlin, Staatliche Museen Preussischer Kulturbesitz, Kupferstichkabinett (II, 54)

72. Antonio da Sangallo the Younger: Model for St Peter's, 1539 ff., from the south

73. Antonio da Sangallo the Younger: Model for St Peter's, 1539 ff., cross-section, engraving by Salamanca

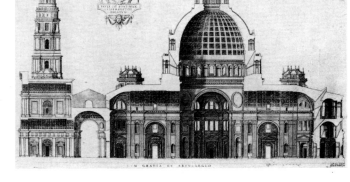

of building, were now walled up. They would have been hardly visible above the new floor. It was then that the piers were given the square form, chamfered on the side under the dome, which we see today [74].

Sangallo's new model of 1539 was a peculiar compromise between the central and the basilican plan [72, 73, 16C]. The dome, the Greek cross, and the four corner towers had to be taken over from the preceding stage of building, but the façade of this completely central structure is pushed out to double the distance on the east, so that there is now an almost independent façade flanked by two huge towers and only loosely connected with the nucleus of the building.

At first sight this solution seems to do justice to all the diverging tendencies, since it has Bramante's Greek cross surmounted by the dome within a longitudinal general plan. But the disadvantages of such a composition are obvious. The doubling of the length of the east arm splits the building; an independent façade is a contradiction in terms. Besides, in view of the lack of funds the project remained utopian.

In the elevation the incongruities stand out even more clearly. The height of the façade towers is artificially increased in order to establish a relationship with the dome, but the other towers rise like stumps from the roof and look

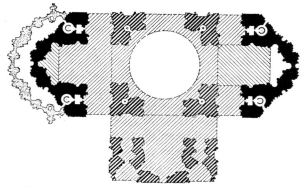

Built before Michelangelo

Rebuilt under Michelangelo

Vaulted by Sangallo

Started by Raphael and Sangallo, razed by Michelangelo

Vaulted by Michelangelo

74. Rome, St Peter's, construction 1506–64

merely superfluous. The articulation of the arms of the cross is just as unsatisfactory; their countless engaged columns, loggias, and aedicules are pulled together inadequately by the weak horizontals of the cornices.

Sangallo had already abandoned Bramante's structural ideas – though not his formal repertory – in his project for the dome of S. Giovanni dei Fiorentini. The model of 1539 carries this development a step farther. In section, the dome recalls that of Florence. The contour is that of a pointed arch, yet this steep dome rests, like Bramante's hemisphere, on pendentives and a drum; the interior, like that of the Pantheon, is coffered. On the outside, the base of the dome is surrounded by two tiers of arcades, the lower of which forms the drum, while the upper serves only to conceal the

springing of the dome and to give it the outer appearance of a hemisphere.[26]

As regards the exterior ends of the arms of the cross, which played so great a part after Bramante's death, Sangallo decided on the same ambulatories for the choir and the other arms, and this would have involved the final removal of Rossellino's choir. Yet he made the walls of the ambulatories so thick that they themselves look like independent spaces connected with the arms of the cross by narrow openings. The tendency to create new and confusing spaces, as Michelangelo rightly observed later, can be seen also in the introduction of galleries over the ambulatories.

A fresco by Vasari in the Cancelleria shows the state of St Peter's at that time [75]. To the left there is the Quattrocento choir vaulted by Bramante; in the middle, the great vault of the south arm of the cross, and in front of it the exterior wall of the ambulatory, designed by Raphael and continued at a leisurely pace by Peruzzi and Sangallo after 1520. To the right the nave of old St Peter's rises above one of the Early Christian mausolea and the obelisk of Nero's circus. The fresco, made a year before Sangallo's death, shows that under his direction considerable progress had been made in the vaulting of the area around the crossing, and especially to the east. When Michelangelo took over after Sangallo's death, he radically altered the plans for the exterior elevation and the eastern part of the church, but he retained Sangallo's complex – yet structurally sound – system of subsidiary vaults around the core.[27]

Michelangelo's criticism of Sangallo's model, which has come down to us through Vasari, strikes straight at the weakness of the design. Sangallo tried to be on the safe side all the way round. He retained the formal repertory of Bramante and Raphael twenty-five years after Raphael's death, since it was regarded as peerless; he chose the Gothic

75. (left) Old and New St Peter's, fresco by Giorgio Vasari, 1546. Rome, Cancelleria

76. (top right) Antonio da Sangallo the Younger: Rome, Palazzo Farnese, plan, and section of vestibule

77. (far right) Antonio da Sangallo the Younger: Rome, Palazzo Farnese, plan of ground floor, final project, c. 1541. Florence, Uffizi (A 248)

78. (bottom right) Antonio da Sangallo the Younger (French copy): Rome, Palazzo Farnese, plan of ground floor, c. 1525– 30. Munich, Staatsbibliothek (cod. icon. 190)

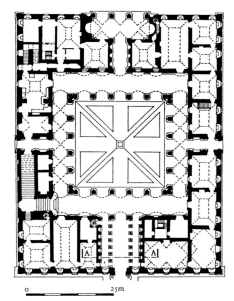

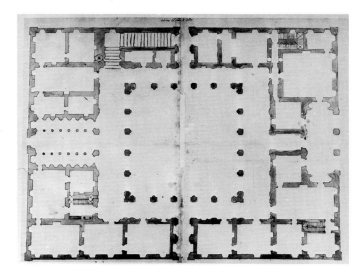

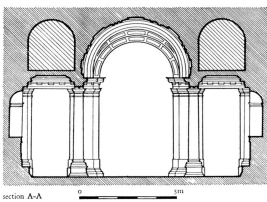

section A-A

construction for the dome which he, as a Florentine, was familiar with, instead of the ancient and as yet untested construction by Bramante, though he tried to salvage Bramante's 'more beautiful', unmedieval hemispherical contour for the exterior view. He provided the classical centralized plan with a separate façade. The walls were reinforced to gain stability and the decorative parts multiplied to increase the richness of the exterior. But all these efforts led to nothing but duplication and sterile repetition, not to a fusion of the structure with the surface of the building.

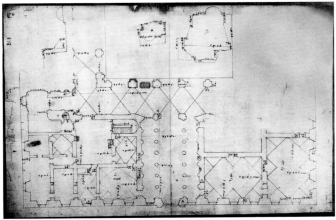

THE PALAZZO FARNESE AND OTHER WORKS

Sangallo's most important surviving work is the Palazzo Farnese [76], the first of a long series of papal family palazzi in Rome. Its effect in the general view of the city, its courtyard, and its furnishings were unsurpassed by any later building.

The palazzo we see today is the product of a complicated and not yet fully elucidated building history.[28] In 1495 the later Pope, Paul III, had acquired an older cardinal's residence on the site of the present building, which he had thoroughly renovated from 1517 on. Even this first Palazzo Farnese, which Pope Leo X visited in 1519, is described in a contemporary document as great and costly;[29] yet before 1530, the Cardinal embarked on an enlargement of it.

Under Clement VII, Alessandro Farnese was the most powerful member of the College of Cardinals; his retinue numbered more than three hundred persons. According to Vasari the Cardinal decided on a plan for an alteration with two staircases submitted by Antonio da Sangallo. The idea was that the two sons of the Cardinal, Pier Luigi and Ranuccio Farnese, should have apartments befitting their rank with separate entrances. This project, certainly modified after Ranuccio's death in 1529, seems to have been carried on rather slowly.

After the election of Cardinal Alessandro to the papacy, in 1534 Sangallo 'entirely changed the original design, seeing that he now had to make a pontiff's rather than a cardinal's palazzo. Thus, having razed some of the neighbouring houses and the old stairway, he remade the stairs anew and ascending more commodiously, and he enlarged the court on every side, and similarly the whole palace.'[30] There is evidence for these changes in a number of drawings by Sangallo and his circle. A sheet in a French sketchbook, now in Munich, gives the ground floor before the alteration [78]; Sangallo's drawing Uffizi 248 shows his final scheme with the new stairs [77]. While both drawings represent the aisled vestibule and the two rooms on its right, they differ entirely in the arrangement of the rooms on the left side.[31]

Work on Sangallo's revised project seems to have made slow progess during the first years of the new Pope's reign. In 1540 the new stairs were not yet built, although the old

79. Antonio da Sangallo the Younger: Rome, Palazzo Farnese, vestibule, 1517

ones had been demolished.[32] In 1541 Duke Pier Luigi Farnese, now the owner of the palazzo, concluded a new agreement with the contractors: old vaults were to be pulled down, new vaults to be made; mouldings were to be altered; provision was made for demolitions and new foundations; the prices for the carving of the mouldings and the new roofs and ceilings were to be determined later because Sangallo 'does not yet know how they are to be made'.[33] Now the building advanced rather more speedily. In January 1546 a stone-carver reported to Sangallo that one corner of the façade was then 7.7 m. (23 feet) high; on the garden side the cellar was finished and the walls of the ground floor were under construction.[34] In March 1547, six months after Sangallo's death, 'the front façade is almost completed up to the top cornice; only the cornice is missing; the colonnade all around [i.e. the court] is in place'; the kitchens on the garden side of the ground floor are finished, the piano nobile of the right wing will 'shortly be habitable'.[35] Nevertheless four years later Vasari wrote in the first edition of his Lives that 'the Palazzo Farnese, where the new stairs and ceilings were made after the revised design [of Sangallo], will never be unified nor seem to be by the same hand'.[36]

Sangallo's 'new design', developed after 1534 and not yet entirely worked out in 1541 when the contract was made, practically entailed a new building. Of the first palazzo of 1517 ff. only the vestibule [76, 79], the two rooms to its right, and three arcades on the façade side of the court remain [80]. They show the forceful Raphaelesque style characteristic of the Sangallo family around 1520. The engaged columns of the piers in the court had a close analogy in the ambulatory of the southern apse of St Peter's; they are equally close to the Doric order in S. Biagio at Montepulciano, designed by Antonio da Sangallo the Elder in 1519. The fleur-de-lis ornament on the capitals in the two old rooms recalls the heraldic dolphins of the Pandolfini in their palazzo in Florence.

The clause 'new vaults to be made' in the contract of 1541 probably refers to the vaulting of the ground-floor portico in the façade wing of the court.[37] For some

reason the old vaults were no longer considered adequate for the more ambitious 'new design'. When Vasari says that 'the court was enlarged on every side', he may refer to the heightening of the portico. Heightening the vaults must, however, have involved the heightening both of the arches between the piers and of the mouldings from which the arches spring. This would explain a unique trait of the Farnese court, namely the double mouldings of the piers [82]. They are without precedent in ancient Roman architecture, and no treatise of the sixteenth century offers an analogy. The irregularity could best be understood as an ingenious response to the intricate problem that confronted Sangallo: the low piers of the first building phase had to be joined to the higher vaults of the 'new design'. The same device had of course also to be applied to the piers which were newly built after 1541 around the court. The resulting effect is that austerity combined with splendour for which the court has so often been praised.

In comparison with the Raphaelesque ground floor, the Ionic order of the piano nobile, executed according to the 'new design', looks impersonal; its capitals are somewhat petty, and the half-columns cannot compete with the powerful piers and the forceful entasis of the Doric order.[38] The piano nobile shows Sangallo's later style, which lacks the power and freshness of his early work.

The façade built according to the 'new design' of 1541, with its thirteen bays, outdid all the other private palazzi in Rome, even in size [81].[39] The palazzo is conceived as a free-standing rectangular block with four façades and a square cortile; its ground floor forms the base to two upper storeys which are practically equal in importance and form. In the façades the Florentine rustication has been abandoned, likewise the Roman order of pilasters or columns. While a preliminary plan by Sangallo still allows giant pilasters for the two upper storeys, in the execution the flat wall surface is only enlivened by quoins, window surrounds, and cornices. In the treatment of detail, Sangallo reverts to the formal repertory of the first quarter of the century, as in St Peter's. Entirely in the Raphael tradition, and anachron-

80. Antonio da Sangallo the Younger: Rome, Palazzo Farnese, arcade of the ground floor, 1517

81. Rome, Palazzo Farnese, façade by Antonio da Sangallo the Younger, designed 1541, finished by Michelangelo, designed 1546

istic at the time of building, are the aedicules of the piano nobile with their alternating pediments. In order to adapt the aedicules to the round-headed windows of the third storey, their architrave is eliminated except for impost blocks over the columns.

The effect of Sangallo's façade comes from its size, not from its design. With its uninterrupted mouldings and the long row of identical openings, it is in the tradition of the Palazzo Medici, while Bramante and Raphael had adopted

for their façades the tradition of the Palazzo Rucellai.

Sangallo's façade was given its ultimate form by Michelangelo. Antonio's design for the crowning cornice did not appeal to the Pope; thus in 1546 a competition was launched to provide another, and Paul III decided on Michelangelo's design [83]. It is typical that the Pope invited three painters to compete alongside Sangallo and Michelangelo, namely Perino del Vaga, Sebastiano del Piombo, and Vasari. The greater concern for visual effect rather than for 'correctness'

82. Rome, Palazzo Farnese, courtyard, ground floor and first storey by Antonio da Sangallo the Younger, second storey by Michelangelo

83. Rome, Palazzo Farnese, façade, and Piazza Farnese as designed by Michelangelo, engraving by Nicolas Beatrizet, 1549

in the theorists' sense can also be seen in the fact that Michelangelo's design for the cornice was first tried out with a model ten feet high, i.e. as big as the cornice was to be, over a corner of the palazzo before the commission was formally confirmed.

The finished cornice diverges only in height from Vitruvian theory, and, it may be added, from Sangallo's design. Yet the whole effect of the façade is due to the massive projection of the cornice and the deep shadow it casts. The flatness of Sangallo's façade was furthermore modified by Michelangelo, who designed the middle window of the piano nobile and the armorial bearings above it.

Unlike the façade and courtyard, the famous aisled vestibule [76, 79] preceded Sangallo's 'new design' of 1541. Here, where there were neither great masses nor great surfaces to be dealt with, we see Sangallo at his best. The lavish detail looks neither playful nor overdone. The ancient structural and ornamental forms are adequate to the function as an entrance hall. An aisled vestibule had already occurred in Raphael's projects and Sangallo's drawings for the Villa Madama [38]. In the Villa Madama, the hall was to open as a loggia towards the entrance steps; in the Palazzo Farnese, the visitor entering by the portal is impressed by the unexpected spaciousness and the wealth of ornament. In form and detail, the ceiling recalls Peruzzi's loggia in the Palazzo Massimo. But while Peruzzi separates tunnel-vault and flat roof and sets them in contrast, Sangallo unites them in a logical system of aisles.

A special problem arose in the planning of the Palazzo Farnese with the placing of the staircase. It appears that its curious arrangement parallel to the left-hand side of the palazzo was a last-minute decision. It entailed several blind windows in the side façade, but considerable space was saved in the main range towards the piazza.

The rear range of the palazzo was barely begun when Sangallo died in 1546. A plan dated 1549 shows the ground floor as it then was, with the alterations Michelangelo had made, or had it in mind to make. Michelangelo's idea of building a second staircase in the right wing was probably felt to be too expensive and was therefore abandoned. The garden front, built after Michelangelo's death, diverges still more from his designs. He had intended to open the three bays of the piano nobile between courtyard and garden in the form of a loggia so as to get a view on to the garden, the Tiber, and the hills on the other side. However, this storey was closed during building; it contains the gallery later decorated by the Carracci. On the other hand, loggias were introduced on the ground and top floors of the garden front, and the passage between the courtyard and the garden loggia was lavishly decorated in the same style as Sangallo's entrance hall. The work on the two lower storeys, superintended by Vignola, was completed in 1568;[40] an inventory of the palazzo made in that year already mentions the 'galleria'.[41] According to the stately inscription by the second

Cardinal Alessandro Farnese, who was owner of the palazzo at the time, the loggia of the top storey, designed by Giacomo della Porta, was not completed till 1589.

Thus three generations of the family contributed to the palazzo. Artistically too it is a collective work, with contributions from the generation of Raphael down to that of Giacomo della Porta. By far the larger part of the building as it now stands goes back to Antonio da Sangallo, but it was by Michelangelo's top storeys in the courtyard and the façade that it became the most splendid of all Roman palazzi.

*

No architect superintended the work on St Peter's as long as Sangallo. Yet if there is little in the church today which bears the mark of his work, that is not merely a matter of circumstances. The qualities to which Sangallo owed his rapid rise in the Fabrica, his technical talent, his power of grasping the ideas of Bramante and Raphael, his practical and sober turn of mind – those very qualities were an obstacle to the continuation of the huge torso which confronted Sangallo when he took office. Benvenuto Cellini's gibe that Sangallo's buildings lacked greatness and distinction because he was neither a sculptor nor a painter, but only a master carpenter,[42] renders precisely, and in the idiom of the time, what distinguished Sangallo from Bramante, Raphael, and Peruzzi. His buildings and designs are practical and made to last, but what they lack is architectural imagination. Yet it was just by reason of those qualities that he was very much in demand for fortifications and utilitarian building. No architect of the time travelled more than he, or was active in more various enterprises. His fountain at Orvieto was looked upon as a peerless marvel and it is thanks to Antonio that the dome of Loreto, which his uncle had erected on inadequate foundations, was preserved. At the end of his life he restored the ancient cutting between the basin of the Velino and the Tiber valley at Terni.

As a draughtsman he was indefatigable. The Uffizi alone contains nearly a thousand sheets by his hand: meticulous working drawings for the model of St Peter's and rapid sketches for Montecassino, reconstructions of the tomb of Theodoric at Ravenna and trigonometrical computations for the Porta S. Spirito in Rome.[43] In technique, his drawings are always precise, economical, and methodical; he never loses sight of the given situation, the specific conditions of the commission. His method of representation is that of the expert; he consistently keeps in mind the distinction between plan, section, and elevation first recommended by Raphael for architectural drawings. Yet no drawing of his could stand as an independent work of art, as so many of Peruzzi's can. Sangallo's interest was concentrated on the building as such, not on the architectural rendering. He was probably never greatly interested in 'prospettiva'. In his work the separation of architecture from painting is fulfilled. These two arts, till then so closely related, went their own ways.

CHAPTER 5

Lombardy and the Venetian Terraferma

CESARE CESARIANO

During the first quarter of the Cinquecento Lombardy and Emilia, like Venice, remained faithful to the architectural forms of the late Quattrocento. The North Italian predilection for small-scale ornament and coloured incrustation was an obstacle to the adoption of the monumental style of Rome. The situation only changed when the great native families of architects and sculptors, the Lombardi, Solari, and Buon, were ousted by artists who had worked in Rome. In 1524 Giulio Romano came to Mantua, in 1527 Jacopo Sansovino to Venice, and at about the same time Michele Sanmicheli arrived at Verona. It was with their work that the new style found its way into northern Italy.

Lombardy retained the old forms longest. With the departure of Leonardo and Bramante, Milan had lost its eminence. After the fall of the Sforza, Lombardy had become the scene of the struggles between France and the house of Habsburg; between 1500 and 1535 the dukedom changed hands seven times. All the important building enterprises suffered from the unsettled political situation. The great churches of S. Maria della Passione and S. Maria presso S. Celso in Milan, which were begun before 1500, were not completed till nearly 1600, and the cathedrals of Pavia and Como only in the eighteenth and nineteenth centuries.

Only one Milanese building of the early Cinquecento, the atrium of S. Maria presso S. Celso [84], begun in 1513 after a design by Cesare Cesariano, can stand comparison with the contemporary architecture of Rome.[1] Cesariano (1483–1543) published a commentary to Vitruvius at Como in 1521 in which he calls himself a disciple of Bramante, and in the precision of its composition and the classical purity of its forms, his atrium indeed recalls Bramante.

The arcading on pillars was an innovation in Milan; in the cloisters of S. Ambrogio Bramante had employed columns throughout. The detail of Cesariano's pillars, the half-columns fronting them on the courtyard side with their tall bases, and the careful moulding of the entablature can hardly be explained without the prototype of Bramante's cloister of S. Maria della Pace, and the coupled pilasters and pediment on the street front of the atrium recall another building of Bramante's circle in Rome, S. Maria di Loreto. One detail is unique: the beautiful Corinthian capitals, cast in bronze, on the courtyard side. This atrium seems to be the only building of Cesariano's that has survived. His designs for the façade of the church were never executed,[2] and the fortifications which he built in Milan in the thirties, when he was Imperial Architect, were demolished.[3]

THE STECCATA AT PARMA

The cities of Parma and Piacenza, which had belonged to the lords of Milan, the Visconti and the Sforza, in the Quattrocento, were incorporated in the Papal States in the early Cinquecento, and were therefore spared the troubles of Lombardy. This relative political security explains the unusually short time of building of the Madonna della Steccata, the most important Cinquecento church in Parma.[4] It is a typical centrally planned church which houses a miraculous image of the Virgin. Its Greek cross plan [85] and the absence of a campanile are reminiscent of the Consolazione at Todi.[5] It is quite understandable that as early as the second half of the Cinquecento the design should have been attributed to Bramante.[6] But the Steccata was not begun till 1521, seven years after Bramante's death. The architect-in-chief was Giovanfrancesco Zaccagni, the master mason his father Bernardino, who built the foundations and the rising walls after a *disegno* – i.e. a model or drawing – of his son's.

Bernardino Zaccagni (*c.* 1460–1530) had worked on the Benedictine church of S. Giovanni Evangelista at Parma. It is a large basilica with pillars instead of columns which follows the prototype of the neighbouring Romanesque cathedral in its plan and the structure of its vaulting.[7] The Steccata itself is not without medieval reminiscences of the kind. Unlike the Consolazione, tunnel-vaulted compartments have been inserted between the arches of the crossing and the apses, and low square chapels added outside at the corners of the crossing. Thus the thrust of the dome is not, as at Todi, carried direct to the outer walls; the scheme must rather be regarded as a simplified version of the parchment plan for St Peter's.

The exterior view rises in three levels from the apses and corner chapels over the chancel roof to the dome [86]. The comparatively low drum is almost entirely concealed by the members in front of it. One recalls the medieval dome of Parma Cathedral, which 'sinks' in similar fashion behind the roofs of the transept and choir.[8]

84. Cesare Cesariano: Milan, S. Maria presso S. Celso, atrium, begun 1513

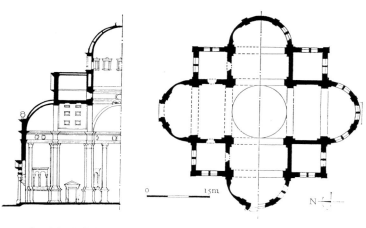

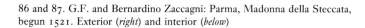

85. (*above*) G. F. and Bernardino Zaccagni: Parma, Madonna della Steccata, begun 1521, half-section and half-plans (before alterations) at ground and upper levels

86 and 87. G.F. and Bernardino Zaccagni: Parma, Madonna della Steccata, begun 1521. Exterior (*right*) and interior (*below*)

In the interior [87], the cruciform plan comes out clearly; the corner chapels are only accessible through low doorways and do not affect the general spatial impression. The pilasters of the arches of the crossing and the transverse arches are ornamented with frescoes, as is customary in northern Italy. The arrangement of the windows is obviously calculated with a view to the painting of the interior.[9] The crescendo from the diffuse but abundant light in the apses through the slightly darker area of the transitional bays to the radiant brilliance under the dome corresponds exactly to the iconographic programme of the frescoes. The shimmering gold leaf of the transverse arches and the gilding of the copper rosettes in the tunnel-vault have a special part to play; the metal to be used here is already mentioned in the contract of 1531, by which Parmigianino was commissioned for the frescoes, and it may be that the idea of making the vault lighter in colour by a lavish application of gold may have originated with the artist himself.[10]

The Zaccagni did not complete the Steccata. After long discussions, father and son had to resign in 1525. At that time one of the arms of the cross had been roofed, except for the apse, and the rest had risen to about the height of the main cornice. Antonio da Sangallo the Younger, who was at Parma in 1526, the architect Tramello of Piacenza, and Correggio took part in the discussions. Correggio was working at the time on the frescoes in the dome of S. Giovanni Evangelista at Parma. Sangallo's report throws light on the questions involved.[11] He proposed to provide three of the apses with entrances ('in case the whole population of the town should assemble for worship in the church'). Two of the towers (the name given to the corner chapels) were to be open and provided with altars, the other two were to remain closed and serve as vestries. The double windows of the apses were unnecessary – sufficient lighting could be provided by round windows in the apses and the drum and the openings of the lantern of the dome. The outer walls above the already-vaulted chancel bay were too high and statically unsound: he was submitting a sketch for these parts.

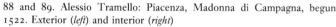

88 and 89. Alessio Tramello: Piacenza, Madonna di Campagna, begun 1522. Exterior (*left*) and interior (*right*)

In the further work on the building, very few of these recommendations were respected:[12] all the corner chapels remained closed, the church was given only one portal, the large windows in the apses were retained, and the crown of the dome was closed so that the lantern is blind. Just as little attention seems to have been paid to Sangallo's design for the roof zone, which was probably an attempt to forestall the 'sinking' of the dome.

Sangallo's report is as enlightening as the reaction it provoked in the building commission, which can be deduced from the building itself. The Steccata was built at the same time as the Madonna di S. Biagio at Montepulciano [51, 52]. Both buildings have the same function, and their plans are closely akin. At Montepulciano, the emphasis lies on pilaster and column, on capital and entablature; the wall surface between these members is bare. At Parma, both the pilasters and the transverse arches in the interior are the boundaries of wall surfaces, and it is on these that the visitor's eye lingers. The difference is certainly due to the difference between brickwork and stonework, but that is not a satisfying explanation. 'Pure' monumentality, the Roman conception of the 'temple', which achieves its effect solely by its architectural forms, is incompatible with the North Italian love of coloured ornament and great frescoes in the vaulting. The building commission did not object to the structural function of the corner chapels as abutments to receive the thrust of the dome being concealed both in the exterior and interior, nor to the apparent 'sinking' of the dome: these points of Sangallo's criticism fell on deaf ears, for the criteria applied in the report by the 'architetto della fabrica di S. Pietro in Roma' were simply incomprehensible to the building commission. The round-headed windows which Sangallo

called 'heretical' were sanctioned by old custom at Parma; the medieval tradition was more deeply rooted and longer-lived there than in Central Italy. Sangallo's ideas of 'perfezione' and 'proporzione' had different meanings for him than for the readers of his report. What the commission was concerned with was not the 'classical' articulation of the building, but the architectural framework of the frescoes, the unity of space and colour, of wall and decoration, and in that respect no Italian church of the time can challenge the Steccata.

TRAMELLO AT PIACENZA

Alessio Tramello, who was called in as consultant by the building commission of the Steccata in 1525, had also been working since 1522 on a centrally planned church, the Madonna di Campagna at Piacenza [88, 89].[13] Tramello planned it, and superintended work on it till it was completed. The building commission forced no *pentimenti* on him. His central church is more homogeneous but also more prosaic than the much bigger Steccata.

The plan is a Greek cross with flat terminations to the arms [90].[14] As in the Steccata, chapels are added to the corners of the crossing, but they are domed and open into the church. In that way more light and air is given to the interior than in the Steccata. The main dome rests on free-standing pillars and not on solid walls, and both outside and inside the vertical articulation is more clearly stated. The outer shell of the main and minor domes is, after the Lombard manner, octagonal and topped with a high lantern. Further reminiscences of Lombardy come out in the tall, broad windows in the drum, through which the light passes

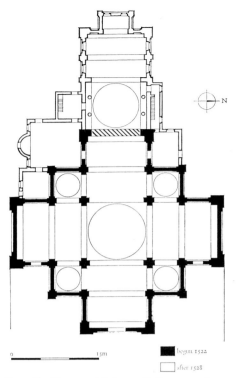

90. Alessio Tramello: Piacenza, Madonna di Campagna, begun 1522, plan

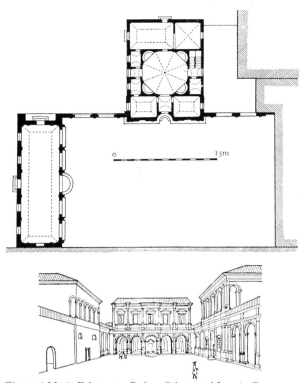

91. Giovanni Maria Falconetto: Padua, Odeon and Loggia Cornaro, 1524, plan and sketch

almost unhindered. This abundance of light is a draw-back for the decorations which cover walls and vaulting: Pordenone's frescoes in the dome almost vanish in the brilliant light. Tramello's church, however, is inferior to the Steccata in care for gradations of architecture, painting, and lighting.

In spite of the similarity in their plans, the two churches have very different antecedents. The five-domed scheme of the Madonna di Campagna grew out of a system that Tramello had already employed in the nave of S. Sepolcro at Piacenza; its prototypes are Byzantino-Venetian. On the other hand, the Steccata cannot be imagined without some knowledge of Bramante's design for St Peter's. A comparison between the two churches shows how essential a part the round forms of dome and apse play in enhancing the monumental effect of the 'Roman' central plan. At the same time, such a comparison brings out how widely North Italian buildings of this kind differ from the Roman type.

FALCONETTO AT PADUA

The work and personality of Giovanni Maria Falconetto have many things in common with those of Cesare Cesariano. Falconetto, born in 1468 at Verona, also began his career as a painter; like Cesariano he had also been to Rome.[15] Falconetto's drawings and reconstructions of ancient buildings correspond to Cesariano's Commentary on Vitruvius; some of them came into the possession of Palladio. From 1524 till his death in 1535, Falconetto was engaged on architectural work for the city of Padua and for the Venetian humanist Alvise Cornaro, who lived there. It is in the buildings which he designed for Cornaro that we encounter

for the first time the classicism which is so characteristic of Venice and the terraferma, the most important representative of which was to be Palladio.

A loggia and what is known as the Odeon [91, 92] have survived from Cornaro's town palazzo in the courtyard of the present Palazzo Giustiniani. The five-bay loggia forms the back of the courtyard, the three-bay front of the Odeon occupies the middle of one long side. Both buildings look like illustrations to a treatise on ancient building. The classical orders have seldom been imitated so closely as in this *forum Cornaro*, which was to be the meeting place of the client's friends; it also served for theatrical performances.[16]

Yet the correctly classical apparatus of form does not create a three-dimensional articulation of the fronts. The relief of the pilasters and niches is strangely shallow; in the loggia the relationship between the engaged Doric columns facing the pillars of the arcades and the Ionic pilasters of the upper storey remains a little vague. The relationship between wall and order recalls Roman buildings of the turn of the century, for instance the Cancelleria. The octagonal room in the middle of the Odeon, with its flat walls alternating with niches, shows that Falconetto had visited Rome about 1500; there are rooms of a very similar shape in the parts of the Golden House which had recently been discovered. The brilliant stucco and fresco decoration of the loggia and Odeon is one of the finest works of the 1530s, and in no way inferior to the decoration of the Villa Madama.[17] An inscription over the architrave of the loggia contains the name of Falconetto and the date 1524. A little later, Falconetto designed two town gates for Padua: the Porta S. Giovanni bears the date 1528, the Porta Savonarola that of 1530, and Falconetto is again named as the architect in the inscriptions.

92. Giovanni Maria Falconetto:
Padua, Loggia Cornaro, 1524

In both gates the archways have domical vaults. The high attics served as a parapet for the cannon mounted over the vault. Both sides of the Porta Savonarola and the city side of the Porta S. Giovanni [93] are articulated, like a Roman triumphal arch, by four columns on high pedestals; in both gates the lateral doors on the outer side are blind. The rusticated outer side of the Porta S. Giovanni has a flat order of pilasters, which would certainly have suffered less under bombardment than the almost free-standing columns of the Porta Savonarola. It is interesting that Falconetto should have abstained from rustication in the later gate and also articulated the outer side as a triumphal arch: the ancient Roman form meant more to him than the defensive strength of the gate. There was no prototype in antiquity for the combination of rustication and pilasters, while the smooth-faced ashlar and the columns could find their sanction in Roman arches. The side openings of the Porta S. Giovanni are treated as aedicules and crowned with elaborate pediments. Over the side archways the Porta Savonarola has straight – hence 'more correct' – lintels, and in the panels above there are roundels with busts; the Arch of Constantine has circular reliefs in the same place.

93. Giovanni Maria Falconetto:
Padua, Porta S. Giovanni, 1528

94. Giovanni Maria Falconetto and others: Luvigliano, Villa dei Vescovi, begun *c.* 1535

Alvise Cornaro certainly had a considerable share in the design for the remarkable villa of the bishops of Padua at Luvigliano which has traditionally been attributed to Falconetto [94].[18] The terracing of the hill on which it stands and the loggias of the piano nobile look back to Bramante's Belvedere Court, the massive rustication of the ground floor to the Porta Julia. There is a striking contrast between the orders and the rustication, which is entirely in the manner of Bramante; the order of the piano nobile triumphs over the 'as yet unshaped' natural forms of the base.[19]

The villa was not completed till after Falconetto's death. Comparing the somewhat coarse detail with that of the buildings at Padua, we can see how much the effect of Falconetto's work owes to its careful and delicate detail. Falconetto's view of antiquity was, so to speak, near-sighted; his prime interest was in detail, and in his own buildings he indulged in it as faithfully as he could. In the city gates he was able to adopt the form of the ancient triumphal arch *in toto*, yet even there scholarly theory seems more important than the living work in hand. It is no coincidence that

Falconetto's reconstructions of the Roman theatre at Verona, which have come down to us in a codex of the Biblioteca Comunale, are reminiscent of architectural utopias of the nineteenth century.[20]

It is clear that the commissions from Cornaro first enabled Falconetto to devote himself to architecture. Cornaro's intellectual interests were mainly concentrated on Stoic philosophy – at the end of his long life he wrote a treatise on self-control. And the buildings he commissioned from Falconetto, however faithful they may be to antiquity, are not without a prosaic touch. It may be said that this orthodox interpretation of antiquity illustrates one extreme of the post-classical movement of about 1530. We shall see the other extreme in the 'heretical' works which Giulio Romano, thirty years his junior, was executing at the same time for the Duke of Mantua. In both cases architect and patron were of about the same age. Thus the difference in style may well be a difference of generations too, nor is it mere chance that Cornaro, the Stoic humanist, employed Falconetto, whereas the capricious extravert Gonzaga Duke of Mantua employed Giulio.

CHAPTER 6

Sanmicheli

Michele Sanmicheli (1484–1559) is the only great architect of the Italian Renaissance who may have known ancient Greek buildings. As military engineer to the Republic of Venice he was active on the fortifications of Corfu, Crete, and Cyprus. Apart from Venice his main activity was at Verona. He visited Rome when he was young, and Bramante's Roman works formed his style.[1]

He belonged to a family of stonemasons which originated on Lake Como. His father had settled at Verona, where he worked on the Loggia del Consiglio. Little is known of his son's training and early travels. In 1509, at the age of twenty-five, Sanmicheli became chief architect of Orvieto Cathedral, which seems to show that his training as a stone-mason was completed. He erected an altar in the cathedral and worked on the upper parts of the façade, but his designs for the campanile were never carried out. In the documents of 1513 we read that 'Sanmicheli had been sent to Rome with a design for the façade in order to obtain Antonio da Sangallo's advice'. The office of works of the cathedral must have appreciated Sanmicheli; in spite of a chronic scarcity of funds, he received in 1521 the large bonus of 100 florins over and above his salary in order 'to prevent him leaving Orvieto, which would mean that work on the building would come to a standstill'.[2]

The anxiety of the cathedral building commission was not quite unfounded. In 1526, Sanmicheli had travelled through North and Central Italy with Antonio da Sangallo the Younger for several months in order to work out a detailed report on the state of the papal fortifications.[3] In 1530 at the latest he entered the service of Venice; in 1531 a letter from the Consiglio dei Dieci, the most important authority in the Republic, states that Sanmicheli was 'indispensable for the fortifications built in all our lands and towards the sea'.[4] At that time his salary was 120 ducats a year; later it was raised to 300 ducats.

Our blitz-hardened time is only too apt to forget that until the eighteenth century fortifications were just as much part of the duties of an architect as religious and domestic building. All the cities of the Middle Ages and the Renaissance were fortified: Giotto designed part of the city walls of Florence, Francesco di Giorgio, Dürer, and Leonardo wrote treatises on fortifications, and city gates by Bramante, Sangallo, and Falconetto have already been mentioned. While most of these constructions fell victim to later extensions of the cities, Sanmicheli's gates at Verona give a vivid idea of their functions. His Porta Nuova and Porta Palio are among the masterpieces of the Renaissance.

Sanmicheli was in charge of the maintenance and moder-nization of the walls of his native city for more than thirty years. The fortress of Verona protected Venetian territory against attack by land; its citadels were no less important for the security of the republic than the coastal forts on the islands of Cyprus and Crete.

CITY GATES

In the Porta Nuova [95, 96], built in the thirties, the actual archway is combined with two artillery towers at the sides in a transverse block.[5] The powerful outer walls were a protec-tion against artillery fire, and at the same time served as abutments to take the recoil of the guns mounted on the vault. There may be echoes of the Porta Maggiore in Rome in the rustication of the façade; Serlio observes that the vigorous rustication of gates and fortifications is the best expression of their purpose. When two side passages were pierced in the nineteenth century, the gate forfeited its character as a defensive structure. The city side was greatly altered at that time. On the outer side, only the central part was rusticated originally; the adjoining wall surfaces were smooth. The coupled Doric order, the pediment, the trophies and inscriptions make this front the real show side. In addition to the main archway, the city side has four narrower passages for foot traffic and two windows for the wide ramps that lead up to the roof through the thickness of the wall. The triglyph frieze, restricted on the outer side to the middle, on the city side runs over the whole breadth of the gate to the coupled pilasters at the corners.

As its plan shows [97], the Porta Palio, built some twenty years later, was not intended as an emplacement for artillery.[6] For that reason three archways could be made on the outer side and the pediment over the centre left out [98]. In the interior of the gate, the passages meet in a groin-vaulted hall opening on to the town in five arches. The scheme of the articulation shows familiarity with Falconetto's gates at Padua, but Sanmicheli couples the columns, and, as he had already done in the Porta Nuova, replaces the slender Corinthian order by the heavier and sturdier Doric. The block of the gate is broader and the horizontal members stronger than in the Porta Nuova; the architrave does not project. The very flat rustication emphasizes the horizontal joints of the masonry, but not the relief of the single block of stone. There is a harmonious balance between the verticals of the fluted columns and the horizontal courses of the wall.

Unlike Falconetto's gates, which still echo medieval gate-houses with their tall attics, Sanmicheli's structures hardly rise above the encircling walls. But the Doric order, with its strong relief, brought out the double function of the gate as a fortification and a triumphal arch far more convincingly than was the case at Padua.

The decoration of the Porta Palio is more vigorous than Falconetto's, more harmonious and better balanced than that of the Porta Nuova. The latter, with its striking rustication, belongs to the same phase of style as Giulio Romano's buildings at Mantua. The harmony and monumentality of the Porta Palio, on the other hand, are typical of Sanmicheli's late style. In other ways too Italian architecture about 1550 abandoned the emotional forms of the second quarter of the century.

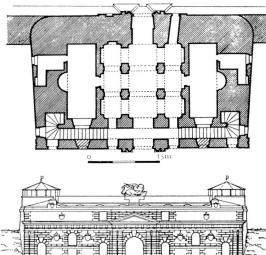

95. (*left*) Michele Sanmicheli: Verona, Porta Nuova, 1533–40

96. (*above*) Michele Sanmicheli: Verona, Porta Nuova, 1533–40, plan and elevation

PALAZZI IN VERONA

Sanmicheli's palazzo façades recall the scheme of Bramante's Palazzo Caprini. In Rome itself, the scheme had disappeared as early as Raphael's Palazzo Branconio dall' Aquila, but the terraferma and Venice continued the use of engaged columns or pilasters in the piano nobile and the rustication of the ground floor up to the end of the eighteenth century.

In the palazzi of the terraferma the courtyard plays a very minor part as compared with Rome or Florence. The building lots are for the most part oblong, and their depth is sometimes three or four times the width of the façade. The courtyard is often no more than a long passage leading from the street to the servants' quarters at the back. Thus 'great'

architecture is confined to the façade and the salone in the piano nobile.

Of the four palazzi built by Sanmicheli at Verona, only one, the present Palazzo Guastaverza, can be dated with certainty. The patron, Bonaventura degli Onorii, obtained permission to begin building in 1555.[7] The Palazzo Pompei (originally Lavezola) probably belongs to the same date.[8] The Palazzo Canossa was built some twenty years earlier; building was in progress in 1533.[9] The date of the unfinished Palazzo Bevilacqua can only be determined on stylistic grounds.[10]

The façade of the Palazzo Bevilacqua has five bays to the right and one to the left of the entrance [99]. The façade would be symmetrical if one assumes that four of the eleven

97. (*below*) Michele Sanmicheli: Verona, Porta Palio, c. 1555–60, plan

98. (*right*) Michele Sanmicheli: Verona, Porta Palio, begun c. 1555

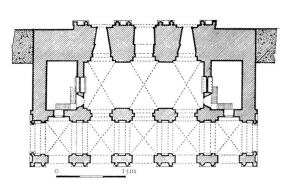

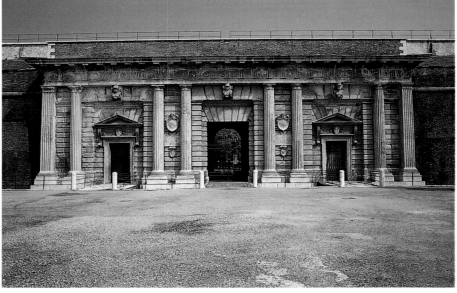

99. Michele Sanmicheli: Verona, Palazzo Bevilacqua, *c.* 1530

bays originally planned are lacking.[11] The sumptuous ornament and complex composition are unique in every sense, and not only in Sanmicheli's work.

The ground floor has rusticated Tuscan pilasters, the piano nobile fluted Corinthian half-columns. On both floors wide and narrow bays alternate, on the piano nobile also high and low round-headed windows. An unprecedented feature is the device by which Sanmicheli transforms his rhythm of wide and narrow bays (b–a–b–a, etc.) into a system of three bays grouped as a triumphal arch. Of the four half-columns of a b–a–b bay, the inner and outer pair have either straight or spiral flutings;[12] in the neighbouring group, the relationship between the pairs is reversed. Thus the triple groups are linked together over the whole façade. The result is a system which can be read off both as b–a–b etc. and as A–B–A.[13]

The lavishness of the decoration is in keeping with the complexity of this scheme. The balustrade stretching across the whole width of the piano nobile rests on jutting modillions; these modillions are at the same time to be understood as triglyphs of the Doric order on the ground floor. The sills of the ground-floor windows are ornamented with a meander pattern; they rest on winged, sphinx-shaped corbels. The keystones over the windows are carved to represent antique busts. Winged figures fill the spandrels of the great windows on the piano nobile, and garlands wind from capital to capital over the small windows. In the rich scroll frieze of the main entablature and on the corbels of the ground floor there appears the pinion of the eagle, the emblem of the Bevilacqua.

The motifs of the decoration may be ancient, but nothing could be less like antiquity than their composition. In the *horror vacui* of the façade, in the complexity of its convoluted patterns, in the ambiguity of its forms, we can sense that same 'heresy' as can be seen in Peruzzi. A characteristic feature is the difference in the relationship between openings and order in the two storeys. In the piano nobile the columns are raised high above the window-sills by tall pedestals

100. Michele Sanmicheli: Verona, Palazzo Canossa, begun *c*. 1532

Bramante and Raphael, Sanmicheli deprives the single bays of their independence by carrying the mouldings of the window imposts and the bases of the windows right across the whole storey and making them run behind the coupled order. There are no projections. Thus the front of the piano nobile seems to consist of two flat strata, one in front with the pilasters, their bases and entablature, and one behind with the windows, their cornices, and the flat course under the openings of the mezzanine.

The focus of the composition of plan and elevation [101] is the three-bay loggia of the façade. The portal of this *atrio* leads to a deep vestibule which is of the same width and length as the loggia. The vaulting of these two units supports the salone of the piano nobile. The vestibule, in its turn, opens into the courtyard loggia; the staircases are situated at its sides.[15] This middle block is of two storeys, flanked by four-storeyed side wings. There are servants' staircases to the two mezzanine floors. One detail may throw light on the ingenious combination of plan and elevation: the vaulting of the courtyard loggia is slightly lower than that of the adjoining vestibule; in that way it was possible to insert, above the loggia, a low mezzanine floor which communicates with the intermediate floors of the wings. The openings between the lower and upper loggias of the cortile front are therefore truly mezzanine windows; the corresponding windows in the façade, on the other hand, are blind, since the vault of the vestibule rises behind them.

Sanmicheli again employed the tripartite scheme for the plan of the later Palazzo Pompei. Once again the façade has seven bays [102]; the width of the vestibule and salone is

101. Michele Sanmicheli: Verona, Palazzo Canossa, begun *c*. 1532, section, elevation, and plan of ground floor

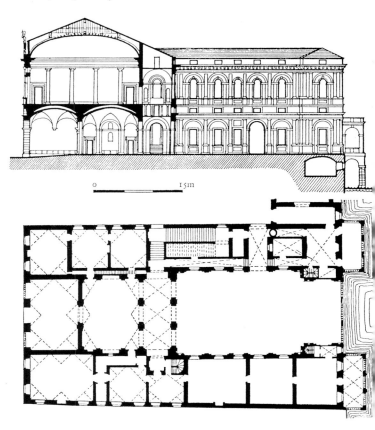

standing on the balustrade; on the ground floor, the relationship is reversed, and it is the windows that are raised so high that their sills reach nearly half way up the pilasters.

The façade is one of the most important examples of the reaction against the high classical style; it owes part of its charm at any rate to a thoroughly classical formal repertory used to express something utterly unclassical. The works of Sanmicheli which are most akin to the Bevilacqua façade are the early Petrucci Chapel at Orvieto, which is discussed below, and the Porta Nuova. The chapel shows the same love of rhythm in the composition and the recession of the wall behind order and ornament. The Porta Nuova is echoed in the treatment of the rusticated Doric order. Thus the Palazzo Bevilacqua was probably one of Sanmicheli's first works at Verona.

The façade of the Palazzo Canossa is much quieter [100].[14] The triumphal arch motif of wide and narrow openings is replaced by bays of equal width. The piano nobile has coupled pilasters, the order has completely vanished from the ground floor, and the relief of the wall is shallower throughout. The three central bays of the ground floor open on to the street like a pillared loggia; Sanmicheli may have seen this motif in the Palazzo del Te at Mantua, which was built not long before. The antecedents of the coupled pilasters in the piano nobile are the coupled columns of the Palazzi Caprini and Caffarelli in Rome. But unlike

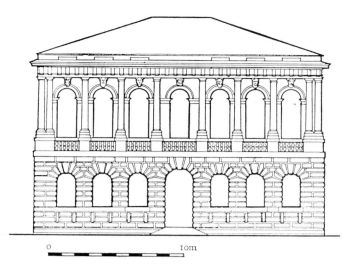

102. Michele Sanmicheli: Venice, Palazzo Pompei, c. 1555, façade

determined by the three central ones. But in this case the two units occupy the entire depth of the block; the vestibule and loggias of the Palazzo Canossa have been suppressed. Though equally careful in arrangement, the plan and elevation are less differentiated; there are no mezzanines, and the decoration, especially in the courtyard, is very quiet. This greater simplicity may be due to the instructions of a thrifty patron, but the famous façade also shows that the artist handled his artistic means more economically than in his early buildings. The piano nobile has fluted Doric columns, like its near contemporary, the Porta Palio; they cut across the springing line of the round window arches, but the order of columns and the wall surface are more clearly distinguished than in the Palazzo Canossa. There is no hint of the complex rhythm and the *horror vacui* of the Palazzo Bevilacqua. The scheme could not be plainer. On each side of the broader middle bay there are three identical, narrower bays; at the corners a pilaster adjoins the column. Thus the triumphal arch theme is replaced by symmetrical grouping, motifs are identical, not alternating, the emphasis is on frame and centre, which gives a stable instead of an unstable balance, and clarity replaces ambiguity. A more striking contrast to the Palazzo Bevilacqua could hardly be imagined.

The façades of the Palazzo Guastaverza at Verona and the Palazzo Roncali at Rovigo also show that in his later life Sanmicheli returned to his earlier preference for the classical principle of rows of identical bays.

PALAZZI IN VENICE

The Palazzi Cornaro[16] and Grimani[17] in Venice are also late works. The plans conform to the usual Venetian scheme [103]; from the main entrance in the façade a long passage leads to the courtyard at the back of the very long and narrow building plot. The situation of the Palazzo Grimani on the Canal Grande may be the reason why the ground floor is not astylar; its Corinthian pilasters support the Corinthian columns of the piano nobile [104]. The outer bays of the façade are flanked by coupled orders which, in their turn, enframe the triumphal arch motif in the centre.

This detachment of the side parts is as new as the close grouping of the three central bays. The fluting of the columns, the cornices of the mezzanine floors, and the balustrade are reminiscent of the Palazzo Bevilacqua, but the composition, though equally ornate, is much less complex. As in the Porta Palio, vertical and horizontal members, stressed centre and enframing sides, are in perfect balance, so that the whole gives an impression of stability and calm. Hardly another architect of the Cinquecento handled the ancient orders with such mastery, or made them so expressive, as Sanmicheli. The Doric is absolutely right in the Porta Palio; in the façade on the Grand Canal it would have looked grim and heavy. The Corinthian pilasters on the ground floor are a deviation from the rule which would, in their place, have dictated the Doric or at most admitted the Ionic; the repetition of the order on the piano nobile is again a breach of the rule. But the use of the more ornate Corinthian order in both storeys, with the heightening of its relief from the flat pilaster to the round column, is precisely the feature which gives the Grimani façade its distinction and splendour.

In both storeys the pilasters and columns cut across the entablature of a smaller order. The smaller pilasters are not fluted. Thus here again there is a new and effective distinction between the flat wall of the façade and a great order set in front of it. This motif, which was to play so great a part in Palladio's work, can hardly be derived from Michelangelo's giant order in the palazzi on the Capitol. The precursors of the minor order in the Palazzo Grimani are rather to be sought in a series of North Italian buildings, beginning with Alberti's façade of S. Andrea in Mantua, and continuing in Sanmicheli's Veronese palazzi.

And finally the palazzo presents the aesthetic and practical solution of a problem which had already preoccupied Sanmicheli in the Palazzo Canossa. The high arch of the main portal leads into the tunnel-vaulted 'nave' of the vestibule; the lower side entrances lead into flat-roofed 'aisles', which rise as far as the entablature of the minor order. Thus the elevation of the group of entrances corresponds to the section of the triple vestibule. No other

103. Michele Sanmicheli: Venice, Palazzo Grimani, begun c. 1556, plan of ground floor

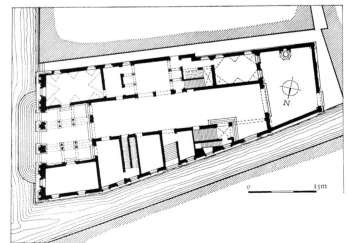

Cinquecento palazzo has this organic unity of façade and entrance hall.[18]

CHURCHES AND CHAPELS

Two of the churches which are unquestionably Sanmicheli's work are round, the other two octagonal. The Cappella Petrucci at Orvieto and the Cappella Pellegrini in the church of S. Bernardino at Verona are mortuary chapels; the chapel at Fumane belongs to the villa of the Della Torre family; S. Maria di Campagna is an important pilgrimage church three miles south-east of Verona. This list illustrates in many ways the function and form of religious building in the second quarter of the century – the indifference to parish or monastic churches, the predominance of memorial building, and finally the preference for the centralized plan. The predilection for the circular form also shows how deeply Bramante's Tempietto had influenced Sanmicheli's work.

The small funerary chapel of the Petrucci in S. Domenico at Orvieto, probably Sanmicheli's earliest architectural work,[19] consists of an octagonal room and a miniature choir under the sanctuary of the Gothic church [105]. The altar of the chapel, and the double flights of steps leading down to it, show that it was in regular use. The striking articulation of the walls by niches and Tuscan pilasters in so small a chapel, its function as a burial place, and even the position of the altar, recall late Roman hypogea in Rome. It may be that Sanmicheli wished to imitate a confessio or a catacomb. The idea would provide the simplest explanation of the peculiarities of the Petrucci Chapel.

The plan and function of the circular Pellegrini Chapel at Verona [106][20] also recall late Roman mortuary buildings, especially the imperial mausolea attached to old St Peter's. Like them, it is connected with the church only by a small antechamber; there is no articulation of the exterior; the interior, with its triumphal arch motif and fluted columns, repeats the formal repertory of the Palazzo Bevilacqua, which was built about the same time. Above the wide spacings of the main order, the drum has freestanding columns; a hemispherical cupola rests on their architrave – an arrangement which looks back to Bramante's design for the drum of St Peter's.

The Madonna di Campagna[21] is the only great Cinquecento church to realize Alberti's ideal of a free-standing, round 'temple' [108]. True, the church does not stand in the 'form', as Alberti had intended, but outside the city walls, like the centrally planned churches of Todi and Montepulciano; like them, it houses a miraculous image. A low Tuscan colonnade surrounds the base of the gigantic cylinder; the smoothness of its walls is broken only by the Ionic pilasters and the windows of the drum [107]. The restraint of the exterior does not prepare the visitor for the subtle refinement of the interior, an octagon with pillars and arches bearing an octagonal domical vault which is concealed under

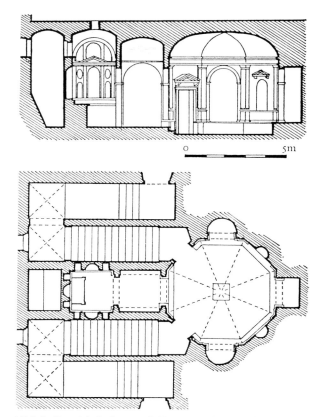

105. Michele Sanmicheli: Orvieto, S. Domenico, Petrucci Chapel, c. 1516, section and plan

the hemisphere of the outer shell [109]. Following an ancient Venetian tradition, the exterior shell of the dome is of wood. In the interior, three of the bays on the transverse and longitudinal axes open as portals, while the fourth leads into the choir. Altars mark the intervening bays. The choir is actually a second, smaller, centrally planned church on a Greek cross plan. The hemispherical dome over the crossing touches the drum of the main vault. The transverse axis of the choir is smaller and its dome lower than that of the big

106. Michele Sanmicheli: Verona, S. Bernardino, Pellegrini Chapel, probably begun in 1527, plan and section

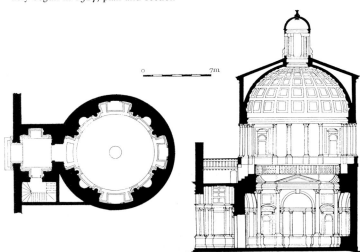

107. (*above*) Michele Sanmicheli: Verona, Madonna di Campagna, begun 1559

108. (*below*) Michele Sanmicheli: Verona, Madonna di Campagna, begun 1559, section and plan

cylinder; seen from the outside, the choir looks like a subsidiary annex.[22]

If one enters the church through the portal on the town side, the miraculous image in the choir chapel is seen in the frame of the arch opposite. The broad, high octagon which surrounds the viewer is like the first of a series of rooms with the high altar standing at its end. The lengthwise sweep from the door to the altar is hardly less important for the general effect than the height of the main dome.

The strong stress on the longitudinal axis, however, conflicts with the principle of a purely centralized plan. The miraculous images at Todi and Montepulciano stand under the dome, though not under its centre. In the Madonna di Campagna, the dome, in the exterior view, certainly keeps its place as the crown of the building, but in the interior the high altar is set so far out of the octagon that the arrangement of dome and altar may be called eccentric.

In view of the Madonna di Campagna, it is easy to understand why the architects of the Renaissance, for all their admiration of the Pantheon, shrank from adopting the circular form for their great churches. Except for its portico, the exterior view of the Pantheon is neglected; in a Renaissance pilgrimage church the exterior and interior were equally important. The ancient vaulting technique with concrete was unimaginable at Verona about 1550; Sanmicheli had no alternative but the double shell. For static reasons, the contour of the two shells had to differ.[23] The foot of the heavy inner shell had to be set comparatively low, that of the lighter outer shell comparatively high.

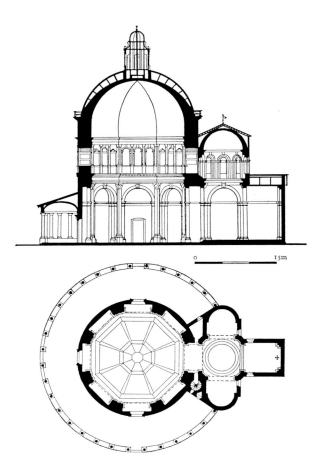

The architect whose aim it was to realize in the Madonna di Campagna the ideal of a 'modern' Pantheon had to take into account the aesthetic conditions which a Renaissance pilgrimage church had to fulfil, and the structural possibilities at his disposal. The compromise, and in particular the discrepancy between the exterior and interior, are and remain unsatisfying.[24] From the outside, the Doric peristyle looks too low, the cylinder rising above it too high; the balustrade is not weighty enough for the necessary transition between the dome and the cylinder; the plain zone between the windows in the drum and the balustrade – which corresponds to the difference in height between the spring of the interior and exterior domes – looks senseless.

Yet these weaknesses were innate in the choice of the architectural composition. They became inevitable as soon as an 'ideal' rotunda was to be crowned by a dome visible from a great distance. Plans such as the quatrefoil or the Greek cross permit a genuine gradation of the building both horizontally and vertically. Their rectangular crossing can be closed by a dome on pendentives; the reduction of volume from the cube of the substructure by way of the cylinder of the drum to the hemisphere of the dome is satisfying both structurally and aesthetically. A domed building on a circular plan admits no gradation of the kind, since drum and dome have to be of the same diameter.

On the other hand, the conscious care devoted to plan and structure are entirely in keeping with Sanmicheli's other buildings. The removal of the altar from the main unit of space recalls his early Petrucci Chapel at Orvieto; he had already got to grips with the problem of the centralized plan in the Pellegrini Chapel. It is quite possible that in the building of the Madonna di Campagna, Sanmicheli's plans were really respected, and they were available at the laying of the foundation stone in 1559. The responsibility for the partly very crude detail and the awkward lantern must rest with the craftsmen.[25]

Of all the architects of the Cinquecento, Sanmicheli cultivated the heritage of Bramante longest and most intensely. His central compositions are inconceivable without the prototype of the Tempietto, his palazzo façades without that of the Palazzo Caprini. It would, however, be a mistake to regard Sanmicheli as a mere copyist or epigone. His Palazzo Bevilacqua is no less 'modern' than the contemporary post-classical buildings in Rome. His gates and the Pompei and Grimani façades are among the few buildings of the Cinquecento which created new types for others to follow. They offered new and practical solutions of building problems,

109. Michele Sanmicheli: Verona, Madonna di Campagna, begun 1559

they fulfilled the ideal of a meaningful use of the ancient orders, so that the modern function of the building could be given adequate expression.[26]

The true heir of Sanmicheli was to be Palladio: without him, Palladio's development cannot be imagined. Sanmicheli's treatment of ornament, his avoidance of colour effects, his interest in the composition of the façade, his adoption of the Roman rotunda, his form of drum and dome developed out of Bramante's design for St Peter's – all these features were continued in Palladio's work.

In concluding this chapter, the most beautiful of the Baroque churches in Venice must be mentioned. The dome of S. Maria della Salute consists, like that of the Madonna di Campagna, of a spherical outer and an octagonal inner shell. In both churches, a large octagon is combined with a centrally planned choir; the plans of the two choirs are also akin. By surrounding the octagon with an octagonal ambulatory, Longhena created the harmony which Sanmicheli's rotunda lacked; it is obvious, however, that the architectural principles of the Madonna di Campagna had their effect on the planning of the Salute.

CHAPTER 7

Giulio Romano

At Mantua, the works of Giulio Romano (1499?–1546),[1] who was a little younger than Sanmicheli, are contemporary with Sanmicheli's buildings at Verona. Both architects owe their determining impulses to Rome, Sanmicheli obviously to the Bramante circle, and Giulio Romano as Raphael's favourite pupil to Raphael. He collaborated in the Vatican Stanze and Logge and in the Villa Madama. After Raphael's death he took over the workshop in collaboration with Giovanfrancesco Penni.

Giulio Romano was one of the few great architects of the century to be born in Rome. The inseparability of structure and decoration which was so characteristic of Raphael's mature style is also a fundamental trait of Giulio's work. His buildings are conceived as an aesthetic whole, and in many cases the share of the architect in the whole can hardly be distinguished from that of the stucco-worker or fresco-painter. To that extent, Giulio is the most important representative of the trend which has been called 'painter's architecture'. He shares with Peruzzi the conscious contrasting of classical and anti-classical form. Both Giulio and Peruzzi show their knowledge of the canon of the orders, but often employ quite heretical forms in the same building. Contemporaries admired as fertility of invention the surprise and shock imparted by this style, and its contradiction in terms. For the connoisseur the work now became a riddle, an experiment, in which the artist and the viewer shared equally.[2]

From his arrival at Mantua in 1524 till his death, Giulio was responsible for all the artistic enterprises at the court of the Gonzaga. His masterpiece was the Palazzo del Te, a large *villa suburbana*, which he designed and decorated with the assistance of his pupils. But he also made plans for new districts in the city, superintended the alteration of the ducal residence, and set the scenes for the state reception of the Emperor Charles V and the new duchess. Art at Mantua in the second quarter of the Cinquecento is practically synonymous with his name. As Vasari tells us: 'Nobody in that city could build without an order from Giulio.'[3]

Giulio's particular architectural thinking is revealed in two buildings in Rome erected before he left to settle in Mantua: the Villa Lante on the Gianicolo[4] and the Palazzo Maccarani in the Piazza S. Eustachio.[5] Like Bramante's Palazzo Caprini, the Palazzo Maccarani has five bays, the ground floor is rusticated, and the piano nobile is articulated by a coupled order [110]. But in the Palazzo Maccarani, the openings on the ground and mezzanine floors are oblong. The string course lies like a beam on vertical strips of rusticated blocks, and the gigantic voussoirs of the botteghe are wedged in between these strips. The window-sills of the piano nobile rest exactly on those points in the string course where it is not supported by the ground floor. A similar contradiction can be seen in the entrance doorway, where the voussoirs of the straight lintel project far out from the façade.[6] At first it looks alarmingly unsteady, until it becomes clear that they

are held fast by the parts of a broken pediment. In addition to orthodox window frames, there are in the piano nobile quite illicit pilasters without capitals, and on the upper floor segmental arches over the windows instead of straight entablatures. The courtyard, enlarged and altered, preserves the original articulation of the piano nobile on its long side. True, the coupled pilasters have capitals, but in themselves they are unusually slender, and therefore 'too tall'. The surrounds of the mezzanine openings are to be looked at as vertically sliced balusters. The charm and fancifulness of this architecture can only be appreciated by the expert who is familiar with the classic repertory of form and its use in the Palazzo Caprini, and he alone can grasp the eccentricity of the Palazzo Maccarani.

Giulio's summons to Mantua was arranged by Baldassare Castiglione, the Gonzaga's agent for cultural affairs in Rome. He recommended Giulio, argued out the terms of his appointment, and actually travelled to Mantua with him in 1524. The Marchese, later Duke Federigo II, born in 1500, as the son of Isabella d'Este, was familiar with the great art of the Renaissance, and loaded Giulio Romano, who was his contemporary, with tokens of his favour. In August 1526 the artist was appointed Superiore Generale of all public buildings; even before that the Duke had presented him with a house, and granted him the citizenship of Mantua. Four months later he appointed him *Superiore delle Strade*.[7] The salary for this position, which Giulio retained till his death, was 500 ducats a year, while Sangallo and Peruzzi, as architects of St Peter's at that time, were paid 300 a year. The new quarters planned by Giulio made Mantua a modern city. Vasari called the new streets 'dry, clean, fair, and pleasing'.[8]

The site of the Palazzo del Te was on an island outside

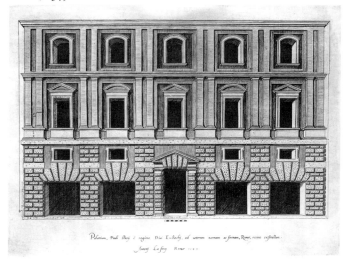

110. Giulio Romano: Rome, Palazzo Maccarani, 1519–20, engraving by Lafreri, 1549

the city walls which had, from time immemorial, housed the stables and provided pasturing for the famous Gonzaga stud. According to Vasari, Federigo's first idea was to have a mere pied-à-terre for refreshments and rest after riding. It was from these modest beginnings that Giulio Romano evolved the elaborate scheme of the present building [111].

The letters exchanged between the client and the artist during building show Giulio as architect, artist, contractor, and clerk of the works. They show how eager the client was to have the building completed as soon as possible; again and again Giulio had to explain delays due to the lack of reliable workmen, to sickness, and to work elsewhere. Federigo's persistence becomes easier to understand if we think of all the villas of the time which remained unfinished or took decades to complete. Most likely the Marchese wished to outvie his sister Eleonora of Urbino, with her great villa near Pesaro. By the end of 1534 the structural and decorative work on the Palazzo del Tè was practically finished.[9]

Vasari speaks of 'a square building with an open turfed courtyard and four entrances. The first entrance, which is seen at once by the visitor coming from the town, leads into a very large loggia opening on to the garden; two other portals lead into various rooms decorated with painting and stucco'.[10] These brief sentences, which are followed by seven pages on the furnishings and the iconographical programme, are no real preparation for the surprises the villa has in store. Firstly the proportions are unusual. The exterior

111. Giulio Romano: Mantua, Palazzo del Te, begun 1525, plan

112. Giulio Romano: Mantua, Palazzo del Te, begun 1525, façade

looks like a low, single-storeyed block, four times as wide as it is high.[11] Both façades looking towards the town have a giant order of Doric pilasters [112], but the intervals between the pilasters and the portals are unequal, so that different systems collide at the corners. Porches and windows are vigorously rusticated, and the detail is just as bizarre as in the Palazzo Maccarani. On the town side is the 'very large loggia' described by Vasari, while the west entrance leads into a tetrastyle vestibule which has flat-roofed aisles and a tunnel-vaulted nave. The scheme of the triple vestibule occurs as the 'atrium' in Fra Giocondo's 1511 edition of Vitruvius; Giulio Romano probably adopted it from the projects for the Villa Madama, which he knew well.[12] The combination of columns, architrave, flat ceiling, and coffered tunnel-vault (the model for the coffers was the Basilica of Maxentius, not the Pantheon) is obviously intended to recall ancient buildings. But the first impression the visitor receives is not that of a 'classical' kind of architecture; the columns and pilasters are coated with a thick crust of rustication. One is led to imagine the marble columns, apparently still in the rough, as they would be when smoothed. The architrave over the columns has been carefully smoothed, but in the centre of each intercolumnar space there is a quite un-motivated 'keystone' with a rusticated surface. It is hardly possible to avoid the impression that these keystones were 'by mistake' left undressed. This 'unfinished' effect seems almost stranger to the expert than to the general visitor; after all, the dressing of columns and architrave was routine work for the stonemason.

In the corners of the courtyard, as on the exterior of the palazzo, different systems collide [113]. The wall surfaces between the half-columns on the north and south sides are of the same width, but on the east and west sides there is an alternation of wider and narrower wall sections, a variant of Bramante's scheme in the Upper Belvedere Court. Between the half-columns, rubbly rustication and fine ashlar stand side by side.[13] On two sides of the courtyard the triglyphs of the entablature look as if they were slipping down. The

114. Giulio Romano: Mantua, Palazzo del Te, begun 1525, Sala dei Cavalli

113. Giulio Romano: Mantua, Palazzo del Te, begun 1525, courtyard

115. Giulio Romano: Mantua, Palazzo del Te, begun 1525, garden loggia

general effect is that the surface is unfinished; the individual member does not seem to have found its final place; the situation is provisional and unstable. As in the Palazzo Maccarani, the viewer constantly feels tricked.

The coloured ornament which must have further brought out the fantastic and restless composition of the façade no longer exists. What an essential part it played in the total effect can be seen in the interior, which, in spite of centuries of neglect and repeated repainting, is tolerably well preserved. In the frescoes of the Sala dei Cavalli [114], the Duke had his favourite horses portrayed. They stand life-size and uncannily alive in front of the pilasters and niches of the painted architecture. The niches contain figures of the gods of Olympus in grisaille, i.e. intended to produce the effect of marble. The mixture of several kinds of reality is just as essential an element of this style as the juxtaposition of completely formed and quite amorphous details. The wooden beams of the ceiling in the Sala dei Cavalli seem to be intertwining.

The interplay of illusion and reality reaches its climax in the frescoes of the Sala dei Giganti. The visitor feels that he is surrounded by tottering walls; they are the rocks collapsing on the giants who have been conquered by Zeus. The god with his thunderbolt appears high above the clouds. A monopteros, carried by the clouds, is hovering at an inaccessible height in the crown of the vault – Olympus in the guise of a Tempietto. The picturing of chaos and terror recalls Hieronymus Bosch. There is not a single vertical or horizontal accent for the eye to rest on; the bounds of the hall seem to yield to the frightful pressure from above. The architect has abandoned the language of architecture. All he cares about is the expressive value, the emotion which the room is to awaken in the visitor.

The Sala dei Giganti was created thirty years after Bramante's Tempietto and fifteen after the Sala delle Colonne in the Farnesina. Looked at from this standpoint, Bramante and Peruzzi seem closer to the master of the Parthenon than to Raphael's pupil.

The whole garden front of the Palazzo del Te is arcaded [116]; the central part contains a three-bay loggia, the vaulting of each bay being supported on four columns [115]. In this loggia, the visitor, emerging from the riot of the Sala dei

116. Giulio Romano: Mantua, Palazzo del Te, begun 1525, garden façade, drawing, c. 1570. Düsseldorf, Kunstmuseum (FP 10922)

117. Giulio Romano: Mantua, Palazzo Ducale, Cortile della Cavallerizza, façade of the Estivale, *c.* 1539

Giganti, is surrounded by light walls and white-stuccoed columns. The columns are impeccable in form and proportion. The vaulting recalls the decoration of the Augustan age. Giulio Romano here displays his familiarity with Alberti and the principles of classical architecture. The segments of a huge entablature with classical mouldings lie over the groups of columns, so that there is no immediate connection between columns and round arches. A similar combination of columns, architrave, and round arch is to be seen in the lower loggias on both sides of the central section, which actually form shallow balconies. As can be seen from the plan, this is a purely aesthetic 'curtain wall', like the Gothic triforium.

If we stand in front of this façade, the rusticated tetrastyle vestibule can be seen through the portal of the loggia and across the courtyard. The contrast is intentional. Wherever one turns in this building, there are clashes of finished and unfinished, orthodox and heretical, fortissimo and pianissimo. It seems as if the forces at work, the conflict between order and chaos, were held suspended for a moment by the architect's spell.[14]

In the city residence of the Gonzaga Giulio designed, in addition to a number of interiors, the so-called *Estivale*, the south front of the present Cortile della Cavallerizza [117].[15] The building, erected in 1538–9 and originally free-standing, was intended as a kind of terrace for performances and tournaments. The seven-bay façade[16] returns to the scheme of the Palazzo Caprini, but in the Duke's palazzo the piano nobile is also rusticated, and in the strangest fashion. Still more, there is movement even in the calmest of classical orders. The Doric columns twist spirally about their own axes.[17] Their rusticated bases project from this wall, needing

the support of brackets which are wedged in between the arches of the ground floor. Under the weight of the string courses the arches are bent into a segmental shape, and the pediments over the windows of the piano nobile become flat relieving arches. Here again the relationship of supporting and supported members is one of frozen movement, and not of enduring harmony.

118. Giulio Romano: Mantua Cathedral, after 1540, plan

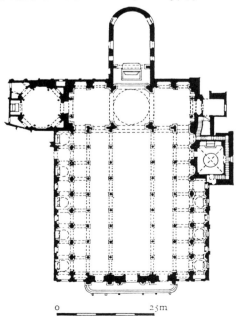

0   25m

GIULIO ROMANO · 81

119. Giulio Romano: Mantua Cathedral, after 1540

form a minor order. In the middle of the bay, the architrave is broken by round-headed arches in the same way as in the outer aisles of Mantua Cathedral.

It is illuminating that so fertile and inventive an artist should have adopted in these buildings traditional forms from the Early Christian basilica and Bramante's Belvedere Court. The forms of the Palazzo del Te are calculated for a near view; given the large scale and the liturgical requirements of the two churches, Giulio had to turn to other means if he was going to produce the effects of contrast which are typical of his conception of architecture. The contrast between vaulted and flat-roofed aisles in the cathedral, the confusing composition of the interior of S. Benedetto, the mixture of old and new elements, are no less surprising than the suite of rooms in the Palazzo del Te. But the studied effects of surprise and contrast look petty in buildings the size of S. Benedetto, for on that scale the eye needs clarity, balance, and permanence.

It is true that Giulio's hands were bound in these commissions: existing parts of buildings had to be worked in and the old frontages had to be maintained. Yet if both churches awaken conflicting feelings in the viewer, that cannot be entirely ascribed to external circumstances. The element of caprice which plays such a determining part in Giulio's style cannot be transposed into the key of monumentality.

The style, however, was ideally right for Giulio's own house, which Vasari admired at Mantua in 1541.[19] The ground floor houses the workshops, the piano nobile the living rooms whose frescoes have recently been rediscovered. Behind the attic a low mezzanine floor is concealed. The façade is entirely in the palazzo style [121], a demonstration of the architect's relation to the court and the nobility. The ground floor appears as a rusticated base, and the portal with its depressed arch interrupts the row of square windows. It is remarkable that Giulio has refrained in the piano nobile from using engaged columns and pilasters; the articulation consists of blank arches with the window frames and pediments recessed in them. The keystones of these arches

Giulio's position and influence remained unchanged when Cardinal Ercole Gonzaga became regent during the minority of Francesco III after Duke Federigo's death in 1540. For the first time, Giulio Romano was faced with problems of religious architecture: he was entrusted with the renovation of Mantua Cathedral and the abbey church of S. Benedetto Po (Polirone), not far from Mantua. Neither building tells us clearly what was the condition before renovation and what is Giulio's part in it.[18] In the cathedal [118] the medieval outer walls were preserved, and work was confined to the double-aisled interior. The flat-roofed nave with its Corinthian columns and architrave recalls old St Peter's. The inner aisles have lavishly decorated tunnel-vaults, while the outer ones have flat coffered ceilings [119]. This curious alternation between flat ceiling and tunnel-vault is continued in the chapels off the outer aisles; from every second bay a round arch leads into a vaulted chapel. From the adjoining bays architraved passages lead into flat-roofed units.

In S. Benedetto, also, the exterior was renovated. For the façade and sides of the church [120] Giulio adopted the triumphal arch motif of Bramante's upper Belvedere Court. In the interior, the vaulting of the thirteenth century was retained, but the medieval system of alternating heavier and lighter piers was completely altered. The major piers were faced with pilasters; the minor ones were removed, and each was replaced by two low columns which, with their architrave,

120. Giulio Romano: S. Benedetto Po (Polirone), abbey church, after 1540

121. Giulio Romano: Mantua, the architect's own house, *c.* 1540

the piano nobile, a shallow niche with a small statue takes the place of a window. Finally, the relationship of arch and pediment is reversed in the two storeys; in the portal, the pediment frames the arch, in the piano nobile the arch frames the pediment.

The blind arches of the piano nobile, in spite of their comparatively shallow relief, make the façade the most striking in the whole length of the street. It has a *grandezza* which no Florentine or Roman artist's house of the sixteenth century possesses. Yet it shows no advance over Giulio's earlier buildings in Rome and Mantua. It is a strange fact that there is no real development in Giulio's style. Till his death he employed the forms which, by the virtuosity of their treatment, had made him Raphael's most beloved pupil.

By 1540 these forms were out of date in Rome. When Giulio died in 1546, Mantua was on the way to becoming a provincial town; the age of the small princely courts was approaching its end. Compared with contemporary Roman architecture, or with the palazzi of Palladio and Sanmicheli, Giulio Romano's late work is not free of a touch of provincialism.

The 'Mantuan style' which Giulio did so much to create had less influence on Italian architecture than on that of the transalpine countries. Through Primaticcio, who worked for a short time on the Palazzo del Te, Giulio exercised a lasting influence on the Fontainebleau school, and in 1536 the Duke of Bavaria had his palace at Landshut built in the Mantuan style.[20] In Italy itself, Giulio's style was continued into the seventeenth century, but only by his Mantuan successors. Today the Estivale is the narrow side of an oblong courtyard; on the three sides which were built later, Giulio's pupil G. B. Bertani adopted the motif of the twisted columns with slight alterations.[21] The courtyard was just finished when Rubens arrived at Mantua, and in his predilection for rustication and twisted columns we may see a late throw-back to Giulio Romano.

support the crowning cornice, which is richly ornamented, but does not project. The simple and apparently logical system is interrupted only in the central bay, where the string course of the ground floor is pushed up by the voussoirs of the doorway, so that a horizontal band is suddenly transformed into the gable over the portal. Above the pediment, which gives a marked stress to the central bay on

CHAPTER 8

Jacopo Sansovino

It is one of the oddities of Italian art history that it was a Florentine architect who gave the main square of Venice its final form [122], and that this Florentine succeeded the last of the many Lombards who had worked as architects of the Venetian Republic in the Quattrocento and Cinquecento.

Jacopo Tatti, surnamed Il Sansovino (1486–1570), began as a sculptor in Andrea Sansovino's workshop in Florence. According to Vasari, he was in Rome from 1506 to 1511, where he lived in Giuliano da Sangallo's house, but returned to Florence in 1511 and stayed there until 1518. For the state entry of Leo X in 1515 Sansovino designed a wooden façade for the cathedral of Florence as a facing to the incomplete Gothic façade, and he worked on the triumphal arches erected on the same occasion.[1] The Pope, impressed by Sansovino's work, engaged him for the façade of S. Lorenzo, for which Giuliano da Sangallo and Raphael also were then preparing the designs. Later the commission passed to Michelangelo.[2] In 1518 Sansovino returned to Rome, and soon after won the competition for S. Giovanni dei Fiorentini over the heads of Peruzzi, Raphael, and Antonio da Sangallo the Younger. In 1520 he was paid for a model of the church, but the actual building, which Sangallo directed, never rose above its foundations.[3]*

Of all these projects we have only documentary evidence. According to Vasari, Sansovino's façade for Florence Cathedral had coupled Corinthian columns on tall pedestals; it was articulated like a triumphal arch, with statues in round-headed niches and reliefs. There are good reasons why this description should recall Giuliano da Sangallo's designs for the façade of S. Lorenzo (cf. p. 44), for the formal repertory in both cases is that of the Bramante circle. The precursor of the combination of coupled columns, statues in niches, and reliefs may have been the Santa Casa at Loreto [24], on which Sansovino's teacher Andrea had worked for a long time.

When Sansovino went to Venice in 1527 after the Sack of Rome, his acquaintance with Cardinal Grimani and Pietro Aretino was all to the good. In the first few years he was busy on strengthening the domes of St Mark's, which had, for many years past, been supported by provisional structures. In 1529, after the death of Bartolomeo Buon of Bergamo, Sansovino succeeded him as *Proto dei Procuratori di Supra*. The office was the most eminent the republic had to bestow on an architect, and the holder was responsible for the neverending work on St Mark's, and for the Procurators' Offices on the Piazza, the Procuratie Vecchie, begun by Bartolomeo and completed by Sansovino in 1538. At first his salary was eighty ducats, but in 1530 it was raised to a hundred and eighty and in 1540 to two hundred.[4]

The Procurators were also responsible for the Library of St Mark's, originally housed in the church, and later removed to the Doges' Palace. In 1537 the Procurators decided to house the library in a large new building, projected since 1536 and intended to face the Doges' Palace on the Piazzetta. Not much is known about the genesis of the plan, but Sansovino was certainly appointed architect-in-chief from the very beginning.

The reconstruction of the Piazzetta was as important for Venice as Michelangelo's slightly later replanning of the Capitol was for Rome. The Capitol and the Piazzetta had been places of execution in the Middle Ages; they now became the forum for acts of state. In both cases the project comprised not only the façades, but also their relationship to the width and depth of their site. In both cases the ground floor is designed as a loggia; it is hardly possible to know in either case whether the decision was based on local custom or on rules laid down by Vitruvius and Alberti. In Venice, the housing of banks and goldsmiths' workshops in the loggias of the new building is in keeping with the principles of these theorists.[5]

Sansovino's Library of St Mark's is not as high as the Doges' Palace facing it, but each of its two storeys is higher than the corresponding loggia of the Gothic building. The delicate Gothic tracery of the Doges' Palace faces the ponderous articulation of the library, where the massive cornices emphasize the horizontals just as much as the broad, flat wall over the loggias of the Doges' Palace. For all their differences, the two façades look equally weighty.

122. Venice, Piazza S. Marco, plans (A) before *c.* 1530, (B) *c.* 1600

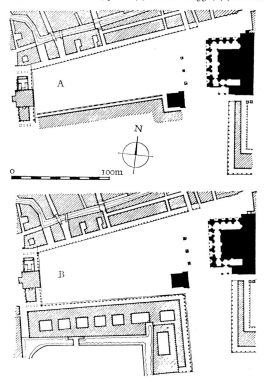

123. Jacopo Sansovino: Venice, Library of St Mark's, begun 1537, façade

The library was begun in the corner adjoining the campanile [123].[6] Three bays of the narrow side on the Piazza and the adjoining arcade of the main front on the Piazzetta seem to have been complete by 1540. In December 1545, the vault covering five bays of the upper storey collapsed, though it was strengthened by tie-rods. The Procurators suspected negligence in the supervision of the works, and Sansovino was removed from office and spent a short time in prison. He himself attributed the disaster to an unusually severe frost. In the end the Procurators granted him a loan of a thousand ducats to make good the damage, which was to be repaid at the rate of a hundred ducats a year. He also had to stand guarantee for any costs in excess of the estimate.[7] A year later, the damaged parts were reconstructed, but the masonry vaults of the upper storey were replaced by a timber roof with false vaulting underneath. In 1547 Sansovino was reinstated in his office as Proto. By 1554 the sixteen arches on the Piazzetta were completed and the interior decoration well advanced. In 1558 the books were moved in. The last five arches on the Molo were not built till 1588–91, under Vincenzo Scamozzi.

On the ground floor of the library a tunnel-vaulted loggia runs in front of botteghe. The shape and moulding of the piers, which are faced with Doric half-columns, recall the Doric order in the courtyard of the Farnese Palace before its alteration.[8] Sansovino certainly knew the Roman palazzo, which was begun in 1517. The combination of pilaster and engaged column in the corner piers of the library recalls

another building of the Sangallo group, which must have been familiar to Sansovino: the Madonna di S. Biagio at Montepulciano, begun in 1518. Thus it is not merely a coincidence that Sansovino's Doric order produces the same effect of splendour and monumentality as the Roman buildings of Raphael's time. Sansovino enhanced this effect by placing reclining figures in the spandrels of the arches, in the way of the Roman triumphal arches, and giving the entablature the unusual height of one third of that of the columns. In the general view of the Piazzetta, the ponderousness of the entablature is an essential feature in the effect of the library.

In the fenestrated walls of the upper storey, the openings had to be narrower and the wall surfaces wider than in the open loggia on the ground floor. Sansovino gave the round-headed windows small, free-standing columns as supports; the entablature of this smaller order is cut across by the engaged columns – also Ionic – of the main order. The smaller columns are fluted, the larger ones smooth. The bases of the latter rest on independent pedestals, those of the small order on the coping of the window balustrade.[9]

The crowning cornice with its balustrade is still more weighty and ornate than that of the ground floor. The putti and garlands of the frieze are a 'Roman' motif. Sansovino produced in it a variation of the terracotta frieze which was placed over the upper storey of the Farnesina in 1521, and the small windows of the mezzanine too are worked into the decorative scheme in the same ways as in the Farnesina.

From the central bay of the ground floor a tunnel-vaulted staircase leads up to the main storey, whose rooms occupy the whole width of the building. The main hall is in the corner facing the campanile. It corresponds to seven arches of the façade and may be regarded as one of the most outstanding and beautiful interiors of the Cinquecento [124]. In the long walls, round-arched windows alternate with lower, painted niches, above which the window imposts are continued as mouldings. In the same way as in the Ionic order of the façade, there is therefore a consonance between two similar systems of different height. The decoration of the sham vaulting is also remarkable; it is divided into squares by ornamental bands, each of which contains a painted tondo. The scheme proceeds from the sections of the walls, but it does not become architectural painting. On the other hand, in the vestibule leading into the main hall, painting is entirely subordinate to structure; stone pilasters support the ornate coffered ceiling, and even the windows are framed in stone aedicules. The vigorous relief of this wall structure provides the transition between the three-dimensional forms of the façade and the painted walls of the salone.*

The magnificent decoration was the work of a number of painters, including Titian, Tintoretto, and Paolo Veronese, and of the sculptors Alessandro Vittoria and Danese Cattaneo. The whole may well have been designed by Sansovino himself.

As pointed out already by Vasari and Palladio, Sansovino's library naturalized the new Roman style in Venice. Palladio called it 'the richest and most ornate building since antiquity',[10] and Jacob Burckhardt still regarded it as 'the most splendid work of secular architecture in modern Europe'.[11] For the first time in Venice, the classical orders were correctly applied, and the relationship of weight and support in columns, pillars, and entablatures was clearly articulated.

Until the sixteenth century the campanile of St Mark's indicated the junction of the Piazza and Piazzetta. On both sides the buildings abutted on to the tower. It is true that Sansovino adopted for the main façade of the new library the frontage of the older, humble buildings, which had been determined by the campanile, but he left a space between the corner of the new building and the campanile. The front of the library on the Piazza was not constructed on the foundations of the building which had preceded it but set back, so that the Piazza now became wider by about 24 m. (80 feet) at the campanile and 13 m. (43 feet) at the other corner of the square [122]. At the other end of the Piazzetta, Sansovino demolished the workshops and shops which flanked the two columns. Only then was the view opened on to the Canal Grande and S. Giorgio Maggiore.[12]

On the side of the campanile facing St Mark's was erected the loggia designed by Sansovino and begun in 1538, which served as the assembly room of the patricians during

124. Jacopo Sansovino: Venice, Library of St Mark's, begun 1537, salone

125. (*above*) Jacopo Sansovino: Venice, Zecca, begun 1536

126. (*right*) Jacopo Sansovino: Venice, Palazzo Corner della Cà Grande, begun *c.* 1545

the Councils of State.[13] The Loggetta, originally called the Ridotto dei Nobili, is a one-storey, three-bay hall; on the façade, round-arched openings alternate with free-standing coupled columns. The scheme – a variant of the triumphal arch motif – can be seen in Giuliano da Sangallo's designs for the façade of S. Lorenzo in Florence. Sansovino had obviously used it before in his wooden sham façade for the cathedral of Florence.

The Zecca, the mint and treasury of the Republic,[14] situated on the Molo, was built about the same time as the library and Loggetta. On the ground floor of the Zecca, the pillars and arcades consist of rusticated blocks of marble [125]. The Doric columns of the upper storey seem to be composed of alternating broad and narrow drums; they stand in niches and not in front of the wall. The scheme of the ground floor is another derivation from Bramante's Palazzo Caprini. But while Bramante doubled the columns in the piano nobile, Sansovino doubled the window lintels. The threefold horizontal of entablature and window lintels, and the absence of any ornament, invest the façade with a strange

and sombre monumentality which gives perfect expression to the function of the building.

The third storey was not added till about 1560, probably by Sansovino himself.* In this storey the engaged columns do not stand in niches. The 'bands' by which they are clamped to the walls stretch sideways to the window jambs, and the windows themselves are crowned with pediments. A comparison between the two storeys shows how greatly this apparently trivial alteration impairs the general look of the façade.[15]

Vasari regarded the façade of the Zecca as the first appearance of rustication in Venice; in this connection he lays stress on the *fortezza* of the building. *Fortezza* is also the epithet that Serlio repeatedly uses for rustication.[16] In the Zecca, the rustication, and the emotions it is expected to arouse in the spectator, are in perfect keeping with the function of the building. Similar expressive trends can be observed in Giulio Romano's buildings, which were erected not much earlier, though Giulio Romano's use of rustication is far more capricious than Sansovino's. It is very probable

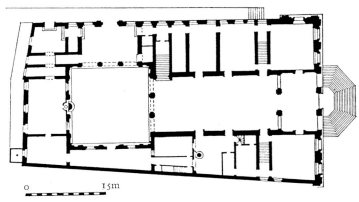

127. Jacopo Sansovino: Venice, Palazzo Corner della Cà Grande, begun
c. 1545, plan

that the Mantuan works were familiar to Sansovino – it is
certain that he knew Sanmicheli, who was in the service of
the republic – and rustication plays an important part
in Sansovino's work.

Sansovino's Palazzo Corner della Cà Grande [126, 127]
was built in the thirties of the century, about the same
time, therefore, as Sanmicheli's Palazzo Canossa at Verona
[100].[17]* It is tempting to regard the two palazzi as variations
on a single theme, just as Bach's sons composed variations on themes of their father. The basic theme is again
Bramante's Palazzo Caprini: the ground floor of both façades
is rusticated and the piano nobile articulated by a coupled
order. In contrast to Sanmicheli, who uses shallow relief
for coupled pilasters, cornices, and window surrounds,
Sansovino allows the articulation to project vigorously from
the wall. The pilasters are replaced by columns, the windows
of the ground floor are provided with aedicules, those of the
mezzanine floor are framed by capriciously large brackets;
in the upper storeys, the bases of the columns and the
balustrades are separated by recesses. Thus the bright,
projecting members stand out against the shadowed wall.

In both palazzi the three central bays of the ground floor
are opened to form an entrance hall. This motif first occurs

in Giulio Romano's Palazzo del Te and is probably derived
from it. In the Palazzo Corner the vaulting of the entrance
hall is independent of the bays of the façade. From the hall
a long passage leads into a courtyard which is unusually
spacious for Venice and, truly Venetian in situation and
function, stands on the rear, short side of the building. The
courtyard is striking not only for its size, but for the careful
and identical articulation of all four walls – probably a
reminiscence of Sansovino's early years in Rome. The
extensive use of rustication in the articulation of the courtyard
probably also goes back to the impression he received from
the Palazzo del Tè.

In the Palazzo Corner Sansovino created a type which was
to be a model for the palazzi of the great Venetian families
till the eighteenth century. We can judge how unusual the
size and sumptuousness of this palazzo was in the sixteenth
century from the mere fact that the family who occupied it
soon went by the surname of 'Corner della Cà Grande'.

To the end of his life Sansovino continued to employ the
classical repertory of form which he had made his own in
Rome. Certain characteristic elements of form are recurrent
in his late work: the coupled columns occur in the façade of
S. Geminiano on the Piazza, which was demolished under
Napoleon I, but often appears in *vedute* by Guardi and
Canaletto, and in the aisled hall of the Scuola Grande della
Misericordia,[18] which has in both storeys of the façade the
triumphal arch scheme of the Loggetta; and in the façade
and courtyard of the Villa Garzoni, near Ponte Casale,
Sansovino repeats the Doric order of the library.[19] Unlike
Michelangelo and his contemporary and friend Titian,
Sansovino did not develop a late style, and his last works are
less important and original than the library or the Palazzo
Corner. The forms that were innovations in the thirties, and
were certainly created to a large extent by Sansovino or
under the influence of his work, soon became public property
in Venice, and Sansovino's late works are at times difficult to
distinguish from those of his pupils and successors. Yet
Sanmicheli's Palazzo Grimani shows that this formal repertory offered possibilities for new and brilliant solutions of
traditional architectural problems.

CHAPTER 9

Michelangelo

When Michelangelo Buonarroti (1475–1564) received his first architectural commission in 1516, his fame had already spread beyond the frontiers of Italy. Four years before, he had completed the frescoes in the Sistine Chapel; for the past ten years he had been engaged on the tomb of Julius II, a work which was to occupy him in all for twenty years.

To the end of his life Michelangelo described himself as a sculptor, and always tried to put forward that pretext in order to refuse commissions for buildings or paintings. Wherever he accepted such commissions, the sculptor's manner of thinking and working becomes obvious. Yet it would be a mistake to regard Michelangelo's buildings as a sculptor's architecture and to take that as the sole explanation of their highly personal character. Bramante and Raphael were active as painters, Giuliano da Sangallo and Jacopo Sansovino as sculptors, Palladio as a stone carver, before they took up architecture. Thus Michelangelo's career is in no way exceptional. The universality of his work is in keeping with a tradition that can be traced at least as far back as Giotto and Giovanni Pisano, if not farther. Besides, Michelangelo himself painted the illusionist architecture in the Sistine Chapel and he designed the architectural framework projected for the sculpture in Julius II's tomb. When seen in this connection, his insistence on his training as a sculptor seems rather to be an early sign of modern specialization than a relic of earlier customs.[1]

FLORENCE

THE FAÇADE OF S. LORENZO

During the pontificates of the Medici popes Leo X (1513–21) and Clement VII (1523–34), Michelangelo was at work on three important projects connected with S. Lorenzo, the family church of the Medici in Florence. The interior had been finished about 1470. For the façade, which has remained in the rough, Brunelleschi had planned a marble facing after the model of S. Miniato or S. Maria Novella. After the state re-entry of the Medici into Florence in 1515, Leo X decided to complete the façade, so that it should stand as a monumental witness to the renewed glory of his house. Vasari writes that the Pope ordered Raphael, Baccio d'Agnolo, and Andrea Sansovino to submit designs. They have vanished; on the other hand, several designs for the marble facing of the façade by Giuliano da Sangallo, whom Vasari does not mention in this connection (cf. above, p. 44), have been preserved. Giuliano died in October 1516. In December 1516 Michelangelo, who had probably taken part in the discussions during Giuliano's lifetime, received a commission from the Pope for a wooden model of the façade. In January 1518 the agreement for it was concluded in Rome.[2] Some of the vicissitudes of the model, the product of a year of labour, can be traced in Michelangelo's drawings.

Even before the agreement was signed, new quarries were opened in the Carrara Hills for the supply of marble. Michelangelo spent more than two years in building a road to the quarries, organizing the work in them and supervising transport to Florence.

In his first designs he adopted Sangallo's scheme: the contour of the façade corresponds to the basilican cross-section of the church, the two-storey nave rises above the single-storey aisles. The classical vocabulary of form characteristic of Roman buildings of the second decade of the sixteenth century also recalls Giuliano's – paired free-standing columns, round-headed niches, aedicules, the central pediment – and the sumptuous decoration with reliefs and the life-size statuary to which, as we know from the sources, the Pope attached great value.

The model described in the contract of 1518 is probably identical with the one preserved in the Casa Buonarroti [128]. It differs in two respects from the first designs. Instead of the flat marble facing planned at first, a two-storey vestibule was to cover the whole width of the church façade; from outside it would have looked like a second transept. It was also to have been far richer in statuary than was originally planned. The contract mentions eighteen life-size statues – twelve in marble and six in bronze – and nineteen reliefs, thirteen of them with life-size figures. The whole of this huge programme was to be completed in eight years.

The closest analogy to this wealth of sculpture is to be found in the Gothic cathedrals of Tuscany. But while Giovanni Pisano had at hand a large workshop of many – in the medieval sense – 'anonymous' workers, the statuary and reliefs of the S. Lorenzo façade, as the contract implies, were all to be the work of Michelangelo. Considering the

128. Michelangelo: Model for the façade of S. Lorenzo, Florence, 1517. Florence, Casa Buonarroti

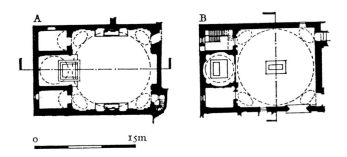

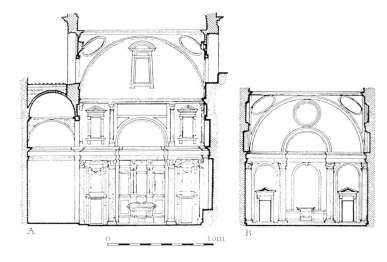

129. (A) Michelangelo: Florence, S. Lorenzo, New Sacristy, begun 1519, plan; (B) Filippo Brunelleschi: Florence, S. Lorenzo, Old Sacristy, after 1421, plan

130. (A) Michelangelo: Florence, S. Lorenzo, New Sacristy, begun 1519, elevation; (B) Filippo Brunelleschi: Florence, S. Lorenzo, Old Sacristy, after 1421, elevation

new conception of the style and personality of the artist and the demands which Michelangelo made on the quality of his own work, the practicability of the scheme must have seemed doubtful from the start. True, Michelangelo regarded the scheme as no more visionary than his first studies for the tomb of Julius II. The design of the façade had a great deal in common with them; in both cases the architectural members between the huge statues and reliefs would merely have acted as their frame and foil. Only once had Michelangelo been able to represent in its entirety this conception of the relationship between the human body and the architectural framework, and that was in the Sistine frescoes. That he was prevented from translating them into the reality of stone and bronze was not entirely due to the changing moods of his patron or to financial and political difficulties.

The actual problems involved in the design can no longer be recognized in the Casa Buonarroti model. In 1518, when the contract was signed between the Pope and the artist, there were wax models of the statues and reliefs in the niches. They have vanished, and in the 'empty' façade the classical rhetoric of the columns and round panels looks like an academic study in style. It is therefore no matter for surprise if historians were very long reluctant to identify this model with Michelangelo's design.

THE NEW SACRISTY OF S. LORENZO

In spite of all the laborious and costly work, the design of the façade was abandoned in 1520 on grounds which have not yet been clarified. To make up for this, the Pope granted Michelangelo a commission for the tombs of the princely members of the house of Medici in S. Lorenzo. Brunelleschi's Old Sacristy was the family mausoleum of the older generations of the family; it therefore seemed reasonable to turn the New Sacristy on the opposite wing of the transept, which had been planned long before, into a mausoleum too.[3]

Though identical in plan, there is a great difference between the elevations of the two chapels [129, 130]. In the New Sacristy [131], an attic storey has been added between the pilaster order and the pendentive zone. The dome

is hemispherical, and not, like Brunelleschi's, a shallow umbrella vault. It is the first Renaissance dome to reproduce the coffer motif of the Pantheon. The great height of the space makes it look sparer and narrower, the more so as the order of pilasters, which was restricted to the wall of the choir in the Old Sacristy, is carried round all four walls in the New. Finally, Michelangelo filled the bays between the grey pietra serena pilasters with powerfully profiled architectural ornament, which, with its paired pilasters, niches, pediments, and volutes, contrasts with the main order both in style and scale.

Even Vasari felt that Michelangelo's complicated scheme was at odds with the tradition of the Quattrocento and the rules of classical architecture. This can be illustrated by a comparison between Brunelleschi's and Michelangelo's doorways. The doors of the Old Sacristy are framed in columns and pediments; the columns stand on the same level as the observer, and their height is calculated in such a way that it is possible for him to feel a relationship between it and his own, or even to imagine himself framed in the aedicules. The round-arched terracotta reliefs over the doors differ from the aedicules in material, colour, outline, and depth – they are typical wall-ornament. On the other hand, the door frames of the New Sacristy [132] are meagre and almost abstract, their marble frames supporting tall, oblong tabernacles, also of marble, framed in pilasters and crowned by segmental pediments. Thus the low door becomes a subsidiary member dominated by the taller tabernacle above it. The tabernacles and their frames are so heavy that the lintels on which they rest have to be supported by brackets, thus forfeiting their true function and becoming the bases of the tabernacles.

By suppressing the aedicules of the doors, Michelangelo has made it impossible for the observer to discover a measurable relationship between architecture and the human body. The architecture bears its own scale within itself, namely in the over-life-size figures on the sarcophagi, which tower over the observer in exactly the same way as the weighty tabernacles under which he enters the sacristy. It is a feature of this architecture that it dwarfs the beholder.

Raphael's Chigi Chapel in S. Maria del Popolo, Rome [32–4], was still under construction when Michelangelo

131. Michelangelo: Florence, S. Lorenzo, New Sacristy, begun 1519

132. Michelangelo: Florence, S. Lorenzo, New Sacristy, begun 1519, detail

began work on the New Sacristy. The visitor enters the Chigi Chapel under one of the four arches which support the dome, so that the relationship between architecture and the human body is made clear and comprehensible. The image of God the Father in the summit of the dome in the Chigi Chapel is also related to the spectator in gesture and scale. But the architecture of the New Sacristy is as remote from the observer as the statues, which inhabit a different sphere from him as he stands looking up at them. No image in human likeness looks down on him from the dome; the ribs between the coffers guide the eye irresistibly into the lantern, whose windows are so large that the light devours the solid forms. Thus the lantern looks immeasurably high.

The Medici Chapel is the only architectural interior to have been designed by Michelangelo himself and executed under his personal supervision. When he moved to Rome in 1534, the decoration and statuary were not yet finished. The seated and reclining figures on the tombs were not put in place till 1545, and in 1559 the idea of completing the decoration of the chapel in accordance with Michelangelo's ideas was finally abandoned. The double tomb planned for the entrance wall and its marble architecture were not executed.

THE LAURENTIAN LIBRARY

Immediately after his elevation in 1523, the second Medici Pope, Clement VII, commissioned Michelangelo to prepare designs for a library to be installed in the west cloister wing of S. Lorenzo. The Biblioteca Laurenziana [133], as it stands today, contains the manuscripts and books belonging to the famous private library of the Medici, founded in the fifteenth century, which Clement removed from the family palazzo to the cloisters and opened to the public.

Work began in 1525. When Michelangelo left Florence in 1534 it was not yet finished. It was continued by Tribolo, Vasari, and Ammannati on verbal instructions from Michelangelo, and had progressed so far by 1571 that the library could be opened. Thus the present building combines parts executed by Michelangelo himself with others built much later in a more or less correct interpretation of his instructions.

According to the Pope's instructions, the two-storey Quattrocento cloister was to remain unaltered by the addition of the library. That explains certain features of Michelangelo's project. The reading room was to constitute a new third floor added upon the older parts of the cloisters, since there was no other way to provide it with adequate lighting;

133. Michelangelo: Florence, S. Lorenzo, Library, begun 1525, section and plan

its walls were to stand on those of the pre-existing upper storey.[4] Thus the length and width of the hall were fixed in advance. In the upper storey, between the cloister and the Old Sacristy, a vestibule, called the *ricetto*, was separated off to house the staircase leading to the reading room. The position of this anteroom, which is contiguous with the high wall of the transept, involved difficulties of lighting. In Michelangelo's first project, the reading room and the ricetto were equal in height; the windows of the ricetto were to be placed either in the vaulting or in skylights. But the ricetto as we see it today is lighted by windows in the clerestory.

The reading room [134] is 46.20 m. long, 10.50 wide, and 8.40 high (152 by 35 by 28 feet). The furnishings and decoration are original. There are two blocks of seats separated by a central passage; their backs serve as reading desks for the benches behind them. The books lie chained on the desks. The desks are lighted from both sides by the comparatively close-set windows in the long sides. The windows are framed in pilasters, and the system of bays they form governs the articulation of the ceiling and the floor. The pilasters bear the cornice, which is carried without projections round the room and supports the cross-beams of the heavy wooden ceiling.

These pilasters, which articulate the walls and correspond to the beams, are a heritage of the Quattrocento. But no Quattrocento interior has any such treatment of the wall-bays between the pilasters to show. It consists of a triple recession of layers, the farthest back containing the window frames, a middle one with the quadrangular blind frame of the upper storey and the tall oblong panels in which the windows are set, and a front one with the pilasters and their running base. The mouldings of the frames are of pietra

serena, the wall surfaces of white stucco. This back and forward movement imparts to the wall a quite unprecedented depth of relief. The difference of function between supporting members and walls between them becomes perfectly clear in the juxtaposition of three- and two-dimensional forms. At the same time Michelangelo solved a structural problem. In view of the older walls of the storey beneath, he had to reduce the weight of the reading-room walls as much as he possibly could. By the system of the frames and layers in the articulation of the walls, the volume and weight of the intervening bays between the pilasters was reduced to a minimum. Thus the pilasters act as the fronts of the pier-

134. Michelangelo: Florence, S. Lorenzo, Library, begun 1525

like sections of the wall between the windows, which actually support the ceiling and take on a genuine structural function.

When Michelangelo left Florence in 1534, only the walls of the reading room were standing; the floors, the seats, and the ceiling were not added till *c.* 1550. But the designs for them were so precise that both the structure and the ornament of the reading room may be regarded as Michelangelo's own work. The ricetto, on the other hand, remained a torso till the twentieth century. The top range we see today was completed in 1904, and it was only then that the three windows looking on to the cloisters were finished, while in the interior, the articulation, which on this range till that time had only been completed on the south wall, was carried round the other three walls. The staircase was built in 1559 by Ammannati; Michelangelo had sent him a clay model of it in 1558.

THE RICETTO

The first designs, made in 1524, show two flights of stairs placed against the side walls of the ricetto and forming a bridge in front of the reading-room door. In 1525 Michelangelo decided to remove the stairway to the middle of the vestibule; it was to start in three flights and unite in a single flight in its upper part. An attempt was made by Tribolo about 1550 to carry out this plan, using the steps lying in the ricetto, which had been made according to Michelangelo's instructions. It came to nothing. Although Ammannati used some of the steps in his construction, the staircase of today cannot be identified with the scheme of 1533–4, since the older steps had to be fitted with pieces of different stone. Besides, in answer to Vasari's inquiry in 1555 about the design for the staircase, Michelangelo replied that he had forgotten all about it. Thus the clay model sent to Ammannati in 1558, after which the staircase was built, is a new design made by Michelangelo between 1555 and 1558.

Ammannati certainly endeavoured to translate Michelangelo's ideas into reality as far as he possibly could.

135. Michelangelo: Florence, S. Lorenzo, Library, begun 1525, ricetto staircase

But the scanty material he had at hand, the comparatively small clay model and Michelangelo's instructions, could give no more than a general idea of the form; the details were left to his judgement.

The staircase takes up half of the floor of the ricetto, which measures 9.50 by 10.30 m. (31 by 34 feet). The lower section of nine steps is in three parallel flights [135]. The treads of the central flight are convex, while those of the side flights, separated off by balustrades, are straight. The three lowest steps of the central flight are wider and higher than those above them; they lie like concentric oval slabs on the floor of the ricetto, the lowest step surging outwards. At the ninth step the three flights unite in a landing for the top section of the staircase. The convex tenth step lies on the landing in the same way as the lowest step does on the floor of the ricetto.

The room in which the staircase is housed, almost perfectly square in plan, is just as unusual as the staircase itself. Its extraordinary height (about 14.6 m. or 44 feet) is a result of the alteration in the plan mentioned above, after Michelangelo's proposal to use skylights for the lighting of the ricetto was rejected. For the middle storey of the three, Michelangelo had projected paired columns from the start. The columns stand in narrow recesses in the wall; in the bays between the paired columns there are deep oblong niches with projecting pediments, while the panels above are ornamented with flat, blind frames [136]. The strangeness of this articulation consists in the fact that the wall is not treated as a plane. The sections of the wall that frame the paired columns project so far that they appear as three-dimensional blocks. On the narrow sides of the recesses there are pilasters corresponding to the columns.

Each of the four walls is crowded with six free-standing columns and three massive wall-bays. The space seems to be bounded by three-dimensional elements, and not by a continuous wall. The shell of wall behind these members is so thin that it can just be made out on the plan; in actual fact the timber roof intended for the ceiling was not to have rested on the outer walls, but on the paired columns. In the third storey, which was added after the revision of the scheme, the system of the main storey is reduced to two dimensions; paired pilasters stand over the columns, and square frames over the recesses. While the play of forces in the main storey stands out clearly, it can only be read off in the third storey in its projection on the wall-plane.

The richly modelled main storey stands on the much plainer walls of the lowest, which contains the staircase and the entrance door. The low doorway is flanked by huge volutes which stand out from the wall under the columns and belong to the middle rather than to the lowest storey. In the same way as in the New Sacristy, the rising walls seem inconceivably high to the visitor standing in the lowest storey; he cannot conceive a rational relationship between them and his own height. The bases of the paired columns stand above the level of the staircase, and their capitals far above the lintel of the reading-room door. Thus still greater prominence is given to the columns of the middle storey, whose unbroken verticals control the whole effect of the room, while the horizontal cornices, with their many projections, hardly affect the general impression at all.

136. Michelangelo: Florence, S. Lorenzo, Library, begun 1525, ricetto

The verticals of the walls are in contrast with the horizontal strata of the steps. But even in the staircase the beholder seems to be faced by superhuman forces. The width of the steps increases from the top downwards, so that to anyone descending the staircase it seems to be flowing out into the room, while to anyone mounting it, the lowest steps seem to be flowing towards him. The dramatically agitated, rounded and weighty forms which characterize the staircase bear the imprint of Michelangelo's latest style, while the articulation of the walls goes back to an earlier phase. The walls were approaching completion when Michelangelo left Florence in 1534.

The contrast between the high anteroom and the long reading room was not intended at the start. In the first designs there is an order of paired columns on the walls of the reading room too. It was only after the change of plan which involved the heightening of the ricetto that Michelangelo decided on the quieter system of pilasters and the cornice without projections for the reading room. The motif of the paired columns was confined to the ricetto, and so gave it a far greater expressive force.

Even contemporaries realized that the composition and details of the Laurenziana were a revolutionary breach with tradition. That is true not only of its formal vocabulary. If the spatial organization of the ricetto seems oppressive, steep, and overpowering, if the columns look as if they were wedged into the wall, it is because the architecture is meant to awaken definite emotions in the observer. In his sonnets, Michelangelo has expressed his vision of the figure imprisoned in the block, which the sculptor liberates. Similar ideas find visual expression in the relationship between wall and column in the structure of the Laurenziana. The dramatic force of the stairway, which has been described so often, is one of these innovations. Bramante's open-air stairway in front of the Belvedere exedra in the Vatican led to no destination outside its own concentric steps [10, 11]. In the ricetto stairway the lower treads swell outwards while the upper ones seem to draw the observer irresistibly upwards into the reading room by the force of their own diminuendo. Another characteristic feature is the transformation of the traditional aedicule motif in the middle storey of the ricetto; the framing pilasters broaden upwards, so that the wider upper part of the frame looks heavier than the narrower lower part. The divergence between this slant of the frames and the vertical edges of the wall again awakens a feeling of a huge weight cramped in space.

We have already seen a similar emotional appeal in the architectural forms of Giulio Romano's Palazzo del Te, which was built at the same time. Giulio Romano leaves the observer uncertain whether the building is still under construction or already in decay. His bizarre ideas are meant to nonplus the observer in the same way as 'black humour' does. But for Michelangelo the forces working in the stones are a parable of the tragedy of human life.

Like Giulio Romano, Michelangelo adopts the formal vocabulary of Bramante and Raphael, but the new meaning he gives it can only be understood when it is compared with its prototype, the classical model. Thus the motif of paired columns had already made its appearance in the Palazzo Caprini; but unlike Bramante's beautiful balance between horizontals and verticals and between two storeys which, for all their differences of form, are equally weighty, the horizontal members in the ricetto are formally so weak that the paired columns of the main storey dominate the whole room.

In classical architecture, the column is the image of the harmonious balance of forces created by the architect. There are reasons why it often appears in illustrations to treatises in anthropomorphic form. Like man, it can be represented as a free-standing organism independent of its surroundings. The columns of the ricetto can hardly be comprehended as independent individuals if only because they are paired. Although they stand free of the wall, they give such a strong impression of a vertical scaffolding that they could be compared with Gothic piers. Finally, by their height and position in the wall, they achieve a dramatic expressiveness which is quite unclassic.

ROME

The Medici Pope Clement VII died not long after Michelangelo settled in Rome. His successor, Pope Paul III Farnese, entrusted to Michelangelo during his pontificate the most important building schemes Rome had to offer.

In December 1537 Michelangelo was awarded Roman citizenship on the Capitol. A month later work was begun on the rearrangement and reconstruction of the Capitoline buildings after the transferral there of the equestrian statue of Marcus Aurelius from the Lateran by papal order. Michelangelo was to continue work on the Capitol till his death. Although it was not completed till the seventeenth century, the piazza with its three palazzi must be regarded as the most important town-planning scheme in Rome during the sixteenth century, and Michelangelo's most important work in the field of secular architecture.

In 1546, after the death of Michelangelo's younger contemporary Antonio da Sangallo, who had kept his position as domestic architect to the Farnese after the elevation of Paul III, Michelangelo took over the superintendence of the Palazzo Farnese and the office of architect-in-chief of St Peter's. Work on St Peter's had been in progress since 1506, and on the Palazzo Farnese since about 1516. Michelangelo altered both buildings, and he largely defined their present shape. The dome of St Peter's, which was executed for the most part after his design, stands as a magnificent witness to the renewed strength of the Catholic Church after the troubles of the Reformation. It dominates the view of Rome and was the model for countless other domes *urbis et orbis*.

THE CAPITOL

Since medieval times, the seat of the city government of Rome had been in the Piazza del Campidoglio, the square which had been formed after the decay of the ancient temples in the shallow depression between the two knolls of the Mons Capitolinus.[5] The east side of the piazza was occupied by the castellated Palazzo del Senatore, the nominal head of the city administration. On the north side was the long flank of the Gothic church of the Franciscans, S. Maria in Aracoeli. Facing it was the fifteenth-century Palazzo dei Conservatori, with the offices of the guilds in the ground floor. A steep path led down into the city from the open west side.

Michelangelo altered the façades of the Senatore and Conservatori palazzi, but left the palazzi themselves in their original place. Further, by 'duplicating' the Palazzo dei

Conservatori on the north side, he reduced the size of the piazza and eliminated the church from the general view.

The development of the plans for the rebuilding of the Capitol has never been satisfactorily elucidated. In the sources, Michelangelo's name does not appear till 1539, when the statue of Marcus Aurelius was put in place and a retaining wall built below S. Maria in Aracoeli. In 1544 a three-bay loggia and a flight of steps were added to the transept of the church; in that way the church, which was also used for the official religious services of the city authorities, was provided with a new approach from the piazza. Soon afterwards, the double stairway in front of the Palazzo del Senatore was begun; in 1550–3 a three-bay loggia and stairway were added beside the Palazzo dei Conservatori [137]. This system of three great stairways is obviously executed after a uniform scheme which may have existed when Michelangelo set the equestrian statue in its place. It is likely, though not proved, that this plan already provided for the alterations to the two palazzi.

The last stage of building, which gave the piazza the form we see today, was begun in 1561, three years, that is, before Michelangelo's death, when Pope Pius IV had earmarked considerable funds for the purpose and ordered a thorough-going restoration of the Palazzo del Senatore. The base and placement of the Marcus Aurelius statue were again changed, the balustrade along the west side of the piazza was built, and the new façade of the Palazzo dei Conservatori begun in 1563. A patrician friend of Michelangelo's, Tommaso dei Cavalieri, was put in charge of the work on the Palazzo del Senatore, and the working drawings for the Palazzo dei Conservatori were made by the architect Guidetto Guidetti 'in accordance with Michelangelo's instructions'. The works commissioned by Pius IV were certainly based on a comprehensive plan by Michelangelo. It is probably this scheme which has come down to us in Étienne Dupérac's engravings [138], which were published after Michelangelo's death. They show the Capitol 'quod S P Q R impensa ad Michaelis Angeli Buonaroti eximii architecti exemplar in antiquum decus restitui posse videtur'. The engravings, of course, can hardly be taken as an exact reproduction of a drawing by Michelangelo's own hand; so far as we know, he

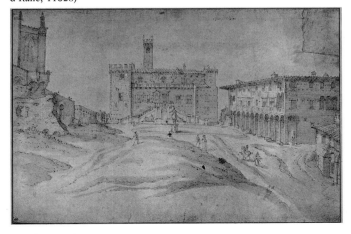

137. Rome, Piazza del Campidoglio, drawing, *c.* 1555. Paris, Louvre (École d'Italie, 11028)

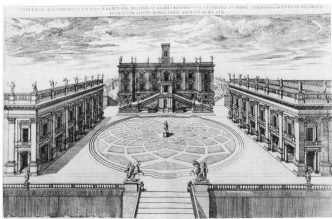

138. Michelangelo: Project for the Piazza del Campidoglio, Rome, engraving by Étienne Dupérac, 1569

139. Michelangelo: Rome, Piazza del Campidoglio, Palazzo dei Conservatori, begun 1563

never embodied his ideas in a definitive design for any of his buildings. Dupérac certainly tried to combine the recognizable parts of the as yet unfinished buildings with what he knew or conjectured about Michelangelo's intentions. He obviously rendered correctly the outstanding features of the project.

The simplest explanation of the discrepancies between the engravings and the actual buildings [139] is that Michelangelo's successors had to fill in the gaps according to their own judgement. Dupérac's engraving was probably the authority for the parts built later.

The façade of the Palazzo dei Conservatori was completed in 1584, that of the Palazzo del Senatore about 1600. The executant architect was Giacomo della Porta. The old tower of the Palazzo del Senatore was damaged by lightning in 1577 and re-erected in its present place by Martino Lunghi in 1583, in the same place as in Michelangelo's plan but not to his design. In the same years Porta completed his work on the *cordonata*, the ramp leading up to the piazza, with its balustrade. The building called the Palazzo Nuovo, the 'duplicate' of the Palazzo dei Conservatori, was not built till the seventeenth century, between 1603 and 1654.

It is in the palazzi on the Campidoglio that the so-called giant order made its first appearance in Roman Renaissance secular building. The eight great pilasters of the two-storey Palazzo dei Conservatori rise to bear the main cornice irrespective of the horizontal division behind them. The columns and cornices of the ground-floor loggias form a subsidiary system to the primary one. Michelangelo's giant order provides a solution both simple and radical to a problem which had preoccupied architects since the time of Alberti, namely how to combine the antique system of columns or pilasters and cornices with the division of storeys in a modern palazzo, with its windows and string courses, in such a way that the vertical members rising from the ground would be able to support the cornice, as they do in classical architecture.

As the plan shows [140], the pilasters are the fronts of piers whose intervals correspond to the sequence of the ground-floor rooms. The partition walls between the rooms combine with the piers to form a uniform system of load-bearing walls which recalls the framework of modern concrete buildings. The construction was so stable that it enabled Michelangelo to provide the ground-floor loggia with a flat stone ceiling and to dispense with arches and vaulting. The ceiling over each bay is supported by four columns, two on the façade, and two in the rear wall of the loggia. These columns with the partition walls of the adjoining rooms form the 'skeleton' of the ground floor. Yet each bay of the loggia is a practically independent structural unit inserted into the giant order. The functions of the greater and lesser orders can be read off on the façade itself. The pilasters and crowning cornice lie in the foremost plane of the wall, the strips of piers appearing left and right beside the giant pilasters in an intermediate one, while the string course of the ground floor and the wall of the piano nobile are in the rear. There are no projections in the main cornice over the pilasters; on the other hand the cornice of the lesser order clasps the pier-strips at the side of the pilasters. At this point the pier absorbs the architrave of the ground floor.

In the same way as in the reading room of the Laurenziana, the material employed for the supporting members differs from that of the non-bearing walls. For pilasters, columns, cornices, and pier-strips travertine is employed, for the rest fine brickwork, so that instead of the harsh contrast of dark grey members and white surfaces so characteristic of Florence, there is the softer Roman contrast of light grey and brick red.

In the three-storey Palazzo del Senatore, Michelangelo treated the ground floor as the rusticated base for the giant order.[6] The pilasters of the latter form a kind of screen to the older building, which is largely preserved behind the façade; they have no structural function.

The double-ramped stairway leading up to the piano nobile rises in front of the ground floor, so that it does not cut across the great pilasters. The stairway and the high placement of the giant order are an expression of the status of the Palazzo del Senatore. It towers above the façades of the side buildings, which 'stand on the ground'. The visitor who approaches the Capitol from the cordonata faces the equestrian statue and sees behind it the high portal of the Palazzo del Senatore.[7]

On plan, the fronts of the Palazzo dei Conservatori and its duplicate, the Palazzo Nuovo, are at acute angles with that of the Senatore and at obtuse angles with the cordonata balustrade. Thus the piazza is trapezoid in plan, a result of the preservation of the frontages of the two old buildings. But the strict symmetry of the twin palazzi, which is, together

140. Rome, Capitoline Hill, angled view and plan

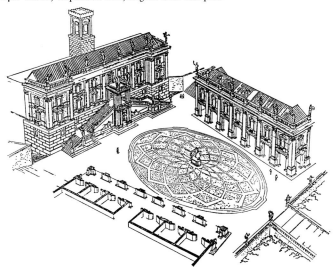

with the giant order, the real innovation in the scheme, makes the observer first perceive the piazza as a rectangle. As Dupérac's engravings show, Michelangelo's plan for the palazzi had provided for three concentric rings of oval steps leading down to the middle of the piazza; the pavement surrounded by the oval was to have had a stellate pattern radiating from the base of Marcus Aurelius's statue. Owing to the combination of the oval and trapezium, the spandrels in the corners of the latter give the illusion of being of equal size, which means that the trapezium is seen as a rectangle. Further, since the longitudinal axis of the oval is at right angles to the Palazzo del Senatore and the balustrade of the cordonata, the observer simply assumes that the transverse axis too meets the fronts of the side palazzi at right angles; hence the latter look parallel. Thus the oval ornament of the pavement makes the observer overlook the 'irregular' trapezoidal form and see the piazza as a regular figure, i.e. as a rectangle.[8]

The ornament of the pavement has another and immediately visible function. The great oval, which contains the oval base of the statue, and the lines of the ornament radiating from and sweeping back to it, make the statue look far bigger than it is. This illusory magnification is a characteristic of Michelangelo the sculptor. By 'monumentalizing' the scale of the statue, i.e. by adapting it to the scale of the surrounding buildings, the statue of the Roman emperor becomes the real theme of the architectural composition. Moreover, the numerous other statues associated with the project, such as the river-gods of the stairway of the Palazzo del Senatore or the figures on the balustrade, become integral parts of the scheme.

In the history of town planning, Michelangelo's reconstruction of the Capitol occupies a place of its own. Its situation on the historic hill in the centre of ancient Rome was unique; it could find a parallel nowhere else. The piazza has no definite antecedents[9] and has found no successors. The Piazzetta in Venice and the Campidoglio are among the most beautiful and the most splendid examples of the characteristically Italian municipal square spreading in front of the town hall. Each of these piazze is bounded by relatively uniform façades; it is, in fact, a kind of 'piazza-salone'. The ancient statue of the Emperor became the model for all the equestrian figures which were erected as symbols of absolutist power in the open squares of European capital cities from the late sixteenth century to the nineteenth.

THE PALAZZO FARNESE

Michelangelo's share in the Palazzo Farnese has been discussed in an earlier chapter. When he took charge of the building in 1546, the rear wing of the court was just begun; in the façade wing of the piano nobile a few rooms to the right of the central axis were ready for occupation. Michelangelo left unaltered Sangallo's Ionic order of the loggia on the court side, but the entablature was heightened and decorated by a frieze with garlands, masks, and fleurs-de-lis. The heightening of the entablature made it possible to raise also the vault of the loggia, which thus springs from an unusually high level [141]. The result is the spacious, hall-like corridor in front of the state rooms of the palazzo, is true of a project for the rear wing of the court which is reproduced in an engraving dated 1560 and ascribed to Michelangelo himself [142]. This project was to open the piano nobile in the rear wing as a loggia. According to Vasari, Michelangelo had planned a bridge to unite the gardens behind the palazzo with the Farnesina gardens on the other side of the Tiber, which were rented by the Farnese at the time. Just as the piazza in front of the palazzo was to play its part in the architectural composition, the open space behind it was to enter into the architectural whole. The purpose of the three-bay loggia was on the one hand to reveal to the spectator standing on the piano nobile in the façade range a view over the river and gardens, and on the other to make the court visible from the gardens. It is characteristic of Michelangelo that only the piano nobile was to be provided with open arcades and that the top floor, which is articulated by pilasters and windows, was not. If the observer standing in the court has the feeling that he is in a room entirely enclosed by walls, that is due to a great extent to the shape of the floor of the court.[11]

ST PETER'S

When Michelangelo succeeded Sangallo as architect-in-chief of St Peter's in 1546, he embarked on a task which, to many of his contemporaries, seemed beyond human powers.[12] The administration of the Fabbrica of St Peter's took it for granted that the building would be continued at enormous expense in accordance with the model made by Sangallo in 1539–43 [16C]. It must have been a shock to them when Michelangelo, immediately upon taking up office, had two models made which presented a totally different design. It was only by the support of the Pope that he was able to get his scheme accepted. For that matter, even the successors of Paul III always took Michelangelo's part in his clashes with the officials of the Fabbrica. Since he refused in advance any payment for his work, his position was invested with a very

141. Michelangelo: Rome, Palazzo Farnese, vault of loggia in the piano nobile, after 1546

which find their climax in the great salone. The present size of the salone was probably already defined by Sangallo, but its pavement and ceiling were only completed around 1550. The room has five windows on the main and three on the side façades, and its height corresponds to two storeys of the façade; thus the windows of the third storey are the openings of the clerestory of the salone.[10]

Michelangelo also designed the crowning cornice of the façade and the top storey of the court [81, 82]. His work on the Palazzo Farnese has been recorded in contemporary engravings. A view of the recently completed façade with the piazza in front of it was published by Lafreri in 1549 [83]. The engraving shows, in the pavement of the piazza, a large chequered pattern, with the width of its square fields corresponding to the bays of the façade. We know that houses standing on the site of the present piazza were acquired by the Farnese before 1549. Thus the layout and size of the piazza are closely related to the building itself. The geometrical pattern in the engraving would have given the piazza a clear and definite scale governed by the architecture; it is as much a part of the architectural composition as the oval ornament in the pavement of the Campidoglio. Thus the engraving may illustrate an unexecuted design for the pavement of the Piazza Farnese by Michelangelo. The same

142. Michelangelo: Project for the rear wing of the Palazzo Farnese, Rome, engraving by Antonio Lafreri, 1560

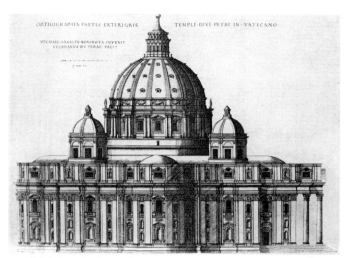

143. Michelangelo: Rome, St Peter's, from the north, engraving by Étienne Dupérac, 1569

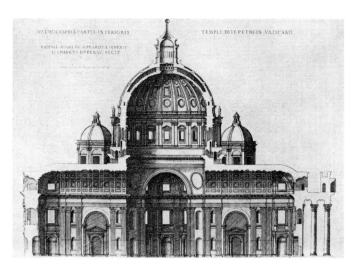

144. Michelangelo: Rome, St Peter's, longitudinal section, engraving by Étienne Dupérac, 1569

high moral prestige. Eventually he received 50 ducats a month, but the payment was made by the papal treasury rather than the Fabbrica. Thus he was free from pressure by petty officials.

Michelangelo solved the structural problems which had proved insoluble to his predecessors. He promoted building operations with such unswerving resolution that at his death the completion of the building could be regarded as certain. When he died in 1564, the south arm of the cross was finished, in the north arm only a part of the vaulting was incomplete, and there was little work left to do on the drum of the dome. The north and south arms built by Michelangelo form the transept of the present church.[13] The west arm of the cross, the present chancel, was built in the late sixteenth century after the demolition of the Rossellino-Bramante choir; in accordance with Michelangelo's project, it is identical in plan and elevation with the other two arms.[14]

Sources for the evolution of Michelangelo's project and the progress of work during his term of office are his own sketches, documents, accounts, and many views of the unfinished building, as well as three engravings by Dupérac which appeared soon after Michelangelo's death and re-produce the plan, section, and elevation of St Peter's [143, 144]. The interpretation of these sources is still to a certain extent controversial. As in the case of the Capitol, Michelangelo left no definitive and binding model. Dupérac's engravings show the north and south arms of the cross as executed by Michelangelo; the attic is shown after its alteration under Michelangelo's immediate successors. There is no doubt that Dupérac's reproduction of the west arm corresponds to Michelangelo's intentions. Contradictions in the drawing of the eastern façade, on the other hand, make it probable that no definite plans for this part had been made when Michelangelo died.[15]

The first thing to strike one in comparing Michelangelo's plan with the plans of his predecessors is the strengthening throughout of the outer walls [16D, 74]. This is a result of the radical simplification of the structural system. The four great piers of the dome are not surrounded, as they were, by

a host of rather confusing subsidiary chapels, but by the square of the outer walls, from which only the apses of the arms of the cross project. The ambulatories of the arms of the cross as well as the campanili have been eliminated, the arms shortened, and the eight 'counter-piers' which receive the sideways thrust of the dome merged with the outer walls [145].

When Michelangelo declared that he had restored Bramante's plan,[16] that can only be taken literally in so far as the dome, like that of Bramante, was to rise above the intersection of a Greek cross with tunnel-vaulted arms terminating in apses. What Michelangelo did not adopt was Bramante's system of minor domes, which, in their structural function and spatial multiplicity, definitely recall antique thermae. The balanced grouping of minor domes and campanili, of higher and lower chapels, was incompatible with his goal of simplicity in structure and unity in the whole. The outer walls were now raised to the same height all round and were articulated by the same paired giant Corinthian pilasters which Bramante had designed for the piers of the dome in the interior [146]. The attic over the main cornice was also carried round the whole building, and it conceals the vaulting of the arms of the cross. A pedimented portico was to be added to the east arm of the cross as a façade; its columns were to be of the same height as the pilasters articulating the walls and the pediment would have risen only slightly above the attic.

The perfect concord between interior and exterior is a definite innovation in the design. The articulation of the outer walls is identical with that of the walls bounding the interior. The true 'façade' of the building is actually its whole exterior. Michelangelo restored Bramante's purely centralized plan, since his own would have presented the same view on all sides. The entrance portico would hardly have interrupted the continuity of the exterior walls.

In 1558–61 Michelangelo had a wooden model made for the main dome which has been preserved [147]. The dome itself was erected by Giacomo della Porta in 1588–91 [148]. Like the dome projected by Michelangelo, it is double-

145. (*left*) Michelangelo: Rome, St Peter's, north transept, designed 1546, nearly finished by 1564

146. (*bottom left*) Michelangelo: Rome, St Peter's, south apse, designed 1546, finished by 1564, and dome, designed 1558–61, executed 1558–93

147. (*top right*) Michelangelo: Model for the dome of St Peter's, 1558–61. Rome, Vatican City

148. (*bottom right*) Michelangelo and Giacomo della Porta: Rome, St Peter's, dome, 1588–91

shelled, but it is steeper than Michelangelo's hemisphere and slightly pointed.[17] Since Porta altered the outer shell of Michelangelo's model in the same sense, Dupérac's engravings, which show the model before this alteration and in its relation to the building as a whole, reproduce Michelangelo's ideas better than the model itself and the finished dome.

In its hemispherical form – though not in its structure – Michelangelo's dome is reminiscent of the Pantheon and of Bramante's project of 1506 [20, 147]. Like Bramante's, it rises above a colonnaded drum. But in Michelangelo's dome, the columns of the drum are paired and flank the windows instead of screening them. To the eye the rhythmic sequence of paired columns and windows looks like a continuation of the paired pilaster motif of the outer walls. While the verticals dominate the drum, the hemisphere of the cupola gives the impression of a resting form in which the upward movement of the verticals comes to an end. Its ribs taper upward and lead to the point at which the foot of the lantern cuts across them. Just as the dome rests on the horizontal cornices of the drum and its attic, the lantern rests on the horizontal ring of the summit of the dome. In this way an equilibrium is achieved between verticals and horizontals; the huge pilasters of the outer walls and the profile of the dome, as well as the festoons on the attic of the drum and the little dormers of the dome, all play a role in achieving this effect.

Michelangelo's model of 1558–61 was the product of years of thought and experiment. Soon after taking up office he wrote to Florence asking for the measurements of the Brunelleschi dome. Unlike Bramante and Sangallo, he obviously had a double-shell structure in mind from the start. In the first studies, both shells have a steep 'Gothic' outline, and the early drawings for the drum and lantern recall the cathedral of Florence. It can be gathered from Dupérac's engravings that the ratio of height between the dome and the lantern was not finally settled till after 1561, i.e. till after the completion of the model. It is typical that Michelangelo should have used the model as a 'visual reference' and have revised his plans again at the last moment; in this case formal and structural considerations stood in a close reciprocal relationship.

The minor domes which appear in Dupérac's engravings are quite incompatible, both in outline and detail, with Michelangelo's style. The formal vocabulary points to Vignola, who was Michelangelo's successor at St Peter's. Various attempts have been made to explain the discrepancy. It is not unlikely that Michelangelo meant to omit the minor domes; in that case what Dupérac reproduced was one of Vignola's new and personal ideas.[18] On the other hand, the possibility that Michelangelo had planned minor domes, but left no designs for them, must be taken into account. In that case, Vignola would have 'completed' Michelangelo's design for Dupérac.[19]

The minor domes which were executed were designed by Porta; the northern one was erected shortly before the main dome, the southern one soon after. They are not substantially different from the design shown in the engravings, but the profile is steeper, the drum and ribs have vigorously projecting outlines, and instead of the insignificant lantern Porta copied Michelangelo's lantern on the New Sacristy of S. Lorenzo.

The main dome of St Peter's is sustained by Bramante's piers [21], and, as Bramante intended, it dominates the exterior view of the church. Michelangelo devised the practical methods by which Bramante's ideas were realized, and it is due to him that the ring of walls enclosing the interior was merged with the dome in one artistic whole, within which the individual members have a perfectly clear structural and aesthetic function. The mutual response between the paired pilasters thrusting up from the ground and the mighty entablature is found again in the interlacing of verticals and horizontals in the attic of the drum. This polarity of upward-soaring and supporting members at rest finds its ultimate expression in the dome. The steeper, taller outline of Porta's outer shell makes the completed dome rather lighter and the verticals rising to the dome rather more pronounced than Michelangelo had intended, yet the dome we see today is so far in accord with Michelangelo's ideas that we may contemplate it as his work.

LATE ARCHITECTURAL PROJECTS

In 1559 Duke Cosimo I of Tuscany applied to Michelangelo for designs for the church of the Florentine colony in Rome – the building begun under Leo X had never risen above its foundations.[20] A wooden model was made after the design selected by the Duke which has come down to us in two engravings and several copies of drawings. Preliminary studies by Michelangelo's own hand have also been preserved [149]. These projects had no influence on the present church, which was built under the supervision of Giacomo della Porta.[21]

149. Michelangelo: Project for S. Giovanni dei Fiorentini, Rome, plan. Florence, Casa Buonarroti (124)

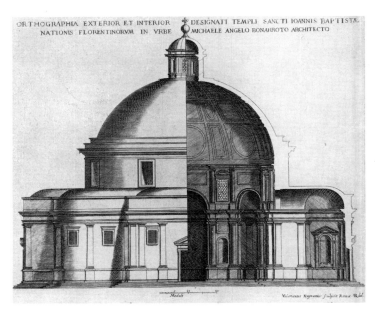

150. Michelangelo: Final project for S. Giovanni dei Fiorentini, Rome, section and exterior elevation, engraving by Valérien Regnart

Michelangelo's final project [150, 151] provided for a circular domed area surrounded by eight lower vestibules and chapels, alternately rectilinear and oval.[22] The plan looks like a conglomeration of eight huge wall sections whose inner faces, each set with paired columns, form the cylinder under the dome; from them emerge the walls surrounding the subsidiary chapels and vestibules. The oddly amorphous shape of the piers of the dome is due to

the configuration of the enclosed space. The conception of the design does not originate in the 'positive' form of the piers, but in the 'negative' form of the space, the angular shape of the vestibules and choir, and the oval of the diagonal chapels.

The eight subsidiary chambers are not connected with each other, but are only open towards the centre in eight arches, which are equal in height but not in width. Broad

151. Michelangelo: Final project for S. Giovanni dei Fiorentini, Rome

152. Michelangelo: Rome, S. Maria Maggiore, Sforza Chapel, c. 1560–73, section, plan, and detail of plan

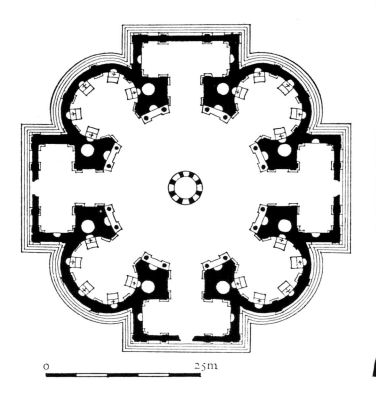

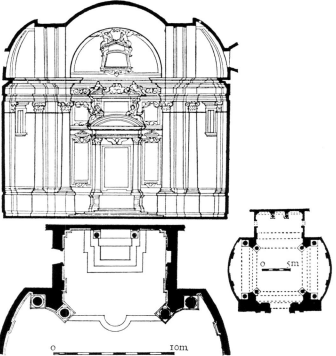

153. Michelangelo: Rome, S. Maria Maggiore, Sforza Chapel, c. 1560–1573

arches in the main bays lead to the vestibules and choir; those of the oval chapels in the diagonals are narrower.[23]

While the conception of the interior is founded on space, that of the exterior proceeds from the plastic volume of the building. The hemisphere of the dome rises above a ring of walls of alternately rectilinear and curved outlines. The rectilinear vestibules and the choir project rather farther to the outside than the oval chapels of the diagonals; thus the exterior view resembles centrally planned buildings of the Greek cross type. The articulation consists only of plain Tuscan pilasters; the attic and the drum of the dome are not articulated. The dome is closely akin to that of the Pantheon. The profile is semicircular, there are steps at its base, and the shell is uninterruptedly smooth.[24]

The memorial chapel of the Sforza in S. Maria Maggiore, begun about 1560 and consecrated in 1573, is the only building in which Michelangelo was able to realize his late conception of space [152].[25] The measurements are unusually large for this type; height, width, and depth measure about 18 m. (60 feet) each.[26] These proportions would have been ideally suitable for a square or a cross-shaped plan with a dome over the crossing. But Michelangelo brings the 'crossing' forward, close to the wall of the aisle of the church, with which it is connected by a narrow and short tunnel-vault. The transepts of the chapel have vaulted

apses; in plan their walls are noticeably flattened segments of a circle which adjoin the *outer* side of the crossing piers [153]. The fourth arm of the cross, which houses the altar, is rectangular in plan, and the width of the tunnel-vault is greater than its depth. Free-standing columns are set in front of the diagonal faces of the crossing piers. The vault over the crossing looks like a swelling sail. Between the narrow springers of the arches and the capitals of the columns, huge impost blocks are inserted [154]. Their mouldings are continued in a flattened form round the walls.

The architecture of the time provides no analogy to the seemingly random curve of the crossing vault and the apses; they discourage geometrical definition. These curves are not determined by the geometrical form of wall-planes or arches, but by the enclosed space, by the configuration of the volume bounded by walls and arches. One element of the 'content' of this space consists in the travertine columns, 9.5 m. (30 feet) high, which stand free in the space like monuments.[27] The monochrome of the walls, the markedly low relief of their articulations, the abundant light streaming from high windows,[28] the peculiarly smooth transitions between the sections of the vaulting – these are all means which help to bring home to the observer the sculptural quality of the space. As the plan shows, that interior is extended as far as the available area allows; at the same time the flattened segmental curves of the apses and vaulting convey to the observer the impression that the shallow shapes of the walls and arches define the available space with the greatest possible economy.

THE PORTA PIA

The Porta Pia [155] is named after Pope Pius IV (1559–65); it stands at the end of the present Via XX Settembre, an ancient traffic artery which the Pope had widened and levelled [43].[29] Michelangelo's name appears in the agreement concluded with a building contractor for the gate; according to Vasari, the Pope had selected the least costly of the three

154. Michelangelo: Rome, S. Maria Maggiore, Sforza Chapel, c. 1560–1573, capitals and entablature

155. Michelangelo: Rome, Porta Pia, begun 1561

designs submitted by Michelangelo. After the deaths of Michelangelo and the Pope, work was still in progress. In their present form, the outer face and the attic of the gate date from the nineteenth century; we cannot gain from Michelangelo's drawings any idea of the attic he had designed himself.[30]

Michelangelo's preliminary studies, which are only concerned with the frame of the passageway, derive from the type of the aedicule portal. In the execution, the passageway is the central bay of a three-bay front, its high relief standing out against the smooth brick planes at the sides. The straight lintel bending into obtuse angles at the corners is spanned by a flattened lunette after the fashion of a relieving arch; the cornice above it, supported by the framing pilasters of the passageway, is spanned in its turn by a broken segmental pediment, which is again crowned by a much broader triangular pediment.

The treatment of the detail is equally compressed and unusual. The vertical flutings of the pilasters rise beside the horizontal strata of the passageway jambs; the segmental pediment rolls inwards into volutes. A garland hangs on these volutes with the ponderous marble block bearing the papal inscription floating above it. The cornice and capitals are represented by plain blocks. However difficult the analysis and description of these forms may be, it would be a great mistake to regard them as mere improvisation on Michelangelo's part. As the many drawings show, they are the fully ripened fruit of precise preliminary studies. They are, of course, quite alien to the classical orders: in detail and composition they could not be more personal.

In the distant view from the city, the accumulation of heavy, shadow-casting forms leads the eye to the pediment group over the passageway. On the other hand, the passageway itself, when one walks through it, seems oppressively

156. Michelangelo: Rome, S. Maria degli Angeli, remodelling begun 1561

cramped and low in comparison with the height and weight of the pediment. The preliminary drawings themselves show the contrast between a cramped opening and a strong and weighty frame which can be seen in the doorways of the New Sacristy.

S. MARIA DEGLI ANGELI

Pius IV also commissioned Michelangelo to convert the tepidarium of the Baths of Diocletian into a church. The interior [156], which is about 59 m. long, 24 m. wide, and 30 m. high (194 by 79 by 99 feet), is unique in one respect, namely that the ancient vaulting and the eight granite columns, 14 m. (46 feet) high, which support the vaulting, have remained unaltered.

The initiator of the enterprise was a Sicilian priest who, as early as 1541, had conceived the idea of converting the great hall in the centre of the vast remains of the baths into a church to be consecrated to the Virgin and the Angels.

In a papal bull dated 1561, Pius IV assumed the responsibility for the building. The church was to contain the Pope's tomb, and the adjacent buildings were ceded to the Carthusian Order for the erection of a monastery.[31] The name of the new church, S. Maria degli Angeli, tallies with the Christian name of the Pope, Giovan Angelo; moreover the thermae were situated on the Strada Pia, which leads to the Porta Pia.

It was already noted with surprise in a contemporary account that Michelangelo placed the high altar on the transverse, not the longitudinal, axis of the great hall, so that the hall seems to be the transept of the church. The square rooms in front of the short sides and the rotunda opposite the new chancel were converted into vestibules and provided with porches. In this way it was possible to reduce the

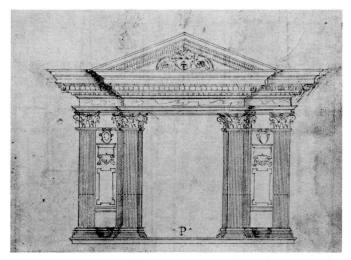

157. Michelangelo: Rome, S. Maria Maggiore, Sforza Chapel, *c.* 1560–1573, elevation of the façade towards the aisle of the church (demolished), drawing by A. Pagliarino, *c.* 1582

rebuilding to the insertion of partition walls and the construction of the lengthy chancel of the Carthusians. The high altar in front of the chancel was flanked by two free-standing columns, so that the chancel was practically cut off from the hall.

In the eighteenth century the church was renovated in a Late Baroque style: new columns were set up at the entrance to the chancel and between the hall and the vestibule, the portals of the short sides were replaced by large altars, and polychrome ornament was applied to the walls. Further, an ornate stucco entablature was carried round the hall. Michelangelo's spatial organization remained practically unaltered, but the impression the church makes on the visitor of today is not the one he intended. The walls and vault were originally stuccoed in white, and the only note of colour was struck by the reddish granite of the eight giant columns standing in front of the walls.

As in the Sforza Chapel and the plans for S. Giovanni dei Fiorentini [149–50, 153–4, 157], Michelangelo obviously conceived the interior space as the true aesthetic subject of his design. He abandoned decoration and colour just as consistently as he relegated the chancel and vestibule to subordinate chapels which are of no importance in the spatial picture. Free of additions and coloured ornament, the shape of the great hall was to stand out in 'white' purity. The fenestration plays its part too. The round vestibule is illuminated only by the lantern, the chancel windows are few and small, but the eight great ancient openings of the clerestory remained practically unaltered.[32] The subsidiary rooms are shadowy, but the huge hall is flooded with daylight falling from above.

Michelangelo's remodelling is far removed from any attempt at an archaeological restoration of the interior of the hall. He probably knew perfectly well that antique interiors – even those of the thermae – were decorated with polychrome stucco or marble: the brightness and variety of the Baroque decoration of S. Maria degli Angeli approximated far more closely to the original state of the tepidarium than the austere monochrome of the sixteenth-century church.

*

In spite of all their differences, the designs for S. Giovanni dei Fiorentini, the Sforza Chapel, and S. Maria degli Angeli show that interest in spatial configuration which is characteristic of Michelangelo's late architectural works. These unique spaces have no true forerunners or successors in the Cinquecento. Their plans are no longer combinations of simple geometrical forms – the square, polygon, semicircle, Greek cross. The curve of the apses of the Sforza Chapel consists of a random segment of a circle; in plan, the diagonal chapels of S. Giovanni dei Fiorentini are in the new elliptical shape first used by Peruzzi; the contours of the dome piers of S. Giovanni elude any kind of geometrical definition.

The monochrome of these interiors was an essential part of their particular quality. It has been preserved in the Sforza Chapel, and there is documentary evidence of it for S. Maria degli Angeli; in St Peter's and S. Giovanni it can be deduced from the reproductions of Michelangelo's designs.

The motif of columns standing free in front of the wall appears in unprecedented monumentality in the 'column monuments' in the Sforza Chapel. In S. Maria degli Angeli extant antique columns were used by Michelangelo in a similar way. The motif recurs in the columns of the loggias of the Capitoline palazzi. Free-standing columns appear in the preliminary studies for the Porta Pia as an alternative to the pilasters which were eventually executed.

Since Vasari, what has been regarded as characteristic of Michelangelo's work lies in the unconventionally novel and quite personal forms. Whether that is praise or blame will depend on the critic's outlook. Michelangelo's 'licences' arise from his independent approach to the commission in hand; they are not arbitrary, but the expression of his disregard of traditional schemes and the traditional apparatus of form. Michelangelo's architectural projects are never visionary – on the contrary, they take full account of the client's wishes and local conditions. Works left unfinished at his death, such as the dome of St Peter's or the Capitol, were finished practically as Michelangelo had conceived them, less from respect for the 'divino' than because Michelangelo's design was regarded as the best solution of the task in hand.

CHAPTER 10

Rome 1550–1600

THE PERIOD FROM 1550 TO 1575

In comparison with Brunelleschi, for instance, Michelangelo devised no new types; his buildings are so extraordinary in their dimensions, or bear so unmistakably the imprint of his hand, that no newcomer could fall heir to his style. In the works of the generation of Roman architects which succeeded Michelangelo, his influence is mainly traceable in the decorative detail. For the most part, however, that generation continued the heritage of Raphael, Peruzzi, and especially of Antonio da Sangallo the Younger.[1]

That also applies to the two architects who succeeded to the superintendence of the work on St Peter's after Michelangelo's death. Pirro Ligorio and Jacopo Vignola had been engaged on papal buildings before; they had also worked for the two great cardinals whose architectural enterprises during the pontificates of the period surpassed those of the Curia in size and importance. Ligorio's Villa d'Este at Tivoli and Vignola's Palazzo Farnese at Caprarola are princely country seats in every sense of the term. In the age of dawning absolutism the type of villa which had developed in the late Quattrocento, and which had already achieved monumentality in the Villa Madama, became indispensable as a complement of the city residence. The development culminates, of course, in Versailles, the country residence of the French kings. Like the great palazzi in the city, the country houses were planned to accommodate the large retinue of the owners who dwelt there during the summer months and who used them as the stage for receptions and other festivities. The fortifications which were essential down to the early sixteenth century, even for papal residences, could now be dispensed with; they were replaced by spreading gardens and ornamental fountains.

In Rome itself, a number of cardinals built summer residences in the second half of the sixteenth century, and their size and importance can be judged by the seventeenth- and eighteenth-century plans of Rome. The only one still standing is the present Villa Medici, begun by Cardinal Ricci. The Farnese Gardens on the Forum and the Palatine succumbed to the archaeological excavations of the nineteenth and twentieth centuries. The Villa d'Este on the Quirinal hill was incorporated in the new papal palace about 1600. As a rule, the villas were secluded from the streets by high walls; their main fronts – in museum-like fashion decorated with antique reliefs and statues – faced the gardens [158, 160]. Antique statues stood at the intersections of garden paths, and the whole complex included grottoes, fountains, waterfalls, and quickset mazes.

PIRRO LIGORIO

Pirro Ligorio's architectural work – he was born about 1510 at Naples and died in 1583 at Ferrara – has not yet been fully investigated.[2] He began work as a painter. Paul IV, himself a native of Naples, appointed him Surveyor of the Works at the Vatican Palace, an office which he retained under Pius IV. He was obliged to resign his appointment as architect-in-chief of St Peter's after a year's work, since, as Vasari relates, he had not kept strictly to Michelangelo's plans. After 1565, Ligorio seems to have been employed only by the house of Este, till 1567 in Rome and later at Ferrara.

Ligorio was a dedicated antiquarian, epigraphist, and excavator, and his detailed compilations are one of our main sources for the knowledge and interpretation of antiquity in the sixteenth century. There is a flavour of nineteenth-century historicism about his own buildings, since what he aimed at was a 'scientifically accurate' reproduction of antique architecture.[3]

It is from that point of view that his remodelling of the Belvedere Court in the Vatican must be understood [5–8, 9]. Work on Bramante's project, which, after the Sack of Rome, was restricted to the maintenance of what was left standing, progressed vigorously under Julius III and Pius IV. In the upper court, the exedra was reduced in size by the insertion of a corridor and given an upper storey. Bramante's round staircase, the radius of which was calculated for the original form of the exedra, was removed and replaced by a double stairway with straight steps planned by Michelangelo. Under Pius IV a semi-domical vault, known as the Nicchione, was built over the exedra. Further, the west wing of the upper court was built and all the façades were coated with stucco. An inscription running round the whole records the achievements of Pius IV.[4]

In the lower court, the steps to the upper terrace, already planned by Bramante, were executed, and the west wing begun.[5] The insertion of semicircular steps on the narrow side under the Stanze provided seats for an arena for open-air tournaments; an engraving of 1565 shows the ceremonial opening of this arena on the occasion of the wedding of one of the Pope's nieces.

Ligorio had published in 1553 a small volume, *Antichità di Roma*, describing the construction of antique circuses. With its surrounding buildings, the Belvedere Court too became a 'circus' with exedrae on both sides. The wall behind the theatre steps of the lower court was to be enriched by a lavish decoration of statuary *alla antica*. The stucco on the façades of the upper court is also in keeping with antique practice, when brickwork was entirely coated with stucco.[6]

Further, Ligorio began for Paul IV a small villa on a rise in the Vatican gardens which is known as the Casino di Pio IV [9, 159–61]. On the whole, the structure and decoration are pretty well preserved; no other building gives so clear an idea of the peculiar character of the Roman villa in the Cinquecento.[7]

At the centre of the complex is an oval courtyard [162]; the surrounding wall is interrupted on the narrow sides by the small gatehouses through which the visitor enters the villa, and on the long sides by architraved loggias. The loggia on the uphill side serves as a vestibule to the actual two-

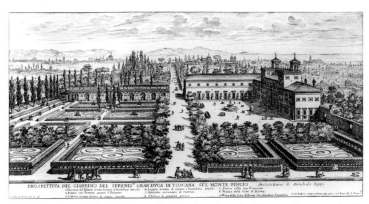

158. Rome, Villa Medici, palace and gardens, looking south, engraving by G.B. Falda

159. Pirro Ligorio: Rome, Casino di Pio IV, begun 1559, looking west, engraving by G. Venturini

storey Casino; the lower loggia opposite, a one-storeyed hall, has a tall, pedimented attic. The façades over the two loggias look like pages out of a picture-book [159]. Instead of an articulation by pilasters and half-columns, the walls are covered with reliefs, inscriptions, escutcheons, statuary, aedicules, and festoons. Ligorio probably found the model for this decoration in buildings of the early Empire. In his compilations there are records of diggings he made at Hadrian's Villa at Tivoli, which show that he was familiar with many buildings which are no longer extant.

In his design for the Casino, Ligorio may also have had in mind Pliny the Younger's famous letter with the description

of his villa, Laurentina. That can be seen not only in the elimination of monumental exteriors and the turning of the main fronts to the court, but also, and especially, in the oval shape of the courtyard itself.[8] Finally, there are reminiscences of antiquity in the materials employed, the lavish use of tessellation, the costly marble columns, and the stucco coating of the brickwork. The profuse stucco and fresco ornament in the interior, on which Federigo Barocci, Santi di Tito, and Taddeo Zuccari collaborated, comprises secular themes treated *alla antica* and religious subjects.

In Rome, Pius IV's Casino is the most important example of those antiquarian trends which we have already seen in

160. Pirro Ligorio: Rome, Casino di Pio IV, begun 1559, façade

161. Pirro Ligorio: Rome, Vatican, Casino di Pio IV, begun 1559, plan

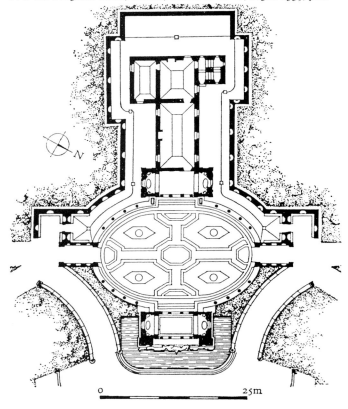

Raphael's Palazzo Branconio dall'Aquila and Peruzzi's cortile of the Palazzo Massimo. Ligorio harks back to the poetic and formal tradition of antiquity in the same way as Raphael in his designs for the Villa Madama, but while Raphael assimilated the heritage of antiquity in his own masterly fashion, Ligorio's villa looks like a book of quotations in which antique forms are reproduced with a maximum of accuracy. The result is an engaging curio. Further, a comparison with the Villa Madama shows the Casino as an example of the closer-knit, compacter formal idiom of the middle of the century.

A second summer seat on which Ligorio worked is the Villa d'Este at Tivoli, already mentioned. Unlike the small Vatican Casino, it is a building of considerable size. The main emphasis lies on the fountains and the gardens rather than on the actual architectural forms [163]. The villa was under construction from about 1560 until the death of the client, Ippolito d'Este, in 1572.[9].

Dupérac's famous engraving of 1573 shows the whole group in bird's-eye view. At the top of the hill stands the Cardinal's palazzo; below it, on the slope and in the flat land further down, are the gardens, divided by a central walk into nearly identical halves. Zigzag paths lead up from the garden beds to the terrace in front of the palazzo. The slope with its terrace looks like a great ornamental pattern composed of lozenge-shaped parts, and the many and various fountains which are the glory of the villa are embedded in the geometry of the gardens. The first impression the visitor was meant to receive as he moved along the paths was indeed that of a

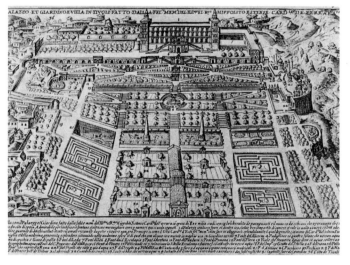

162. (*above right*) Pirro Ligorio: Rome, Casino di Pio IV, begun 1559, courtyard

163. (*right*) Pirro Ligorio: Tivoli, Villa d'Este, *c.* 1565–1572, engraving by G. Lauro, 1641

164. (*below*) Pirro Ligorio: Tivoli, Villa d'Este, *c.* 1565–1572, Fountain of Tivoli

geometrical pattern; the paths led to the grottoes, which contained mythological, dynastic, or heroic scenes. The antique torsos of the Este collection were 'restored', i.e. adapted to this programme, and placed in the grottoes. The best known example of programmatic architecture is the socalled Rometta, which appears in the top right-hand corner of the Dupérac engraving. It is a representation of the ancient city of Rome, with a miniature Tiber flowing round an island. The figure of Rome enthroned in the centre of a group of ruins has a counterpart in the large, seated figure of the Tiburtine Sibyl in the 'Fontana di Tivoli'; in the 'Fontana di Aniene' there is a reclining figure of the near-by river Aniene from which the water for the entire villa is drawn.

The architectural setting of the fountains and grottoes is rusticated throughout [164]. The pavement is pebble-mosaic, and the walls are encrusted with 'sponge-stone', the calcareous deposit of the streams flowing in the neighbourhood of Tivoli. There are also rusticated fountains in the crypto-porticus, the lowest storey of the palazzo. At every point there is a deliberate fusion of art and nature.

No clear idea of Ligorio's part in the work on the villa can be gained from the documentary sources, but his employment as the antiquarian of the house of Este, the learned programme, and the stylistic kinship with Pius IV's Casino leave little room for doubt that he was the originator of the design of the villa. He had greater freedom to work on a generous scale here than in the Casino of Pius IV or the Vatican Court, where he was bound by pre-existing parts of the building.

Geometrical gardens with labyrinths and zigzag paths, rusticated grottoes and fountains are recorded in Rome and Florence as early as the first half of the sixteenth century;[10] the importance of the Villa d'Este lies in the fact that the entire repertory typical of the villa in the later sixteenth century has here been realized for the first time on a large scale and to an overall plan. Though considerably impaired, the iconographical and architectural programme has been preserved to the present day, in spite of later changes including the removal of the antique sculpture and the romantic decay of the villa.[11]

The villa, as a new type, was less dependent on traditional usage and established requirements than churches and palazzi, so that the personality of the architect and his patron had greater freedom of expression. Apart from Michelangelo, there is hardly a more personal design in Cinquecento architecture than that of Pius IV's Casino. Ligorio's wilfulness, as Vasari hints, was the reason for his dismissal from his work on St Peter's, and therefore, in all probability, for his removal to Ferrara. His extremely personal style was not very well suited to monumental building.

VIGNOLA

The monumental buildings left unfinished by Michelangelo were not continued by Ligorio, but by Vignola, who was appointed to St Peter's at the same time as Ligorio in 1564, though at first at only half Ligorio's salary. Giacomo Barozzi (1507–73), generally known as Vignola from his birthplace near Bologna, was probably brought to Rome by the younger

Cardinal Alessandro Farnese. In all probability it was the patronage of that powerful cardinal that finally brought him to St Peter's and the Capitoline palazzi. Unlike Ligorio, in whose work decoration is more important than structure, Vignola kept strictly to traditional standards and elements of architectural composition. His formal repertory continues the Sangallo tradition. His Emilian origin is traceable only in a few decorative details.

Vignola's treatise on the five orders, published in 1562 and repeatedly reprinted and translated, became the vademecum of the architects of the seventeenth and eighteenth centuries. As long as columns and pilasters remained essential features of the more monumental kind of building, Vignola's *Regola*, in its simplicity and precision, was indispensable, and it came to the end of its usefulness only when stone was ousted by the new building materials – iron, glass, and concrete.

The *Regola delle Cinque Ordini* is not a treatise in the sense of Vitruvius and Alberti. Except for a short introduction, the book contains only thirty-two plates with explanatory captions. Each order is illustrated by four to six plates; each plate shows two columns with their architraves. These plates are followed by illustrations of pillared arcades with half-columns of the respective order and details of the bases, capitals, and mouldings. The unit of measurement is given by a *modulo:* in the actual work of building, all that had to be determined was the ratio between the *modulo* and the local unit of measurement.

As Vignola explains in his foreword, he had, after an exhaustive study of ancient buildings, selected the proportions 'which are generally regarded as most beautiful and most pleasing to the eye'. He goes on to say that his plates

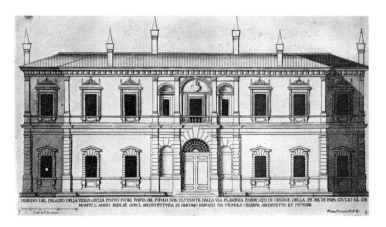

are patterns for the working architect. In the large engravings, details stand out clearly, while the rough woodcuts in Serlio's treatise, which had appeared twenty years earlier, were of little use to the practising architect. The success of Vignola's book shows that the *Regola* fulfilled a need. In the second half of the sixteenth century, a standardization took place of the very forms illustrated in the *Cinque Ordini*. While the architects of the late Quattrocento and early Cinquecento drew single capitals or architraves and varied them in their own practice, later in the century certain examples, such as Bramante's capitals in St Peter's were accepted as the rule and copied again and again.[12]

Vignola, like many other Renaissance architects, began as a painter. In 1538 and 1539 he received payments for work in the Vatican. In 1541 Paul III appointed him architect of S. Petronio in Bologna,[13] but he was not able to take up the appointment till 1543, since from 1541 to 1543 he was at work with his fellow-countryman Primaticcio at Fontainebleau on casting bronze figures of the antique statuary in the Vatican from plaster moulds. Vignola's seven years' term on S. Petronio has left little trace on the building; on the other hand, two designs for the façade have been preserved which, like Peruzzi's drawings, made twenty years before, are an odd mixture of Gothic and Renaissance forms. The façade was never built since the building commission could come to no decision on any of the large number of designs submitted.[14]

His first biographer, Egnatio Danti, writes that Vignola did work on the Palazzo Bocchi in Bologna. An engraving dated 1545 probably shows the design for the façade which was begun in that year [165]. The rusticated basement and the window frames of the ground floor recall the Palazzo del Te at Mantua; bizarre details such as the busts over the mezzanine windows, the inscriptions on the basement, and the metopes under the balustrade may have been inspired by ideas of the patron, a famous humanist who wished to turn his house into the seat of an academy. The portal and the top storey have been copied almost literally from an illustration in Serlio's treatise. The ornamental tops of the mezzanine windows are to be found in later designs by Vignola, and are a characteristic feature of his work.[15]

With its rusticated window-surrounds and the rusticated blocks through which the columns of the portal rise, the façade of Vignola's first Roman building, the Palazzina of Julius III's villa [166, 167], recalls the Palazzo Bocchi. The articulation of the centre of the façade is an innovation; its three bays are composed in the guise of a triumphal arch and executed in freestone, so that this part of the front

165. (*left*) Giacomo Barozzi da Vignola: Project for the Palazzo Bocchi, Bologna, engraving, 1545

166. (*top*) Giacomo Barozzi da Vignola: Rome, Villa Giulia, begun 1551, façade, engraving by Ferrerio

167. (*right*) Giacomo Barozzi da Vignola: Rome, Villa Giulia, begun 1551, façade

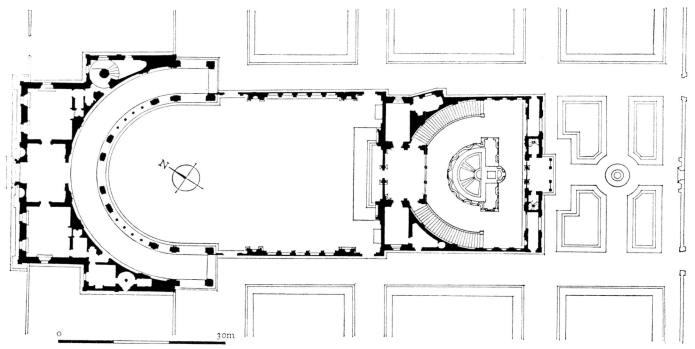

168. Giacomo Barozzi da Vignola: Rome, Villa Giulia, begun 1551, plan

stands out in higher relief than the flat brick walls at the sides.

The villa is situated outside the city walls, and it is this situation which explains both the reminiscences of fortified buildings and the triumphal arch motif of the façade. The portal – the only entrance – leads into a walled papal enclosure [168] and is thus similar to the Vatican. There is nothing of the kind in Roman architecture about 1550, though there are details reminiscent of Giulio Romano and of Serlio's treatise. The façade as a whole is a novel and thoroughly considered solution of the commission in hand.

As Vasari relates, he himself and Bartolommeo Ammannati collaborated with Vignola on the design and construction of the villa. The architectural history and the attribution of its various parts have not been fully elucidated.[16]

The vestibule of Vignola's two-storeyed Palazzina leads into a semicircular courtyard loggia [169]. The other three sides of the court are single-storeyed and obviously in the style of Ammannati. Antique statues stand in the niches of the long sides. The façade facing the entrance wing is decorated with stucco reliefs; originally, it had a small doorway leading to a loggia, which is also by Ammannati and which looks down on a lower, profusely decorated nymphaeum. At that point, at the very heart of the complex, there flow the waters of the Aqua Vergine, the ancient aqueduct which Julius III had restored and conducted to his villa.[17]

Pope Julius's villa can hardly be compared to the Villa Madama and Pius IV's Casino, since it is situated in a valley and not on a hillside. Yet here too the differences in level are an essential element in the plan. The visitor approaching from the two-storeyed Palazzina enters a single-storeyed courtyard. It is only from Ammannati's loggia that he first catches sight of the nymphaeum [170], which is situated far

below the level of the first court. Its lowest storey, the Fontana Segreta of the Aqua Vergine, can only be reached by stairways concealed in the walls. The account books show that this arrangement was planned from the start; the earthworks round the Palazzina and the Fontana Segreta were begun at the same time. The semicircular stairway leading down from the loggia to the nymphaeum, on the other hand, was not originally provided for, as many *pentimenti* show. Ammannati was only called in after work had begun, and he altered the original plan at this point.

As Vasari's narrative hints, the patron was responsible for a good many of the details. Certainly it was not always easy for the working architects to fall in with Julius III's proposed alterations: the Pontiff was obviously far less concerned about the breaks and the unsatisfactory transitions they involved than the architects who had to alter or restrict their plans.

Vignola's artistic personality found far freer range of expression in the Palazzo Farnese at Caprarola. Situated in the hereditary estates of the Farnese, Caprarola belonged to the dukedom of Castro and Nepi, which Paul III had created for his son Pier Luigi Farnese. During his period as Cardinal, Paul had started a pentagonal fortress on the hill overlooking Caprarola. The Rocca, probably a single-storey building, determined the ground plan of the palazzo built by Vignola for the younger Cardinal Alessandro Farnese, the Pope's

169. (*above right*) Giacomo Barozzi da Vignola and others: Rome, Villa Giulia, begun 1551, first courtyard

170. (*right*) Giacomo Barozzi da Vignola and others: Rome, Villa Giulia, begun 1551, second courtyard with the Fontana Segreta

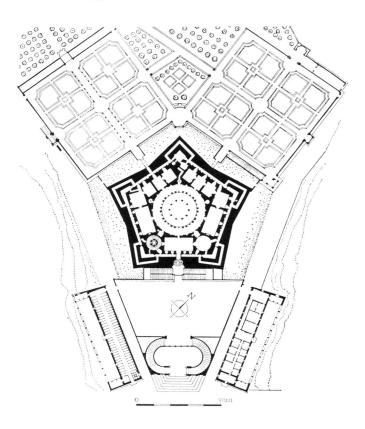

grandson [171]. It was of this palazzo that Montaigne wrote in 1581 that there was nothing else like it in Italy. 'This building is surrounded by a deep moat hewn out of the tufa; it is pentagonal in form but looks like a pure rectangle. Inside, however, it is perfectly round.'[18]

This is an exact description of the unusual form of the building. The multi-storeyed façade seen by the traveller approaching from Caprarola looks at first sight like that of a 'regular' palazzo, i.e. of a palazzo built on a rectangular plan [172]. The circular court ('inside it is perfectly round'), however, gives the polygon a 'regular' form in the interior [173]. The combination of circle and polygon appears more than once in the plan: in one corner of the pentagon is the famous round staircase [174], in the corresponding angle the round chapel. The difficulties presented by this unusual plan have all been mastered with elegance and restraint. But what most aroused the admiration of contemporaries was the skilful disposition and arrangement of the rooms, not the lavishness of the frescoes on the ground floor and the piano nobile. Thus, for instance, visitors driving in through the basement storey can alight and walk directly to the round staircase; a circular driveway under the court brings the carriage back to the entrance. On the piano nobile, the five central bays of the façade form an open loggia facing east, which was therefore cool in summer. The smaller rooms in the other wings were provided with heating facilities and could therefore be used in colder weather.

The design of the state rooms, incomparable in size and decoration, is undoubtedly the work of Vignola [175]. The articulation must be looked at as a uniform, carefully graded system. The ground floor is treated as a basement throughout; the piano nobile in general has single pilasters, but double half-columns on the piers in the courtyard and double pilasters on the walls around the ambulatory of the court and in the chapel; the great loggia on the façade again has single pilasters. The arrangement of single and double members is governed by the scheme b–a–b, a leitmotif in Vignola's architecture.

171. (above left) Giacomo Barozzi da Vignola: Caprarola, Palazzo Farnese, begun 1559, plan

172. (left) Giacomo Barozzi da Vignola: Caprarola, Palazzo Farnese, begun 1559, façade

173. (top right) Giacomo Barozzi da Vignola: Caprarola, Palazzo Farnese, begun 1559, courtyard

174. (*above*) Giacomo Barozzi da Vignola: Caprarola, Palazzo Farnese, begun 1559, staircase

175. (*left*) Giacomo Barozzi da Vignola: Caprarola, Palazzo Farnese, begun 1559, Sala di Ercole

176. (*below*) Giacomo Barozzi da Vignola: Piacenza, Palazzo Farnese, begun 1558, plan

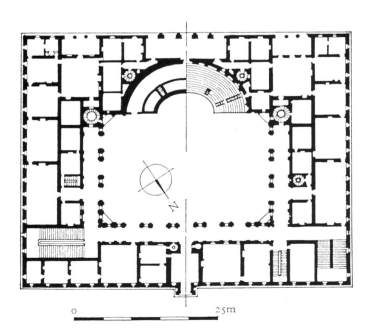

177. Giacomo Barozzi da Vignola: Bologna, Portico dei Banchi, begun *c.* 1561

Vignola also designed the plan for the huge palazzo which was begun by the Farnese in 1558 at Piacenza, the capital of the new dukedom of Parma and Piacenza. The projects far outstripped the means of the dynasty; after many interruptions, work was stopped soon after 1600 and the court removed to Parma. The finished part represents hardly a third of the total project; in the cortile, the impressive freestone incrustation which had been planned was abandoned, and the building looks like a vast ruin.

The only possible comparison to this huge scheme in contemporary Italian architecture is the Vatican Palace. The existing designs show a rectangular plan with frontages of about 111 m. and 88 m. (335 and 190 feet), and with 23 and 17 bays respectively [176]. On one side of the court there was to have been a theatre with fifteen semicircular tiers of seats.[19] The centre of the city front, like that of the Villa Giulia, was to have a triumphal arch motif and a tower, while the fronts looking on to the garden and the Po were provided with open loggias like the garden front of the Palazzo Farnese in Rome.

The scheme recalls that of the Vatican in so far as it combines elements of the palazzo, fortress, and villa. A moat was planned in front of the city façade with a drawbridge leading up to the main portal. On the garden front, on the other hand, with its loggias, there was to be no trace of fortification. The Villa Madama was the model for the theatre in the court; the articulation of the court arcades repeats the motif of the Upper Belvedere Court.

The palazzo at Piacenza was commissioned by Margaret of Parma, the natural daughter of Charles V and the wife of Duke Ottavio Farnese. At almost the same time, in 1561,

Margaret's step-brother, Philip II, conceived the idea of the Escorial. Both buildings stand witness to the ambitions of the house of Habsburg. Francesco Paciotto, the fortifications architect, who had competed with Vignola for the commission, later made projects for the Escorial. It is therefore not by chance that the Escorial has a number of typological and formal elements in common with the great scheme for Piacenza.[20]

On one of his journeys to Parma and Piacenza, Vignola probably designed the Portico dei Banchi in the city of Bologna, where he had worked earlier [177]. The portico, one of the great achievements of urban architecture in sixteenth-century Italy, is almost as important for the general view of the main piazza of Bologna as Sansovino's Libreria for the Piazzetta in Venice. The narrow side of the piazza opposite the Palazzo del Comune consisted of a number of buildings varying in height and width, with arcades and shops on the ground floors. Vignola faced these *banchi* with a uniform portico-façade harmonizing with the rest of the piazza. The round-arched arcades of the ground-floor loggias and the low mezzanine are framed in Corinthian pilasters. The only articulation of the two upper storeys consists of pilaster strips; the windows have the ornamental tops characteristic of Vignola.[21]

ECCLESIASTICAL ARCHITECTURE

After the Sack of Rome, religious building in the city, with the exception of the construction of St Peter's, had come to a standstill. Except for some minor confraternity churches, only one religious building of any size was erected in the

178. Giacomo Barozzi da Vignola and Giacomo della Porta: Rome, Gesù, begun 1568

second quarter of the century, and that was the hospital church of S. Spirito in Sassia,[22] the work of Antonio da Sangallo the Younger, built between 1537 and 1545. S. Spirito is the first Roman example of the flat-roofed single-aisled church with chapels which had been developed in Florence in the late Quattrocento. Sangallo's church had an important influence on the future, since the tendency to broaden the nave as far as possible resulted in fundamentally new spatial forms in the third quarter of the century.

The Roman mother-church of the Jesuit Order, Il Gesù, begun by Vignola in 1568, shows the full development of the

type [179]. The tunnel-vaulted nave, nearly 18 m. (60 feet) in width, has four chapels on each side, and the end walls of the transept are aligned with the outer walls of the chapels. The domed crossing is followed by a bay of the same width as the nave and the broad apse.[23]

On entering, the visitor has the impression of a wide and high hall bounded on both sides by huge double pilasters [178]. The tunnel-vault rises above a cornice which runs continuously from the façade to the piers of the crossing. Between the coupled pilasters, low, round-arched openings lead into the chapels. While the nave is brightly lit from the

179. Giacomo Barozzi da Vignola: Rome, Gesù, begun 1568, plan and section

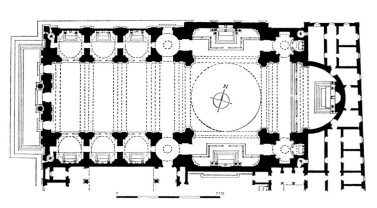

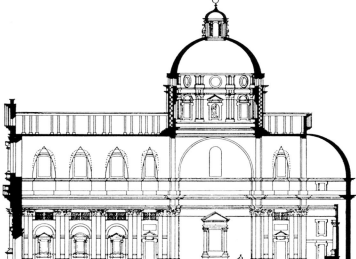

180. Giacomo della Porta: Rome, Gesù, façade, begun 1571, engraving by Villamena

181. Giacomo Barozzi da Vignola: Rome, Gesù, project for the façade, engraving by Mario Cartaro, 1573

façade windows and the lunettes of the tunnel-vault, the chapels are comparatively dim. Above them is the gallery, the 'coretti', which are cut off from the nave by gratings.

The comparison betwen the Gesù and Alberti's S. Andrea at Mantua, which is so often drawn in literature, only holds good up to a point. In S. Andrea, the transverse tunnel-vaults of the chapels act as abutments to the main vault, while in the Gesù the side-thrust of the main tunnel-vault is conducted outwards to buttresses resting on walls between the chapels. Unlike the chapels in S. Andrea, which rise to the height of the crowning cornice, the low, saucer-domed chapels in the Gesù are of no importance for the spatial effect of the nave or for the statics of the vault.

In a church of the importance of the Gesù, a dome over the crossing was indispensable; as far as might be, the diameter of the dome had to be equal to the width of the nave. The plan shows that Vignola fulfilled these requirements by continuing the row of chapels into the piers of the crossing; the four low, narrow chapels in the corners between the transept, nave, and chancel are, as it were, hollowed out of the piers. The result is a simple, clear configuration of various spatial elements; the dome seems to rest on the surrounding walls, and not on three-dimensional piers. At the same time, these small chapels form a convenient passage between the nave and the transept.

The foundation stone of the building was laid on 26 June 1568, after years spent in discussing the situation, size, and shape of the church. Certain details in the history of the plan have never been cleared up. Nanni di Baccio Bigi had submitted a design for the church as early as 1550. In 1554 Michelangelo also was called in. In addition, financial difficulties retarded the beginning of construction. Work started only when Cardinal Alessandro Farnese agreed to make larger contributions in 1568. The Cardinal was enthusiastically in favour of Vignola's plan, which the Order accepted with reluctance. Building was directed by the Jesuit Father Giovanni Tristano, an architectural expert who had already worked on several churches of the Order. It must have come as a surprise when in 1571 the Cardinal decided to have the façade executed after a design by Giacomo della Porta [180]. Several plans submitted by Vignola [181] must have failed to satisfy him.

When Vignola died in the summer of 1573, the nave, with the two piers of the crossing belonging to it, had risen as far as the crowning cornice. The great tunnel-vault and the façade were finished in 1577. After the purchase of several more plots of land, it was possible to carry on with the building, and the church was consecrated in 1584. Vignola's ground plan certainly remained in force till the church was completed. The vaulting of the nave and the façade, on the other hand, are Porta's work. Porta also directed building operations after 1573; his formal idiom can be recognized particularly in the choir and the dome.

After consultation with the Order, in 1568 the Cardinal wrote to Vignola: 'The church is to have a single nave, not a nave and aisles, and there are to be chapels on both sides'; further, 'the church is to be entirely vaulted over'. The rest he left to Vignola's judgement. What the Cardinal was actually aiming at was a wide, open space not cluttered up with additions, thereby partaking of a tendency which became general after the middle of the sixteenth century. The same trend can be seen in contemporary churches in Milan, Florence, and Venice. In France and Germany it resulted a little later in the removal of Gothic rood screens and altars from cathedrals. It is only partly true that the Gesù and the Jesuit churches of the seventeenth century were determined by rules laid down by the Council of Trent; it was probably rather the new ideal of a church with a spacious interior clearly bounded but imposing no definite perspectives, which developed about the middle of the sixteenth century, that influenced the ideas of the Council.[24]

In engravings of the early seventeenth century the great tunnel-vault over the nave of the Gesù is stuccoed in plain white and quite unadorned [182]. The grey travertine of the twin pilasters was faced with marble in the nineteenth century. In the middle of the seventeenth century the vault was decorated with the polychrome stucco and frescoes which have made of the Gesù a model of decorative art of the Baroque. On the other hand, the stuccoes and altars of the side chapels, which are in any case hardly visible from the nave, were made at the time of building. Thus, in its original form, the interior corresponded exactly to the ideas and instructions of the Council of Trent. In its monochrome it recalls the Sforza Chapel or Michelangelo's designs for S. Giovanni dei Fiorentini.

While Vignola, in the Gesù, contributed largely to forming

182. Giacomo Barozzi da Vignola and Giacomo della Porta: Rome, Gesù, begun 1568, montage of engraving by Villamena

183. Giacomo Barozzi da Vignola: Rome, S. Andrea in Via Flaminia, 1550–c. 1553

the type of the Baroque longitudinal church, he also enriched the conception of the centrally planned church in a way which was to become of prime importance for the architects of the seventeenth and eighteenth centuries: he was the first to create an ecclesiastical building on an oval plan.[25] Even in his first Roman building, the small memorial chapel of S. Andrea in Via Flaminia (1550–c. 1553) [183, 184, 185A], which is part of the group of the Villa Giulia, the rectangular interior is vaulted over by an oval dome. A more thorough-going design is the plan, probably dating from 1559, for a chapel for the conclave in the Belvedere Court of the Vatican, which is planned as an oval interior enclosed in a rectangle.[26] In the last ten years of his life Vignola put into practice the *concetto* of a purely oval space in the church of the confraternity of S. Anna dei Palafrenieri [9, 185B].[27] Like the chapel of the conclave project, S. Anna is a 'double shell' building, which combines two stereometric figures: an interior oval enclosed in a square shell of masonry.[28]

As the sixteenth- and seventeeth-century plans of Rome show, S. Anna stood free to the view on three sides. A dome was certainly anticipated in the original project. In the early sixteenth century in Rome these prerequisites would have resulted in a 'regular' centrally planned building, possibly of the same type as S. Eligio degli Orefici, also a confraternity church. The curious form of S. Anna can be explained neither by the function nor by the situation of the building, but only by assuming it to be a specific *concetto* of the architect. Unlike those of Bramante, Vignola's plans do not emerge from the concept of a stereometric structure, conceived as a uniform figure, in which interior and exterior are mutually related; on the contrary the interior is unrelated to

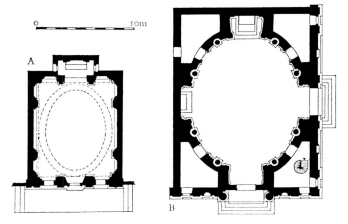

184. (*left*) Giacomo Barozzi da Vignola: Rome, S. Andrea in Via Flaminia, 1550–*c.* 1553

185. (*above*) (A) Giacomo Barozzi da Vignola: Rome, S. Andrea in Via Flaminia, 1550–*c.* 1533, plan of ground floor; (B) Giacomo and Giacinto Barozzi da Vignola: Rome, S. Anna dei Palafrenieri, begun 1565, reconstruction of original plan

186 and 187. Giacomo and Giacinto Barozzi da Vignola: Rome, S. Anna dei Palafrenieri, begun 1565. Interior (*right*) and exterior (*bottom right*)

the exterior, the space to its shell, and even the articulation to the structure. Similar trends clearly appear in Peruzzi's drawings, but Vignola was the first to turn the *concetto* into reality. In this context there come to mind the varying connections of the circle and polygon at Caprarola.

The interior oval of S. Anna is articulated by eight columns set in the wall [186]. The intercolumnar spaces, where the altars and niches are situated, are wider than those in the diagonals with the low entrances into the subsidiary chapels.[29] Thus in the same way as in the round court of Caprarola, a rhythm of alternating narrow and wide intercolumniations articulates the wall. The main front of S. Anna [187] and the side façade on the via Angelica, a street laid out shortly before the church, have the flat pilasters which are Vignola's trade-mark. The two fronts – they are, after all, the sides of a rectangle – have, in spite of the difference of length, five bays each. The disposition of these bays differs as much as that in the interior. Thus in this centrally planned building, not only is the interior unrelated to the exterior, but the system of the main façade is also unrelated to that of the side façade. In Bramante's plans for St Peter's, in Leonardo da Vinci's designs for centrally planned buildings, or even in S. Maria presso S. Biagio at Montepulciano, on the other hand, 'all parts are equally grouped round one point',[30] and in such a way that 'every individual form seems logically related to all the other elements . . . by its situation in the total plan'.[31]

Vignola's 'invention' had successors in Rome and northern Italy in the sixteenth century. The importance of the oval plan in the work of Bernini and Borromini and in Austrian and German architecture of the seventeenth and eighteenth centuries cannot be taken into consideration here.

THE PERIOD FROM 1575 TO 1600

In the last quarter of the sixteenth century, building activity in Rome rose almost to fever-pitch. The two popes Gregory XIII (1572–85) and Sixtus (1585–90) were both men of energy and initiative and had at heart the continuation and completion of St Peter's (cf. above, pp. 98–101), of the Gesù, and of the Capitoline palazzi; new wings were added to the Vatican, and in the Belvedere Court Sixtus V built the new library between the lower and upper terraces, which destroyed Bramante's great architectural perspective. With the same ruthlessness, Sixtus V demolished the ancient Lateran Palace and replaced it by a new and dull building. Many of the present main vistas of the city are due to this Pope and the new streets he cut through it [43] – the via Sistina still bears his name. He set up the obelisks in the Piazza del Popolo and in front of S. Maria Maggiore and the new Lateran Palace, and had the obelisk in front of St Peter's removed to its present site. The erection of the obelisks as a *point de vue* at the ends of the new streets and in front of great churches

was not purposeless. Their *interpretatio christiana* was part of a programme for the 'restauratio' of Rome in which the political and religious trends of the Counter-Reformation were mingled with a close study of sources and monuments characteristic of the period. Thus a large number of old churches was repaired or renovated; 'confessiones' – imagined to be a feature *more antico*, i.e. as open crypts – were constructed in front of the high altars to house the relics of patron saints;[32] and Sixtus V crowned the columns of Trajan and Marcus Aurelius with figures of St Peter and St Paul.

GIACOMO DELLA PORTA

In the Roman architecture of the last quarter of the century, the first name that comes to mind is that of Giacomo della Porta (1533?–1602). As 'architetto del popolo romano' he became surveyor of the works on the Capitol after Michelangelo's death. During Vignola's lifetime, Cardinal Alessandro Farnese commissioned Porta to design the façade of the Gesù [180]; he executed the transept, dome, and choir of the church, which was completed in 1584 [179]. In 1573, after Vignola's death, he was appointed architect-in-chief of St Peter's, where he built the mortuary chapel for Gregory XIII and the corresponding one for Clement VIII. Both chapels had been planned in 1569 at the latest, to judge from Dupérac's engravings, to have minor domes, the

188. Giacomo della Porta: Rome, S. Maria ai Monti, begun 1580

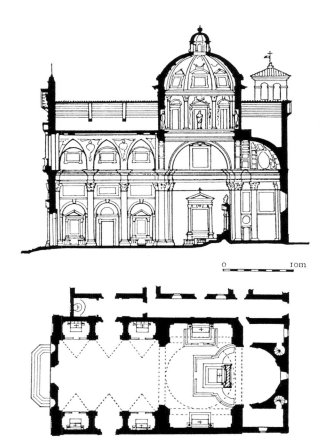

189. Giacomo della Porta: Rome, S. Maria ai Monti, begun 1580, section and plan

conception of which probably goes back to Vignola. Finally, after the demolition of the so-called Rossellino-Bramante choir, Porta built the west arm of the crossing[33] and vaulted the main dome in 1588–90.[34] He also succeeded Vignola in the final work on the Palazzo Farnese.

In all these buildings Porta appears as a thoroughly reliable if not very inspired architect, with a brilliant command of the problems of construction and a sympathy for the buildings already begun. He is 'the chief disciple of Michelangelo in the later sixteenth century. On his own, Porta rarely exhibits the grandiose power and magnificence of Michelangelo'.[35] His buildings are marked by a sober monumentality: the detail is less subtle than Vignola's. Porta's model is not to be sought in antiquity; his capitals, portals, and window surrounds are a standardized simplification of Michelangelo's formal idiom at St Peter's and the Capitol.

The comparison between Porta's Gesù façade and Vignola's, which was not executed, but has been preserved in an engraving, is one of the standard tasks in the teaching of architectural history [180, 181].[36] Porta's language is by far the blunter. By reducing the number of niches and statues and duplicating all members next to the main portal, he deprived the single members of their individuality. Stepped up both in relief and height, Porta's scheme leads to a climax in the centre bay, where one finds the portal, the emblem of the Jesuits, the double pediment, the large upper window, the shield with the Farnese arms, and finally the Holy Cross.

Vignola had tried to preserve as much as possible the equilibrium of an ancient temple front. Compared with

Porta's ponderous double pilasters, Vignola's rhythmic system of niches, portals, and pilasters is far more complex, the interplay of verticals and horizontals subtler, the treatment of the surface richer. Many characteristic elements of Porta's final design already occur in Vignola's various projects for the façade. It was left to the younger architect to accomplish the synthesis of his predecessor's ideas. It is tempting to assume that Vignola's classical training prevented him from reaching this synthesis. By doubling the pediment over the main portal Porta certainly abandoned what may be called the utopia of the ancient temple front applied to the Christian church. The central portal and the window above it receive such a powerful emphasis from their size and framework that the central bay of the façade looks like one vertical unit.

In a similar way, Della Porta stresses the vertical members in the small church of S. Maria ai Monti [188], which he designed himself, and which was begun in 1580. Its plan is a simplified variant of that of the Gesù: three chapels on each side of the nave, a transept aligned with the chapels, a semicircular apse [189]. It is just because of this similarity that the differences stand out. The entrances to the chapels are framed in single and not in double pilasters as in the Gesù, and these pilasters correspond to projections in the entablature. Owing to these interruptions in the horizontals, the nave is not, as in the Gesù, a uniform hall, but a space with vertical divisions. Moreover, the ratio between the inner length and inner height of the interior is different (Gesù about 8:3, S. Maria ai Monti about 2:1).

In 1591 the Theatine Order began the building of its own

Roman mother church, S. Andrea della Valle, near the Gesù. It took nearly thirty years to complete, but its main elements must have been established from the beginning. Quite early the church was regarded as a rival to the Gesù, and it is in fact related to it in size and type. Father Fabrizio Grimaldi (1543–1613), a native of southern Italy, collaborated with Della Porta in the design; the contribution of Della Porta is proved convincingly not only by the sources but by style.[37] For all its relationship to the Gesù, the interior shows the same tendency to vertical emphasis as S. Maria ai Monti. The pillars resemble those of the Campidoglio façades; the pilasters, again not coupled, have half-pilasters recessed a little on both sides [190], and these bundled pilasters, which are expressed in a projection in the main architrave, are carried through the vault as transverse arches. The entrances to the chapels rise almost to the height of the architrave, so that their *outer* wall – again in striking contrast to the Gesù – is seen as the actual spatial boundary. The steeper proportions of the dome and choir underline the stressed verticality of the nave. The bearing function of the pillars is emphasized by the grouped pilasters and can be interpreted dynamically; the spacious hall of the Gesù, bounded by a balanced system of double pilasters and an unbroken entablature, can be interpreted statically.

Della Porta was also interested in the problem of the centrally planned church. An unrealized project for the church of the university of Rome shows a rotunda with a comparatively steep dome.[38] In 1582, Della Porta began the memorial church of S. Maria Scala Coeli, next to S. Paolo alle Tre Fontane, an octagon vaulted by a flattened dome,

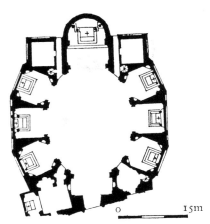

191. Francesco Capriani da Volterra: Rome, S. Giacomo degli Incurabili, begun 1592, plan

with alternating broader and narrower sides. Three of the broader sides swell out into semicircular apses; the fourth contains the entrance.[39]

More impressive than these centrally planned buildings, in which Della Porta returns to traditional types of plan, is the façade of the church of S. Atanasio dei Greci, founded by Gregory XIII. The two-storeyed front of the nave is flanked by three-storeyed towers. This is the first double-towered façade in Rome, though the idea already appears in the early designs for St Peter's and later in Vignola's projects for the Gesù. The upper parts of the façade of SS. Trinità dei Monti, which is of the same type and was built shortly after

190. Giacomo della Porta and others: Rome, S. Andrea della Valle, begun 1591

192. Francesco Capriani da Volterra: Rome, S. Giacomo degli Incurabili, begun 1592

193. (*left*) Francesco Capriani da Volterra: Rome, S. Giacomo degli Incurabili, begun 1592

194. (*bottom left*) Francesco Capriani da Volterra: Project for the plan of S. Giacomo degli Incurabili, Rome, 1590. Stockholm, Nationalmuseum (inv. no. CC 2071)

195. (*bottom right*) Workshop of Francesco Capriani da Volterra: Project for the plan of S. Giacomo degli Incurabili, Rome. Vienna, Albertina (Rom 349)

S. Atanasio, may also have originated in a design by Della Porta.[40]

Della Porta simplified Vignola's subtle compositions; his system of articulation is more easily intelligible, his decoration 'modern', i.e. rather Michelangelesque than antique, and his buildings lack the speculative element which comes out for example in Vignola's predilection for the oval. It was not only his masterly command of his métier but his turning away from Vignola and his profound understanding for the late works of Michelangelo which made Della Porta the leading Roman architect of the seventies and eighties. At first sight his work does not look particularly individual; his peculiarly 'Roman' style – Della Porta was the only prominent architect of his time to be born in Rome – becomes clear if his *œuvre* is compared with those of Vignola's followers who worked beside him in the city.

OTHER ARCHITECTS

Francesco Capriani da Volterra (*c.* 1530–1594) and Ottavio Mascarino (1536–1606) may be regarded as Vignola's pupils. In 1565–6 Capriani was active at Guastalla, the residence of a branch of the Gonzaga, in 1570–80 on the

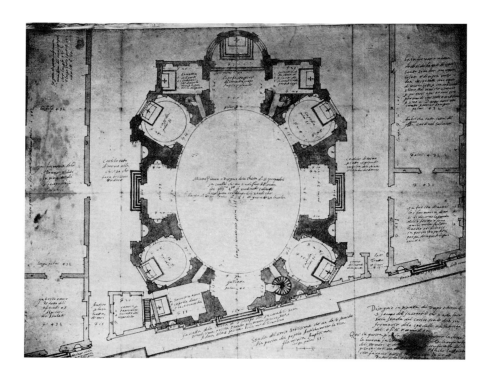

196. Francesco Capriani da Volterra: Project for the Palazzo Gaetani, Rome, 1581, plan of ground floor. Florence, Uffizi (A 6733)

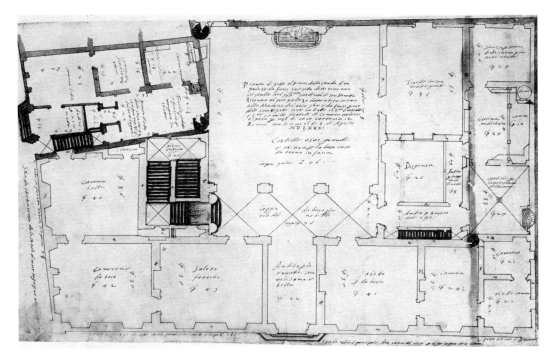

Villa d'Este at Tivoli, and subsequently for the Gaetani in Rome.[41] In Volterra's most important Roman work, the hospital church of S. Giacomo degli Incurabili on the Corso,[42] the oval plan appears for the first time in an ecclesiastical building on a large scale (along axis of the oval *c.* 25.5 m. or 83 feet 8 in., short axis *c.* 18.7 m., or 61 feet 4 in.) [191]. The side-thrust of the dome covered by a timber roof is borne by volutes. There is no outer shell. In the interior [192, 193], the main cornice, as in the Gesù, is broken at both ends of the long axis, i.e. at the entrance and at the choir, by tall arches which reach up into the zone of the vaulting. Thus the long axis is given a marked predominance. The entrances to side chapels are stepped after the fashion of a triumphal arch.

The building differs in many important respects from Volterra's project of 1590, which has been preserved in Stockholm [194]. The double pilasters which, in the drawing, articulated all the piers in the oval interior, are only present in the finished building as a frame for the entrance and the choir; the openings leading to the side chapels are flanked by single pilasters. In this way greater stress is given to the longitudinal axis, the piers lose some of their plastic force

197. Francesco Capriani da Volterra: Project for the Palazzo Gaetani, Rome, 1581, façade. Florence, Uffizi (A 6722)

198. Ottaviano Mascarino: Rome, Quirinal Palace, courtyard, 1577–85

and structural expression, and the rhythm of the wall comes from the grouping of the pilasters. A similar change can be seen in the exterior. Instead of the multiple, somewhat skimpy articulation of the façades of the courtyard in the design there are now unadorned, unarticulated walls; the exterior is merely a shell for the interior. Obviously these changes reflect Volterra's final design; they appear, together with an

199. Ottaviano Mascarino: Rome, Quirinal Palace, staircase, 1577–85

unexecuted project for the façade, in a drawing of 1595–6 [195], and they are an open rejection of the 'classical' ideal of identical treatment of the interior and exterior of the building. That ideal is still apparent in Volterra's earlier designs which adopt a large number of details from the famous Bramante project for St Peter's, which had become known through Serlio. The choice of an oval plan for the church is certainly incomprehensible without Vignola's pioneer work, but Volterra first aimed at uniting the new spatial form with piers which were already out of date in the late sixteenth century. He then resolved this incongruity, and, in doing so, created the model for the oval churches of the seventeenth and eighteenth centuries, which were based on the completed building of S. Giacomo.

With the exception of the Palazzo Borghese, which will be considered later, Roman palazzo façades conform to the type of the Palazzo Farnese; the architect's hand can be traced mainly in the details of the portals and window surrounds. A characteristic example may be seen in Volterra's dated design of 1581 for Cardinal Enrico Gaetani's palazzo [196, 197], which is distinguished from many other similar buildings by the shape of the balcony over the main entrance.[43] The detailed text to the plan shows the disposition of the various rooms: on the ground floor, on either side of the courtyard, storerooms, the kitchen, the huge chimney, and the hearth; on the façade 'salotti' and 'camere' (living rooms and bedrooms); on the piano nobile the 'sala grande' and the 'galleria' for state receptions. The great hall was to measure 15.5 by 8.7 m. (51 by 29 feet), the gallery, at the time an indispensable part of the palazzo, 14 m. by 6 m. (46 by 20 feet). According to the text accompanying this plan, two nephews of the Cardinal were to live in the palazzo too; in all probability the second floor was intended for them.

Like his countryman Vignola, a friend of his youth, Ottaviano Mascarino (1536–1606) of Bologna began his career as a painter.[44] Soon after the elevation of Gregory XIII, himself a native of Bologna, Mascarino went to Rome; from 1577 to 1585 he was active on the Vatican and Quirinal buildings as the Pope's architect. According to a remark made by Della Porta in 1593, Mascarino and Volterra were regarded as 'the best architects . . . he makes no distinction between the two of them, and both could be put in the same box and taken out by chance, and there are none better in Rome'.[45]

The Vatican Palace was considerably enlarged during the pontificate of Gregory XIII. On the side of the Cortile di S. Damaso facing the Piazza S. Pietro, the second wing, begun under Pius IV, and adjoining Bramante's loggias at right angles, was completed; the forms of the older wing were adopted practically unaltered [9]. Further, under Gregory XIII the west range of the Belvedere Court was completed after nearly eighty years of building, and a fourth storey added, which Bramante had not planned; it is known to visitors to the Vatican Museum as the Galleria delle Carte Geografiche. For the most part, these enterprises were carried out under Mascarino's supervision. He realized Bramante's ideas in the Belvedere Court just as Della Porta had realized Michelangelo's ideas for the Campidoglio and the dome of St Peter's; the architectural details have been 'modernized' and the rooms arranged in accordance with

200. (*right*) Giacomo Barozzi da
Vignola and others: Rome,
Palazzo Borghese, façade, begun
c. 1560

201. (*bottom right*) Martino
Lunghi the Elder: Rome, Palazzo
Borghese, courtyard, 1586
(begun earlier)

their new functions, but the basic conception of Bramante's original designs 'never ceased to be the guiding principle . . . it is to the credit rather than to the detriment of Bramante's conception that it excited future generations not only to complete a project that might have remained inchoate, but to find in it the opportunity to express the changing climate of taste and requirements of function'.[46]

In the Quirinal, the summer residence of the popes since Gregory XIII, Mascarino erected the two-storeyed loggia which remains as the north range of the present courtyard [198]. Originally flanked by two flat projections, it was the garden front of a free-standing villa of the Farnesina type: when the complex was enlarged, it was deprived of that function. Towards the end of Gregory XIII's reign it was provided with the towering Belvedere which still crowns the whole Quirinal group. The individual forms of the loggia and the Belvedere are closely connected with those of the façade of Caprarola; even Mascarino's famous oval staircase [199] is unimaginable without Vignola's circular staircase at Caprarola [174].[47] Mascarino also adopted Vignola's ideas in several designs for oval churches.[48] It is therefore surprising that two generally reliable seventeenth-century authors should attribute to him one of the most original buildings of his time, the nave of S. Salvatore in Lauro, a nave with four flat chapels on either side, and with a tunnel-vault supported by double columns. The motif of columns standing free in front of the wall probably derives from Michelangelo's church in the Baths of Diocletian. The double columns invest the comparatively small space with a monumentality unequalled in Mascarino's other work.[49]

Another successor of Vignola was Martino Lunghi the Elder, a Lombard (before 1540?–91). His name first appears in 1568 in the building records of the Dominican church of S. Croce, founded by Pius V in his birthplace, Bosco Marengo, near Alessandria, and begun in 1566.[50] The plan

202. Domenico Fontana: Rome, Lateran Palace, begun 1586

and elevation of S. Croce have many details in common with Vignola's Roman churches – indeed Vignola, who worked on the Vatican Palace and St Peter's under Pius V, may have collaborated in the designs. It is likely that Lunghi, who had probably been working in Genoa, was first summoned to Bosco Marengo to supervise building operations. The motif of the tripartite lunette window which dominates the façade already appears in Antonio da Sangallo's designs for St Peter's, and is frequent in Vignola's late work.[51] From 1569 Lunghi was active in Rome; in the early years of Gregory XIII's reign he conducted work on the Vatican and Quirinal, which was taken over in 1577 by Ottaviano Mascarino.

In 1578, the year after its medieval predecessor had been struck by lightning, Lunghi was commissioned to rebuild the tower of the Palazzo del Senatore on the Campidoglio [140]. The most important building on which he worked, however, is the Palazzo Borghese, though it is very difficult to identify his part in it. The main façade [200] was erected soon after 1560, i.e. about the same time as Caprarola; the client, also a native of Bologna, was a protégé of Cardinal Alessandro Farnese. There are analogies in Vignola's work to the details which diverge from the Roman idiom. The façade is five-storeyed, like that of the Palazzo Farnese at Piacenza (see above, p. 116). The portal, flanked by free-standing columns, tallies with a plate in the *Cinque Ordini* which shows a project by Vignola for the portal of the Cancelleria. The central window is emphasized by a blind arch, flanking pilasters, and pediment. Thus the central axis in both storeys is articulated on its own, as in the Villa di Papa Giulio. It has

been suggested that the design for the façade should be attributed to Vignola, and that its weaknesses may be explained by the fact that he did not supervise the execution.[52]

The fame of the Palazzo Borghese is due less to its façade than to its courtyard with the double columns [201]. This motif, which is to be found quite frequently in contemporary Genoese and Lombard architecture, is without precedent in Rome and had few successors there. The account books give no clear indication of whether the double columns were already part of the courtyard side of the façade range, which was begun about 1560, or were only introduced by Lunghi, who took charge of the second stage of building in 1586. The latter seems more probable to me, the more so as the documents of Bosco Marengo show that Lunghi was in touch with Genoa. In any case, Lunghi continued the motif along both side ranges – to that extent, at least, one of the finest courtyards in Rome is his work. The high aesthetic quality of the courtyard is certainly difficult to place in Lunghi's verified work, for instance the façade of S. Girolamo degli Schiavoni.[53]

The one Roman architect of the late sixteenth century who was famous in his lifetime is Domenico Fontana (1543– 1607). That fame was admittedly based above all on the removal and re-erection of the obelisk in the Piazza di S. Pietro, an engineering achievement which was admired by experts and the general public alike.[54] But Fontana kept up an uncommonly widespread activity in architecture too. It contributed to his good fortune that Cardinal Felice Peretti, in whose service he was, became, as Sixtus V, the most

203. Domenico Fontana: Rome,
Vatican Library, 1587–9

zealous and energetic patron of architecture of the period, and entrusted his architectural projects to Fontana. Thus Fontana played a most important part in the three papal palaces, the Vatican, the Quirinal, and the Lateran, the latter a new building constructed to his design [202]. He laid out new streets; together with his brother Giovanni, he conducted to Rome the first new aqueduct it had had since antiquity, and, with the Moses Fountain of the Acqua Felice, gave the city its first monumental water-display. The new Vatican Library in the Belvedere Court [9, 203] and the Pope's mausoleum, the Cappella Sistina adjoining S. Maria Maggiore, are his work too.

When Sixtus V died in 1590 not all his plans had been realized,[55] yet what remains of the five years of his pontificate is astounding enough as an achievement both of organization and finance.[56] Even as a cardinal, Sixtus had obviously come to realize Fontana's talent for organization in the building of his Villa Montalto-Peretti.[57] That talent even covered stylistic 'organization'. The time-limits set by the Pope were so narrow that they could be kept to only if the formal vocabulary was standardized and reduced to a small number of types. This is the explanation of the uniform, even monotonous character of this thoroughly derivative and entirely unoriginal architecture, which adopted its types from established models and its articulations from Vignola's *Cinque Ordini*. Fontana's lack of imagination was admirably suited to the impatience of the Pope, who cared only for efficiency

and never took time to consider the slow maturing of an artistic idea.

And yet it would be a mistake to judge the achievement of the client and his architect merely as *multa non multum*. When the Pope had the small Presepe Chapel in S. Maria Maggiore (since ancient times identified with the crib of Bethlehem) removed to the centre of his mortuary chapel, and the shrine of the Host erected above it, with himself kneeling before the sacrament, he invested the building with a historical and theological significance which cannot be judged by purely architectural standards of criticism. The same may be said of the obelisk brought to Rome by Augustus and erected by Sixtus in front of the choir of S. Maria Maggiore. The inscription records the birth of Christ in the reign of Augustus, the Flight into Egypt, the Pax Augusta, and the crib brought from Bethlehem to Rome, the centre of the ancient and the Christian worlds; thus the cross on the obelisk symbolizes the triumph of Christianity over paganism as well as the manifold relationships between these monuments.[58]

Soon after the Pope's death Fontana went to Naples, where he remained in the viceroy's service till his death. But his Neapolitan designs, for instance the Palazzo Reale, lack the austerity and sober gravity which were peculiar to Sixtus V and his buildings. Fontana's nephew, Carlo Maderno, who took over his work in Rome, had a greater affinity to Della Porta than to his uncle.[59]

CHAPTER 11

Northern Italy: Genoa, Milan, and Piedmont

GALEAZZO ALESSI IN GENOA

Like Palladio and Vignola, Galeazzo Alessi (1512–72), a native of Perugia, is one of the great architects of the period. His buildings are of a typological and stylistic importance for Genoa and Milan equal to Palladio's palazzi and villas for the Veneto. However, unlike his great contemporaries, Alessi wrote no treatise; this may be one of the reasons why we have no satisfactory account of his *œuvre* and his career.[1]

Alessi's first buildings in Genoa show him in full command of the repertoire of contemporary Roman architecture. S. Maria di Carignano, a centrally planned church situated on a hill commanding a panorama of the city, cannot be imagined without Sangallo's and Michelangelo's projects for St Peter's. The plan of the Villa Cambiaso (1548), with its three-bay loggia flanked by projecting wings, follows a type which originated in all probability with Peruzzi. Alessi's familiarity with Sanmicheli's palazzi at Verona is demonstrated by the superb articulation of the façade [204]: Doric half-columns on the ground floor, fluted Ionic pilasters on the upper storey, the doubling of the pilasters giving the order a forcefulness which is reminiscent of Raphael.[2] The disposition of the interior is no less masterly. The great salone is situated above the entrance loggia and the adjoining vestibule, its vaulting reaching up to the roof, so that the room is also lighted by the upper mezzanine windows. Adjoining the rear of the salone is the loggia of the upper storey, its vaulting supported by two pairs of columns [205]. The walls of the loggia show the same combination of monumental austerity and rich ornament as the façade: the soffits of the arches are covered with ornament, termini fill the spandrels between the arches, and the crowning cornice is outstandingly lavish.

The church of S. Maria di Carignano, planned in 1549, stands on a hill which belonged to the Sauli, and a number of anecdotes show that this church which they founded is to be regarded primarily as a monument raised to their own family.[3] Thus there were no historical and liturgical conditions, as there were in St Peter's, to prevent the realization of an ideal centrally planned church. The founders' wishes coincided perfectly with the architect's ideas. In a letter to his patron, Alessi calls the church 'my first-born creation, and of all my daughters the dearest'.

The square plan [206], as in Michelangelo's project for St Peter's, encompasses the Greek cross of the main arms and the four chapels in the angles; from outside, the apse, encased in a rectangle of masonry, appears as a projection. The main dome over the crossing is surrounded by four minor domes and two campanili instead of the originally planned four [207].[4] The tops of the towers reach up as high as the crown of the great dome, while the four minor domes hardly rise above the church roof. The crossing piers are unusually massive [208]; the diameter of the dome is only a little wider than the arms of the crossing. Here Alessi drew his con-clusions from experiences in the building of St Peter's,[5] so that inside the dome looks somewhat cramped; in spite of its height it does not appear to be the centre of the building, but merely a strong vertical accent above the junction of the four arms of the cross. Outside, the arms of the cross are provided with façades; their giant pilasters carry pediments with large lunette windows.

Alessi's strictly classical project was not entirely carried through, even in the execution of the façades, and the lavish sculptural ornament of the seventeenth century finally modified the effect of the original design. All the same, S. Maria di Carignano, along with the churches in Todi and Montepulciano, may be regarded as the finest centrally planned building of the sixteenth century. Like Alessi's other Genoese works, its fame spread far beyond the bounds of Italy, thanks to its inclusion in Rubens's volume of engravings published in 1622 under the title *Palazzi di Genova*.

Although Alessi's activity in Genoa lasted less than ten years,[6] his style had a lasting influence on Genoese architecture. This *stile alessiano* can be identified most clearly in the palazzi in the Strada Nuova, now the via Garibaldi, which according to Vasari was planned by Alessi. This street is the Genoese equivalent to contemporary town-planning enterprises in Venice, Rome, and Bologna.

The Genoese patriciate had lived, from time immemorial, in the crowded districts round the harbour, but the houses, for the most part fortified and cramped, could no longer satisfy the new demand for decorum and comfort. Spanish ceremonial demanded *grandezza* even in the architectural background of life. In 1550 the Doge issued a decree ordering the layout of a new street *in ornamentum civitatis* in a comparatively vacant area at the the edge of the old town. A committee of seven patricians supervised the necessary expropriations, demolitions, and ground-levellings. In 1558 the first building sites were sold, the profits going to the renovation of the cathedral and the construction of the Molo. Between 1558 and 1570 eleven of the fifteen palazzi in the street, which was 225 m. (250 yards) long and 7.5 m. (25 feet) broad, were finished. Originally the street ended at a garden wall. It was therefore not planned as a thoroughfare.[7] All the frontages are aligned along the street [209]; alleys 3.5 m. (12 feet) wide separated each palazzo from its neighbour. Obviously the height as well as the width of the façades was prescribed, and the portals of opposite palazzi had to face each other. However the owners were free to arrange the interiors as they wished – all the palazzi have two main storeys with mezzanines – and there are variations in the placing of the staircases, in the height of the storeys, and in the courtyards; moreover the rise in the land to the rear led to numerous differences in the arrangement of vestibules, courtyard arcades, terraces, and staircases.

For several buildings, the architectural history and the architect are unknown.[8] The street was laid out by Bernardino da Cantone (mentioned between 1537 and

204. (*above*) Galeazzo Alessi: Genoa, Villa Cambiaso, 1548, façade

205. (*right*) Galeazzo Alessi: Genoa, Villa Cambiaso, 1548, loggia

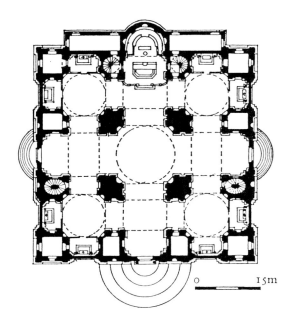

206. (*above*) Galeazzo Alessi: Genoa, S. Maria di Carignano, designed 1549, plan

207. (*right*) Galeazzo Alessi: Genoa, S. Maria di Carignano, designed 1549

208. (*below left*) Galeazzo Alessi: Genoa, S. Maria di Carignano, designed 1549

209. (*below right*) Genoa, Strada Nuova, begun 1558

1576), who was employed by the city administration and had also worked under Alessi on S. Maria di Carignano.[9] Other architects mentioned in the sources are the brothers Giovanni and Domenico Ponsello, who had also worked on the church, Giovanni Battista Castello, il Bergamasco, and the brothers Giovanni and Rocco Lurago.[10] Castello's works (c. 1510–1569) are notable for their excellent stucco-work on the façades and vaults.[11] The Palazzo Doria Tursi has always been admired for its imaginative handling of the rise in level behind the façade: a straight flight of steps leads from the vestibule into the long, colonnaded courtyard, and from the back of the courtyard another flight leads to a landing, from which branching flights lead to the loggias of the piano nobile. This plan was later repeated in the famous courtyard of Genoa University.[12]

The function and the special quality of the Strada Nuova emerge best when it is compared with the palazzo façades on the Canal Grande in Venice. In both cases the feudal nobility had created its own adequate expression in architecture. This process, which took several centuries in Venice, was completed by the Genoese nobility in a single resolute act. It seems to me that the whole project was also based on a perfectly conscious artistic conception. In spite of many differences, the two rows of ten façades erected in the first stage of building look like a single composition; for all the many variants, a rational plan stands out clearly, as Vasari, the first to appreciate the Strada Nuova, realized. His attribution of the layout as a whole to Alessi seems thoroughly credible, and it has been restated recently by the leading authority on the subject.[13]

The biggest palazzo designed by Alessi for a Genoese patron stands in the centre of Milan [210]. The client, Tommaso Marino, had acquired a fortune in Milan by banking and tax-farming; in an inscription on a building he calls himself Duke of Terranuova, a title which he had acquired for the huge sum of 300,000 scudi.[14] The size and luxury of this town mansion of a *nouveau riche* are unprecedented among the patriciate of the period: the area it covers approximately equals that of Sixtus V's Lateran Palace in Rome; the three-storey façades [211] are respectively of seventeen and eleven bays, of a width of 62 m. and 54 m. and a height of 23 m. (203 and 177 feet, 75 feet); the salone, situated between two courtyards, is about 22 m. long and 11 m. wide (72 by 36 feet).[15] The façade has the same

210. (*above*) Galeazzo Alessi: Milan, Palazzo Marini, begun 1558, plan

211. (*right*) Galeazzo Alessi: Milan, Palazzo Marini, begun 1558, façade

212. Galeazzo Alessi: Milan, Palazzo Marini, begun 1558, courtyard

'classical' system of articulation as the Villa Cambiaso in Genoa, yet in the present case the subordinate elements take on a curious life of their own, so that ornament drowns structure. The window aedicules on the ground floor are squeezed in as an Ionic minor order between the Doric half-columns of the main order. The architrave of the aedicules consists of boldly projecting stones, and the shafts of the columns stick in their blocks. On the piano nobile the pilasters of the window surrounds taper downwards, and the gaps in the broken pediments open on to grotesque human or animal heads which, in their turn, act as brackets for the surrounds of the mezzanine windows. On the top storey the pilasters of the main order taper too, and the flutings, laid on as strips, converge downwards. Further, in place of an orthodox capital there is a ⊓-shaped block at the top of the pilaster, bearing a gigantic head framed by brackets.

Every pair of the twenty-four columns of the courtyard supports an architrave which forms the impost of the round-arched arcade, so that the heavy piers of the upper storey stand on the intercolumnar spaces of the ground floor [212]. The contrast between the profuse ornament of the Ionic piers and the plainness of the Doric columns is intentional. For the theorist, the Ionic order is feminine, the Doric masculine; accordingly, there are lion's heads on the brackets over the Doric columns, but caryatids in the Ionic upper storey.

The stylistic sources of this 'painterly' architecture are to be found in the work of the Raphael circle, for instance the stuccoed façade of the Palazzo dall'Aquila, the Vatican logge, or again in Giulio Romano's works in Rome and Mantua. In Rome, the painterly trend as it appears in the middle of the century, especially in the work of Pirro Ligorio,[16] yielded to the more austere style of Michelangelo and Vignola. In Lombardy, on the other hand, with its innate love of the lavish decoration of flat surfaces, it flourished. This Lombard delight in ornament may also explain why the anthropo-morphization of architectural members (cf. Alessi's termini in the courtyard of the Palazzo Marino) did not remain confined to the decoration of villas and public fountains, as it did in Rome.

Alessi's name appears in the documents of nearly all the important buildings which were in progress in Milan about 1560. His prestige was, in all probability, based on the effect of the Palazzo Marino. Further, Alessi was able to enter into the heritage of the two most important architects active in Milan before his arrival.

CRISTOFORO LOMBARDINO AND DOMENICO GIUNTI IN MILAN

On the death of the last Sforza in 1536, the dukedom of Milan passed into the hands of the Spanish branch of the house of Habsburg. After the political situation had settled down, it became possible to continue building work which had been suspended during the long wars.

In the thirties and forties the most outstanding architect was Cristoforo Lombardi or Lombardino (first mentioned in 1510; d. 1555), who had been active since 1510 as a sculptor, but from 1526 till his death was architect-in-chief of the cathedral.[17] As the building of the cathedral lagged during his term of office, Lombardino had time to take on other commissions, including the preparation of designs for the façade of the Certosa di Pavia and the supervision of their execution.[18] In 1545 he collaborated with Giulio Romano on projects for the façade of S. Petronio at Bologna.[19] In Milan there is verified evidence of his work on the Palazzo Stampa di Soncino[20] and the church of S. Caterina alla Chiusa,[21] now demolished. His work is notable for a surprising classical 'purism', which shows that Lombardino had been in Rome about 1515; it is the same phase of style as can be seen in Giuliano da Sangallo's designs for the façades of S. Lorenzo in Florence and that by Cola dall' Amatrice for S. Bernardino at L'Aquila (cf. above, p. 44). The most impressive Milanese example of this style is the great dome over the centrally planned church of S. Maria della Passione,[22] begun by Battagio in 1489 [213]. The exterior has the high tiburio – in the present case octagonal and two-storeyed – embracing the vaulting which had been traditional in Lombardy since the Middle Ages. The sides of the octagon have Lombardino's characteristic articulation by twin half-columns, round-arched and rectangular niches, and aedicules, and there are traces which show that the remaining surfaces were ornamented by painting. The tiburio, traditional in form but modern in articulation, surrounds an eight-sided domical vault, which is steeper than is usual in Lombardy. The articulation of the interior of the dome is also an innovation. The angles between the chapels are set with half-columns whose entablature projects. They continue into the drum as wall-strips, and into the vault of the dome as ribs. Thus, unlike older Lombard usage, there is a marked stress on the vertical aspects of the dome. Its curve recalls Sangallo's almost contemporary project for St Peter's, but Lombardino is more consistent than Sangallo, since he omits the coffering of the dome. The decorative scheme of the Pantheon dome is not suited to a domical vault.[23]

From 1533 to 1555 Lombardino worked on S. Maria presso S. Celso, superintending the enlargement of the church by aisles and an ambulatory.[24] At that time the form of the façade, itself enlarged by these additions, must have been discussed too. A sketch in the Victoria and Albert Museum shows a project of the kind which stylistically and chronologically finds its place in Lombardino's œuvre [214].[25] The façade is treated as a two-storeyed flat portico. For the unusual use of the Corinthian order for the ground floor the project had to conform to the existing Corinthian atrium. The consistent purism with which the scheme of the antique temple front is here transferred to a Christian church can only be paralleled in this period in the work of Palladio.

In 1547 the Viceroy of Milan, Ferrante Gonzaga, acquired the Villa Simonetta, which was situated outside the town gates. Ferrante was conducting a lively correspondence with the humanist Paolo Giovio, who himself possessed a famous villa on Lake Como. After a visit to the Villa Simonetta, Giovio wrote to its owner 'there is a wealth of flowing water there. There are fish-ponds, aviaries, and all kinds of menageries such as Varro and Columella report in ancient times.... We have given this lovely place the name nymphaeum, because it is the name given by an ancient Roman to his own estate, which was surrounded with flowering gardens and much water.... Master Domenico da Prato will assuredly find a thousand delicious concetti to adorn the

213. Cristoforo Lombardino: Milan, S. Maria della Passione, dome, completed probably c. 1550

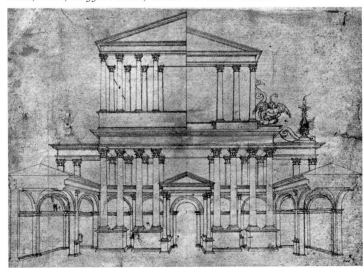

214. Cristoforo Lombardino: Project for the façade of S. Maria presso S. Celso, Milan, c. 1550. London, Victoria and Albert Museum

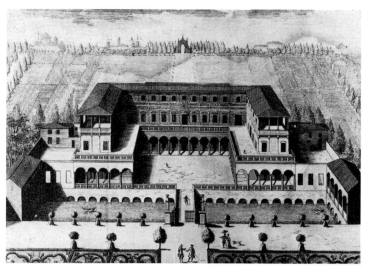

215. Domenico Giunti: Milan, Villa Simonetta, garden façade, after 1547, engraving by del Re

216. Domenico Giunti: Milan, Villa Simonetta, façade, after 1547

place . . . above all he must see that the entrance side looks dignified and stately.'[26]

The architect mentioned here was Domenico Giunti of Prato (1506–60), whom Ferrante Gonzaga had already employed in Sicily and had brought to Milan in 1546.[27] The Simonetta is the only well-known secular building by Giunti [215]. He considerably enlarged the layout of 1547 by building side wings which created a U-shaped forecourt for the old façade. To the ground floor of the courtyard and the narrow sides of the new wings he added a columned loggia; on the top was a terrace which opened a view on to the adjoining fish-ponds, gardens, and service ranges. The original rear became the new façade [216]; it was invested with the 'dignità e pomposa vista' required by Giovio by means of a new three-storeyed portico. The ground floor has round-arched arcades on pillars with Doric half-columns, the piano nobile Tuscan columns and an architrave, the second storey Corinthian columns carrying a timber ceiling.[28]

The owner's delight in country life, the literary culture of

217. Domenico Giunti: Milan, S. Angelo, 1552–5

his circle, and the skill of a classically trained architect combined to create a work which was no less near to antique models in function and form than the Villa Madama or Pius IV's Casino. Stylistically Giunti's portico façade[29] is closely related to Lombardino's almost contemporary design for S. Maria presso S. Celso [214]. The Roman analogy to this Milanese classicism is Pirro Ligorio's archaeological style.

Ferrante Gonzaga and his architect played an important part in the general layout of the city. When the fortifications were renovated, the suburbs which had developed outside the medieval walls were incorporated in the city itself. In the centre, the piazza in front of the cathedral was enlarged by the demolition of the old church of S. Tecla. Since the Franciscan monastery of S. Angelo had been sacrificed to the new bastions, the viceroy founded a new building within the walls, which was designed by Giunti and begun in 1552. Work proceeded so rapidly that the new church of S. Angelo could be consecrated as early as 1555.[30] In this case Giunti recast on very original lines the type of the aisleless friary church which was familiar to him from his native Tuscany [217]. The nave is spanned by a tunnel-vault. The partition walls between the chapels are set with fluted Ionic pilasters, and the transept is cut off from the nave by a comparatively low triumphal arch and broad pilasters. An important element in the spatial effect is the illumination by large round windows in the penetrations of the vaulting and the tall clerestory above the cornice. In spite of the long row of chapels, one has an impression of a wide, spacious hall. The transept too has a tunnel-vault, but its axis runs at right angles to that of the nave, so that it becomes an almost independent spatial element, the actual content of which is the high altar – a disposition which is perfectly adapted to the functions of a Minorite church. The transept and choir serve the liturgy, the nave the sermon. As in most Franciscan churches, the exterior is quite plain. The importance of the building lies in the plain, functional, yet novel disposition of the interior, which is not only admirably suited to its purpose, but also modern, since it anticipates certain peculiarities of the Gesù.

In a similar fashion, a traditional theme is reformulated in
S. Paolo alle Monache [218].[31] S. Paolo belongs to the
Lombard type of aisleless convent churches in which the
congregation is separated from the choir by a high, transverse
wall.[32] The attribution of the church to Giunti, suggested by
Baroni, is supported by the 'classical', i.e. windowless, wide
tunnel-vault, the uninterrupted cornice, and the giant Corinthian half-columns between the shallow chapels. The
monumental simplicity of the interior recalls S. Andrea at
Mantua.

ALESSI'S LATER WORKS IN MILAN

Cristoforo Lombardino died in 1555 and Domenico Giunti,
who in 1556 had accompanied his patron, Ferrante Gonzaga,
to Mantua, in 1560. These dates coincide with Galeazzo
Alessi's arrival in Milan. Although Alessi had kept his house
in Perugia, and had been in Genoa, Brescia, and Rome in
the course of these years, Milan remained the real head-
quarters of his activity from 1557 to 1569.[33] His one com-
petitor, Vincenzo Seregni (1509–94), who had been in the
cathedral office of works, made a name only in commissions
for civic works; in important ecclesiastical buildings he was
overshadowed by Alessi.[34] Thus, for instance, in 1565 Alessi
was appointed surveyor of the works of the S. Maria presso
S. Celso, an appointment in which Seregni had succeeded
Lombardino in 1555. Alessi designed the façade of the
church, which was completed long after his departure from
Milan by Martino Bassi [219, 220].[35] A comparison between
the design and the execution shows that Bassi retained the
fundamental features of Alessi's conception, but reduced the

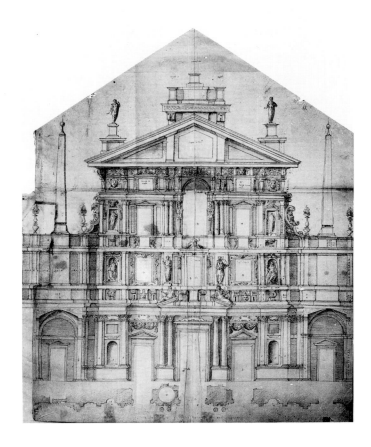

218. (*below*) Domenico Giunti: Milan, S. Paolo alle Monache, 1549–51

219. (*above right*) Galeazzo Alessi: Project for the façade of S. Maria presso
S. Celso, Milan, before 1570. Milan, Biblioteca Ambrosiana

220. (*right*) Galeazzo Alessi and others: Milan, S. Maria presso S. Celso,
façade

221. (*left*) Vincenzo Seregni and others: Milan, S. Vittore al Corpo, 1560–after 1580

222. (*below*) Galeazzo Alessi: Milan, SS. Paolo e Barnaba, 1561–7, plan

decoration and its relief. In the two attic zones, harsh and rather primitive forms replace Alessi's subtle details. Unfortunately the flanking obelisks, which were an important feature in the design, were greatly reduced in height.

The voluminous, 'didactic' programme of statues and reliefs on the façade recalls Giuliano da Sangallo's and Michelangelo's designs for S. Lorenzo in Florence. S. Maria presso S. Celso is the one great Italian church façade of the Cinquecento on which a programme of the kind was actually executed. As in the façade of the Certosa di Pavia, executed a century earlier, the Lombard delight in the decorative enlivening of the wall surface was greater than the need to equate the church façade with an antique temple front, which had practically been the orthodox rule for Italian architects since Alberti. The classical orders, the columns, architrave, and pediment, are little more than a foil for the sculpture.

The system of columns which Alessi's predecessor in office had designed about 1550 for the same façade excluded any possibility of decoration. It is hardly possible to imagine a greater contrast than that between the 'classical' project of a Lombard and the peculiarly 'Lombard' façade of Alessi, the Central Italian. The committee were obviously satisfied with Alessi's work, for they also commissioned designs from him for the interior furnishings of the church.[36]

Alessi's role in the great Olivetan church of S. Vittore al Corpo, Milan, begun in 1560 and completed after 1580 by Martino Bassi, has not yet been clarified. His name appears in the documents, yet how Alessi collaborated with Seregni, who had been working on the monastery buildings since 1553, remains an open question.[37] The aisled basilican nave and the monks' choir behind the altar [221] repeat the scheme of other churches of the order, like the apses of the transepts. The centralized arrangement of the transept and the choir recall the centrally planned Lombard churches of the late Quattrocento, and the comparatively cramped

crossing of Alessi's church in Genoa. The diameter of the dome is less than the width of the nave; as in S. Angelo, the piers of the dome advance into the nave and create a clear distinction between nave and crossing.

It is obvious that liturgical considerations played their part here, as in S. Angelo, in the disposition of the transept and choir. In medieval churches, the monks' choir reached as far as the first bays of the nave, and it was separated from the transept and the congregation in the nave by walls and high stalls. The high altar in the choir was barely visible from the nave, and a special altar for the lay congregation stood in front of the monks' choir.[38] In S. Angelo and S. Vittore, on the other hand, the monks sit in the choir behind the high altar, which is separated from the congregation only by a low balustrade and is therefore in full view from the nave. The differences in level in the pavement explain this arrangement. The chancel area is separated from the congregation by two steps; in S. Angelo these steps are situated between the front piers of the crossing, in S. Vittore between the rear piers.

In the projects for ecclesiastical buildings of the late fifteenth and early sixteenth centuries liturgical consider-

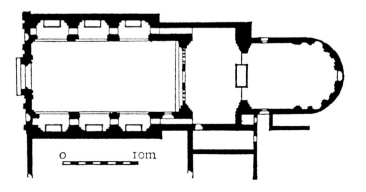

0   10m

ations played no great part. The central plan, the form preferred by the period, was in any case not suited to liturgy; the longitudinal buildings followed the traditional scheme. On the other hand, the placing of the choir stalls behind the altar in the two Milanese churches indicates a close collaboration between the architect and the clergy; the consequences for the liturgy must have been considered in great detail. The innovations correspond to the reforming aims of the Council of Trent.[39]

These tendencies find their clearest expression in Alessi's church of SS. Paolo e Barnaba, built between 1561 and 1567 [222].[40] The building was commissioned by the Milanese branch of the new religious order of the Barnabites, a foundation of the Counter-Reformation authorized by Pope Paul IV in 1556. The sources confirm that Alessi's project was only accepted after several sittings of the chapter, and there is hardly any doubt that one of the points at issue was the shape of the choir.

In S. Barnaba too the high altar stands between the rear piers of the crossing and in front of the monks' choir [223]. These piers, however, advance so far into the interior that they must be regarded less as supports of the crossing vault than as vertical members of the triumphal arch which frames the altar, and at the same time marks the boundary between the crossing and the choir. The front crossing piers project far less, and for that reason the arch they support, which separates the tunnel-vault of the nave from the crossing vault, is higher and wider than the triumphal arch. The spectator standing in the nave sees the front arch as a frame to the triumphal arch, and that, in its turn, as a frame to the high altar. A similar calculation lies behind the gradations of the vault and the pavement. The peculiar trough-shaped vault over the crossing, i.e. over the liturgical area in front of the high altar, is higher than the vault of the nave, but it

draws the eye upward far less than a dome would.[41]

In S. Barnaba, the crossing piers, the arch under the vault, and the vault itself owe their shape far more to their part in the total spatial effect than in S. Vittorio and S. Angelo. The 'liturgical area' with the high altar is the real content of this spatial picture.[42] Finally, the unusually delicate stucco decoration, carefully matched with the architectural members, is important in this spatial effect.

Other works by Alessi in Milan are the façade of the church of S. Raffaelle and an organ loft in the cathedral. Further, he prepared designs for the Sacro Monte of Varallo, the earliest of the three 'Sacred Hills' in Lombardy. Here the Stations of the Cross form a monumental processional way to the top of the hill.[43]

*

Alessi is mentioned for the last time in Milan in 1568. He spent the last years of his life in Perugia, where he held the honorary office of Prior in 1571. It may have contributed to his leaving Milan that Archbishop Carlo Borromeo passed the great architectural commissions to Pellegrino Pellegrini, who was summoned to Milan in 1564, and was fifteen years younger than Alessi.

In the same year, 1564, the Council of Trent published its enactments on reform. Cardinal Carlo Borromeo, born in 1538, had, in his function as Secretary of State to his uncle, Pius IV, taken a leading part in the concluding stage of the Council. He showed an unflagging energy in putting into action reforms in his archbishopric, which he took over after the death of the Pope in 1565. It is mainly due to Borromeo's activity that ideas put forward at the Council of Trent had an earlier and more lasting influence on ecclesiastical building in Lombardy than in Rome. Borromeo visited practically all the parishes and religious communities in his vast diocese in

223. Galeazzo Alessi: Milan, SS.
Paolo e Barnaba, 1561–7

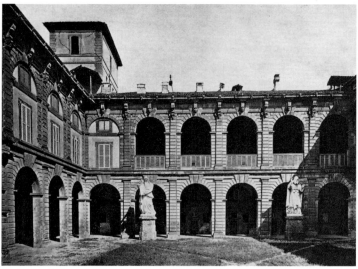

224. Pellegrino Pellegrini: Milan, Palazzo Arcivescovile, Canonica, designed 1564

225. Pellegrino Pellegrini: Pavia, Collegio Borromeo, courtyard, designed 1564

person.[44] What he saw and heard on these long journeys was not without influence on his *Instructiones* for the building and furnishing of churches, published in 1577, the most important Counter-Reformatory expression in literary form of a theme which, since Alberti, had been left entirely to the architects.[45]

The style of the *Instructiones* is typical of Borromeo – terse and clear, relating throughout to practical aims and comprehensible even to a country priest. Although the liturgy always takes precedence over aesthetics, the architect's work is never dismissed as negligible. Thus at the beginning of the book it is stated that the suitable site for the church is 'to be determined by the judgment of the bishop with the assent of the architect appointed by him'. In principle the churches are to be cruciform, 'as we see in the great Roman basilicas'. In exceptional cases departures from this rule by the architect may be approved by the bishop. In the chapters on the 'cappella maggiore' with the high altar and the clergy choir, there is a description of the arrangement that has already been noted in S. Angelo, S. Vittore, and S. Barnaba. In this connection, therefore, the *Instructiones* codify a type already established in Milan and familiar to the Archbishop. Borromeo may also have had in mind the Milanese churches of S. Ambrogio and S. Maria presso S. Celso when he explicitly recommended an atrium in front of the church.[46]

PELLEGRINO PELLEGRINI

In many respects, Carlo Borromeo's connection with his architect Pellegrino Pellegrini (1527–96) resembles Domenico Fontana's with Sixtus V.[47] In 1564, before his own return, the Cardinal announced from Rome the arrival of Pellegrini in Milan.[48] He stood resolutely by his protégé until his own death, and gave him the commissions for all the major buildings he founded. In 1567 he had Seregni dismissed against the will of the Fabrica del Duomo and Pellegrini appointed chief architect of the cathedral.

Like Fontana, Pellegrini combined an expert knowledge of architecture with great organizing capacity. In his buildings, he simplified Alessi's formal vocabulary. His own style is less elegant and more sober, but what really distinguishes him from Fontana is his wealth of ideas. His range of modes of expression can be seen in the Canons' Courts in the archiepiscopal palace in Milan [224] and the Collegio Borromeo in Pavia [225], which he designed in the first year of his work for Borromeo. Jacob Burckhardt describes the pillared arcades of the Canonica as 'a tall, rusticated double hall, in which glum rustication is at last taken seriously. Either the architect or S. Carlo himself wished the courtyard to have an air of gloomy majesty; only one lower and one upper storey, though both of tremendous height'.[49] At Pavia, on the other hand, the courtyard arcades have architraves on paired columns; the motif of the Palazzo Marino has been adopted here, though its profuse sculptural ornament has been suppressed. For that reason, Pellegrini's arcades, unlike Alessi's, look light and almost weightless. The façade of the Collegio is less attractive. On the ground floor low rectangular windows alternate with higher round-arched niches, but on the upper storeys only the central bay is stressed by a high round arch crowned by a pediment. A third system appears in the double-bay flat projections flanking the façade, with windows lighting the two staircases. In a smaller building, this accumulation of motifs might have been regarded, in the idiom of the time, as 'capriccioso', but in a façade of seventeen bays it produces an effect of restlessness or lack of discipline.

In 1569, a year after the beginning of work on the Gesù in Rome, Carlo Borromeo laid the foundation stone for the Jesuit church of S. Fedele, Pellegrini's most important ecclesiastical building in Milan. Pellegrini owed this commission to the Cardinal too; the Vicar General of the Order in Rome wished to entrust the project to Father Tristano.[50]

The plan of S. Fedele [226] is as unusual as its elevation. The nave, 26 m. (50 feet) wide, consists of only two square bays [227]. Its vaults are supported on semicircular wall-arches and transverse arches which, in their turn, rest on six giant free-standing columns.[51] The structural elements and the enclosing walls have nothing in common except the continuous Corinthian architrave which projects far beyond the columns: 'The construction is of such a kind that the entire nave can be imagined without the enclosing walls.'[52] The wall sections between the columns are articulated in the b-a-b motif of a triumphal arch.

The eastern parts of the church were built to a different plan in the seventeenth and eighteenth centuries, but Pellegrini's project has been preserved in drawings.[53] They show a transept whose end walls are aligned with the nave, a dome over the square crossing, and a semicircular apse. Instead of the high Lombard tiburio which was actually executed, a lower Roman dome with a drum, a spherical outer shell, and a lantern was planned.

The interior of S. Fedele surpasses the Roman Gesù in brightness and clarity. In both churches the aim of the architect was a wide space, without anything to hinder a free view of the high altar. But while Vignola places the walls bearing the vault *behind* the walls enclosing the nave, Pellegrini takes the opposite course by placing the structural elements in the interior, i.e. in front of the walls. In the Gesù the side altars stand in deep chapels screened from the nave by arches; in S. Fedele they stand in shallow niches which open towards the nave in tall arches, and therefore appear as an articulation of the wall and not as subsidiary spaces.[54]

It is very interesting to note that the articulation of the walls of the Gesù may be regarded as a recasting of Bramante's pilaster system in St Peter's, while S. Fedele is a direct reversion to the antique. Pellegrini was in Rome in 1564.[55] At that time the building of S. Maria degli Angeli in the Baths of Diocletian was progressing rapidly. Carlo Borromeo was certainly familiar with his uncle's favourite enterprise, and for Pellegrini it was as important as the work of Michelangelo. Thus it follows without difficulty that, three years after Pellegrini's stay in Rome, he took up, in his plans for S. Fedele, the motif of the free-standing columns bearing the imposts of the vaulting. In S. Maria degli Angeli the lower edge of the architrave is 14 m. (46 feet) above the pavement, in S. Fedele 13.40 m. (45 feet); thus the springers of the vault are roughly of the same height in both churches. The Caesarean dimensions of the thermae columns could not, of course, be repeated in the Jesuit church, and Pellegrini

227. Pellegrino Pellegrini: Milan, S. Fedele, begun 1569

mastered the problem by placing his columns on pedestals 3.30 m. (11 feet) in height. The vaults are saucer-shaped, which makes them lighter than a groin-vault and gives the separate bays a certain independence.

Pellegrini's church obviously satisfied all the liturgical and aesthetic requirements of his clients. It is clear from the documents that the Milanese Jesuits approved the design of the church just as much as the Cardinal, who made the building possible by subventions and enabled his own architect to undertake the work. When the *Instructiones* appeared, S. Fedele was still under construction. They are so generalized that they in no way inhibited the architect's artistic freedom, and even a church like S. Fedele, built on a system so immediately influenced by antiquity, could be adapted to them.

In Jesuit church building, however, S. Fedele had no successors. The settlements were obliged to submit the projects for their churches to the Vicar General in Rome, and all the prominent members of the order were trained in Rome. It was therefore no more than a matter of course that the Roman mother church should become the architectural model for the churches of the order.

Pellegrini's round church of S. Sebastiano in Milan, founded by the city after the great plague of 1576, is a striking example of how little the *Instructiones* inhibited the architect's artistic freedom [228].[56] In this case the tradition

226. Pellegrino Pellegrini: Milan, S. Fedele, begun 1569, plan

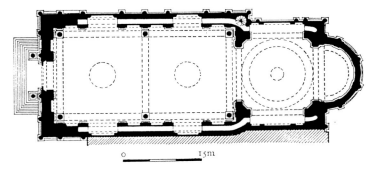

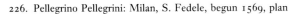

0   15m

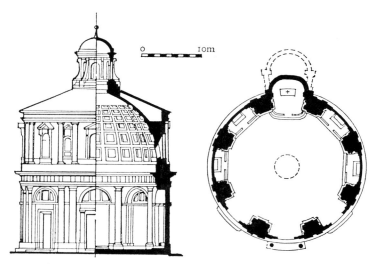

228. Pellegrino Pellegrini: Milan, S. Sebastiano, begun 1577, half-elevation and half-section of original project, and plan (the choir altered later)

for centrally planned churches which went back to the Middle Ages carried the day over the ideological scruples of the *Instructiones*, according to which 'the round form, frequently used by the ancients for the temples of their gods, has rarely been used by Christians'. Once again Pellegrini reverted directly to the antique model; the circular plan as well as the construction and decoration of the dome are inspired by the Pantheon and not by Bramante's Tempietto.[57]

During his long term of office as architect-in-chief of the cathedral of Milan, i.e. Carlo Borromeo's own church, Pellegrini built the high barriers between the choir and the ambulatory, and the crypt under the choir known as the *scurolo*. His share in the many designs for the façade in the later sixteenth century has still to be investigated; he was certainly the first to advocate vigorously a façade in the 'new' style. The four portals of the aisles, begun while he was in office, are preserved in the neo-Gothic façade.[58]

THE REBUILDING OF S. LORENZO IN MILAN: MARTINO BASSI

The greatest enterprise in ecclesiastical architecture in Milan in the sixteenth century was the restoration of an Early Christian rotunda. On 5 June 1573, as we read in the chronicle, 'the church of S. Lorenzo, one of the oldest and most beautiful churches in Milan, collapsed.... The whole city wept because the finest building it possessed was lying in ruins and might never be restored'.[59] The fear was groundless, especially thanks to the efforts made by Carlo Borromeo to assemble the means for rebuilding, measuring the ruins and preparing plans for restoration.

The superintendence of the works was entrusted to Martino Bassi (1542–91), who has already been mentioned as Alessi's successor at S. Maria presso S. Celso.[60] Bassi, who became chief architect of the cathedral in 1587 when Pellegrini was called to Spain, did not live to see the completion of S. Lorenzo; when he died, the vaulting of the dome was in progress.

Carlo Borromeo had given orders that there should be no alteration in the plan of the old church; the sixteenth-century

building stands on its ancient foundations [229]. Thus S. Lorenzo presents a unique phenomenon – the late antique quatrefoil plan determines the highly complex spatial configuration of an interior defined by walls built in the Cinquecento [230]. The root problem of the restoration was the dome, which was over 20 m. (65 feet) in width, and the construction of its eight supports. The four towers in corners of the quatrefoil, which take up the side-thrust of the domes, survived the collapse and have retained their function.

Bassi's plan for a domical vault was repeatedly modified and only adopted after long discussion. In contrast to other projects, Bassi first wished to abandon the drum; he was ultimately persuaded to insert openings in the foot of the dome which, from the outside, look like windows in a drum. This drum is actually a Lombard tiburio surrounding the vault, and from the outside the dome rising from it looks too low. The interior [231] gains by the massive Doric piers of the dome and the projecting main cornice, which give it a gloomy monumentality. The old building must have looked as transparent and weightless as S. Vitale at Ravenna.

Some of the projects entered for the rebuilding have been preserved.[61] Their wealth of ideas almost rivals that of the ideas for St Peter's. Bassi's first scheme was a low spherical vault after the fashion of the Pantheon (with an open oculus). One project [232], perhaps by Pellegrini, has a notably steep dome not unlike that of Florence Cathedral in outline, but on a circular plan; for the corner towers, two storeys were to be added to the old stumps. The actual rebuilding of S. Lorenzo is a belated echo of Bramante's plan for St Peter's, which in its turn had been reminiscent of the late antique central plan of S. Lorenzo.[62]

ASCANIO VITOZZI IN PIEDMONT

In 1584, Duke Carlo Emanuele I of Savoy appointed Ascanio Vitozzi (c. 1539–1615), a native of Orvieto, as his architect and engineer. Vitozzi had taken part in several campaigns

229. (*below*) Martino Bassi: Milan, S. Lorenzo, rebuilt after 1573, plan

230. (*right*) Martino Bassi and others: Milan, S. Lorenzo, rebuilt after 1573

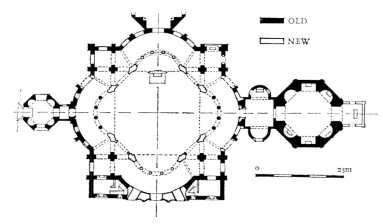

232. (*left*) Pellegrino Pellegrini(?): Project for S. Lorenzo, Milan, cross-section and plan. Milan, Musei Civici (Raccolta Bianconi, vol. IV, 24)

233. (*above*) Ascanio Vitozzi and others: Vicoforte di Mondovì, S. Maria, begun 1596

and was experienced in fortifications; nothing is known of his training as an architect. His activity in Turin was comprehensive, but there are few records of it.[63] His chief work, the pilgrimage church at Vicoforte di Mondovì, begun in 1596, the largest centrally planned building of the late Cinquecento in Italy, was only completed in the eighteenth century.

Detailed evidence of the history of the planning of the church and the forms which Vitozzi had in mind for the Madonna di Vico exists in the sources and preliminary sketches. The Duke, the client for the church, wished to make it the funerary church of the house of Savoy, though it is difficult to disentangle religious from dynastic motives. The process of the design is characteristic of Carlo Emanuele; in addition to the plans prepared at Turin, he had others sent from Genoa, Rome, and Milan. The whole collection looks like a pattern-book of church plans current about 1600; in addition to the rotunda, the octagon, and the square, basilican plans were proposed with and without chapels attached to the aisles, as well as a single-aisled church with chapels.[64] All the projects include a large dome; it is, however, interesting that the idea of placing the altar with the miraculous image under the dome first appears at a late stage of planning.

In Vitozzi's project, which the Duke ultimately decided to execute, the miraculous image is placed in the centre of an oval space 36 m. long and 24 m. wide (120 by 80 feet) [233, 234]. On the diagonal axes four large chapels adjoin the oval, on the transverse axis the vestibules, on the longitudinal axis the choir at one end, the entrance at the other. The lavish decoration of the exterior was necessary since the building was a pilgrimage and votive church: there are giant orders on the three entrance sides, four towers flanking the ends of the oval, and carefully articulated tripartite lunette

234. Ascanio Vitozzi: Vicoforte di Mondovì, S. Maria, begun 1596, plan

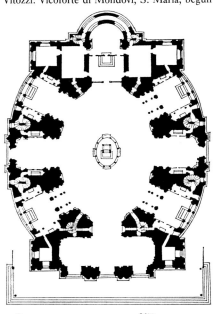

0   25m

231. Martino Bassi: Milan, S. Lorenzo, rebuilt after 1573

235. Ascanio Vitozzi and others: Vicoforte di Mondovì, S. Maria, begun 1596

windows in the diagonals between the side portals and the towers.[65]

In spite of a certain eclecticism in some details, Vitozzi's plan was a thoroughly original solution of the problem in hand.[66] With the miraculous image in the centre of the oval, the visual and liturgical function of the high altar is preserved in the choir. The tripartite lunette windows provide a wealth of light for the chapels destined for the tombs of the Duke's family and separated from the main space by the arrangement of the columns and screen walls. The lavish articulation of the portals of the transverse axis turns three sides of the church into twin-towered façades; since the choir apse is also flanked by towers, the three-dimensional body of the church allows the plan, an oval interlocked with a cross, to stand out clearly. At the same time the ideal, already stated by Alberti, of the free-standing, wholly visible centrally planned church is realized; with its towers and gigantic dome the church dominates the hilly country surrounding it [235].

The historical roots of Vitozzi's design lie in Rome. There is nothing comparable to it in Piedmontese architecture of the Cinquecento. But the Madonna di Vico is distinguished from its Roman models by the peculiarly unconventional and independent interpretation of the adopted form. From that point of view Vitozzi may be regarded as the pioneer of the great Piedmontese Baroque architecture.

CHAPTER 12

Palladio

Since the eighteenth century, the name of Andrea Palladio (1508–80) has stood for architectural perfection. There are Palladian buildings in Russia and in the United States. Travellers visit the little town of Vicenza for the sole purpose of seeing Palladio's works.

Yet the fact that no Renaissance architect has had so much research lavished on him in the last generation cannot be entirely explained by his quality and his fame. The general interest in the Cinquecento has been, if anything, on the decline, and our knowledge of Pellegrini or Alessi has on the whole remained stationary, while recent publications on Palladio would stock a small library.[1] The reasons for the present interest in Palladio lie in particular qualities of his work. It is curiously abstract; it can be visualized independently of its environment, and therefore lends itself to imitation. Many of his works conform to the present trend to smooth surfaces, right angles, and plain cubic forms. Equally, many of his buildings have remained practically unaltered, so that it requires no historical imagination to see them in their original form. Finally, Palladio founded his own enduring fame by a book of illustrations and comments on his own work.[2]

THE QUATTRO LIBRI DI ARCHITETTURA

In the history of architecture, Palladio's treatise occupies a key position. It combines the humanistic literary tradition of the editions and commentaries of Vitruvius with the illustrated pattern-books written by architects for practical use.

In his *Dieci Libri di Architettura*, Alberti uses the language and title of his classical model; he writes for humanists and cultivated clients, but not for working architects. Unlike rhetoric, dialectics, and grammar, architecture was not one of the seven liberal arts. A new Vitruvius, Alberti appeals to the reader as a writer, not as an architect; the classical form of the book is at least as important as its contents. Serlio's and Vignola's treatises, on the other hand, are addressed to the practical architect. The concise Italian texts merely serve as explanations to the illustrations; they lay no claim to literary merit and assume no particular scholarship in the reader.

Palladio was familiar with the monuments of antiquity and the literary tradition established by Vitruvius, since he had himself written a little book, *Antichità di Roma* (1554), and had illustrated Daniele Barbaro's commentary on Vitruvius (1556). Yet there was nothing of the learned humanist in the author of the *Quattro Libri*. Born in Padua, the son of a miller, he had been trained as a stonemason in Padua and Vicenza. In 1534 he married a carpenter's daughter. Even as late as 1542 he appears in the records as *lapicida*. Even as *architector*, the name first given him in 1540, and then from 1545 on, he was not a representative of the liberal arts.

Thus when Palladio writes, at the beginning of his book, that in the study of architecture, which he had practised from his youth, Vitruvius had been his 'maestro e guida', 'il solo antico scrittore di quest'arte', that is on mere literary flourish, nor is it possible to miss the echo of Dante. Just as Dante was inspired by Virgil, the author of the *Quattro Libri*, speaking as a writer and an architect, finds his inspiration in Vitruvius. In going on to say that the book is meant to help the reader 'to avoid errors, barbarous (i.e. Gothic) devices, excessive costs, and premature dilapidation of buildings' Palladio is speaking to the client as well as to the architect.

The title-page summarizes the contents of the book: 'After a short treatise on the five orders and indications of the most important requirements in building, the present volume proceeds to deal with private buildings, streets, bridges, squares, sport halls, and temples'. The 'short treatise' refers to Book I, which is on more or less the same lines as the corresponding chapters in Serlio and Vignola. Book II contains 'designs for many houses, urban and rural, by Palladio, with illustrations of Greek and Roman houses'. Thus Palladio's own buildings take their place beside the buildings of antiquity; in fact they bear the stamp of antiquity as illustrations of ancient private houses built according to Vitruvius's text.

A typical example – the convent of S. Maria della Carità in Venice, designed by Palladio – is illustrated with the caption 'Atrio Corinthio' [236]. Palladio adds the remark that he had tried to reproduce the house of antiquity, and, in doing so, had given it a Corinthian atrium.[3] The vestry beside the atrium 'serves as a tablinum, the name given at that time to the room in which they preserved the portraits of their ancestors'. Considering the previous reconstruction of the antique house with a tetra-style atrium, and the one which follows with a roofed atrium, the convent building must be regarded as an archaeological reconstruction.

The only authority Palladio had for these reconstructions was Vitruvius's text, which is, in his own words, 'most difficult and obscure and to be used with great caution'.

236. Andrea Palladio: Venice, convent of S. Maria della Carità, Atrio Corinthio, after the *Quattro Libri*, 1570

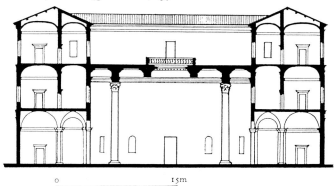

237. Andrea Palladio: Project for the Rialto Bridge, Venice. Vicenza, Museo Civico

Nor did the ruins of Imperial Rome, which he had seen, have much to offer him for the Greek and early Roman premises described by Vitruvius. Thus what the illustrations actually show are modern architectural compositions. Their style belongs to the Cinquecento; what Palladio had learnt from Vitruvius and existing monuments – whether rightly or wrongly – was fused in them with the forms and types of the sixteenth century to create a new unity.

It is in Book III, 'Edifici pubblici', that the elements of this synthesis are most clearly demonstrated. After a technical and historical introduction, the section on bridges describes Caesar's bridge over the Rhine and other examples, ancient and modern. It concludes with a stone bridge 'di mia invenzione', a superb rendering of Palladio's project for the Rialto in Venice [237]*. The type of the basilica is illustrated by the Basilica Portia in Rome and Palladio's Basilica at Vicenza. The comment in the text states that both buildings serve the same purpose, namely jurisdiction and the conduct of public affairs, however widely they may differ in form. In the ancient basilicas, the colonnades were in the interior, in the modern form they are on the exterior.

Book IV, 'Ancient Temples in Rome and other Places in Italy and Elsewhere', contains, with one exception, no contemporary buildings or reconstructions. There were sufficient monuments extant to illustrate the types of ancient sacred architecture. Bramante's Tempietto at S. Pietro in Montorio, the only 'modern' building to find a place in Book IV, represents the Doric peripteral rotunda. The selection of ancient monuments is essentially the same as Serlio's, though the woodcuts in Palladio's treatise are made with far greater care. They are only based in part on Palladio's own measurements; he often makes use of older drawings.[4] Architects of the twentieth century may feel some surprise when they read in the preface to this book that 'Anyone can see by studying ancient temples the forms and decoration that should be used for churches' (i.e. Christian churches), but in that sentence Palladio prophesied the development of church building down to the nineteenth century. It must, of course, be realized that that development was influenced by the churches he built himself – which are not illustrated in the treatise – and still more by the treatise itself.

Vicenza, and the workmen in the shop in which Andrea di Pietro of Padua spent his apprenticeship as a sculptor's assistant, had little to contribute to the formation of Palladio's personality as an artist. But not far from Vicenza the great buildings were rising which were to make the Veneto the most outstanding architectural centre of Italy. Falconetto was active at Padua, Giulio Romano at Mantua, Sanmicheli at Verona, Sansovino at Venice. When Palladio declares, in the first lines of his book, that he had dedicated his life to the study of architecture from his youth, those were the masters that were foremost in his mind. It was to them that he owed the formation of his critical judgement and his style. The Basilica of Vicenza, Palladio's first monumental work, shows that his style was fully developed by the end of the forties. Ideas and influences can be traced from all four masters, but they give no impression of alien elements: they have simply flowed into Palladio's formal idiom.

In 1538 at latest, the stonemason, then thirty years of age, made the acquaintance of Gian Giorgio Trissino (d. 1550), a humanist who belonged to one of the patrician families of Vicenza, and an amateur architect himself.[5] A travelled man of the world, Trissino recognized the gifts of the young workman. He introduced him to the study of antiquity and patronized him with all the means in his power. In 1541, Palladio – the classical name is an invention of Trissino's – accompanied his patron to Rome. After his return, and in all probability on Trissino's recommendation, he became the foremost architect of the Vicentine nobility.[6] He returned to Rome several times later. He had also studied at first hand the ancient monuments of northern Italy and the south of France. The fact that in 1556 he became one of the founding members of the learned Accademia Olimpica is proof of the respect in which he was held in Vicenza. In 1561 commissions began to come in from Venice, and in 1570 he settled there with his family. It was in Venice too that his *Quattro Libri* was published in 1570, and in Venice again in 1575 that an Italian translation of Caesar's Commentaries appeared with his illustrations. He kept in touch with Vicenza; in the last year of his life he designed the theatre of the Accademia Olimpica. A month before his death he still received fees for his work on the Basilica.

CHURCHES

'We, who worship no false gods, will choose the most perfect and beautiful form for our churches. Since the circle excels all other forms in being simple, homogeneous, everywhere the same, solid and capacious, our temples shall be circular. The circle mirrors God's unity, infinity, his homogeneity and justice' ('Unità, infinita Essenza, Uniformità e Giustizia').

This famous passage appears in Book IV of Palladio's treatise, five years before Carlo Borromeo's *Instructiones*, in which the central plan was expressly rejected as pagan and little suited to a Christian ecclesiastical building. Alberti had already praised the central plan as the most beautiful form of church building. To the architects it remained the ideal of beauty as long as aesthetics dominated the field.[7] But however often round churches may appear in sketchbooks and paintings, actual centrally planned buildings are very rare. These exceptions include Bramante's Tempietto, S. Maria di

238. (*above*) Andrea Palladio: Venice, S. Giorgio Maggiore, begun 1566

239. (*below*) Andrea Palladio: Venice, S. Giorgio Maggiore, begun 1566, section and plan

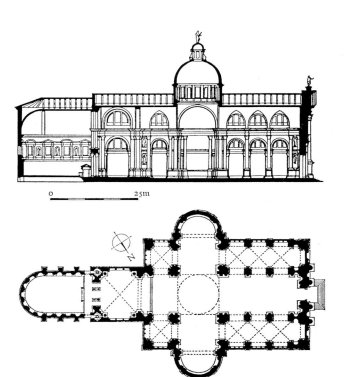

Campagna near Verona, and S. Sebastiano in Milan – all votive churches. The clergy preferred the traditional forms. Many new buildings were erected on old plans, since the centrally planned church is in any case ill-suited to the Christian liturgy.[8]

After the middle of the sixteenth century, the practical liturgical requirements of the clergy overcame the aesthetic ideas of the architects. When Palladio writes, after the passage quoted above, that longitudinal churches had their advantages, it sounds like a farewell to the central plan: 'The entrance lies at the foot of the Cross; it faces the high altar and the choir. At the ends of the arms of the Cross are two more altars or entrances. In the longitudinal church, the worshipper can see before his eyes the tree on which our Saviour hung. This is the form in which I built the church of S. Giorgio Maggiore in Venice.'

S. Giorgio Maggiore, the Benedictine monastery church begun in 1566, is a basilica with a dome over the crossing, transepts terminating in half-domes, and a long chancel [239]. It was Palladio's first great ecclesiastical building. The plan is of a type common since medieval times, but the visitor entering the church finds himself in an unprecedented, highly surprising kind of space, traditionally described as bright, clear, plain, solemn [238]. The vaults and walls are stuccoed in pure white, against which the half-columns, pilasters, and arches stand out in grey.[9] The three-bay nave has a tunnel-vault with lunettes, the aisles have groin-vaults. The piers are solid enough to make a clear separation between the aisles, but they do not look massive. They are a skilfully composed organism of vertical members: giant half-columns on high pedestals towards the nave, lower paired pilasters under the springers of the arcade arches, half-columns between pilasters in the aisles. Pilasters adjoin the giant columns of the crossing. Beyond the crossing, the aisled system of the nave is carried one bay forward; the chancel then continues the nave, but it is longer and wider than the bays of the nave and differs from them by its groin-vault supported by fluted free-standing columns. A characteristic invention of Palladio, which was destined to have a great future, is the group of columns between the chancel and the monks' choir; only here the columns, which in all the other parts of the church stand in front of or are engaged in the wall, are visible from all sides.

All the various forms of vaults and articulations have their precise parallels in the *Quattro Libri*. The creative intention which inspired S. Giorgio Maggiore was an 'antique Christian church'. To Palladio that was natural, not paradoxical; the forms of antique architecture, the most beautiful and stately ever invented, become the expression of the noblest and most sublime creation of architecture, the Christian House of God. If the interior of S. Giorgio envelops the visitor of today with its atmosphere of solemnity, it is difficult to say whether that feeling arises from an immediate impression on entering the church, or because he is already conditioned by the countless churches which descended from Palladio.

It is unnecessary to explain here that, for Palladio's conception of the church façade, the columned portico of the antique temple was the right thing in the right place.[10] But while the antique temple front consists of free-standing, three-dimensional elements, the façade of the Christian church, which is the outer side of the wall enclosing the interior, takes on, of its very nature, the character of the ground of a relief. The nave and aisles in S. Giorgio Maggiore differ in height; the section of the Christian basilica is totally different from that of an antique temple. Palladio was faced with this problem in three Venetian churches, and in all three cases he solved it in the same way: by reducing to a minimum the projection of the nave over the aisles, and setting in front of it a composite giant order; the slopes of the pediment run parallel to the slope of the roof. At the sides there is a lower, flatter Corinthian order with half-pediments. In this way, two 'antique' systems are projected on to the church façade, the members of the central system standing out against the flatter sides by their stronger relief. Both systems have a fully developed entablature, the smaller running behind the giant order. One can even imagine that the centre of the smaller pediment is concealed behind the giant order.

The effort to create the church façade *all' antica* can be traced from Alberti through Bramante's and Raphael's designs for St Peter's down to Vignola and Cristoforo Lombardino. But not even Palladio could nullify the inherent incompatibility. By doubling the system, and by the apparent

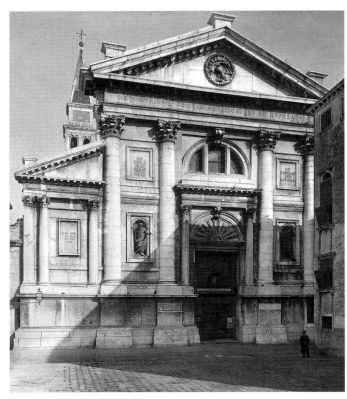

240. (*above*) Andrea Palladio: Venice, S. Francesco alla Vigna, façade, begun *c.* 1562

241. (*right*) Andrea Palladio: Venice, Redentore, begun 1577

concealment of the smaller pediment, he displays the problem, he does not solve it, though his treatment, if complex, is dignified and consistent in itself. That is obvious from the many imitations which continued into the nineteenth century.

When the façade of S. Giorgio Maggiore was completed, after 1600, certain alterations had obviously been carried out in the details. The façade of S. Francesco alla Vigna [240], which was built under Palladio's supervision about the same time as the interior of S. Giorgio, is superior to that of S. Giorgio both in composition and in detail. The side and central parts stand on a common base. The flanking half-pediments are supported by half-columns instead of pilasters, which are employed only at the corners. Thus the smaller system is characterized as a temple *in antis*.

In the Redentore, the latest façade of this type, the larger order is also treated as that of a temple *in antis* [241].[11] In this case the main pediment corresponds to the crown of the vault. Above it rise a tall attic and the roof of the nave, and the buttresses above the half-pediments. The architrave of the lesser order corresponds to the main cornice in the interior. Here, therefore, the façade reflects the structural system of the interior; the roofs are visible above it. In that way the façade, in a quite unprecedented fashion, becomes an integral part of the building. Seen from a distance, the façade, dome, towers, and roofs unite in an admirably balanced composition. On the other hand, the strata of the surface can only be grasped by the observer standing directly in front of the church.

The Redentore was founded by the republic of Venice. During the plague of 1576, the Doge vowed that a church should be built in honour of the Redeemer. After the Senate had voted for a longitudinal and against a central plan, and had approved the design Palladio submitted in accordance with this decision, the foundation stone was laid in the spring of 1577.[12] Since the end of the plague in the summer of 1577, a procession of thanksgiving has taken place every year, crossing over to the Giudecca on a temporary bridge of barges. The participants in the procession, therefore, see the strangely composed church façade facing them at the end of a *via sacra*. The dome in the centre of the picture rises over the altar on which the Doge lays the thank-offering.

The function of the church is also expressed in the configuration of the plan [242]. On entering, the visitor finds himself in a moderately high, oblong room surrounded by half-columns [243]. Opposite the entrance a great arch opens on to the high altar and the area under the dome. Looked at from the crossing, the parts of the wall that support the arch are seen to be the piers of the dome. The result is that the domed space looks wider than the nave, while actually both are equal in width. As in S. Giorgio, the presbytery and the chancel are separated by a screen of columns, but in the Redentore they are arranged in a semi-circle, and their architrave supports the half-dome of an apse.

The liturgical heart of the church, the crossing, is dominated by the circle of the drum and dome and by the semicircles of the crossing arches and apses, the nave by the uninterrupted horizontal of the cornice and the verticals of the columns. In the plan and elevation of the side chapels, the semicircle is again the dominant note.

The plan of the Redentore recalls that of Pellegrini's

243. Andrea Palladio: Venice, Redentore, begun 1577

242. Andrea Palladio: Venice, Redentore, begun 1577, section and plan

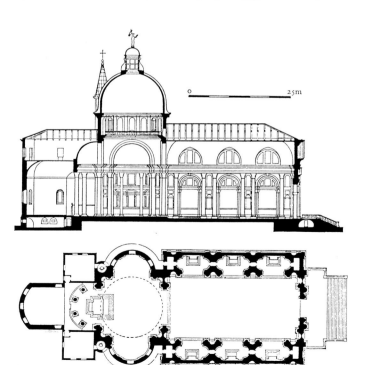

almost contemporary church of S. Fedele at Milan. Pellegrini inserts the antique motif of a vault resting on free-standing columns as if it were some quotation from an old work in a thoroughly contemporary wall-composition. In Palladio's church, ancient and modern can no more be separated than column and wall or space and structure.

The plague which led to the foundation of the Redentore was also the origin of the votive church of S. Sebastiano at Milan. The transactions of the Venetian Senate give the reasons why the Redentore was to be built 'in forma quadrangolare' and not on a central plan: the function of divine service was clearly regarded as more important than the 'ideal' central plan which was practically the rule for votive churches. A curious light is cast on the Senate's decision of 1577 by the fact that fifty years later the city, again menaced by the plague, returned to the central plan in the church of S. Maria della Salute.

SECULAR ARCHITECTURE

The Basilica Palladiana at Vicenza is the medieval senate house, round which Palladio built a two-storeyed loggia [244, 245].[13] On the ground floor, the number of arches was determined by the disposition of the old building; further, in

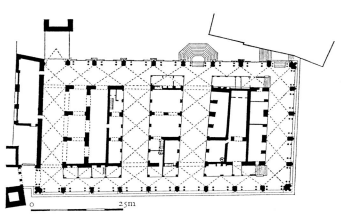

244. (*left*) Andrea Palladio: Vicenza, Basilica, begun 1549

245. (*above*) Andrea Palladio: Vicenza, Basilica, begun 1549, plan

246. (*below*) Andrea Palladio: Vicenza, Loggia del Capitanato, commissioned 1571

deciding on the size of the intercolumniation, three broad passages, varying in width, which ran straight through the building under the great hall, had to be taken into consideration.

Every pier of the loggia is faced by a half-column whose entablature projects from the entablature along the wall. Smaller, free-standing columns are inserted in this main order, their architraves serving as imposts to the round-arched arcading. A similar form of this 'Palladian' motif had already appeared ten years earlier in Serlio's Book IV and in the upper storey of Sansovino's Libreria. In the Basilica, the motif has a practical purpose. By detaching minor columnar elements from the pier, Palladio was able to integrate the old bays, which were unequal in width, into a system of seemingly equal arcades. At the same time, each of the members of the pillar is given its own structural function, but that function, unlike Sansovino's system, which unfolds in a plane, can only be understood if the spectator moves round it. There is yet another difference between the Basilica and the Libreria: in the former the sculptural decoration is confined to the key-stones of the arches and the statues on the attic. The effect of the Libreria is born of the rich Ionic order of the upper storey, that of the Basilica derives from the 'masculine' Doric of the ground floor.

In 1571, more than twenty years after the beginning of work on the Basilica, Palladio was commissioned for the Loggia del Capitanato [246], which stands opposite it, and was the residence of the Venetian 'City Captain' of Vicenza. Building stopped after three bays had been erected. It is uncertain whether Palladio's project had envisaged five or seven bays.[14]

The composite giant order of the Loggia is a superb example of Palladio's late style. In comparison with the clear, unusually careful detail of the Basilica, the forms look coarse and violent. The volume of the pillars is extremely reduced, the window surrounds of the upper storey break into the entablature, uncouth triglyphs support the architraves of the balconies, and the wall is smothered with stucco ornament. Among these restless, intentionally unclassical forms stand the four tall half-columns crowned with their part of the entablature. They look like the remains of an antique building which has had arcades and an upper storey forced into it. The column, the most important and dignified element of ancient architecture, is invested with the greatest dignity and monumentality when it dominates several storeys of a modern utilitarian building. It is in that way that the giant order of Palladio's Loggia should be understood.

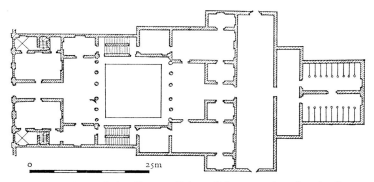

247. Andrea Palladio: Vicenza, Palazzo Valmarana, plan after the *Quattro Libri*, 1570

PALAZZI

In Book II of his treatise, Palladio illustrates five of the palazzi he designed in Vicenza [247].[15] The façades of these palazzi are still standing and correspond substantially to the illustrations, but illustrations of the parts adjoining the rear of the façade ranges bear no resemblance to what is now standing. Here again the treatise proves to be a combination of architectural theory and 'Vitruvian' reconstructions. Palladio's plans and elevations transform the palazzi of the Vicentine patriciate into antique domestic architecture. The courtyard becomes a monumental Vitruvian peristyle. As the present condition of the buildings shows, the clients were perfectly satisfied with a façade. Further suggestions of Palladio's were certainly beyond their means and probably beyond their wishes.

For the patrician of the terraferma, the courtyard was not the same thing as it was for his contemporaries in Rome and Florence. Besides, the medieval tangle of streets and the density of the built-up areas in Vicenza did not allow for large building sites. The street front, the entrance hall, and the rooms on the piano nobile were the true status symbols of the clients.

In the division of the house into two storeys of roughly equal height, and in the fenestration, Palladio's façades are of the same type as those of Sanmicheli in Verona, even though, for Palladio as for Sanmicheli, every building presented a new problem. The rusticated front of the early Palazzo Thiene [248] contains Roman echoes and reminiscences of Giulio Romano's Mantuan style. The classical façade of the Palazzo Chiericati, designed about the same time, with its colonnaded front, was determined by its situation on the 'Isola', an open tract of land on the edge of the town. In designing it Palladio had in mind the two-storeyed portico which surrounded the Roman forum. The façades of the palazzi Iseppo Porto and Barbaran seem closely related to each other, yet there was an interval

248. Andrea Palladio: Vicenza, Palazzo Thiene, begun 1542(?), façade

249. Andrea Palladio: Vicenza, Palazzo Valmarana, begun *c.* 1565, façade

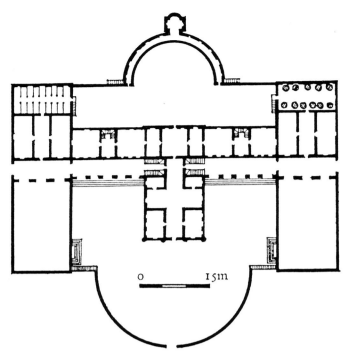

250. Andrea Palladio: Maser, Villa Barbaro, plan after the *Quattro Libri*, 1570

of twenty years between their building. Palladio's work cannot be easily classified and dated by a consistent stylistic development; instead, for each new building he drew on a repertory of fully developed types which already existed in his mind. All the same, the giant pilasters of the façade of the Palazzo Valmarana [249] already show the trend to exaggerated dimensions which is characteristic of his late work and can be seen in the Loggia del Capitanato.[16]

VILLAS

Among the illustrations in Book II there are reproductions of more than twenty villas which Palladio designed for the Venetian and Vicentine nobility [250]. While in his palazzi Palladio adopted and developed the type of the upper-class town mansion, it was he who created the villa type of the terraferma.[17] The social and economic developments which inaugurated the type have only become clear through very recent research. The Turkish advance in the eastern Mediterranean and the discovery of America were the death-knell of Venetian overseas trade. The republic therefore began to take an interest in the agricultural development of its own lands in the terraferma. The great swamps of the river valleys were systematically reclaimed, and country estates became an attractive source of income to the nobility.[18]

Unlike the Roman and Florentine country seats, Palladio's

251. Andrea Palladio: Pojana Maggiore, Villa, begun *c.* 1549

252. Andrea Palladio: Vicenza, La Rotonda, *c.* 1566–70

villas are surrounded by fields and vineyards which belonged to the owner of the villa and were agriculturally productive. Thus the estate includes, beside the villa whose owner enjoyed country life in warm weather, houses for farm-workers, barns, wine cellars, grain stores, and stables. The modest properties on the terraferma could not compete with the terraced gardens, the mazes, the fountains and the grottoes of Rome. But the distinction and simplicity of Palladio's work gave them an incomparable charm which can be felt even today.

The master's house, usually two-storeyed, but occasionally of only one storey, five to seven bays wide, stands as a rule on a slight rise in the land. It is generally distinguished by a pediment over a columned or pillared hall [251].[19] But at its sides, or wherever the terrain permitted, there were low open wings leading to the outbuildings. As Palladio explains,

in this arrangement care had to be taken to prevent the master from being disturbed by the outdoor work, or inter-fering in it himself.

In the placing of loggias and pediments every Palladian villa presents some new variant. The pediment may rise above the roof or be set in front of it. There are two-storeyed loggias or giant orders in front of two storeys. The service wings may be parallel or at right angles to the axis of the house, or may curve away in front of it. The plans of the whole group are always symmetrical, like those of the rooms of the house; in the centre there is a salone.[20] The length, width, and height of the separate rooms, their geometry, are determined by a system of rational proportions which is a characteristic of Palladio's architecture and comes out most clearly in the villas; it stems from Vitruvius and Alberti. 'The geometrical keynote is, subconsciously rather than

253. Andrea Palladio: Vicenza, La Rotonda, *c.* 1566–70, plan and section

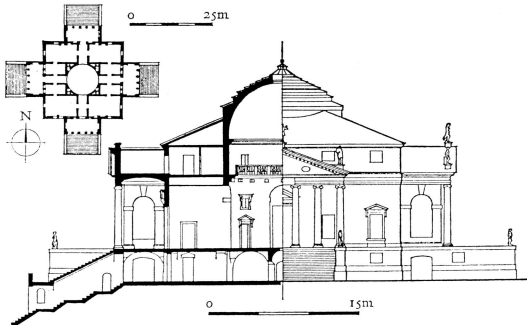

consciously, perceptible to everyone who visits Palladio's villas and it is this that gives his buildings their convincing quality' (Wittkower).

Palladio purposely gave the name 'suburbana' to his most famous villa, La Rotonda [252], which was planned as a country seat for the dignitary of the Church for whom it was built. It is, however, not only the absence of service buildings that distinguishes the Rotonda from the other villas – it is also the only work by Palladio that corresponds exactly to the illustration in the *Quattro Libri*.[21] Only here was the architect able to realize to the full his vision of 'well-building', as Sir Henry Wotton called it. That applies to the situation of the Rotonda on a height 'with gentle approaches' as well as to its form. The plan [253], composed of the simplest and therefore the most beautiful geometrical figures, the square, circle, and rectangle, is symmetrical on both axes. The same porticoes with the same pediments appear on all four sides,

and even the number of steps leading to the loggias is equal. Thus the Rotonda presents the same view from all four sides; in the high round salone in the centre we begin to understand what Palladio means when he ascribes to the circle the divine qualities of *unità* and *uniformità*. If the vault over his room is shaped like a dome, a feature till then confined to churches, that is perfectly consistent.

With all its simplicity, this architecture is highly abstract and in the literal sense of the word 'absolute', i.e. bound by no this-worldly conditions. When Goethe visited the Rotonda, he called it 'habitable, but not homely'. The identity of aesthetic and theological categories which was a peculiarity of the Renaissance conception of architecture could only be achieved if the patron was prepared, as he was in the case of the Rotonda, to accept the aims and ideals of the architect. That is why the Rotonda has become the exemplar of ideal architecture.

254. Antonio da Ponte: Venice, Rialto Bridge, 1588–91

CHAPTER 13

Venice and Padua in the Late Sixteenth Century

In the last years of his life, after Sansovino's death in 1570, Palladio became the most prominent architect in Venice, and was commissioned for public buildings by the senate. After the fires of 1574 and 1577 he submitted reports for the restoration of the Doge's Palace, though the actual work was carried out by Antonio da Ponte, the 'proto' (architect-in-chief) of the Signoria.[1] Da Ponte was active at the same time on the building of the state prison adjoining the Doge's Palace on the Riva degli Schiavoni.[2] The unadorned façade, appropriate to the purpose of the building, is a variant of Sansovino's style. For the Rialto Bridge (1588–91), Da Ponte's masterpiece, he adopted designs by Palladio [237, 254].* The stone bridge replaced a wooden drawbridge. Its width and height had to be calculated for the shipping on the Canal Grande, and the building of shops on the bridge, the open arch over its centre, and the side pavements were also prescribed. The bridge as executed is plainer than Palladio's more ambitious design, but Da Ponte did full justice to the complex requirements and structural difficulties of the commission. The bridge soon became a landmark of Venice.[3]

Beside the art of the great 'foreigner' Sansovino, and of Sanmicheli and Palladio, Venice had its own native building tradition in the sixteenth century which continued, practically unaltered, the architecture of the late Quattrocento. The outstanding masters of this trend, Antonio Abbondio of Lombardy, named Il Scarpagnino (c. 1481?–1549), and Giangiacomo da Grigi (first mentioned in 1550, d. 1572), collaborated on the Scuola Grande di S. Rocco [255], which was finished after a protracted building period about 1560. It may be regarded as a characteristic example of this local style.[4] The complex adjoining the church contains, in addition to the offices and assembly rooms of the Scuola, the great halls made famous by Tintoretto's paintings. In contrast to Sansovino's and Palladio's 'classical' façades, that of the Scuola is an example of display architecture set in front of a building [256]. The free-standing columns of the two storeys stand on far-projecting pedestals, and the crowning cornice has no relation to the gable behind it. The old Venetian delight in costly stone is expressed in the polychrome incrustation. The staircase leading to the upper hall of the Scuola is an important document in the history of the staircase [257]. Two parallel flights with tunnel-vaults lead, half-way up, to a landing; from there a single, broader and domed central flight turns at 180 degrees to reach the upper storey. For all its simplicity, the arrangement is entirely monumental, and the staircase has an importance similar to those in the ricetto of the Laurenziana and at Caprarola.

In Paduan architecture of the middle of the sixteenth century, local tradition also has more force than the new classical art of Sansovino and Palladio. The church of the abbey of S. Giustina and the cathedral, which were built at this time, are among the largest ecclesiastical buildings in Italy.[5] S. Giustina, S. Sepolcro at Piacenza, S. Salvatore in Venice, and a number of other monasteries were united in

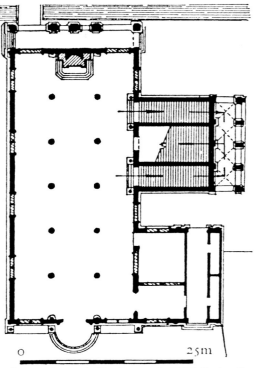

255. Bon, Scarpagnino, and Giangiacomo da Grigi: Venice, Scuola di S. Rocco, c. 1515 ff., 1527 ff., and 1549 ff., plan

256A. Bon and Scarpagnino: Venice, Scuola di S. Rocco, façade, begun 1515

256B. (*above*) Bon and Scarpagnino: Venice, Scuola di S. Rocco, detail of façade

257. (*right*) Bon and Scarpagnino: Venice, Scuola di S. Rocco, staircase, after 1544

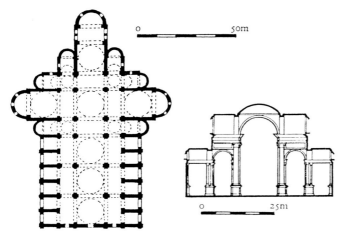

258. (*above*) Andrea Moroni and Andrea della Valle: Padua, S. Giustina, begun 1532, plan and section

259. (*right*) Andrea Moroni and Andrea della Valle: Padua, S. Giustina, begun 1532

260. (*below right*) Andrea Palladio and Vincenzo Scamozzi: Vicenza, Teatro Olimpico, opened 1585, plan

the Cassinese Congregation. The Byzantino-Venetian plan of the cross-domed church, which first appeared in S. Salvatore and was then adopted by the other two churches, is enriched in S. Giustina by a far-projecting transept with apses [258]. The three gigantic bays of the nave [259] are vaulted with low, windowless domes, but the four domes over the crossing, the choir, and the transepts are brightly illuminated by drums and lanterns. Thus there is an effective contrast between the radiant brightness of the eastern parts and the muted light in the nave.

The rebuilding of the cathedral, for which projects had been commissioned from Sansovino and Michelangelo, was ultimately carried out after a design by Andrea della Valle of Padua (d. in Venice, 1577). The plan is a variation on the type of S. Giustina, but in the cathedral the longitudinal axis is stressed with greater force, while the number of domes is reduced. The abandonment of the rhythmic sequence of the vaults certainly impairs the spatial effect.

SCAMOZZI

In 1583, Vincenzo Scamozzi (1552–1616), born at Vicenza, was given the commission for the Nuove Procuratie adjoining Sansovino's Libreria on the south side of the Piazza. Scamozzi adopted the system of the Libreria practically without alteration. By the addition of a third storey, the long façade was given its due relationship to the width of the Piazza.[6]

Further, after Palladio's death, Scamozzi finished the Teatro Olimpico at Vicenza [260]; it was opened in 1585 with a performance of *Oedipus Tyrannus*. The auditorium, with its crowning colonnade and its spendid proscenium (*frons scenae*), is certainly inspired by Palladio's design. Scamozzi supplemented the stage wall by the street vistas visible behind the three doorways.[7]

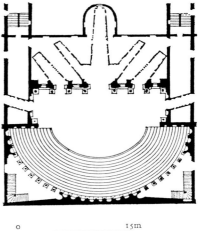

The Teatro Olimpico was fitted into an older building. A few years later, Scamozzi built for Duke Vespasiano Gonzaga at Sabbioneta the first real theatre in modern architecture [261]. The form of the auditorium is taken from Palladio's Olimpico. The seating in the theatre at Sabbioneta strictly followed court protocol. The duke and his family sat in the loggia crowning the auditorium, his entourage filled the semicircular steps, while ordinary spectators stood in the pit. Scamozzi abandoned the stage wall of the proscenium, and treated the stage, as Serlio had already done, as one street vista. Palladio's conception of the reconstruction of the antique *frons scenae* was abandoned. It was taken up later by Inigo Jones.[8]

261. Vincenzo Scamozzi: Sabbioneta, theatre, 1588–90

CHAPTER 14

Tuscany 1550–1600

AMMANNATI

The Florentine sculptor Bartolomeo Ammannati (1511–92), who worked under Sansovino on the sculpture of the Libreria in Venice, shows Sansovino's influence in his very first work of architecture, an arch which he constructed in the palazzo of the Paduan doctor of medicine Marco Benavides, between the courtyard and the garden adjoining it [262].[1] With its vigorous Doric order the arch is an excellent example of a reversion to classical antiquity which was particularly in favour among the humanists of Padua University.[2]

After a short period of work in Urbino, Ammannati went in 1550 to Rome, where he received several important commissions from Julius III on the recommendation of his friend Vasari. His share in the work on the Villa Giulia has already been mentioned. Certain details which the Villa Giulia has in common with the Villa Imperiale at Pesaro built for the Duke of Urbino may have originated with Ammannati, who became familiar with the Villa Imperiale during his work at Urbino.[3] The garden front of the present Palazzo di Firenze in Rome, which Ammannati renovated and enlarged for Julius III's brother, still recalls the Benavides arch in the consistent application of the classical orders; the shallower relief of the courtyard front [263] shows his preoccupation with Vignola's style.

Ammannati's architectural masterpiece is the courtyard of the Palazzo Pitti in Florence, begun in 1560 [264]. The Quattrocento building which had passed into the possession of Duke Cosimo I in 1549 consisted only of the façade range; the courtyard had not risen above its beginnings.[4] But a stately courtyard was indispensable for a princely residence in the Cinquecento: further, the rise in the terrain behind the building and its situation on the outskirts of the city gave the opportunity for an ideal composition of palazzo, cortile, and garden. The old building was enlarged by two rear wings, and a large horseshoe-shaped theatre was built in the garden, its level corresponding to that of the piano nobile. The ground floor and pavement of the courtyard are therefore invisible from the theatre; a one-storeyed retaining wall separates the courtyard from the garden. In planning the layout, it had to be taken into consideration that, looking from the garden, the courtyard should be the show façade of the palazzo.

The three-storeyed cortile is one of the most important Cinquecento examples of the use of rustication [265]. Serlio's advice to restrict rustication to fortifications and buildings of a similar character was by no means followed universally, as can be seen in buildings by Giulio Romano, Alessi, and Pellegrini. While the rustication of Sansovino's Zecca façade in Venice is perfectly adapted to the function of the building, in the cortile of the cathedral Canonica or the Palazzo Marino in Milan it is merely the architect's personal mode of expression.

Ammannati, who had collaborated in the building, knew the façade of the Villa Giulia, which offers one of the few examples of rustication in Roman urban architecture.

262. Bartolomeo Ammannati: Padua, Arco Benavides, 1544

263. Bartolomeo Ammannati: Rome, Palazzo di Firenze, courtyard façade, after 1550

264 and 265. Bartolomeo Ammannati: Florence, Palazzo Pitti, courtyard, begun 1560

266. Bartolomeo Ammannati: Florence, Ponte S. Trinità, 1558-70 (before destruction)

But whereas Vignola's portal follows Serlio's rule, namely that only the Tuscan order is appropriate to rustication, the rustication of the Pitti cortile stretches up to the Ionic and Corinthian orders of the upper storeys. Various kinds of considerations must have led to the divergence from the canon. The *robustezza* of the rustication was well suited to the princely character of the building. The courtyard was the proscenium for the performances in the garden theatre, in which nature and art were combined in the same way as rustication with architecture. And finally the Quattrocento entrance side was already rusticated.

The only later building of Ammannati's which can compare with the Pitti courtyard in monumentality and power of expression is the Ponte S. Trinità in Florence [266].[5] The curve of the three arches of the bridge and the roadway across it is formed of elliptical segments; the elasticity of the flat arches connecting the two river banks is like a taut bow. From ancient times, bridge arches had been constructed as semicircles, or segments of circles, and in the Middle Ages occasionally as pointed arches, but the elliptical curve is present in a design by Vignola as early as 1547 for a small bridge near Bologna.[6] Ammannati may also have seen Michelangelo's vault in the piano nobile of the Palazzo Farnese, the curvature of which resembles the three-centred arch, i.e. the ellipse. We know that Vasari discussed the projects for the Ponte S. Trinità with Michelangelo, and brought back drawings and notes to Florence. It is therefore not impossible that Michelangelo devised the arch of the bridge. Ammannati was solely responsible for its execution, however,[7] and the mouldings and heraldic cartouches show his inimitable, dignified, slow-paced calligraphy.

VASARI

Giorgio Vasari (1511-74), as architect of Duke Cosimo I, had a similar function and status to Pellegrini in Milan and Domenico Fontana in Rome. Diplomatic skill, astounding industry, indefatigable energy, and facility in production made him the ideal court artist. It is due above all to his talent for organization that Florence once more became the capital of European art in the late sixteenth century.

At a time when he was arranging the Palazzo Vecchio as a residence for the Duke, Vasari designed the Uffizi, the greatest Florentine building enterprise of the time; in his own words, 'the loggia of the huge building that stretches to the Arno, of all the buildings that I have erected, was the most difficult and the most dangerous, because it had to be constructed over the river and, as it were, in the air'.[8]

The Uffizi, built before the great enterprises of Sixtus V, like the roughly contemporary Escorial is an early example of the architecture of absolute monarchy [267]. It was erected by order of Cosimo I for thirteen administrative agencies, so that they would abandon their time-honoured offices, which were scattered all over the town, and move into the new building. The documents contain urgent reports on the resistance of the guilds to the move and of the owners of the many houses, shops, and workshops demolished or expropriated to make room for the new building.

Work was begun on the foundations in 1560; in 1564 the range adjoining the Palazzo Vecchio was being used and the narrow side looking on the Arno was nearly complete. After Vasari's death the building was continued by Alfonso Parigi and Bernardo Buontalenti, and finished soon after 1580. According to contemporary documents the total cost amounted to 400,000 scudi.[9] The twelve masons and twenty-four workmen were supervised by a deputy overseer, who acted in Vasari's place. For some parts of the building full-scale wooden models were made according to Vasari's directions. As provveditore, Vasari had a salary of 150 scudi and other benefits.

The chronicle mentioned above reports that the old buildings had been pulled down 'in order to construct the street and the new quarters' for the administration. The loggia corridors on the ground floor of the Uffizi were built for pedestrian traffic and for the clients of the authorities waiting in front of the portals [268]. The street [269], about 140 m. (150 yards) in length and 18 m. (60 feet) in width, lined with uniform four-storeyed façades, which leads from the Piazza

267. Giorgio Vasari: Florence, Uffizi, 1560-soon after 1580, plan and detail

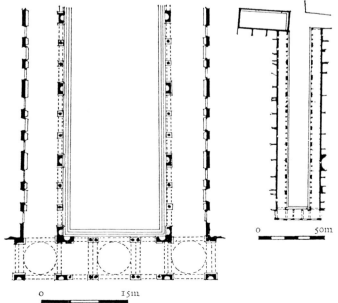

268. Giorgio Vasari: Florence, Uffizi, 1560–soon after 1580, loggia

269. Giorgio Vasari: Florence, Uffizi, 1560–soon after 1580

Signoria to the Arno, is the urbanistic analogy to the Strada Nuova in Genoa; the client in this case was the ruler of the dukedom of Tuscany, while in Genoa it was the patrician oligarchy of the republic. Consequently, the Florentine buildings are uniform and the Genoese façades vary.

Vasari subdivided the long façade into units of three bays. On the ground floor, coupled Doric columns alternate with thicker pillars. In the main storey, flat wall-strips frame each set of three windows. The middle window has a segmental pediment, the side windows triangular ones, so that the central axis of each group of three has a strong central accent. A delicate relief, indispensable to the general effect of the long fronts, is given by the shallow projections of the cornice above the pillars and pilaster strips. Complicated details were impossible in a façade of this length and height. The relief had to be easy to read; more powerful projections with rhythmic backward and forward movements would have produced an effect of restlessness.[10]

The vaulting of the ground-floor loggia is lighted by openings in the mezzanine over the Doric order. Similar windows are to be seen in the coffered tunnel-vault of Bramante's choir in S. Maria del Popolo and in the cortile loggia of Peruzzi's Palazzo Massimo. At this point Vasari could quote 'classical' models. On the other hand, there is

a novel variation of the traditional coffering in the tunnel-vault.[11]

The choice of the Doric order for the ground floor of the Uffizi was, as Vasari writes, the Duke's. For the construction of the architrave, a new kind of iron clamp was used, which Vasari describes in detail.[12]

While he was supervising the work on the Uffizi, Vasari also had a hand in the rebuilding of the medieval Palazzo Comunale of Pisa, which was remodelled in 1561 by Cosimo I to become the residence of the Cavalieri di S. Stefano, an order which he had founded.[13] In his native town of Arezzo Vasari designed in 1566 the abbey church of SS. Fiora e Lucilla, and in 1573 the Logge Vasariane.[14]

Vasari's modernization of the interior of the great Florentine friars' churches of S. Maria Novella (1565–72) and S. Croce (1566–84) is important for sixteenth-century architecture in Europe. It is closely connected with the ideas of the Council of Trent, and parallel to the contemporary work of Carlo Borromeo in Milan. Both 'purified' churches express the new ideal conception of the open, clarified space which was also expressed in the Gesù in Rome. According to Vasari, he acted by order of Cosimo I, who wished, as a Catholic ruler, to follow the path of the great Solomon 'and to have the churches renovated, improved, and beautified'.

270. Bernardo Buontalenti: Pratolino, Villa Medici, begun 1569, painting
by Utens, Florence

So he had to remove the high medieval screens and the
monks' choirs from the nave and to place the choir stalls
behind the new high altar. In S. Croce a tall gilt ciborium
was placed on the high altar; further, in both churches the
old altars in the aisles were replaced by uniform, large
aedicules with new altar paintings.[15] According to contemporary writers, all other monastic churches were cleared in
the same fashion, and looked 'rinate e rimbellite'.[16]

BUONTALENTI

Vasari's work at the Uffizi was completed by Bernardo
Buontalenti (1531–1608), who, in 1586, superintended the
building of the theatre in the upper storey – the first permanent theatre in Florence (though later demolished) – and
designed the famous *tribuna*, the octagonal domed hall in
which the finest pieces of the Medicean art collection were
exhibited.[17] Buontalenti owes his reputation above all to his
technical skill. He built fortresses, harbours, and canals, and
was a fireworks specialist. His greatly admired architectural
masterpiece, the Medici Villa at Pratolino, near Florence,
begun in 1569 [270], was almost entirely destroyed in the
early nineteenth century; according to Montaigne, who visited
Pratolino in 1580, its fountains and gardens rivalled those of
the Villa d'Este at Tivoli, though they had 'quelque peu plus
de mignardise'.[18] Of the Medici Villa at Signa, also designed
by Buontalenti, only the palazzo remains; its plain and
undecorated forms recall Florentine villas of the Quattrocento. His large addition to the Palazzo Vecchio continues
the type of earlier Florentine façades with its coarse rustication and plain windows.

Where Buontalenti shows an inexhaustible wealth of
invention is in his architectural ornament. His native talent
was for decorative detail, and form as a whole and articulation
remain traditional. A famous example is the Porta delle
Suppliche, a side entrance to the Uffizi [271]. The portal is
Michelangelesque in type, but Buontalenti varies the motif
of the broken pediment by reversing the half-pediments, i.e.
by making them sweep up from the centre to the sides. On
the portal of the Casino Mediceo, the tympanum is inhabited
by a bat-like animal whose wings spread out like a shell. The
wavy bands of the archivolts look as though they had been
moulded in clay. The same is true of the swags which hold
the coat of arms in place as the keystone of the arch.[19]

The system of the façade of S. Trinità in Florence, completed in 1594, in which Buontalenti reverts to the Albertian
scheme of S. Maria Novella, looks outdated beside the contemporary façade of S. Susanna in Rome, but the 'pediments, door-frames, cartouches, capitals, and volutes have
been given forms never seen before'.[20] Rome has nothing to
compare with Buontalenti's high altar in S. Trinità and the
staircase leading from the transept to the altar [272]. The
banisters taper downwards instead of upwards, and the steps,
rolled like volutes, are too narrow for use and are merely
there for the visual effect; the actual way up to the altar is at
the side, behind the balustrade.[21]

The weak successors of Cosimo I had neither the energy
nor the means to continue his great enterprises, so that
several of Buontalenti's schemes were abandoned at their
beginnings or never carried out. Among these projects are
the Cappella dei Principi, the mausoleum of the ducal house,
behind the choir of S. Lorenzo, not completed till the

271. (*left*) Bernardo Buontalenti: Florence, Uffizi, Porta delle Suppliche, 1576–7

272. (*above*) Bernardo Buontalenti: Florence, S. Stefano al Ponte, steps leading to choir (formerly in S. Trinità), 1574

273. (*below*) Giorgio Vasari and Bernardo Buontalenti: Florence, Boboli Gardens, grotto, façade, 1556–60 and 1583–93

eighteenth century, the façade of the cathedral, the reconstruction of the choir of S. Spirito, and Buontalenti's stairway and fountain in front of the Palazzo Pitti.[22]

The many models for the façade of the cathedral made after designs by Buontalenti and his competitors are preserved in the Museo dell'Opera.[23] Compared with the contemporary development in Rome, they have the oddly old-fashioned look of Florentine architecture about 1600, when interest was concentrated more on detail than on the organization of the form as a whole. That also holds good of Buontalenti's contemporary Dosio (1533–*c.* 1609) and his pupil Ludovico Cardi, called Cigoli (1559–1613), and the architectural work of the sculptor Giovanni da Bologna (1524–1608). The Michelangelesque motif of columns recessed into the wall had no progeny in Rome; in Florence it survives in Dosio's Cappella Niccolini in S. Croce, and in Giovanni da Bologna's Cappella del Soccorso in SS. Annunziata.[24]

BIZZARRIE

The bizarre grotto behind the Palazzo Pitti conveys some idea of the vanished gardens laid out by Buontalenti at Pratolino; it is one of the most important examples of the fusion of nature with art which is an outstanding characteristic of the Cinquecento. The façade [273] begun by Vasari – the ground floor is a repetition of the Uffizi motif of double Doric columns flanked by pillars – is attached to the passage between the Uffizi and the Pitti. Buontalenti's upper storey can hardly be regarded as architecture; the pumice-stone which hangs from the pediments like stalactites and the mosaic wall make the front look like a freak of nature. Over the architrave of the columns a lunette opens on to the

dark interior of the grotto [274] in which were 'the four roughhewn figures by the divine hand of Michelangelo, which look as if they had been specially made for this purpose. They support the vaulting. Buontalenti also created many figures, human and animal, and had them painted by his pupil Poccetti'.[25] From the first grotto a passage of artificial rocks leads into a smaller one, which ends in a third grotto with a mosaic wall fountain, from which water drips over rock crystal. In the midst of this cave stands the fountain with Giambologna's nude figure of Venus: Anadyomene. It is only when the eye has grown accustomed to the dim light that it becomes aware of the countless shells on the pedestals of the statues and on the walls, the satyrs which look up from the edge of the fountain, the water jets which shoot up round the statue, the seemingly natural forms untouched by human hand on walls and vaults. The grotto represents the birth cave of the Anadyomene. What has been created here, with frescoes, stucco-work, unhewn stone, and flowing water, is the counterpart of the courtly ceremonial in the neighbouring palazzo, a union of nature and art which seems to come from an older, more primitive world.[26]

The strange and intentional contrast between nature not yet shaped and architecture shaped according to the rules of the art can be traced throughout the century. It is first seen in the rusticated base of Bramante's Palazzo Caprini, and in Giulio's Sala dei Giganti and his unfinished, half-hewn columns in the Palazzo del Te at Mantua. Quite similar columns can be seen in the courtyard of Palladio's Palazzo Thiene at Vicenza, and the same building contains a fireplace shaped like the mouth of a huge leafy head, and another like the mouth of Polyphemus. About 1550 the sculptor employed on the building, Bartolomeo Ridolfi, did three similar fireplaces in Sanmicheli's Villa Fumane near Verona.[27] On the ground floor of the studio which Federico Zuccari built for himself in Florence in 1579, 'rough, unhewn' blocks project from the smoothly worked surface, three showing in relief the tools of the painter, sculptor, and architect, and on the

275. Bomarzo, Sacro Bosco, probably 1550–70, miniature tempietto

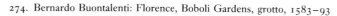

274. Bernardo Buontalenti: Florence, Boboli Gardens, grotto, 1583–93

upper storey two perfectly 'correct' windows flank a panel, now empty, which was intended for a fresco. As Zuccari explains in his treatise: 'These three professions [are] a single science...; this excellent profession [of architecture] in conjunction with two others appears really as one single and complete science....' With his 'scienza' the artist forms out of the raw material of nature the 'perfect' creation of art.[28]

The quickset mazes and the Rometta of the Villa d'Este at Tivoli, or Buontalenti's grottoes adjoining the Pitti, must be regarded in this sense as pictorial architecture. At Pratolino there was an 'artificial mountain, at the top of which is a white horse, leaping, with two wings, and immediately below...there sit the nine muses with Apollo carved in stone'.[29] Thus Pegasus reared on an artificial Parnassus.

The most famous example of bizarre 'pictorial architecture' is the so-called Sacro Bosco of Bomarzo.[30] In this case, what is represented is the opposite of order and rule. There are no straight paths in the gardens – in contrast to the clarity of the scheme in the Villa d'Este, it is intentionally disordered. In the small house which stands on the hillside there are no right angles; all the walls, floors, and ceilings are off the straight. The tortoises hewn in tufa in the garden are as big as the elephants by the side of them, so that even the dimensions are 'irrational'. Not far from a miniature tempietto [275] is the monstrous opening of a huge cave, a Gate of Hell [276], much larger than the portal of the

276. Bomarzo, Sacro Bosco, probably 1550–70, the 'Gate of Hell'

tempietto. The visitor, confronted time and again by extravagance, is encouraged by an inscription to wonder whether so many marvels have been made to deceive him, or to impress him as creations of art.[31] This is a conscious allusion to the ambiguity of all art – it may be truth, and it may be deceit, turning the world upside down, an architectural parallel to the contemporary paintings of Pieter Brueghel.

The client at Bomarzo, Virginio Orsini, who resided in the castle above the garden, was in close contact with the Roman humanists of his day. His letters show that he made a considerable contribution to the design and conception of the complex. The gardens of Bomarzo should not be regarded merely as the capricious idea of an eccentric, for beside the formal canon of Palladio or Vignola, the architecture of the sixteenth century also tolerated the possibility of an uncanonical 'bizzarria', though admittedly the bizarre forms are placed only where they can be justified.

Thus Federico Zuccari, in the last decade of the century, repeated on the front of his Roman residence, in a somewhat milder form, the 'bizzarrie' of the Florentine façade. The real showpiece, however, is the portal in the wall which originally separated the little garden from the street – a huge, grotesque maw flanked by two similar ones for the windows [277]. It is significant that the portal led into the garden, for in such a situation, as in the garden beside the Pitti, fantastic natural forms and forces 'not yet tamed' were acceptable. It is not by chance that Zuccari's gate of the Inferno in a drawing for the *Divina Commedia* is very similar.[32] From ancient times the architect was regarded as the image of God; as God created the order of the world, the architect creates the order of his building. In the world created by God, Hell is the opposite of 'right being'; in the world of the architect, the 'bizzarrie' are the opposite of rule and order.

277. Federico Zuccari: Rome, Palazzo Zuccari, *c.* 1590, garden portal

Notes

Additional notes to the revised edition appear on page 190

Note: For full quotations of the works here abbreviated as Vasari Mil. and as Venturi, *Storia*, see Bibliography section I. B (p. 191) and section III (p. 192).

INTRODUCTION

The editor would like to acknowledge the generous advice and help she has received from Christy Anderson, Bruce Boucher, Madeleine Brown, Georgia Clarke, Paul Davies and Caroline Elam.

1. Peter Murray, *The Architecture of the Italian Renaissance*, London, 1969; *idem, Renaissance Architecture*, London, 1986. Manfredo Tafuri's *L'architettura dell'Umanesimo*, Bari, 1969, is unfortunately out of print.

2. George Hersey, 'The Renaissance Matrix': review of Ludwig H. Heydenreich and Wolfgang Lotz, *Architecture in Italy 1400–1600* and of Hans-Karl Lücke, *Leon Battista Alberti: De Re Aedificatoria* (facsimile of first printed edition, Florence, 1485), *Journal of the Society of Architectural Historians*, XXXVI, 1977, 256.

3. See Arnaldo Bruschi, *Bramante architetto*, Bari, 1969, 989–95. I have discussed this problem in more detail in my recent article, 'Bramante's Tempietto: Spanish Royal Patronage in Rome', *Apollo*, CXXXVI, October 1992, 211–17, especially 211–12 and note 9.

4. Hubertus Günther, 'Bramantes Hofprojekt um der Tempietto und seine Darstellung in Serlios drittem Buch', in G. de Angelis d'Ossat *et al.*, *Studi Bramanteschi: Atti del Congresso Internazionale* (1970), Rome, 1974, 483–501, especially 490–1 and note 19.

5. C. L. Frommel, *Der römische Palastbau der Hochrenaissance*, 3 vols, Tübingen, 1973, 85.

6. Many articles on Italian Renaissance architecture have been cited in the recent exhibition catalogue *The Renaissance from Brunelleschi to Michelangelo*, edited by Henry A. Millon and Vittorio Magnano Lampugnani, London, 1994, 698–715.

7. The following biographical information is drawn from James Ackerman's introduction to Wolfgang Lotz's *Studies in the Italian Renaissance*, Cambridge, Mass. and London, 1977, xvii–xviii; and from the same author's obituary, 'In Memoriam: Wolfgang Lotz', *Journal of the Society of Architectural Historians*, XLI, March 1982, 5–6.

8. A full bibliography of Lotz's writings down to 1974 may be found in his *Studies in the Italian Renaissance* (*op. cit.*, Note 7), ix–xii.

9. Ackerman, 'In Memoriam,' (*op. cit.*, Note 6), 5.

10. Sir John Summerson, *Architecture in Britain 1530–1830*, Harmondsworth, 1953 and later editions. Summerson's contribution to modernist theory is discussed in C. St J. Wilson, *Architectural Reflections: Studies in the philosophy and practice of architecture*, Oxford, 1992, 26, 87–94 and 152–5.

11. For a recent analysis of this theme, see Alina A. Payne, 'Rudolf Wittkower and Architectural Principles in the Age of Modernism', *Journal of the Society of Architectural Historians*, LIII, September 1994, 322–42.

12. Nikolaus Pevsner, *Pioneers of Modern Design from William Morris to Walter Gropius*, Harmondsworth, 1960 and later edns. (first published as *Pioneers of the Modern Movement*, London, 1936).

13. Clarification may be sought in Franz Graf Wolff Metternich and Christof Thoenes, *Die frühen St Peter-Entwürfe, 1505–1514*, Tübingen, 1987; and Christoph Luitpold Frommel, 'St Peter's : The Early History', in Millon and Lampugnani (*op. cit.*), 399–423.

14. See Wolfgang Lotz, 'Notizen zum kirchlichen Zentralbau der Renaissance', *Studien zur toskanischen Kunst (Festschrift für Ludwig Heydenreich)*, Munich, 1964, 157–65.

15. Lotz explains his dissatisfaction with the term mannerism in his 'Mannerism in Architecture: Changing Aspects', in Millard Meiss *et al.* (eds), *Studies in Western Art*, Vol. II, *The Renaissance and Mannerism* (Acts of the 20th International Congress of the History of Art), Princeton, 1963, 239–46.

16. But see the criticisms in James Ackerman's review of C. L. Frommel's *Der römische Palastbau der Hochrenaissance* in the *Journal of the Society of Architectural Historians*, XXXIV, 1975, 74–5.

17. See especially Wolfgang Lotz, 'The Rendering of the Interior in Architectural Drawings of the Renaissance', English translation from the German original of 1965 in *Studies in the Italian Renaissance* (*op. cit.*, Note 7), 1–41.

18. For a survey of the field down to 1987/8 see William Hood, 'The State of Research: Italian Renaissance Art', *Art Bulletin*, LXIX, 1987, 174–86; and Marvin Trachtenberg, 'Some Observations on recent Architectural History', *Art Bulletin*, LXX, 1988, 208–41.

19. I have referred to the fundamental role of the Centro in my review article, Deborah Howard, 'Four Centuries of Literature on Palladio', *Journal of the Society of Architectural Historians*, XXXIX, 1980, 224–41. See also James S. Ackerman, 'Gli studi palladiani degli ultimi trent'anni', in André Chastel and Renato Cevese (eds), *Andrea Palladio: nuovi contributi* (Proceedings of Vicenza seminar, 1988), Milan, 1990, 122–6.

20. See especially 'Sixteenth-Century Italian Squares' and 'The Roman Legacy in Sansovino's Venetian Buildings', in Wolfgang Lotz, *Studies in the Italian Renaissance* (*op.cit.*, Note 7), 74–116 and 140–51.

21. See, for example, Tafuri's last book, *Ricerca del Rinascimento: Principi, città, architetti*, Turin, 1992. Tafuri's achievement and approach is summarized in the obituary by James Ackerman 'In Memoriam: Manfredo Tafuri, 1935–1994', *Journal of the Society of Architectural Historians*, LIII, June 1994, 137–8.

22. See the volumes edited by Jean Guillaume cited in the bibliography.

23. Wolfgang Braunfels, *Monasteries of Western Europe: The Architecture of the Orders*, translated by Alastair Laing, London, 1972; Irma B. Jaffé and R. Wittkower, *Baroque Art: the Jesuit Contribution*, New York, 1972; Richard Bösel, *Jesuitenarchitektur in Italien*, Teil I, 2 vols, Vienna, 1986.

24. Simon Pepper and Nicholas Adams, *Firearms and Fortifications: Military Architecture and Siege Warfare in Sixteenth Century Siena*, Chicago, 1986; Daniela Lamberini (ed.), *L'architettura militare veneta del Cinquecento* (proceedings of seminar held at Vicenza, 1982), Milan, 1988.

25. Brian Pullan, *Rich and Poor in Renaissance Venice: The Social Institutions of a Catholic State, to 1620*, Oxford, 1971; Deborah Howard, *Jacopo Sansovino: Architecture and Patronage in Renaissance Venice*, New Haven and London, 1975, revised edn. 1987; Philip L. Sohm, *The Scuola Grande di San Marco 1437–1550: The Architecture of a Venetian Lay Confraternity* (Ph.D. dissertation, Johns Hopkins University, 1978), New York and London, 1982; Manfredo Tafuri, *Venezia e il Rinascimento: Religione, scienza, architettura*, Turin, 1985; English translation by Jessica Levine as *Venice and the Renaissance*, Cambridge, Mass. and London, 1989; Patricia Fortini Brown, *Venetian Narrative Painting in the Age of Carpaccio*, New Haven and London, 1988.

26. Richard Bentmann and Michael Müller, *Die Villa als Herrschafts-architektur: Versuch einer kunst- und sozialgeschichtlichen Analyse*, Frankfurt, 1970, English edn, translated by T. Spence and D. Craven as *The Villa as Hegemonic Architecture*, New Jersey and London, 1992; James S. Ackerman, *The Villa: Form and Ideology of Country Houses* (A. W. Mellon lectures in the Fine Arts, 1985), Princeton, 1990.

27. David R. Coffin, *The Villa in the Life of Renaissance Rome*, Princeton, 1979; Howard Burns, Bruce Boucher and Lynda Fairbairn, *Andrea Palladio 1508–1580: The portico and the farmyard* (Arts Council exhibition catalogue), London, 1975.

28. David R. Coffin, *Gardens and Gardening in Papal Rome*, Princeton, 1991; Claudia Lazzaro, *The Italian Renaissance Garden: From the Conventions of Planting, Design and Ornament to the Grand Gardens of Sixteenth-Century Central Italy*, New Haven and London, 1990; Margherita Azzi Visentini, *L'Orto Botanico di Padova e il giardino del Rinascimento*, Milan, 1984.

29. Rudolf Wittkower, *Architectural Principles in the Age of Humanism*, London, 1949; and later edns.

30. See Antonio Pinelli, Orietta Rossi, *Genga architetto: aspetti della cultura urbinate del primo 500*, Rome, 1971.

31. C. L. Frommel, *Der römische Palastbau der Hochrenaissance*, 3 vols, Tübingen, 1973.

32. Kathleen Weil-Garris and John F. d'Amico, *The Renaissance Cardinal's Ideal Palace; A Chapter from Cortesi's De Cardinaltu*, Rome, 1980; Peter Thornton, *The Italian Renaissance Interior 1400–1600*, London, 1991; Jean Guillaume (ed.), *Architecture et vie sociale à la Renaissance* (proceedings of colloquium held at Tours, 1988), Paris, 1994.

33. See, for example, Deborah Howard, *Jacopo Sansovino* (*op. cit.*, note 25); and Clare Robertson, *Il Gran Cardinale: Alessandro Farnese, Patron of the Arts*, New Haven and London, 1992.

34. See especially Antonio Foscari and Manfredo Tafuri, *L'armonia e il conflitti: La Chiesa di San Francesco della Vigna nella Venezia del '500*, Turin, 1983; Manfredo Tafuri (ed.), *'Renovatio urbis': Venezia nell'età di Andrea Gritti (1523–1538)*, Rome, 1984; *idem, Venezia e il Rinascimento* (*op. cit.*, Note 25).

35. Christine Shaw, *Julius II: The Warrior Pope*, Oxford, 1993.

36. See, for example, H. Günther, *Das Studium der antiken Architektur in der Zeichnungen der Hochrenaissance*, Tübingen, 1989; and Howard Burns and Arnold Nesselrath, 'Raffaello e l'antico', in C.L. Frommel, S. Ray and M. Tafuri, *Raffaello architetto*, Milan, 1984, 379–450.

37. Myra Nan Rosenfeld, *Sebastiano Serlio on Domestic Architecture: the 16th-century manuscript of Book VI in the Avery Library of Columbia University* (facsimile reprint, with commentary), New York, Cambridge, Mass. and London, 1978; Vitruvius, *I dieci libri dell'architettura tradotti e commentati da Daniele Barbaro* (1567), with introductory essays by Manfredo Tafuri and Manuela Morresi, Milan, 1987; Sebastiano Serlio, *Architettura civile: Libri sesto, settimo e ottavo nei manoscritti di Monaco e Vienna*, ed. Francesco Paolo Fiore, Milan, 1994.

38. Jean Guillaume (ed.), *Les traités d'architecture de la Renaissance* (proceedings of colloquium held at Tours, 1981), Paris, 1988; *idem* (ed.), *L'emploi des ordres à la Renaissance* (proceedings of colloquium held at Tours, 1986), Paris, 1992.

39. See, for example, the recent article by Paul Davies, 'A project drawing by Jacopo Sansovino for the Loggetta in Venice', *The Burlington Magazine*, CXXXVI, August 1984, 487–97.

40. Christoph L. Frommel and Nicholas Adams, *The Architectural Drawings of Antonio da Sangallo the Younger and his Circle*, vol. I: *Fortifications, Machines, and Festival Architecture*, Cambridge, Mass. and London, 1994.

41. See, for example, Howard Burns, 'I disegni', in Renato Cevese (ed.), *Mostra del Palladio* (catalogue of exhibition at Basilica Palladiana, Vicenza), Milan, 1973, 131–54; and *idem*, 'I disegni del Palladio', *Bollettino del Centro Internazionale di Studi di Architettura 'Andrea Palladio'*, XV, 1973, 169–91.

42. See Gabriella Delfini *et al.*, *Fabbriche romane del primo '500: cinque secoli di restauri* (exhibition catalogue, Pantheon), Rome, 1984. The discovery, first cited by Forster and Tuttle (a work known to Lotz), that the surface rustication on the Palazzo del Tè dates from the late eighteenth century should also be mentioned in this context (Kurt W. Forster and Richard J. Tuttle, 'The Palazzo del Tè', *Journal of the Society of Architectural Historians*, XXX, 1971, 283–4.

43. The exception to this paucity of technical research is, of course, the study of fortifications, as mentioned above. See also J. Guillaume (ed.), *Les chantiers de la Renaissance* (proceedings of a colloquium held at Tours, 1983–4), Paris, 1991. Two recent attempts to look at Cinquecento architecture from a more technical perspective are Richard J. Betts, 'Structural Innovation and Structural Design in Renaissance Architecture', *Journal of the Society of Architectural Historians*, LII, 1993, 1–25; and Deborah Howard, 'Renovation and Innovation in Venetian Architecture', *Scroope*, VI, 1994/5, 66–74.

44. A personal and sensitive response to the bewildering developments in the subject over the past two decades is to be found in James Ackerman's reviews of his own articles in *Distance Points: Essays in Theory and Renaissance Art and Architecture*, Cambridge, Mass. and London, 1991.

45. Alexander Tzonis and Liane Lefaivre, *Classical Architecture: The Poetics of Order*, Cambridge, Mass. and London, 1987; George Hersey, *The Lost Meaning of Classical Architecture: Speculations on Ornament from Vitruvius to Venturi*, Cambridge, Mass. and London, 1988; John Onians, *Bearers of Meaning: The Classical Orders in Antiquity, the Middle Ages, and the Renaissance*, Princeton, 1988.

46. Mark Jarzombek, *Leon Battista Alberti: His Literary and Aesthetic Theories*, Cambridge, Mass. and London, 1989; Charles Burroughs, *From Signs to Design: Environmental Process and Reform in Early Renaissance Rome*, Cambridge, Mass. and London, 1990; Christine Smith, *Architecture in the Culture of Early Humanism: Ethics, Aesthetics, and Eloquence 1400–1470*, New York and Oxford, 1922.

47. The literature in these fields is enormous, but a few titles may be mentioned here: Clifford Geertz, *The Interpretation of Cultures*, New York, 1973; Edward Shils, *Tradition*, London, 1981; C. Geertz, *Local Knowledge: Further Essays in Interpretive Anthropology*, New York, 1983; David Cannadine and Simon Price (eds), *Rituals of Royalty, Power and Ceremonial in Traditional Societies*, Cambridge, 1987; Jean-Paul Bourdier and Nezar Alsayyad, *Dwelling, Settlements and Tradition: Cross-cultural perspectives*, New York and London, 1989 (especially the essays by Oliver and Rapoport); Catherine Bell, *Ritual Theory, Ritual Practice*, New York and Oxford, 1992.

48. See, for example, David Woodward (ed.), *Art and Cartography: Six Historical Essays*, Chicago and London, 1987; Dennis Cosgrove and Stephen Daniels (eds), *The Iconography of Landscape*, Cambridge, 1988.

49. The most useful recent publication is Barbara Wisch and Susan Scott Munshower, *Triumphal Celebrations and the Rituals of Statecraft* (Papers in Art History from Pennsylvania State University, Vol. VI, Part I of '*All the World's a Stage . . .': Art and Pageantry in the Renaissance and Baroque*), University Park, 1990.

50. See especially Ennio Concina, *Dell'arabico: A Venezia tra Rinascimento e Oriente*, Venice, 1994. See also the more global treatment in Jay A. Levenson (ed.), *Circa 1492: Art in the Age of Exploration* (exhibition catalogue, National Gallery of Art, Washington D.C.), New Haven and London, 1991.

51. Stephen Greenblatt, *Renaissance Self-fashioning: From More to Shakespeare*, Chicago and London, 1980, 2.

52. Millon and Lampugnani (eds), *The Renaissance from Brunelleschi to Michelangelo* (*op. cit.*, Note 6).

CHAPTER I

1. For Serlio's life and work see A. Blunt, *Art and Architecture in France: 1500–1700* (Pelican History of Art; the edition here quoted is the first, Harmondsworth, 1953), 44 ff., and M. Rosci, *Il Trattato di architettura di Sebastiano Serlio* (Milan, n.d.), 13 ff.

2. See the authoritative survey of Bramante's œuvre by A. Bruschi, *Bramante architetto* (Bari, 1969).

3. Cesare Cesariano's edition of Vitruvius (Pavia, 1521), fol. 70 verso. The edition of Vitruvius published in 1536 at Perugia by Bernardo Caporali is practically a reprint of the Cesariano text; it adds to the passage quoted that the author, i.e. Caporali, had taken part in a symposium with Perugino, Signorelli, and Pinturicchio held at Bramante's house, where Vitruvius's description of the ancient peripteral temple was discussed.

4. Cf. Bramante's alteration of S. Satiro, Milan, and the church of S. Maria delle Grazie di Fornò at Forlì, built in 1450, an imitation on a smaller scale of S. Stefano Rotondo, Rome. See also E. Rosenthal, 'The Antecedents of Bramante's Tempietto', *Journal of the Society of Architectural Historians*, XXIII (1964), 55 ff. According to the inscription on a marble tablet in the crypt, the Tempietto ('Sacellum') was 'erected by King Ferdinand and Queen Isabella of Spain in 1502'. R. Bonelli (*Da Bramante a Michelangelo* (Venice, 1960), 19 and 45), G. de Angelis d'Ossat (*Palladio*, XVI (1966), 83 ff.), and Bruschi (*op. cit.*, 481 and 989) suggested a date *c.* 1510; but see Rosenthal, *op. cit.*, 55, note 2. It should also be noted that Queen Isabella died in 1504.

5. Book III. See also W. Lotz, 'Notizen zum kirchlichen Zentralbau der Renaissance', in *Studien zur Toskanischen Kunst, Festschrift für L. H. Heydenreich* (Munich, 1964), 162 f.

6. The two ancient rotundas appeared already in Giuliano da Sangallo's Codex Barberini, and also later in Serlio and Palladio. As in the ancient buildings, the height of the columns in Bramante's Tempietto tallies fairly exactly with the width of the cella. The use of the Doric instead of the Corinthian order may be connected with Serlio's theory that the 'robuster' Doric order was appropriate to the 'masculine' St Peter's (Book IV).

7. For confirmation, see G. Giovannoni's *Saggi sulla architettura del Rinascimento*, 2nd ed. (Milan, 1935), 152.

8. The seated figure of the Apostle in the altar niche is modern; the relief and mensa, on the other hand, are part of the original furnishings. Early in the seventeenth century the crypt under the Tempietto was renovated and at the same time alterations were made to the altar, porch, dome, and lantern.

9. C. Ricci, 'Il Chiostro della Pace', *Documenti Bramanteschi, Nuova Antologia* (1915), 361 ff.; Bruschi, *op. cit.*, 872 ff. The cloister was commissioned by Cardinal Oliviero Carafa; his name appears in the architrave of the Ionic order.

10. In J. S. Ackerman's authoritative monograph, *The Cortile del Belvedere* (Vatican City, 1954), all the documents and the views of the Belvedere Court are contained and set forth in order. The present description and analysis of its architecture are based on this monograph. See also Bruschi, *op. cit.*, 291 ff. and 865 ff.; H. H. Brummer, *The Statue Court in the Vatican Belvedere* (Stockholm, 1970).

11. For the date of the medal see R. Weiss, 'The Medals of Pope Julius II (1503–13)', *Journal of the Warburg and Courtauld Institutes*, XXVIII (1956), 180 f.

12. In his *Commentari*, Pius II speaks with enthusiasm of the view from the garden loggia of the Palazzo Piccolomini at Pienza; the terraces and staircases of the Belvedere Court also recall a project of 1489 by Giuliano da Sangallo for the palace of the King of Naples (G. Marchini, *Giuliano da Sangallo* (Florence, 1942), 88, and Bruschi, *op. cit.*, 308 and figure 209), which Bramante may have known.

13. The arrangement can be compared to that of Roman triumphal arches.

14. Under construction at the time of Bramante's death, the logge were completed by Raphael; for the chronology see Bruschi, *op. cit.*, 931 ff. The glazing in of the façades has greatly impaired the original architectural effect.

15. L. von Pastor, *The History of the Popes from the Close of the Middle Ages*, 3rd English ed., 36 vols. (London, 1950), VI, 636 ff. and 461 ff., is the best summary of the data of the rebuilding of St Peter's under Julius II. For the medal and the parchment plan see also P. Murray, 'Menicantonio, du Cerceau, and the Towers of St Peter's', in *Studies in Renaissance and Baroque Art presented to Anthony Blunt* (London 1967), 7 ff.

16. In contrast to the usual orientation, the façade of St Peter's is to the east, the choir to the west. For the relation of Rossellino's choir to the new structure cf. F. Wolff Metternich, 'Bramantes Chor der Peterskirche zu Rom', *Römische Quartalschrift*, LVIII (1963), 271 ff.

17. Book III.

18. The measurements given by Serlio in Book III for the designs by Bramante, Raphael, and Peruzzi, which all tally with each other, are as follows:

Interior diameter of the dome	188 palms
Total height of the lantern	36 palms
Total height of the dome	224 palms
Height of the crossing arches	220 palms
Span of the crossing arches	104 palms

Serlio measures the span from pilaster to pilaster; this gives 110 palms from wall to wall, i.e. the width of the nave of old St Peter's. The difference of 4 palms (about 3 feet) seems small in these great dimensions. For the measurements and the slight inaccuracies of Serlio's figures see F. Wolff Metternich, 'Über die Massgrundlagen des Kuppelentwurfes Bramantes für die Peterskirche in Rom', in *Essays in the History of Architecture presented to Rudolf Wittkower* (London, 1967), 40 ff. As Count Metternich has shown, the parchment plan provided for a dome the radius of which was to be equal to the width of the *apse* of old St Peter's (80 palms), whereas the radius of the final scheme equals the width of the *nave* of the Constantinian church.

19. Cf. below, p. 54.

20. Charles de Tolnay, *The Tomb of Julius II* (Princeton, N.J., 1954), 19 and 164, and H. von Einem, in *Festschrift für Hans Jantzen* (Berlin, 1951), 152 ff., have assumed that Michelangelo's design of 1505 for the tomb had in view the site over the confessio, and was therefore intended as the tomb both of the Apostle and the Pope. Yet neither Vasari nor Condivi seems to offer any adequate support for this theory, especially as none of the reconstructions of the Michelangelo design carried out so far contains a proper emplacement for the altar, which was indispensable as the liturgical focus of the building (cf. F. Wolff Metternich in *Der Mensch und die Künste, Festschrift für Heinrich Lützeler* (Düsseldorf, 1962), 443 ff.). We know that Julius II vigorously opposed Bramante's attempts to change the site of the confessio; the determination to preserve the original confessio also comes out in the splendid structure of the *tigurio* designed by Bramante to encase the high altar during the building of the new church; for the back wall consisted of the apse of Constantine's basilica. For the measurements and plan of the *tigurio* see J. Christern and K. Thiersch, *Römische Quartalschrift*, LXIV (1969), 16 ff. and figure 4.

21. F. Tassi (ed.), *Ricordi, prose e poesie di Benvenuto Cellini* (Florence, 1829), III, 367.

22. For the identification of the building see Giovannoni, *op. cit.*, 97, note 2, and Bruschi, *op. cit.*, 1040 ff. The façade was drawn by Palladio. The engraving in the present volume is reproduced from the comprehensive ancient and contemporary views brought out by the French publisher Antonio Lafreri in Rome about the middle of the sixteenth century. For a catalogue of these engravings cf. C. Huelsen, 'Das Speculum Romanae Magnificentiae des Antonio Lafreri', *Festschrift für Leo S. Olschki: Collectanea Variae Doctrinae* (Munich, 1921), 121 ff.

23. Serlio characterizes rustication as 'parte opera di natura e parte opera di artificio' (Book IV, 'dell'ornamento rustico').

24. For documents see the summary in Bruschi, *op. cit.*, 960 ff. According to the legend, the Casa Santa was the place of the Virgin's birth carried from Nazareth to Loreto by angels. The incrustation was completed by Andrea Sansovino under Leo X after a model by Bramante. See also Bruschi, *op. cit.*, 652 ff., for Bramante's design of the large oblong square bounded by the façades of the church of the Santa Casa and the papal palace.

25. Book IV, 'dell'ordine corinthio': 'A temple of this order shall be dedicated to the Virgin as the Mother of Christ.' The encasement of the high altar and the tomb of the Apostle in St Peter's, begun by Bramante about the same time, had, like the Tempietto, the Doric order. See above, Note 6.

26. In Spain, c. 1530, in Charles V's palace at Granada. In France, echoes of the Vatican logge can be seen in the north-west front of Blois (cf. Blunt, *op. cit.*, 10 and plate 8b). In Germany the knowledge of Bramante's designs about 1510–15 can be proved from the work of three artists: a master of the Altdorfer circle at Regensburg (cf. P. Halm, *Münchner Jahrbuch der bildenden Künste*, 3rd series, 11 (1951), 20); in Hermann Vischer, the son of Peter Vischer, who made drawings of Bramante's buildings in 1514–15 (cf. W. Lotz, *Miscellanea Bibliothecae Hertzianae* (Munich, 1961), 157 ff.); and finally in the Fugger Chapel in St Anna at Augsburg (cf. W. Lotz, *Mitteilungen des Kunsthistorischen Instituts in Florenz*, VII (1956), 208).

27. Pastor, *op. cit.*, 360; Ludwig H. Heydenreich, *Architecture in Italy 1400–1500* (New Haven and London, 1996) chapter 12, Note 42.

28. Leo X's papal writ of 1 August 1514: V. Golzio, *Raffaello nei documenti, nelle testimonianze dei contemporanei e nella letteratura del suo secolo* (Città del Vaticano, 1936), 33. Raphael had been at work on the building since 1 April 1514. Fra Giocondo's appointment was confirmed on 1 August 1514: as the elder, he received four hundred ducats, Raphael three hundred, but both bore the title of 'magister operis', while Giuliano da Sangallo was employed as

superintendent and assistant. He had the same salary as Raphael, three hundred ducats a year. Documents for the appointments of Fra Giocondo and Sangallo in Pastor, *op. cit.*

29. A satirical dialogue printed in 1517 describes how St Peter keeps Bramante waiting at the gates of Heaven until the new church is finished. Bramante attempts to throw the blame for the destruction of old St Peter's on Julius II and to make excuses for himself. Cf. Andrea Guarna da Salerno, ed. G. and E. Battisti, *Scimmia* (Rome, 1970), 105–21.

30. For these questions cf. D. Frey, *Bramante-Studien. Bramante's St Peter-Entwurf und seine Apokryphen* (Vienna, 1915), and the plates in T. Hofmann, *Entstehungsgeschichte des St Peter in Rom* (Zittau, 1928). The more recent account of Bramante's share in the planning and building history found in O. H. Förster, *Bramante* (Vienna-Munich, 1956), 209 ff., differs somewhat from the following.

31. Variants:
   (a) Giuliano da Sangallo, Uffizi 9 (cf. Marchini, *op. cit.*, plate XXIb).
   (b) Giuliano da Sangallo, Uffizi 7 (cf. Marchini, *op. cit.*, plate XXIIa).
       Antonio da Sangallo, Uffizi 252 (cf. Hofmann, *op. cit.*, 110).
       Peruzzi, Uffizi 2 [25].
   (c) Giuliano da Sangallo, Codex Barberini (cf. Marchini. *op. cit.*, plate XXIIb).
       Mellon sketchbook, fol. 72 verso [28]; for the sketchbook see H. Nachod, 'A Recently Discovered Architectural Sketchbook', *Rare Books*, VIII (1955); cf. also below, Chapter 2, Note 13).
   (d) Raphael according to Serlio.
       Peruzzi, Uffizi 14 (cf. H. von Geymüller, *Les Projets primitifs pour la basilique de Saint-Pierre de Rome* (Paris, 1875), plate 20, 6).
       Peruzzi according to Serlio [16B].
       Mellon sketchbook, fol. 73 recto (cf. Nachod, *op. cit.*, figure 7, and Förster, *op. cit.*, figure III).

32. Variants:
   (a) Giuliano da Sangallo, Uffizi 8 recto.
   (b) Peruzzi according to Serlio [16B].
   (c) Mellon sketchbook, fol. 70 verso-71 recto (cf. Nachod, *op. cit.*, figure 2, and Förster, *op. cit.*, figure 112).

33. Variants:
   (a) Antonio da Sangallo, Vienna (Frey, *op. cit.*, figure 30).
   (b) Codex Coner, fol. 17 (cf. T. Ashby, 'Sixteenth-Century Drawings of Roman Buildings attributed to Andreas Coner', *Papers of the British School at Rome*, 11 (1904), 1 ff.).
   (c) Giuliano da Sangallo, Uffizi 9 (see above).
   (d) Giuliano da Sangallo, Uffizi 7, variant to the right (see above).
   (e) Giuliano da Sangallo, Codex Barberini, variant to the left (see above).
       Peruzzi, Uffizi 14, variant to the left [26].
   (f) Giuliano da Sangallo, Codex Barberini, right-hand variant.
       Raphael according to Serlio.
       Mellon sketchbook, fol. 72 verso (see above).
   (g) Mellon sketchbook, fol. 73 recto (see above).
   (h) Peruzzi, Uffizi 14 [26].
       Peruzzi, Uffizi 16 (Geymüller, *op. cit.*, plate 20, 5).
       Peruzzi, Uffizi 15 (Frey, *op. cit.*, figure 12).
       Antonio da Sangallo, Uffizi 255.
       Antonio da Sangallo (copy), Munich, Staatsbibliothek, cod. icon. 195 (related solution).

CHAPTER 2

1. V. Golzio, *Raffaello nei documenti etc.* (Vatican City, 1936), 33 f.

2. Bramante's life and work show how small was the part played in the practice of architecture by technical training.

3. Erected as the memorial chapel of Agostino Chigi, banker to Julius II and Leo X, and of his brother Sigismondo. The mosaics in the dome bear the date 1516. Part of the decoration was incomplete when the patron died in 1520; according to a contract dating from that year the work was continued after the existing designs. The marble slabs and the pyramid-shaped monuments were partly renovated by Bernini. For documents on the history of the building see Golzio, *op. cit.*, 101 and 126; J. Shearman, 'The Chigi Chapel in S. Maria del Popolo', *Journal of the Warburg and Courtauld Institutes*, XXIV (1961), 129 ff., and M. Hirst, *ibid.*, 183 ff.

4. In the constellation pictured in the dome, Raphael continued a tradition which went back to the choir of the Pazzi Chapel. Cf. J. Seznec, *The Survival of the Ancient Gods* (New York, 1953), 79 ff.

5. Golzio, *op. cit.*, 222 and 47, note 1; H. von Geymüller, *Raffaello Sanzio studiato come architetto* (Milan, 1884), 57, with the date 1520, not confirmed elsewhere. Vasari called the palazzo 'cosa bellissima'. The façade was stuccoed by Giovanni da Udine (see Vasari Mil., VI, 555, as 'cosa singolare'). Cf. the

floor plan of the palace in Munich, Staatsbibliothek, cod. icon. 195.

6. First attribution to Raphael on an engraving by Alessandro Specchi, 1696. According to Vasari, the author was Raphael's pupil Lorenzetto. The Specchi engraving gives the date as 1515, which may go back to some lost inscription on the building. Reconstruction of the original façade in Geymüller, op. cit., 54; it was twice enlarged and now has seventeen instead of the original seven bays.

7. Baldassare Castiglione was in possession of a letter by Raphael which contained a description of the layout (cf. Golzio, op. cit., 147 ff.). A copy of this letter was recently discovered and published by P. Foster; cf. 'Raphael on the Villa Madama: the Text of a Lost Letter', Römisches Jahrbuch für Kunstgeschichte, XI (1967–8), 307 ff.: 'the form, style and architectural terminology in Raphael's description confirm the hypothesis . . . that the architect of the Villa Madama may have had in mind the creation of a building similar to Pliny's Laurentine Villa'.

After Raphael's death Giulio Romano and Giovanni da Udine continued work on the decoration of the loggia (cf. A. Venturi, Archivio Storico dell'Arte, 11 (1889), 157 ff.). The actual work was probably discontinued soon after 1520. For a detailed description of the villa see Serlio, Book III; for views of the building before the modern restoration see T. Hofmann, Raffael in seiner Bedeutung als Architekt, 2nd ed., 1 (Zittau, 1908), plates IV–XII, XLVII–XLVIII; for further literature see C. L. Frommel, 'La Villa Madama e la tipologia della villa romana nel Rinascimento', Bollettino del Centro Internazionale di Studi di Architettura Andrea Palladio, XI (1969), 47 ff. and n. 63, note 12.

The 'Ninfeo' at Genazzano, probably the remains of a never-completed villa designed for Cardinal Pompeo Colonna, has many traits in common with the Villa Madama; cf. C. L. Frommel, 'Bramantes Ninfeo in Genazzano', Römisches Jahrbuch für Kunstgeschichte, XII (1969), 137 ff. Frommel's attribution to Bramante appears convincing in view of the analogies between the Ninfeo and the parchment plan for St Peter's. Cf. also Bruschi, Bramante architetto (Bari, 1969), 1048 ff.

8. Golzio, op. cit., 79 ff., provided definitive arguments that this letter, although couched in Castiglione's words, was written by Raphael rather than Bramante. The mere fact that Bramante, according to two reliable witnesses, could not write is a strong point against him. Cf. above, p. 11. The text of the letter in Golzio; English translation by V. Wanscher, Raffaello Santi da Urbino (London, 1926), 154 ff. German translation by J. Vogel, Bramante und Raffael (Leipzig, 1910). Cf. also V. Cian, Archivio Storico Lombardo, N.S. VII (1942), 70 ff., and Baldassar Castiglione (Vatican City, 1951).

9. For the organization of the office, see J. S. Ackerman, Journal of the Society of Architectural Historians, XIII (1954), fasc. 3, p. 5, and Lotz, Mitteilungen des Kunsthistorischen Instituts Florenz, VII (1956), 195 and 208 ff.

10. Cf. above, Note 8.

11. In a letter from Lionardo Sellaio to Michelangelo of 22 November 1516, we read 'Raphael applied for an assistant [at St Peter's] and Antonio da Sangallo was assigned to him' (Golzio, op. cit., 51).

12. Book III. Cf. also Golzio, op. cit., 34.

13. For the sketchbook, now in the collection of Mr Paul Mellon, cf. H. Nachod, 'A Recently Discovered Architectural Sketchbook', Rare Books, Notes on the History of Old Books and Manuscripts, VIII, no. 1 (New York, 1955), 1 ff. Nachod's attribution to Domenico de Chiarellis, a member of the office under Bramante and Raphael, is conjectural. The plan of Raphael's project in the sketchbook differs from Serlio's reproduction, since the Rossellino apse is retained and provided with an ambulatory; two colossal towers are added to the front. Serlio's version is an ideal plan, while that in the sketchbook takes account of the progress of the building in 1514.

14. Serlio gives the breadth of the nave in Raphael's plan as 92 palms, in Peruzzi's as 104 palms. The difference can be explained by the fact that Raphael intended the nave to be narrower than the crossing arch; this is confirmed by Antonio da Sangallo's memorandum (cf. below, p. 177). The plan in the Mellon sketchbook, which is probably more reliable than Serlio's woodcut in this respect, shows the niches in the piers walled up on the side of the nave; hence the piers were to be reinforced on that side.

15. The reintroduction of the minor domes explains the piercing of the walls of the Rossellino choir; its apse was to be retained, but its exterior view was to be adjusted to the arms of the cross by the one-storeyed ambulatory placed before it. Cf. [19, 29].

16. Florence, Uffizi 54 and 79; Munich, Staatsbibliothek, cod. icon. 195, fol. 3b.

17. Text in Geymüller, op. cit., 293 ff., Vasari Mil., V, 477 f., and G. Giovannoni, Antonio da Sangallo il giovane (Rome, n.d.), 132 f.

18. The plan facing Raphael's design in the Mellon sketchbook may show Sangallo's counterproject. The nave is wider and is vaulted in the same way as the rooms of Roman baths; it would therefore have been much better lighted by lunettes than by Raphael's tunnel-vault. Four large chapels have been added to the aisle, and the west apse now has the same ambulatory as the arms of the cross. All these differences correspond exactly to the suggested improvement contained in the memorandum.

CHAPTER 3

1. For the town-planning history of Rome, see Pastor, op. cit. (Chapter 1, Note 15), VI, chapter VIII, and VIII, chapter IV; P. Paschini, Roma nel Rinascimento (Storia di Roma, XII) (Bologna, 1940), passim; P. Pecchiai, Roma nel Cinquecento (Storia di Roma, XIII) (Bologna, 1948), passim; P. Romano, Roma nelle sue strade e nelle sue piazze (Rome, 1947–9); G. Giovannoni, 'Topografia e urbanistica di Roma', in Storia di Roma, XXII (Bologna, 1958). Cf. also the appendix 'Zur Urbanistik der Hochrenaissance: Via Giulia und Via Lungara' in C. L. Frommel, Die Farnesina und Peruzzis architektonisches Frühwerk (Berlin, 1961), 163 ff.

2. Vasari Mil., V, 451. For the history and restoration of the palace see R. U. Montini and R. Averani, Palazzo Baldassini e l'arte di Giovanni da Udine (Quaderni di Storia dell'Arte, V) (Rome, 1957); D. Redig de Campos, 'Notizia su Palazzo Baldassini', Bollettino Centro Studi per la Storia d'Architettura, X (1956), 3 ff.

3. For the plan see P. Letarouilly, Édifices de Rome moderne (Liège-Brussels, 1849–66), III, 267. The courtyard was altered several times, but not radically transformed. For similar courtyards in the palazzi Giraud-Torlonia and Alberini, cf. Venturi, Storia, XI, figures 192–7 and 241–2.

4. Sangallo's drawing of the plan of the Palazzo di Giustizia is reproduced in Venturi, Storia, XI, figure 97. For the Palazzo di Giustizia see also A. Bruschi, Bramante architetto (Bari, 1969), 593 ff.

5. For the contract see D. Gnoli, Annuario dell'Associazione Artistica tra i Cultori di Architettura, 1910–11 (Rome, 1912), 70 f. The rent was 150 ducats per annum. An anonymous drawing in the Metropolitan Museum of c. 1560 gives the elevation of two bays of the façade (no. 49.22.82).

6. The legend of an engraving of c. 1550 by Lafreri names Bramante as the architect and adds: 'often taken as a design by Raphael' (cf. Vasari Mil., V, 534). For the authorship see also J. Shearman in Bollettino Centro Internaz. Studi Arch. Andrea Palladio, VIII (1967), 357, 359. The present façade in the via de' Banchi has seven bays, that in Lafreri's engraving only five. The palazzo was enlarged in 1866, when the present side and rear façades were added; the cortile was altered too (cf. Il Buonarroti, 1 (1866), 75 and 135). Letarouilly, Édifices, 1, 106, shows the present plan. The Florentine architect Pietro di Giacomo Rosselli was witness to the signing of the contract. In 1516 Rosselli designed the house of Prospero de' Mocchi in the via dei Coronari; the two buildings, however, differ so widely that they can hardly be ascribed to the same architect. Cf. P. Tomei, L'Architettura a Roma nel Quattrocento (Rome, 1942), 239.

7. As Lafreri's engraving shows, the small square openings over the windows figured in the original building; they belong to the mezzanine rooms above the piano nobile.

8. For the predominance of the centralized plan cf. also W. Lotz, 'Notizen zum kirchlichen Zentralbau der Renaissance', in Studien zur toskanischen Kunst, Festschrift für L. H. Heydenreich (Munich, 1964), 157 ff., and S. Sinding-Larsen, 'Some Functional and Iconographical Aspects of the Centralized Church in the Italian Renaissance', in Acta ad Archaeologiam et Artium Historiam pertinentia, II (1965), 203 ff., with a list of centralized churches, 243 ff.

9. Vasari Mil., 1, 122; G. Mollat, 'Jean de Thororières, architecte de St Louis', Annales de St Louis des Français, VI (1902), 279. According to I. Lesellier, Mélanges, IIL (1931), 239, the architect was Jean de Chenevières. That S. Salvatore was not the French national church, but an independent building, can be deduced from Francesco Albertini, De mirabilibus Romae (1510), ed. Schmarsow (Heilbronn, 1886), 9. A number of fragments of the decoration of S. Salvatore were later used in S. Luigi dei Francesi.

10. This church, which Albertini (op. cit., 8) expressly names as a foundation of Julius II's, was later vaulted by Antonio da Sangallo the Younger; a choir chapel was added about 1550. About 1575 Giacomo del Duca erected a second dome over Sangallo's vault. Cf. M. Zocca, Atti del I Congresso Nazionale di Storia dell'Architettura (Florence, 1937), 100, and S. Benedetti, S. Maria di Loreto (Chiese di Roma illustrate, C) (Rome, 1968), 19 ff. For Sangallo's part in the building, which was probably restricted to the vaulting, cf. also J. S. Ackerman, The Cortile del Belvedere (Vatican City, 1954), 49, note 2.

11. Cf. J. S. Ackerman, Journal of the Society of Architectural Historians, XIII (1954), no. 3, p. 11, note 16. Above the entrance to the church is a group of the Virgin and Child executed for the church by Andrea Sansovino; it is dated 1520.

12. A plan of the same shape is to be found in the anterooms of the Baths of Diocletian, which were repeatedly drawn just at this time.

13. The façade of the Anima, erected under Julius II, is attributed to Andrea Sansovino by A. Venturi in Storia, XI (1), 148 f., while G. Marchini, Giuliano da Sangallo (Florence, 1942), 20, attributes it to Giuliano da Sangallo.

14. The building of the church was approved by Julius II in 1509, the dome was closed in 1536. The façade was completely renovated at the beginning of the seventeenth century, and the interior was twice restored in the twentieth century. The original state of the building can be reconstructed from sixteenth-century drawings; on one of them, Raphael is named as the architect, on another, Peruzzi. Cf. H. von Geymüller, Raffaello Sanzio studiato come architetto (Milan, 1884), 22, and C. L. Frommel, 'S. Eligio und die Kuppel der Cappella

Medici', in *Stil und Überlieferung, Akten des 21. Internationalen Kongresses für Kunstgeschichte, Bonn, 1964* (Berlin, 1967), 11, 41; 'Geymüller's attribution to Raphael remains the most probable of all hypotheses' (Frommel, *op. cit.*, note 27).

15. Plan and elevation in P. Laspeyres, *S. Maria della Consolazione zu Todi* (Berlin, 1869). The contracts and documents published in the *Giornale di Erudizion Artistica*, 1 (1872), 3 ff., and 111 (1874), 321 ff. A visitation report of 1574 mentions a model designed by Bramante; according to the same authority, the vaults planned (at that time) were to bear 'a certain resemblance to new St Peter's'. This can only refer to Michelangelo's centralized plan, which had been in hand since 1549. Whether the model which was at Todi in 1574 was really based on Bramante must remain a matter of conjecture. Cf. also Bruschi, *op. cit.*, (Note 4), 922 ff., and the exhaustive documentation provided by J. Zänker, *Die Wallfahrtskirche Santa Maria della Consolazione in Todi* (thesis, Bonn, 1971).

16. The travertine facing of the north apse was not carried out till early in the twentieth century. Cf. G. Giovannoni, *Bollettino d'Arte*, VII (1913), 32.

17. The faithful reproduction of the Ospedale recalls the efforts of Antonio's brother Giuliano da Sangallo to preserve Brunelleschi's plan for the portal of S. Spirito; both brothers must have felt it incumbent on them to preserve Brunelleschi's heritage; cf. W. Lotz, 'Italienische Plätze des 16. Jahrhunderts', *Jahrbuch 1968 der Max-Planck-Gesellschaft*, 50 ff.

18. For the building history cf. A. Schiavo, *Bollettino Centro Storia d'Arte*, fasc. 6 (Spoleto, 1952), 33, and particularly 47 ff.

19. Cf. the plan of Raphael's project in the Mellon sketchbook [28].

20. See H. von Geymüller, *Der Palazzo Pandolfini in Florenz und Raffaels Stellung zur Hochrenaissance in Toscana* (Munich, 1908). The client was Giannozzo Pandolfini, Bishop of Troia. Raphael was in Florence in 1515 and 1519 (cf. V. Golzio, *Raffaello* (Vatican City, 1936), 36); the plans for the palazzo may have been made during one of these periods. The account of the building history given by Vasari, who saw the palace under construction, is perfectly credible. After the Sack of Rome, work had slackened; after the death of Gianfrancesco da Sangallo in 1530, the palazzo was finished by his brother Aristotile 'to the point at which it can be seen now', which implies that Raphael's plan was not completed (Vasari Mil., VI, 264, and IV, 435). In the present building, only the ground floor can correspond to the original plan. The intention was certainly to give the piano nobile nine bays, but only the four now existing were carried out. The cortile which Raphael doubtless planned must have been abandoned, the finished part shut off by a wall at right angles to the wall of the façade, while the crowning cornice was continued along this wall. Since the name of Pope Clement VII appears in the inscription in the frieze above the wall, this part of the building could have been completed at the earliest in 1524, but probably not before 1530, under Aristotile as chief architect. The right-hand part of the façade never rose above the ground floor; a garden was laid out behind it. Cf. also G. Marchini, in *Raffaéllo. L'opera. Le fonti. La fortuna*, II (Novara, 1968), 480 ff.

21. The details of the window pediments tally almost exactly with those of the nearly contemporary Palazzo Branconio dall'Aquila, the balconies in front of the windows with those of the Palazzo Caprini. Instead of the upright oblong frame between the windows of the piano nobile, round niches with statues must have been planned, as in the Palazzo dall'Aquila. The present frames date from a later stage of building, when the niches were removed. Baccio d'Agnolo adopted the niche motif in his Palazzo Bartolini Salimbeni, Florence, as early as 1520.

22. For Giuliano da Sangallo's designs, cf. Charles de Tolnay, *Gazette des Beaux-Arts*, LXXVI (1934), 24 ff.; Marchini, *op. cit.* (Note 13), 69 ff. and 100; B. Degenhart, *Römisches Jahrbuch der Kunst*, VII (1955), *passim*; Richard Pommer's unpublished M.A. thesis, 1957 (MS. in the Institute of Fine Arts, New York University); W. Lotz, *Journal of the Society of Architectural Historians*, XXII (1963), 5 ff.; and P. Sanpaolesi, *Rivista Ist. Naz. d'Archeologia e Storia dell'Arte*, N.S. XIII–XIV (1964–5), 283 ff. Raphael's designs for the same façade are lost; cf. Golzio, *op. cit.* (Note 20), 36.

23. L. Serra, *Aquila monumentale* (Aquila, 1912), 38. The façade was begun in 1525, the second storey bears the date 1540. According to earlier sources, the façade bore the inscription 'Cola Amatricius Architector Instruxit 1527'.

24. R. Pane, *Architettura del Rinascimento a Napoli* (Naples, 1937), 269. In a contract of 1516 Giovanni Thoma da Como was instructed to execute certain details in the church of S. Maria delle Grazie in Naples, after the model of the marble arches of the Caracciolo Chapel; thus the ground floor, at any rate, of the latter must have been standing in 1516. Yet the contract does not imply, as Pane assumes, that both buildings are to be ascribed to the same master. In a letter from Pietro Summonte to Marcantonio Michiel, dated 20 March 1524, we read that 'the chapel begun by Galeazzo Caracciolo is now to be continued by his son'. In 1557 the decoration of the chapel was not yet finished; cf. *Napoli Nobilissima*, N.S. III (1922), 127 f. The architecture of the chapel has been attributed to Giovanni Tommaso Malvito by C. Thoenes in *Neapel und Umgebung* (Stuttgart, 1971), 132.

CHAPTER 4

1. In the preface to his Book II, 'della Prospettiva'.

2. Very few dates of Peruzzi's early life have been preserved. In 1501 he was assistant to Pinturicchio in the painting of the chapel of S. Giovanni in Siena Cathedral. The first works by him in Rome established by documentary evidence date from 1509 to 1510. Vasari gives the date 1503 for his removal to Rome; there is no other evidence for it. See also C. L. Frommel, *Baldassare Peruzzi als Maler und Zeichner* (Vienna–Munich, 1967–8), 10 f.

3. Vasari's attribution of the Farnesina to Peruzzi is now generally accepted. H. von Geymüller's attempt to associate the architecture of the villa with Raphael must be regarded as a failure.

In Aegidius Gallus's *De Viridario Augustino Chisii*, published in Rome in 1511, there is a detailed description of the frescoes on the ground floor of the Farnesina. At that time the building must have been far advanced, if not complete. Other sources and literature in E. Gerlini, *La Villa Farnesina in Roma* (Rome, 1949), 40 ff., and C. L. Frommel, *Die Farnesina und Peruzzis architektonisches Frühwerk* (Berlin, 1961), 199 ff. In the Villa Le Volte (now Mieli), near Siena, built by Sigismondo Chigi, Agostino's brother, there is an inscription with the date 1505. The composition anticipates certain features of the Farnesina, i.e. the horseshoe plan, the ground-floor loggia between the projecting wings, and the asymmetrical plan. It therefore seems plausible to ascribe it to Peruzzi; see Frommel, *op. cit.*, 106 ff. and 123 ff.

4. For the meaning of the frescoes, cf. F. Saxl, *La Fede astrologica di Agostino Chigi* (Rome, 1934), A. von Salis, *Antike und Renaissance* (Erlenbach–Zürich, 1947), 190 ff., and Frommel, *op. cit.* (Note 2), 46 ff.

5. Cf. also W. Lotz, *Mitteilungen des Kunsthistorischen Instituts Florenz*, VII (1956), 206.

6. See F. Cruciani, *Il Teatro del Campidoglio e le feste romane del 1513* (Milan, 1968), with the texts of the contemporary descriptions and a reconstruction of the theatre by A. Bruschi. A plan of the *theatrum* is to be found in the so-called Codex Coner, a contemporary sketchbook, fol. 23 (see T. Ashby, *Papers of the British School at Rome*, II (1904) and VI (1913); cf. also J. S. Ackerman, *Art Bulletin*, XXXVIII (1956), 55 ff., and I. Lavin, 'The Campidoglio and Sixteenth-Century Stage Design', in *Essays in Honor of Walter Friedlaender* (New York, 1956), 114 ff.). The construction of the Capitoline theatre of 1513 was directed by Pietro Rosselli (see above, Chapter 3, Note 6).

7. That is how Vasari (IV, 595) describes a temporary decorative structure designed by Peruzzi for the occasion of Giuliano de'Medici's nomination as Gonfaloniere della Santa Chiesa. Yet the data he gives tally exactly with the plan of the theatre of 1513; possibly Vasari confused the two ceremonies.

8. Cf. R. Krautheimer, 'The Tragic and Comic Scene of the Renaissance', *Gazette des Beaux-Arts*, 6th series, XXXIII (1948), 327 ff., and R. Klein and H. Zerner, 'Vitruve et le théâtre de la Renaissance italienne', in *Le Lieu théâtral à la Renaissance* (Colloques Internationaux du Centre National de la Recherche Scientifique, 22–7 mars 1963) (Paris, 1964), 49–60.

9. On 1 December 1534, Pope Paul III raised Peruzzi's salary for his work on St Peter's from 150 to 300 ducats per month (L. von Pastor, *Storia dei Papi*, V (Rome, 1959), document 6 in the appendix).

10. Cf. G. Zucchini, *Disegni antichi e moderni per la facciata di S. Petronio* (Bologna, 1933), *passim*, and R. Bernheimer, 'Gothic Survival and Revival in Bologna', *Art Bulletin*, XXXVI (1954), 275.

11. See W. Lotz, 'Die ovalen Kirchenräume des Cinquecento', *Römisches Jahrbuch für Kunstgeschichte*, VII (1955), 26 ff.

12. Cf. H. Wurm, *Der Palazzo Massimo alle Colonne* (Berlin, 1965), and the review by H. Biermann, *Zeitschrift für Kunstgeschichte*, XXX (1967), 251 ff. The palazzo is still in the possession of the family.

13. F. Tassi (ed.), *Ricordi, prose e poesie di Benvenuto Cellini* (Florence, 1829), III, 369.

14. G. Giovannoni, *Antonio da Sangallo il giovane*, 2 vols. (Rome, n.d., c. 1959). The book, published posthumously, is indispensable for Sangallo's biography, buildings, and drawings; the bibliography and the notes are inadequate. Cf. also J. S. Ackerman, *Journal of the Society of Architectural Historians*, XIII, no. 3 (1954), 3 ff.

15. Cf. above, p. 34.

16. Cf. Giovannoni, *op. cit.*, I, 84.

17. Cf. *Plan und Bauwerk*, catalogue of exhibition (Munich, 1952), 15 ff.; H. Siebenhüner, in *Kunstgeschichtliche Studien für Hans Kauffmann* (Berlin, 1956), 172 ff.; E. Rufini, *S. Giovanni dei Fiorentini* (Chiese di Roma illustrate, XXXIX) (Rome, 1957); Giovannoni, *op. cit.*, 214–33 and figures 164, 167–75; J. S. Ackerman, *The Architecture of Michelangelo* (London, 1961), II, 117 ff.; W. Buchowiecki, *Handbuch der Kirchen Roms*, II (Vienna, 1970), 88 ff.

18. Giovannoni, *op. cit.*, I, 79 ff., 347 ff.

19. Pastor, *op. cit.*, V, appendix, documents 20 and 27a.

20. *Ibid.*, 758, note 4.

21. 'La Fabrica di S. Pietro non ha un soldo'; Venturi, *Storia*, XI (1), 520.

22. Pastor, *op. cit.*, 758.

23. *Ibid.*, 759.

24. *Ibid.*, 760. For the following cf. also Giovannoni. *op. cit.*, I, 143 ff.

25. The raising of the pavement, which Geymüller had already inferred from the drawings and K. Frey from the account books, was confirmed in the building itself during the recent excavations. 'The lower part [of the dividing wall] came to light; its height up to the pavement of the present basilica was 2.60 m. The pavement itself is 60 cm. thick; hence the difference of level between the pavements of the old and new edifices is 3.20 m.'; B. M. Apollonj Ghetti, A. Ferrua, E. Josi, E. Kirschbaum, *Esplorazioni sotto la confessione di S. Pietro in Vaticano* (Città del Vaticano, 1951), I, plate CIX and figure 165. Cf. also G. Giovannoni, *Spigolature nell'archivio di S. Pietro in Vaticano* (Rome, 1941), 12, and *Antonio da Sangallo il giovane* (Rome, n.d.), I, 147.

26. A preliminary design by Sangallo (Uffizi A 66) provides for a dome without drum or pendentives. Its outline and structure would have approximated more closely to the dome of Florence Cathedral than as executed. On a design for a centrally planned church (Uffizi 168), Sangallo formulated very clearly the difference between the 'Florentine' and the new 'Roman' construction of the dome: 'This may be vaulted in two ways. The first, or cheaper, is this: the curve of the dome is begun at the same level as the impost of the great arches, and the dome is built as a domical vault. The second way is to make a cornice at the top of the arches constructed to a perfect circle and above this to go on straight so that you may cut in apertures of any kind you want or windows or even roundels. And above the said apertures make another round cornice from which you may begin to spring the dome; but first keep it straight [i.e. 'continue vertically'] for a distance of $2\frac{1}{2}$ times the projection of the cornice.' (Cf. Ackerman, *loc. cit.* (Note 14), 11, and Giovannoni, *Sangallo*, I, 228 f.)

27. During the last years of Sangallo's term the tunnel-vaults adjoining the eastern and southern crossing arches were executed; the southern vault, with its centering still in place, appears in the middle of Vasari's fresco, the east vault is encased by the high walls, also built by Sangallo, which are visible between the nave of the old basilica and the crossing area. Cf. also Ackerman's survey of Sangallo's work for St Peter's (*The Architecture of Michelangelo* (London, 1961), II, 87). Summing up Sangallo's achievement, Vasari wrote in 1550 that 'from now on there will be neither cracks [*sc.*, in the piers] nor will it threaten to become a ruin, as it did under Bramante.' (*Le Vite* (Florence, 1550), ed, C. Ricci, III (Milan–Rome, 1927), 324.)

28. Cf. H. Siebenhüner, 'Der Palazzo Farnese', *Wallraf-Richartz-Jahrbuch*, XIV (1952), 144 ff.; Ackerman, *op. cit.*, I, 75 ff., and II, 67 ff.; and Giovannoni, *op. cit.*, I, 150 ff.

29. Sources in F. Navenne, *Rome. Le Palais Farnèse et les Farnèse* (Paris, 1914), and U. Gnoli, *Mélanges d'Archéologie et d'Histoire*, LIV (1937), 203 ff.

30. Vasari Mil., v, 469. Vasari, who had been commissioned by Cardinal Alessandro Farnese to paint in the neighbouring Cancelleria in 1545, must have known all there was to know about the palazzo.

31. See also Ackerman, *op. cit.*, II, 67 ff. The Munich sketchbook (Staatsbibliothek, cod. icon. 195, fol. 8) was attributed to Philibert de l'Orme by A. Blunt (cf. *Philibert de l'Orme* (London, 1958), 15 ff.). De l'Orme was in Rome during the years 1536 to 1538. But as C. L. Frommel has kindly pointed out to me, the drawing must stem from an earlier date and can be attributed to Jean de Chenevières (cf. above, Chapter 3, Note 9). Professor Frommel is preparing an exhaustive study of Roman palazzi, 1500–50.

The drawing in Munich shows only four of the five piers of the façade wing of the court, and one of the adjoining left wing. Thus the sketch tallies fairly well with Vasari's description of the building before the elevation of Paul III: 'he had built a good part of his palazzo, having made a portion of the first window row [i.e., the second storey] on the front façade, the public room behind it [i.e., the three-aisled vestibule] and started one wing of the court' (Vasari Mil., v, 469).

32. In March 1540, Vittoria Farnese was injured by a fall on the temporary wooden staircase which was then in place (cf. Navenne, *op. cit.*, 257).

33. Cf. Gnoli, *op. cit.*, 209 f.

34. See Vasari Mil., v, 487.

35. See the letter of Prospero Mocchi to Pier Luigi Farnese in A. Gotti, *Vita di Michelangelo Buonarroti* (Florence, 1875), I, 294 f., and Ackerman, *op. cit.*, II, 72.

36. Vasari, *Vite* (Florence, 1550; ed. C. Ricci, Milan–Rome, 1927), I, 325.

37. This is borne out by a contract of 1546 for extensive carving in travertine (5000 scudi for material alone) with appended drawings for measuring the Doric arches and capitals; cf. Ackerman, *op. cit.*, II, 70.

38. The Ionic arcades in the front and rear wings of the piano nobile, originally open, have been walled up in the nineteenth century (E. Lavagnino, *La Chiesa di S. Spirito in Sassia* (Turin, 1962), 51; P. Letarouilly, *Édifices de Rome moderne* (Liège, 1849 ff.), text II, 279; plates II, 130 speaks of 'a regrettable alteration of a rather recent date'). A drawing by Annibale Carracci in Frankfurt (Städel'sches Kunstinstitut, Inv. No. 4064) shows the original aspect of the loggia of the façade wing. In the wings to the right and left, where mezzanines

were accommodated, the arcades were blind from the beginning; the window frames were probably designed by Vignola.

39. In point of scale, only the Cancelleria could bear any comparison with the scale of the new building. The second Cardinal Alessandro Farnese, the grandson of Paul III, was in residence there at the time.

40. J. S. Ackerman kindly drew my attention to a mason's account of 13 April 1557 in the State Archive in Naples (Carte Farnesiane, busta 2036); the document is signed by Vignola as 'architetto del Ill.mo et R.mo Santo Angelo' (i.e. Cardinal Ranuccio Farnese, who was living in the palazzo at the time).

41. *Documenti inediti per servire alla storia dei musei d'Italia* (Florence and Rome, 1878), I, 72 ('Inventario delle statue . . . che sono nella camera grande del cardinale, detta la galleria . . .').

42. Tassi (ed.), *op. cit.* (Note 13), III, 367.

43. Cf. the catalogue of Sangallo's drawings in Giovannoni, *op. cit.*, 407–56.

CHAPTER 5

1. Cesariano's design of 1513 replaced an older model delivered in 1505 by Cristoforo Solari; cf. C. Baroni, *Documenti per la storia dell' architettura a Milano nel Rinascimento e Barocco*, I (Florence, 1940), docs. 248 and 250. The high altar of S. Maria presso S. Celso contains a famous miraculous image; the atrium, therefore, like that of SS. Annunziata in Florence, was intended for the sale of devotional articles and as a meeting place for the congregation before and after processions.

2. Cf. C. Baroni, *L'Architettura lombarda da Bramante al Richini* (Milan, 1941), 118 and figures 89 and 92.

3. *Ibid.*, 118; for Cesariano's biography and his commentary to Vitruvius see the introduction by C. H. Krinsky to *Vitruvius De Architectura* (Munich, 1969), the reprint of the Como edition of 1521.

4. Sources and dates in L. Testi, *Santa Maria della Steccata in Parma* (no place or date [1922]). The foundation stone was laid in 1521, the dome roofed in 1535, and the installation of the sacred image and the consecration took place in 1539. Cf. also B. Adorni, 'Antonio da Sangallo il giovane e la cupola della Steccata', in *Quaderni dell'Istituto di Storia dell'Architettura*, XV, nos., 85–90 (1968), 95 ff.

5. The four apses were originally identical. In the eighteenth century the wall behind the sanctuary was pierced and a square choir added. The frescoed half-dome of the sixteenth century was preserved.

6. Vasari Mil., VI, 487: 'built, it is said, after Bramante's design and instructions'.

7. The nave of S. Giovanni has a groin-vault; the transepts terminate in apses.

8. The statues, volutes, and balustrades of the roof zone date from the seventeenth and eighteenth centuries. After the original designs, the apses were to be crowned with dwarf galleries ('corridoi'), another medieval feature; Testi, *op. cit.*, 15 f. and 25 f. The design also provided for two minor apses in place of the present twin windows; these 'piccole capelle tonde' had already been executed, at any rate on the east side, by 1525 (cf. Testi, *op. cit.*, 24 f). The absidioles would have made the exterior view still more restless and intensified the resemblance to choir schemes of the High Middle Ages. They were demolished in 1523–6.

9. A bequest of a thousand ducats for these frescoes dates from 1524; cf. Testi, *op. cit.*, 117.

10. Contract in Testi, *op. cit.*, 265; Parmigianino began his work in the church with the gilding. For the 8896 pieces of gold leaf supplied to him from June 1534 to April 1539, cf. Testi, *op. cit.*, 122.

11. For his expert's report, cf. Testi, *op, cit.*, 263 f., and Adorni, *op, cit.*, 96 f.

12. The first superintendent was Marcantonio Zucchi, who was succeeded by Alessandro Chierici; the ornamental parts, such as the capitals and mouldings, were mainly the work of Giovanfrancesco d'Agrate, the sculptor.

13. The date of Tramello's birth is unknown. He is mentioned in building documents from 1501 to 1528; he died in January 1529. In 1522 he was commissioned for a model of the Madonna di Campagna; the masonry seems to have been completed as early as 1528. In 1531 Pordenone was commissioned for the frescoes in the dome. Cf. P. Gazzola, 'Opere di Alessio Tramello architetto piacentino', *I Monumenti italiani*, fasc. V (Rome, 1935), *passim*, and J. Ganz, *Alessio Tramello* (Frauenfeld, 1968), 53 ff.; for Tramello's biography cf. *Bollettino Storico Piacentino*, LXI (1966), 58 ff.; cf. also J. Schulz, 'Pordenone's Cupolas', *Studies in Renaissance and Baroque Art presented to Anthony Blunt* (London, 1967), 44 ff.

14. The present chancel and sacristy date from the late eighteenth century.

15. According to Vasari (Mil., V, 319), Falconetto spent twelve years in Rome; but see also G. Gerola in Thieme-Becker, XI (1915), 223 f., and R. Brenzoni in *Atti dell'Istituto Veneto di Scienze, Lettere ed Arti*, CXII (1953–4), 269 ff.; the artist's documented activity in the Veneto is incompatible with a prolonged sojourn in Rome.

16. See G. Fiocco, 'La Casa di Alvise Cornaro', *Bollettino del Museo Civico di Padova*, LVII (1968), 1 ff., and G. Schweikhart, 'Studien zum Werk des Giovanni Maria Falconetto', *ibid.*, 17 ff.

17. According to a contemporary source, the account by Marcantonio Michiel, these decorations were executed 'after drawings by Raphael' (Th. Frimmel, 'Del Anonimo Morelliano', *Wiener Quellenschriften zur Kunstgeschichte* (1888), 10 f.). The decorations have been attributed to Tiziano Minio and dated 1533–8 by W. Wolters (*Pantheon*, XXI (1963), 21 ff. and 222 ff.; see also Schweikhart, *op. cit.*). The impact made by the Cornaro buildings can be gauged from contemporary descriptions; in addition to Michiel, the Casino and Odeon are also mentioned in the foreword to Book IV of the 1543 edition of Serlio, and by Vasari (Mil., V, 322), who says that Cornaro himself designed the Odeon. Cornaro survived Falconetto by thirty-one years; he died in his palazzo in 1566 at the age of ninety-one. In his later years he wrote a treatise on architecture; cf. G. Fiocco, *Alvise Cornaro, il suo tempo e le sue opere* (Vicenza, 1965), 155–67. Schweikhart (*op. cit.*, 35 ff.) has pointed out that the stylistic difference between the loggia and the Odeon justifies Vasari's attribution of the Odeon to Cornaro.

18. Alvise Cornaro was administrator of the bishopric of Padua from 1529 to 1538. A report dated 1543 mentions the as yet unfinished villa with admiration; the execution is less refined than that of Falconetto's other buildings. Schweikhart (*op. cit.*, 35 f.) has suggested that Vasari's attribution of the villa to Cornaro (Mil., V, 324) is trustworthy. The rear façade, in all important details identical with the main front, bears the date 1579 on its steps. During the enlargement the interior was completely altered.

19. Cf. the Serlio quotation, Chapter 1, Note 23.

20. G. Zorzi (*Palladio*, N.S. V (1955), 31) has attributed to Falconetto a number of drawings of ancient buildings contained in volumes of drawings now in the Royal Institute of British Architects which were part of Palladio's estate. Another part of Falconetto's estate seems to have been preserved in MS. 978 in the Biblioteca Comunale at Verona; it contains the drawings for the illustrations in Torello Sarayna's book, *Le Antichità di Verona* (Verona, 1540). The woodcuts in Sarayna's book are by Caroto, who obviously supplemented and completed Falconetto's illustrations (cf. Vasari Mil., V, 323).

CHAPTER 6

1. E. Langenskiöld's book *Michele Sanmicheli, The Architect of Verona* (Uppsala, 1938) has to some extent been superseded by the entries in the catalogue of the exhibition 'Michele Sanmicheli', ed. P. Gazzola (Venice, 1960), below referred to as *Catalogue*. See also the 'bibliografia ragionata' by N. Carboneri in *Michele Sanmicheli, 1484–1559, Studi raccolti dall'Accademia di Agricoltura, Scienze e Lettere di Verona* (Verona, 1960), 195–296.

2. L. Fumi, *Il Duomo di Orvieto e i suoi ristauri* (Rome, 1891), 101.

3. Cf. L. Beltrami, *Relazione sullo stato delle rocche di Romagna, stesa nel 1526 per di ordine Clemente VII per Antonio di Sangallo e Michele Sanmicheli* (Nozze Greppe-Belgioioso) (Milan, 1902).

4. A. Bertoldi, *Michele Sanmicheli al servizio della repubblica veneta* (Venice, 1874).

5. Date on the outer side, 1533, on the city side, 1533 and 1540; in the inscription Sanmicheli is named as architect. In the nineteenth century the parts of the city wall adjoining the gate on both sides were dismantled and the moat was filled up. Its original state can be seen in [96]; cf. also the model illustrated in *Catalogue*, plate 91. The model was made for the exhibition.

6. The date on the outer side is 1557; the city side was completed only after Sanmicheli's death (cf. Vasari Mil., VI, 352). At Verona, Vasari saw a model with a pediment on the outer side 'intended as a parapet for the men serving the guns to be placed on this gate'. Hence the version executed is the result of a change of plan; cf. also *Catalogue*, 192 and plate 156.

7. Cf. R. Brenzoni, *Rivista d'Arte*, XIX (1937), 57 ff.

8. Langenskiöld, *op. cit.*, 12, prefers the thirties as the date for the Palazzo Pompei; but cf. W. Lotz, *Zeitschrift für Kunstgeschichte*, IX (1940), 221 ff. See also *Catalogue*, 108 ff.

9. L. di Canossa, *Studi e ricerche intorno al Palazzo Canossa* (Verona, 1908), 2 ff., and *Catalogue*, 119 f. The palazzo is still in the possession of the family.

10. The traditional date of c. 1530 seems to me right; cf. Langenskiöld, *op. cit.*, 61, *Catalogue*, 122 f., and A. Blunt, *Burlington Magazine*, CIII (1961), 152.

11. The plan of the courtyard is asymmetrical and seems to indicate that the architect's design has only partly been executed. On the other hand it has been pointed out by Blunt (*ibid.*) that the architrave and frieze of the entablature are continued around the corner at the left end of the façade; hence no prolongation of the façade can have been projected, at least not at the time when the corner block of the entablature was put in place.

12. The prototype for the spirally fluted columns of the Palazzo Bevilacqua was obviously the neighbouring late Roman Porta dei Borsari, where the same form appears. Sanmicheli had probably already seen the motif of the alternating fluting, which also occurs on late Roman sarcophagi, in the Temple of Clitumnus near Spoleto. In the Renaissance, this early medieval structure was believed to be Roman; cf. illustration and description in Palladio, *Quattro Libri*, Book III, chapter XXV.

Le Antichità di Verona by Torello Sarayna (Verona, 1540) contains an illustration of the ancient Porta dei Leoni, Verona, that shows columns with alternating spiral flutings in the top storey. Serlio, Book III, fol. 114, correctly gives flat pilasters in his illustration of the same gate. The woodcuts for Sarayna's book were made by Giovanni Caroto after drawings which have been preserved in MS. 978, Biblioteca Comunale, Verona. In the particular drawing in question, the columns of the Porta dei Leoni are not fluted. Caroto therefore 'invented' the spiral fluting in his woodcut. His model may have been the Palazzo Bevilacqua.

13. It only seems paradoxical that the b-bays are framed by one straight and one spiral column. As subordinate parts of the scheme, these bays did not need a symmetrical frame. What is really illogical is the present arrangement of the pediments over the side bays, for no satisfying reading can be devised for them even in a reconstruction of the façade in its original width. The simplest explanation, probably, is that when the building was brought to a provisional end, portions already finished were simply put in the wrong place.

14. The crowning balustrade with the statues was not added till the Baroque.

15. The rear wings of the courtyard leading towards the river belong to the late seventeenth century. When they were added, the main staircase was added too. At that time the original timber roof of the salone was replaced by flat vaulting. Tiepolo's fresco on this ceiling was destroyed during the last war.

16. For the date of the Palazzo Cornaro-Mocenigo a S. Polo, see *Catalogue*, 168 f.; the façade looks like a preliminary study for that of the later Palazzo Grimani. In the rusticated ground floor there are three portals; the two outer ones lead to the rooms in the corner of the palazzo. In the interior, which was very much altered in later renovations, Cinquecento forms are only retained in the vestibule and salone. For the top storey, see next Note.

17. The Palazzo Grimani a S. Luca, today the Corte d'Appello, was begun in 1556 at the earliest for it was in that year that the client, Girolamo Grimani, acquired the site. Work was still proceeding on the piano nobile in 1561. After Sanmicheli's death, Giovanni Giacomo de' Grigi became superintendent of the works. The balustrade in front of the piano nobile and the top storey are by him. G. Boschieri ('Il Palazzo Grimani', *Rivista della Città di Venezia* (December, 1931), 461 ff., cf. also Vasari Mil., VI, 359) has proved that the plan for the piano nobile was altered in 1561; the height of the original plan was reduced. Boschieri, and after him Langenskiöld (*op. cit.*, 89), interprets this reduction as a proof that no third floor was originally planned. Yet the evidence does not seem quite conclusive. It is quite possible that Sanmicheli had a kind of attic in mind; Langenskiöld's reconstruction of the ground floor and first floor (*op. cit.*, figure 33) looks too broad and low. Girolamo Grimani bequeathed the palazzo to his two sons in 1570; one storey to each. This later arrangement may have been the reason for the alterations made in 1561. A high piano nobile with a low attic would have been an advantage to one of the heirs and a drawback to the other. In the Palazzo Cornaro a S. Polo, Langenskiöld (*op. cit.*, 78 ff. and figure 28) also assumes that the top storey was added later, and refers to Bramante's and Raphael's Roman façades. But conditions in Venice were radically different: building land was dearer; most Quattrocento palazzi have three main storeys. Serlio writes (Book IV, fol. 153 verso): 'The practice of building in Venice has not its like anywhere else in Italy. The town has a very large population and building sites are therefore limited;... there is no room whatever for large courtyards and gardens.' He then goes on (fol. 155 and 156) to illustrate two Venetian palazzo façades, both of which have, above the piano nobile, a storey which is not much lower; in both cases the three middle bays are arranged on the triumphal arch pattern. Whether Serlio was influenced by Sanmicheli or vice versa is a question that still awaits investigation. Cf. also M. Rosci, *Il Trattato di architettura di Sebastiano Serlio* (Milan, n.d.), 31, and *Catalogue*, 168 f. and 172 f.

18. Cf. the combination of an aisled vestibule and simple round-arched portal in the palazzi del Te, Farnese, and Pitti, and of a single vestibule and triple-bay portal in Vignola's Casino for Pope Julius's villa.

19. A contract of 1516, which binds Sanmicheli to carve a complex tombstone for the pavement in front of the high altar of S. Domenico, mentions two round openings with grilles in the floor. Obviously the crypt-like chapel was to receive its light through these grilles (cf. M. Kahnemann Mangione, 'La Tomba Petrucci di M. Sanmicheli in S. Domenico in Orvieto', *Arte Veneta*, XV (1961), 59 ff.). Although the underground chapel is not mentioned in the contract it seems safe to assume that Sanmicheli designed the whole *ensemble*. The tomb, still incomplete in 1520, no longer exists. The pavement around the tomb, the landings of the stairs, and the floor of the chapel were tiled with costly majolica; it probably came from the same workshop as the tiles from the Palazzo Petrucci in Siena, which are now in the Metropolitan Museum of Art.

20. Probably begun in 1527, the chapel is mentioned as under construction in 1529 (cf. R. Brenzoni, *Atti Ist. Ven. Sc. Lett. Arti*, CXV (1957), 125 ff.). In 1538 Margarita Raimondi received permission to replace Paolo Sanmicheli, a cousin

of Michele's, then working at the building, by 'another suitable stonemason, who shall complete the chapel' (see G. dal Re, *Madonna Verona*, VIII (1914), 52 ff.). According to Vasari (Mil., VI, 353, 'There is no more beautiful building of the kind in Italy') the chapel was still unfinished when Sanmicheli died. In the nineteenth century it was entirely renovated. Cf. also *Catalogue*, 111.

21. Foundation stone laid in 1559, i.e. the year of Sanmicheli's death. Vasari saw at Verona a model of the church made after Sanmicheli's design. The miraculous image was removed to the church in 1561; in 1562 Pope Pius IV granted indulgences. The dome was not completed till 1667. Cf. the anonymous *Descrizione del tempio della Madonna di Campagna* (Verona, 1823), 3 ff., and *Catalogue* 181 f.

22. Verona is on the west side, the choir on the east side of the church. Thus the visitor coming from the town sees only the big cylinder with the dome.

23. For the static and aesthetic problems presented by a vault of the kind, see G. Giovannoni *Saggi sull' architettura del Rinascimento* (Milan, 1935), 153 ff. In the Madonna di Campagna, the ratio between the height of the domical vault from the springing of the dome to the crown and its width is 3 : 4. In a spherical dome the ratio is 1 : 2.

24. In this connection the sixteenth-century description of the late Roman rotunda adjacent to St Peter's may be of interest: 'The chapel [of S. Petronilla] is an octagon and rotunda [*sic*]. In the rotunda eight altars are inserted in the thickness of the walls, one on each side.' (M. Cerrati, *Tiberii Alpharani De Basilicae Vaticanae* (Rome, 1914), 133.) The circular mausoleum had a single-shell dome of concrete; the altars stood in rectangular niches. Can Sanmicheli have seen a precedent in Roman prototypes of the kind when he submitted his plan? But there was a more obvious example of the combination of circle and polygon dating from the late Quattrocento: S. Maria della Croce near Crema. Crema was a Venetian possession and Sanmicheli had worked on the fortifications of Orzinuovi near by. The important pilgrimage church is, for all its formal differences, the only Renaissance building that can compare with the Madonna di Campagna. The Lombard mantling of the domical vault with a dwarf gallery and a conical helm must, however, have looked out of date in 1550. For Sanmicheli's work at Crema and Orzinuovi, see Verga, *I Monumenti architettonici di Crema e dei dintorni* (Crema, 1939), *passim*, and *Catalogue*, *passim*.

25. For the execution, see Vasari Mil., VI, 355. It should be recalled that the dome of S. Giorgio in Braida and the round chapel in the courtyard of the Lazzaretto at Verona, now a ruin, have always been attributed to Sanmicheli. In the chapel, the altar, visible from all sides of the courtyard, stood in the centre of two concentric colonnades. The interior ring bore the tall drum with the dome, and the peristyle was covered by a lean-to roof, in the same way as in the Madonna di Campagna. Vasari does not mention the chapel in his detailed description of the Lazzaretto (Mil., VI, 359); cf. also *Catalogue*, 175, for S. Giorgio and 144 for the Lazzaretto.

26. Compare, for instance, the very different effect of the Tuscan order in the piano nobile of the Palazzo Pompei and in the Porta Palio. In the latter, the coupling of the columns, and the contrast between them and the relatively low archways, produces an effect of power and monumentality. The totally different relationship in the façade of the palazzo with its equilibrium of vertical and horizontal elements gives an impression of harmony and tranquillity.

CHAPTER 7

1. The date of his birth is uncertain; cf. J. Vogel, *Monatshefte für Kunstwissenschaft*, XIII (1920), 52 ff., and F. Hartt, *Giulio Romano* (New Haven, 1958), 3. In the literature the date 1492 is often mentioned; it comes from Vasari, but there is no documentary evidence of it.

2. Vasari's description of Giulio's art is characteristic: 'proud, assured, capricious, varied, fertile, and universal' (Mil., V, 524).

3. Vasari Mil., V, 549. For Giulio's work in Mantua and the Gonzaga court see also E. Marani and C. Perina in *Mantova: Le Arti*, II (Mantua, 1961), 197 ff.

4. Erected *c.* 1518–20 as the *villa suburbana* of the *datario* Baldassare Turini (Vasari Mil., V, 534). Renovated after the Second World War, it became the Finnish Academy; see Hartt, *op. cit.*, 62 f., A. Prandi, *Villa Lante al Gianicolo* (Rome, 1954), and J. Shearman, 'Giulio Romano: Tradizione, Licenza, Artificio', in *Bollettino del Centro Internazionale di Storia dell'Architettura Andrea Palladio*, IX (1967), 354 ff.

5. Built *c.* 1520 for Paolo Stazi; later the property of the Cenci, now Palazzo di Brazza; cf. E. Gombrich, 'Zum Werke Giulio Romanos', *Jahrbuch der Kunsthistorischen Sammlungen in Wien*, VIII (1934), 79 ff., and IX (1935), 121 ff., Hartt, *op. cit.*, 64, and Shearman, *op. cit.*

6. Cf. on the other hand the portal of the Palazzo Pandolfini [54].

7. The decree appointing Giulio *Superiore delle Strade* prescribes his duties: 'to supervise the level of the streets; to see to it that all basements are lighted by windows, to prevent the erection of chimneys flush with the street, to see that no impediment to traffic is placed in the roadways'. Translation by Hartt, *op. cit.*, 74 f.

8. Vasari Mil., V, 548.

9. Detailed history in Hartt, *op. cit.*, 91 ff.; see also G. Paccagnini, *Il Palazzo Te* (Milan, 1957), and Shearman, *op. cit.*, 360 ff. and 434 ff. The important drawings discovered by Egon Verheyen show the building before its alteration in the eighteenth century; cf. 'Jacopo Strada's Mantuan Drawings of 1567–8', *Art Bulletin*, XLIX (1967), 62 ff.
As K. W. Forster and R. J. Tuttle (*Journal of the Society of Architectural Historians*, XXX (1971), 267 ff.) and E. Verheyen (*Mitteilungen des Kunsthistorischen Institutes in Florenz*, XVI (1972), 73 ff.) have shown, Giulio's original design was considerably changed during the execution. See also Forster and Tuttle, 280 ff., for a detailed account of the thorough restoration of the building and its decoration in the late eighteenth century. At that time, 'all the façades [were] entirely covered with a heavy mixture of cement ... most of the rustication is presently two or three times as thick as it was originally'. Moreover, all extant pavements in the palazzo date from this restoration.

10. Vasari Mil., V, 537. As Shearman (*op. cit.*, 434 ff.) has shown, the walls of an older building, mentioned by Vasari as 'muraglia vecchia' (Mil., 436), were incorporated in the northern wing. This explains a number of irregularities in the façade and the courtyard side of this wing.

11. In the old views of the town, small copses can be seen in front of the two main façades. Obviously the situation of the building on an island, the bridge leading to the island, and the vegetation permitted only certain views, whether near or distant. Today the palazzo stands in a wide suburban piazza, where it looks flat and insignificant. Moreover the original colouring of the façades has perished. The material was brick throughout, stuccoed like Bramante's ground floor of the Palazzo Caprini.

12. The motif of the aisled atrium, which was to become important later in the work of Sanmicheli and Palladio, occurs also in the Palazzo Farnese in Rome; Antonio da Sangallo, like Giulio, knew it from his work on the Villa Madama. For the derivation of the form from Vitruvius and the first edition of the treatise, cf. P. G. Hamberg, *Palladio*, N.S. VIII (1958), 16 ff.

13. This treatment of the surface must be regarded as ironical, if only because the stucco is here *applied* to the wall, while in the ashlar which the stucco imitates the surface is *chipped off*.

14. The pediment over the loggia of the garden façade is an addition of the eighteenth century. Originally there was a low colonnade over the ground floor on either side of the loggia; the crowning attic ran on over the loggia (see Verheyen, *op. cit.*, figure 7).
For the gardens, now gone, and the still existing little Casino della Grotta, see Hartt, *op. cit.*, 153 ff.

15. The building history of the Estivale was not elucidated until the renovation of the whole building in the thirties. Cf. W. Lotz, *Zeitschrift für Kunstgeschichte*, X (1941), 227 ff., and Hartt, *op. cit.*, 187 ff. See *ibid.* 161 ff., and G. Paccagnini, *Il Palazzo Ducale di Mantova* (Turin, 1969), for Giulio's other work in the Palazzo Ducale.

16. For the reconstruction of the façade, now partly concealed by later additions, see Hartt, *op. cit.*, figure 409. Originally the columns of the piano nobile were coupled at the corners.

17. The motif of the twisted columns appears here for the first time in a large-scale building; it goes back to the famous 'Solomonic' columns of the high altar of old St Peter's, and can also be seen – though with composite capitals – in Raphael's tapestry of the 'Healing of the Paralytic', which Giulio probably worked on too. Further, Cardinal Ercole Gonzaga, a brother of Duke Federigo, acquired about 1540 the so-called Mantuan series of Raphael's tapestries, which were hung in the cathedral. Later they were removed to the Palazzo Ducale. Giulio's cartoon of the 'Triumph of Scipio', made in the thirties (Hartt, *op. cit.*, figure 482), is another example of his conception of the column as a form in movement: the victorious Scipio banquets in the midst of Ionic columns which are spiral-fluted, though not twisted.

18. See the detailed discussion of both buildings in Hartt, *op. cit.*, 241 ff. The rebuilding of the cathedral was not completed till 1600. After Giulio's death, his pupil G. B. Bertani worked on it. The renovation of S. Benedetto, on the other hand, was practically finished when Giulio died. In 1547 new stalls were placed in the church, and the new organ was paid for in 1552; cf. A. Bertolotti, *I Comuni e le parrocchie della provincia di Mantova* (Mantua, 1893), 182, and Marani and Perina, *op. cit.*, II, 211 ff.

19. Giulio acquired the building site in 1538. Work was obviously complete by 1544. Thorough-going alterations took place in 1800; how far they went is a matter of controversy. F. Hartt obviously assumed that the asymmetrical façade of today originally had three bays on each side of the portal; thus the fourth bay on the left-hand side of today would go back to 1800. The earlier literature, on the other hand, assumed that the façade was originally of five bays and that the entrance was shifted in 1800. Cf. the detailed discussion of the sources in Hartt, *op. cit.*, 236 ff. The traditional assumption of a façade of five bays has again been strongly supported by Marani and Perina, *op. cit.*, II, 214 and note 140. Of the 'coloured stucco which luxuriates over the entire front' (Vasari Mil., V, 549)

nothing remains. For the second famous artist's house at Mantua, Mantegna's, cf. Ludwig H. Heydenreich *Architecture in Italy 1400–1500* (New Haven and London, 1996).

20. Cf. E. Hergen, 'Wirkunget und Einflüsse des Palazzo del Te nördlich der Alpen', in *Festschrift für Harald Keller* (Darmstadt, 1963), 281 ff.

21. The east wing on the lake shore was finished in 1556; the north wing was still in construction in 1572; the Galleria della Mostra, the west wing, was not built till *c.* 1600. For the building history, cf. C. Cottafavi, *Ricerche e documenti sulla costruzione del Palazzo Ducale di Mantova* (Mantua, 1939), 5 ff. For Bertani, see Marani and Perina, *op. cit.*, III (Mantua, 1965), 3–70; for his work in the Palazzo Ducale cf. also Paccagnini, *op. cit.*, *passim*.

CHAPTER 8

1. Vasari Mil., XII, 494 ff. Milanesi's text is based on a *Vita di Jacopo Sansovino* published soon after the artist's death (no place, no date), and not the shorter text of the Vasari edition of 1568 (cf. *Vita di Jacopo Tatti detto il Sansovino*, ed. G. Lorenzetti (Florence, 1913), 79 f.). For Sansovino's decorations for the state entry of Leo X, cf. Lorenzetti, *op. cit.*, 95 f., and W. Lotz, *Journal of the Society of Architectural Historians*, XXII (1963), 3 f.

2. Lorenzetti, *op. cit.*, 96 f.; for Michelangelo's projects see Chapter 9.

3. See above, Chapter 4, and Lotz, *op. cit.*, 7.

4. H. R. Weihrauch, *Studien zum bildnerischen Werke des Jacopo Sansovino* (Strasbourg, 1935), 42, and M. Tafuri, *Jacopo Sansovino e l'architettura del '500 a Venezia* (Padua, 1969), 9.

5. Vitruvius, *De architectura*, V, I, speaks of the Roman fora: 'Distribuuntur circaque in porticibus argentariae tabernae...'. Alberti, *De re aedificatoria*, VIII, 6, writes in practically the same terms. Cf. W. Lotz, 'Sansovinos Bibliothek von S. Marco und die Stadtbaukunst des Renaissance', in *Kunst des Mittelalters in Sachsen, Festschrift Wolf Schubert* (Weimar, 1967), 336 ff., idem, 'Italienische Plätze des 16. Jahrhunderts', in *Jahrbuch der Max-Planck-Gesellschaft* (1968), 41 ff., and Tafuri, *op. cit.*, 44 ff.

6. G. Lorenzetti, 'La Libreria Sansoviniana di Venezia', *Accademie e Biblioteche d'Italia*, II (1929), 73 ff.; also in his *Vita di Jacopo Tatti* (cf. Note 1), 110 ff. See also Tafuri, *op. cit.*, 54 f. and note 76 for the chronology of the building.

7. G. Gaye, *Processo e atti...per il crollo della Libreria* (Venice, 1855), and L. Pittoni, *Jacopo Sansovino scultore* (Venice, 1909), 168 ff.

8. Cf. Lotz, *op. cit.* (Note 1), 9; see also above, p. 58.

9. The motif of the small columns placed within the large order, which reappears not much later in Palladio's Basilica at Vicenza, again comes from Raphael; it occurs, for instance, in the Benediction Loggia in the background of the fresco of the 'Fire in the Borgo' in Raphael's Stanze. Cf. also W. Lotz, 'Palladio e Sansovino', in *Bollettino del Centro Internazionale di Studi sull' Architettura Andrea Palladio*, IX (1967), 13 ff.

10. *Quattro Libri*, preface to Book 1.

11. *Die Kunst der Renaissance in Italien*, § 53.

12. In planning the new Procurazie, Scamozzi adopted the scheme of the Libreria, but increased the number of storeys to three. Scamozzi also wished to add another storey to the Libreria itself, but the plan would have involved a drastic change in the harmonious proportions of Sansovino's building and was turned down by the Procuratori di Supra. Cf. F. Barbieri, *Vincenzo Scamozzi* (Vicenza, 1952), *passim*, and Tafuri, *op. cit.*, 54.

The medieval Ospizio Orseolo, which was torn down and replaced by the Procuratie Nuove, appears still in the print of 1577 with the celebrations of the victory at Lepanto; cf. plate XIII in *Studies in Renaissance and Baroque Art presented to Anthony Blunt* (London and New York, 1967).

13. Cf. G. Lorenzetti, 'La Loggetta al campanile di S. Marco', *L'Arte*, XIII (1910), 108 ff. An older loggia on the same site was destroyed by lightning in 1537. In a letter from Pietro Aretino to Sansovino, dated 20 November 1537, there is mention of a model of the loggia. The building was roofed in 1539. According to a document of 1602 (cf. Lorenzetti, *op. cit.*, 119) the intention was to build loggias on all four sides of the campanile. In the seventeenth century, the attic was widened by one bay on both sides; at the same time the openings on the narrow sides were closed. For the sculpture of the Loggetta, cf. Weihrauch, *op. cit.*, 54 ff., for its function see Tafuri, *op. cit.*, 65 ff.

14. For the building history of the Zecca, cf. R. Gallo, 'Contributi su Jacopo Sansovino', *Saggi e Memorie di Storia dell'Arte* (Fondazione Cini), I (1957), and Tafuri, *op. cit.*, 72. The older building was demolished in 1535–6. In 1536, Sansovino submitted three models. Work was in progress by 1537. In 1542, workshops were rented out on the ground floor of the new building, but in 1558 it was decided to hand over these rooms to the Zecca. The second storey was completed in 1548. The entrance to the Zecca is from the Piazzetta; the ground floor towards the Molo had botteghe which were walled up in 1580, obviously in order to obtain more space for the Zecca itself.

15. The reason given for the addition of a top storey, decided on in June 1558

and begun three months later, was that the piano nobile was too hot in summer. No architect is named, but in view of the circumstances it can only have been Sansovino. Cf. Gallo, *op. cit.*, and Tafuri, *op. cit.*, 72.

16. In Book IV (1537), we read in the chapter 'dell'ornamento rustico' that the Doric order could be combined with rustication and the result would be 'parte opera di natura e parte opera di artefice'. The Doric columns with rusticated bands and rusticated voussoirs echoed the work of nature, the capitals and the plain parts of the column shafts the work of man: 'la quale mistura, per mio aviso, è molto grata all'occhio, e rappresenta in se gran fortezza'.

17. For the Palazzo Corner, cf. Gallo, *op. cit.*, 86, Lorenzetti, *op. cit.* (Note 1), 115, and Tafuri, *op. cit.*, 28 ff.

18. For S. Geminiano, cf. Gallo, *op. cit.*, 97, and Tafuri, *op. cit.*, 145 and 157; for the Scuola Grande della Misericordia, cf. Lorenzetti, *op. cit.* (Note 1), 116, and Tafuri, *op. cit.*, 12 ff.

19. For the Villa Garzoni at Ponte Casale, probably built in the forties, cf. L. Puppi, in 'Prospettive', *Rassegna di Architettura, etc.*, no. 24 (1962), 51 ff., Lotz (cf. Note 1), 10, B. Rupprecht, 'Die Villa Garzoni des Jacopo Sansovino', *Mitteilungen des Kunsthistorischen Instituts Florenz*, XI (1963), 2 ff., L. Puppi, *Bollettino* (*op. cit.*, Note 9), 95 ff., and Tafuri, *op. cit.*, 99.

CHAPTER 9

1. The present account of Michelangelo's work in architecture is substantially based on J. S. Ackerman's outstanding study, *The Architecture of Michelangelo*, 2 vols., 2nd ed. (London, 1964). Ackerman has collected and clarified the literature, in particular the work of Charles de Tolnay. A *catalogue raisonné* of Michelangelo's buildings with an extensive pictorial documentation, excellent pictures of the buildings, and reproductions of all Michelangelo's architectural drawings may be found in *Michelangelo architetto*, ed. P. Portoghesi and B. Zevi (Turin, n.d. [1964]). With regard to these publications references to literature have been largely omitted in the following Notes.

The two versions of Vasari's *Vita di Michelangelo* have been edited and exhaustively commented by P. Barocchi: vol. I Testo, vols. II–IV Commento (Milan-Naples, 1962). The edition also provides extensive excerpts from the pertinent literature.

2. For the text of the contract, see G. Milanesi, *Le Lettere di Michelangelo Buonarroti* (Florence, 1875), 671.

3. According to the memoirs of G. B. Figigiovanni, Prior of S. Lorenzo, the New Sacristy was begun on 4 November 1519; cf. A. Parronchi, in *Atti del Convegno di Studi Michelangioleschi, Firenze-Roma 1964* (Rome, 1966), 322 ff. See also C. F. Frommel, 'S. Eligio und die Kuppel der Cappella Medici', *Stil und Überlieferung, Akten des 21. Internationalen Kongress f. Kunstgeschichte, Bonn, 1964*, II (Berlin, 1967), 41 ff.

4. The conditions laid down by the Pope made it impossible for Michelangelo to return to the nave-and-aisles type of Quattrocento libraries (cf., for instance, S. Marco, Florence, or the Biblioteca Malatestiana at Cesena). There may, however, be an echo of this older type in Michelangelo's original project of a nave-and-aisles arrangement of the desks in the reading room.

5. Cf. Ackerman, *op. cit.*, I, 54 ff., and II, 49 ff., and G. de Angelis d'Ossat and C. Pietrangeli, *Il Campidoglio di Michelangelo* (Milan, 1965), a book published à propos the Michelangelo celebrations of 1964.

6. The rustication of the basement as executed is far flatter than Michelangelo intended it to be. As Dupérac's engraving shows [138], the two upper storeys were to be of the same height and have the same fenestration. As executed, the top floor is lower, and its square windows give it the look of a mezzanine to the piano nobile. This impairs the effect of the giant order very considerably. Cf. also the drawing in Christ Church, Oxford, published by T. Buddensieg, *Zeitschrift für Kunst-geschichte*, XXX (1969), 177 and figures 6–7.

7. The canopy over the landing of the stairway, which appears in Dupérac's engraving, was not executed. It would have given greater stress to the portal, and also have emphasized, with its smaller order, the effect of the giant pilasters.

8. Cf. W. Lotz, 'Italienische Plätze des 16. Jahrhunderts', *Jahrbuch der Max-Planck-Gesellschaft* (1968), 54 ff.

The effect of the oval as here described cannot be fully appreciated today on the Campidoglio itself. The present pavement of the piazza, executed in 1940 and intended to reproduce the pattern shown by Dupérac, does not fully correspond to that of the engravings. The single oval ring executed in 1940 was opened to the spandrels of the piazza in order to provide level cross-connections across the corners between the access streets and the oval itself. On the other hand, Dupérac's engraving shows that the three oval rings originally planned were to be uninterrupted. The illusion of the identity of the spandrels would thus have seemed far more pronounced than it is today.

9. The layout of the piazza at Pienza, which has often been mentioned in this connection (cf. Ludwig H. Heydenreich *Architecture in Italy 1400–1500* (New Haven and London, 1996), belongs to the prehistory of the plan, but it was

not the model for the Campidoglio. At Pienza the piazza is also trapezoidal in shape, but the buildings surrounding it vary in height, articulation, and size. Further, there is no statue in the centre of the piazza. The view over the landscape by means of the diverging façades at the sides, as described by Pius II, has no analogy on the Capitol, since the fronts of the palazzi run towards the Palazzo del Senatore [140]. The view of the forum in Dupérac's engraving is an invention of the engraver's.

10. In a document dated 27 August 1547, Michelangelo is expressly described as the architect 'fabricae palatii . . . Ducis Parma et Placentiae'; cf. A. Schiavo, *La Vita e le opere architettoniche di Michelangelo* (Rome, 1953), 276. Whether the unusual size and height of the salone in the piano nobile were already designed by Sangallo remains an open question. Unlike the older rooms on the right-hand side of the façade, the salone is two storeys in height; this may have been decided in 1541, when Sangallo altered the original plan.

11. A comparison of Michelangelo's top storey with the much 'lighter' one of the Cancelleria shows the important part played in the general effect by the weighty pediments and the high relief of the pilasters. The notion that the top storey of the court was not designed by Michelangelo but by Giacomo della Porta (R. Bonelli, *Da Bramante a Michelangelo* (Venice, 1960), 85) is refuted by the caption of the 1560 engraving of the court, in which only Sangallo and Michelangelo are named as its architects and in which the storey appears in its present form. Bonelli restated his opinion, but without the attribution to Porta, in *Michelangelo architetto* (see Note 1), 618; it is ex silentio accepted by G. de Angelis d'Ossat in *Michelangelo: Artista, Pensatore, Scrittore*, ed. M. Salmi (Novara, 1965), 369.

12. Speaking of a chapel, Rabelais wrote in 1548 that it was 'désolée, minée et descouverte comme est à Rome le temple de Saint-Pierre' (*Pantagruel*, Quart Livre, chapter XLV).

13. In the interior, the cool monochrome of grey travertine and white stucco is impaired by the brightly coloured marble facing of the seventeenth century. It must also be mentioned in this connection that the lighting planned by Michelangelo was altered in della Porta's execution of the dome: 'Michelangelo's purpose was to bring a diffused light into the dome from invisible sources to create a mysterious effect' (Ackerman, *op. cit.*, II, 110).

14. To the east, the section of Constantine's nave which had been separated by the provisional wall was preserved till the seventeenth century.

15. As H. A. Millon and C. H. Smyth (*Burlington Magazine*, CXI (1969), 484 ff.) have shown, the 'present attic order was introduced by his successors' after Michelangelo's death. Michelangelo's design of the attic is preserved in an engraving published in 1564 by Vincenzo Luchino. The attic over the southern arm of the cross, executed as shown in the engraving, was at a later time changed to conform to the altered design which was first executed over the northern arm.

For the façade shown in Dupérac's engravings see C. Thoenes, 'Bemerkungen zur St Peter-Fassade Michelangelos', in *Festschrift Kauffmann, Munuscula Discipulorum* (Berlin, 1968), 331 ff.

16. 'Anyone who, like Sangallo, departed from Bramante's plans departed from truth; any unbiased observer can see that in his model' (letter from Michelangelo, dated 1555 by Milanesi, *op. cit.* (Note 2), 535, but in all probability written in 1546/7, i.e. shortly after Michelangelo's appointment; see E. H. Ramsden, *The Letters of Michelangelo* (London, 1963), II, 69 and 237 f.).

17. For the development and dating of Michelangelo's project for the dome and the execution of the double-shell dome by Giacomo della Porta, the most important authority is R. Wittkower, *La Cupola di S. Pietro di Michelangelo* (Florence, 1964); also Ackerman, *op. cit.*, I, 97 ff., and II, 107 ff. H. R. Alker (*Michelangelo und seine Kuppel von St Peter in Rom* (Karlsruhe, 1968), 17 ff.) has tried to prove that the outer shell of the model was altered after 1561 by Michelangelo himself; hence the executed dome would correspond to Michelangelo's final design. Attractive though this theory is, Alker's arguments are not conclusive. His measured drawings of the model and its competent analysis should specifically be mentioned.

18. This opinion, which was put forward by John Coolidge, is supported by an exterior view of St Peter's, probably made earlier than Dupérac's engravings 'secondo il disegno del Buonaroti', which shows the church without minor domes. The four small domes beside the apses of the transepts shown in the view are not, as Ackerman supposed, minor domes, but overhead lights for the spiral staircases in the 'counter-piers'. Cf. J. Coolidge, 'Vignola and the Little Domes of St Peter's', *Marsyas*, II (1942), 63 ff. (particularly 78 and figure 12: reconstruction of the exterior view without minor domes); Ackerman, *op. cit.*, II, 113; R. Wittkower (ed.), *Disegni de le ruine di Roma e come anticamente erono* (Milan, [1963]), 27, reviewed by C. Thoenes, *Kunstchronik*, XVIII (1965), 18 f.

19. Ackerman favours this view, *op. cit.*, II, 114.

20. See above, p. 52.

21. Cf. H. Siebenhüner, 'S. Giovanni dei Fiorentini in Rom', in *Kunstgeschichtliche Studien für Hans Kauffmann* (Berlin, 1956), 172 ff.

22. For the description and reproduction of Michelangelo's projects, cf. Ackerman, *op. cit.*, II, 121.

23. Peruzzi had already conceived a centralized plan with oval chapels in the diagonal axes and alternately narrow and wide openings towards the area under the dome in a project for S. Giovanni dei Fiorentini (Uffizi A510); cf. W. Lotz, *Römisches Jahrbuch für Kunstgeschichte*, VII (1955), 21. It is uncertain whether Michelangelo knew these projects.

24. It is notable that all the reproductions of the model show a single-shell dome. A vault of this shape with a span of over 25 m. (80 feet) could only have been cast in concrete. It may be that Michelangelo's drawings gave no clear indications for the dome; it has already been pointed out that even in St Peter's he left the definitive plan of the shape and contour of the dome and lantern undecided till the end.

25. Cf. Ackerman, *op. cit.*, I, 109 f., and II, 122 ff.; begun to a commission from Cardinal Guido Ascanio Sforza (d. 1564); according to Vasari, Tiberio Calcagni (d. 1565) was entrusted with the execution of Michelangelo's designs. The chapel, which Vasari described as unfinished in 1568, was consecrated in 1573. There seems to be no reason to doubt that the execution (probably by Giacomo della Porta) was in line with Michelangelo's intentions. The earliest known views of the building are in Francesco Pagliarino's *Zibaldone* (between 1578 and 1581; Milan, Castello Sforzesco, Cod. Trivulzio 179, unpublished); a drawing in the *Zibaldone* shows the elevation of the façade of the chapel towards the side aisle of the church, which was demolished in the eighteenth century [157]. A memorandum of 1577 concerning the Capitoline buildings mentions the price of travertine which had been used for the 'facciata' and the columns of the chapel; cf. P. Pecchiai, *Il Campidoglio nel Cinquecento* (Rome, 1950), 253.

26. Cf. S. Maria del Popolo, Chigi Chapel, inner width 7.04 m. (23 feet), summit of dome 14.08 m. (43 feet); S. Lorenzo, New Sacristy, inner width 12 m. (39 feet), summit of dome 25 m. (80 feet).

27. The unprecedented use of travertine for columns in the interior is characteristic of Michelangelo's predilection for monochrome. The tombs of the two Sforza cardinals, erected about 1580, and the modern decoration impair the intended effect.

28. The lighting we see today does not correspond to the original. Two windows were broken out at the side of the altar; when the adjacent Borghese Chapel was built the corresponding lunette window of the Sforza Chapel was walled up.

29. For reproduction and description of preliminary drawings see E. MacDougall, 'Michelangelo and the Porta Pia', *Journal of the Society of Architectural Historians*, XIX (1960), 97 ff.

30. Since the gate, which once stood flush with the Aurelian Walls and towered above them, was isolated in modern times, the original function as a passageway has become unrecognizable. The unimpressive old outer side of the gate, known to us in drawings, was destroyed in the nineteenth century.

31. The foundation stone of the church was laid in 1561. The first mass was not said till 1565, and the building was not finished till about 1590, under Sixtus V.

32. The large volutes round the windows, which can be seen in [156], belong to the seventeenth century.

CHAPTER 10

1. Cf. M. G. Lewine, 'Roman Architectural Practice during Michelangelo's Maturity', in *Stil und Überlieferung in der Kunst des Abendlandes* (Akten des 21. Internationalen Kongresses für Kunstgeschichte, Bonn, 1964) (Berlin, 1967), II, 20 ff.; also H. Hibbard, 'Maderno, Michelangelo and Cinquecento Tradition', *ibid.*, 33 ff.

2. Cf. D. Coffin, *The Villa d'Este at Tivoli* (Princeton, N. J., 1960), and C. Lamb, *Die Villa d'Este in Tivoli* (Munich, 1966), 85 ff.

3. Cf. Lamb, *op. cit.*, 92, and E. Mandowsky and C. Mitchell, *Pirro Ligorio's Roman Antiquities* (Studies of the Warburg Institute, XXVIII, London, 1963).

4. For details, see J. S. Ackerman, *The Cortile del Belvedere* (Vatican City, 1954), 73 ff. The ground plan of Michelangelo's stairway is preserved in a drawing in the Metropolitan Museum; see C. de Tolnay, *Stil und Überlieferung* (Note 1), II, 67.

5. For Ligorio's designs for the west corridor, cf. Ackerman, *op. cit.*, 87 ff., and the drawing attributed to Sallustio Peruzzi in the Phyllis Lambert Collection, New York [7]; cf. W. Lotz, *Kunstchronik*, XI (1958), 96 ff. The west wing was completed only about 1580.

6. Stucco coating of a façade appears for the first time in Bramante's Palazzo Caprini; cf. above, pp. 22–3.

7. See W. Friedlaender, *Das Kasino Pius des Vierten* (Leipzig, 1912), and C. Elling, *Villa Pia in Vaticano* (Copenhagen, 1947).

8. For Pliny's letter on the Laurentina, cf. D. Coffin, 'The Plans of the Villa Madama', *Art Bulletin*, IL (1967), 119: '. . . Pliny compares the shape of the central court of his Villa to the letter D. . . . However, the passage . . . is a result of later philological criticism. Most of the Italian late fifteenth century and early sixteenth century editions of the *Letters* . . . use the letter O to describe the form

of the court in Pliny's Villa.' In early-sixteenth-century printing, however, the letter O – like the court of the Villa Madama, which Coffin connects with it – is circular in shape; but later in the century O took the shape of an oval. Thus I should like to regard the oval court of the Casino as a 'literal' copy of the Laurentina court. Ligorio may also have thought of the oval shape of the circus arena or, as Elling (*op. cit.*, 31 ff.) has suggested, of the ancient naumachia.

9. The beginning of actual building work was preceded by large purchases of land and ground-levellings. Cf. the documents in Coffin, *op. cit.*, 8 ff.

10. A letter from Annibale Caro dated 13 July 1538 gives a full description of the garden of Giovanni de' Gaddi in Rome, where there were grottoes with antique ornament, pergolas, and elaborate fountains: 'tra il piovere, il gorgogliare, e il versare, e di questa fonte, e dell'altra, oltra al vedere, si fa un sentir molto piacevole, e quasi armonioso, congiunto un altro maggior suono, il quale si sente, e non si scorge donde si venga'; A. Caro, *Lettere Familiari* (ed. A. Greco), I (Florence, 1957), 105 ff.

11. For the original condition of the villa as shown not only in Dupérac and his explanations, but in contemporary descriptions, cf. Lamb, *op. cit.*, and Coffin, *op. cit.*

12. Early in the Cinquecento it was possible to place side by side, in a Doric entablature, metopes of different shapes, as in the Tempietto, or to employ different capitals side by side, as in the court of the Palazzo Medici-Lante in Rome; in the second half of the century the Corinthian capital in the crossing of St Peter's was copied for the Gesù (see Hibbard, *op. cit.*, 39), which has the same form of capital throughout.

13. Pastor, *op. cit.*, v, 730; cf. also details in M. Walcher Casotti, *Il Vignola* (Trieste, 1960), I, 259 ff. For Vignola's sojourn in France see also S. Pressouyre, 'Les Fontes de Primatice à Fontainebleau', *Bulletin Monumental*, CXXXVII (1969), 225 ff.

14. For the subject of Gothic in the Renaissance, see R. Bernheimer, 'Gothic Survival and Revival in Bologna', *Art Bulletin*, XXXVI (1954), 263 ff.; also *ibid.*, 272 ff., and Walcher Casotti, *op. cit.*, I, 57 ff., for Vignola's designs for S. Petronio.

15. Cf. J. K. Schmidt, 'Zu Vignolas Palazzo Bocchi in Bologna', *Mitteilungen des Kunsthistorischen Instituts Florenz*, XIII (1967), 83 ff. The design shown in the engraving was altered in the execution. The ground floor is the only part left standing from the first stage of building. Instead of the pilasters which appear in the engraving, the portal has Tuscan columns which are partly encased in rusticated blocks; the balcony above the portal and the upper storey belong to a later stage of building.

Until now the engraving had only been known in a variant bearing the date of 1555 and the arms of Pius IV (1561–5); the version published by Schmidt shows the arms of Paul III; the Pius IV version gives the executed portal.

16. The villa was begun soon after the elevation of Julius III (1550–4), and practically completed at the time of his death. The profuse antique decoration was removed to the Vatican later in the sixteenth century; as we see it today, the building is the result of many restorations. For a review of the copious literature, see now F. L. Moore, 'A Contribution to the Study of the Villa Giulia', *Römisches Jahrbuch für Kunstgeschichte*, XII (1969), 171 ff.; for a fully documented history of the building and its decoration see T. Falk, 'Studien zur Topographie und Geschichte der Villa Giulia in Rom', *ibid.*, XIII (1971), 101 ff.

17. A portrait medal of the Pope, with Vignola's Palazzina and the nymphaeum on the reverse side, bears the inscription FONS VIRGINIS VILLAE JULIAE; see Moore, *op. cit.*, figures 3 and 4. For Ammannati's share see also below, pp. 164, 166.

18. Michel de Montaigne, *Voyage en Italie par la Suisse et l'Allemagne en 1580 et 1581*; for Caprarola, see Lotz, *Vignola-Studien*, 35 ff., Walcher Casotti, *op. cit.*, I, 71 and 156 ff. (cf. review by C. Thoenes, *Kunstchronik*, XV (1962), 151 ff.), and L. W. Partridge, 'Vignola and the Villa Farnese at Caprarola', *Art Bulletin*, LII (1970), 81 ff. As the documents discovered by Partridge prove, Vignola also designed the street which leads through the town of Caprarola to the palazzo and the semicircular ramps that lead from the street to the palazzo. Before building was begun, the Cardinal ordered full reports and several designs from Vignola and Francesco Paciotto, who was engaged on the Farnese fortifications in Parma and Piacenza. It is clear from these sources that the round cortile was an idea of Vignola; Paciotto had proposed a decagonal court. The work began in 1559 under Vignola's supervision, and when he died in 1573 the Cardinal abandoned the idea of appointing another architect in his place, since the building was practically finished (cf. Fulvio Orsini's letter of 6 September 1573, in A. Ronchini, *Atti e Memorie della Deputazione di Storia Patria per la Provincia di Emilia*, N.S. IV, part II (1880), 54 f.).

19. Cf. Walcher Casotti, *op. cit.*, I, 78 ff. and 162 ff. At Piacenza, Vignola had to take Francesco Paciotto's designs into account too: cf. G. Kubler, 'Francesco Paciotto, Architect', in *Essays in Memory of Karl Lehmann* (New York, 1964), 176 ff. (Spanish translation: 'Francesco Paciotto, arquitecto', in *Goya, Revista de Arte*, nos. 56–7 (1963), 86 ff.). Paciotto proposed to build the theatre in the court in wood; Vignola's proposal to build it in stone as a permanent structure

was, however, accepted. This part of the building never got beyond its beginnings. For the early history of the building and Vignola's plans, see now P. Dreyer, 'Beiträge zur Planungsgeschichte des Palazzo Farnese in Piacenza', *Jahrbuch des Berliner Museen*, VIII (1966), 160 ff.; cf. also A. Terzaghi, 'Disegni originali del Vignola per il Palazzo Farnese di Piacenza', in *Il Palazzo Farnese e la chiesa di S. Agostino in Piacenza* (Piacenza, 1960). As Dreyer points out, Vignola first planned a fortified villa reaching to the Po. The drawings made by Vignola's son Giacinto to his father's instructions are at Windsor and in the State Archives at Parma.

20. Consult, however, Kubler, *op. cit.*, 188.

21. In Vignola's design, the two windows over the street openings were to be provided with balconies; these, however, were subsequently omitted, along with the clock towers over the same bays. The rather monotonous façade of today would have gained emphasis and the contour would have been effectively enriched. The attribution to Vignola is made as early as Egnatio Danti's biography of Vignola of 1583 ('built under Pius IV'). Bolognese guide-books of the seventeenth century give the date 1562, which may have appeared on the façade at an earlier time. For Vignola's drawing of the original project in Berlin, cf. Walcher Casotti, *op. cit.*, 61 f. and 147 f., and W. Lotz, 'Italienische Plätze des 16. Jahrhunderts', *Jahrbuch 1968 der Max-Planck-Gesellschaft*, 57 ff.

22. M. J. Lewine gives a list of the churches built in Rome between 1527 and 1575, *op. cit.* (Note 1), II, 20. For S. Spirito in Sassia, *ibid.*, 22, and E. Lavagnino, *La Chiesa di Santo Spirito in Sassia* (Turin, 1962).

23. The measurements of the plan could not be simpler. Exactly half of its total length of 320 palms (71.36 m., or 234 feet 1 in.) is occupied by the nave; the transept also is 160 palms in length, the chapels 40 palms. For the early architectural history of the Gesù cf. J. S. Ackerman and W. Lotz, 'Vignoliana', in *Essays in Memory of Karl Lehmann* (New York, 1964), 14 ff. and its attached bibliography. The profuse Baroque decoration, and in particular Bacciccia's great fresco in the vault, have radically altered the general effect of the interior.

24. Nanni di Baccio Bigi's Gesù project of 1550 shows a remarkably wide nave with a timber ceiling, six chapels on each side, and a comparatively narrow transept. This project, which was obviously regarded as the model as early as March 1568, was intended for another site (cf. P. Pirri, 'La Topografia del Gesù di Roma, etc.', *Archivum Historicum Societatis Jesu*, X (1941), 177 ff.). The present site was not definitely decided on till just before the foundation stone was laid.

25. Though designs for oval churches existed as early as Peruzzi; cf. p. 49. Vignola may have become familiar with Peruzzi's ideas through Serlio. On this point, cf. W. Lotz, 'Die ovalen Sakralbauten des Cinquecento', *Römisches Jahrbuch für Kunstgeschichte*, VII (1955), 35 ff.; also Ackerman, 'Vignoliana' (*op. cit.*, Note 23), 12.

26. For this and the following point, cf. Lotz, *op. cit.*, 40 ff. Vignola's design for S. Maria del Piano at Capranica, showing an oblong interior with exedrae on the short sides, precedes the plan for the conclave chapel with its 'pure' oval. The plan of S. Maria del Piano was published and dated (before 1559) by K. Schwager, *Zeitschrift für Kunstgeschichte*, XXXI (1968), 249 f.

27. M. Lewine, 'Vignola's Church of Sant'Anna dei Palafrenieri, Rome', *Art Bulletin*, XLVII (1965), 199 ff. (containing new references to sources and important observations on the building and the reconstruction of its original state; cf. [185B]). Excerpts from the building accounts were published by A. Cicinelli, *S. Anna dei Palafrenieri in Vaticano* (Chiese di Roma illustrate, CX) (Rome, 1970), 31 ff.: cornerstone 1565; façade under construction 1566; the columns framing the portal 1567; window grilles 1571–2; interior columns and main cornice 1576; provisional wooden roof and consecration 1583. The clerk of the works was – as in all Vignola's late works – his son Giacinto. The façade and vaulting were completed in the eighteenth century. The interior was disfigured by the restorations of 1842 and 1902–3.

28. For the original function of the 'irregular spaces' in the corners, cf. Lewine, *op. cit.* (Note 27), 211.

29. In addition to the main portal, there was a side entrance to the church in the right-hand side wall. Opposite the main entrance, the altar of St Anne stood in a niche, and there was a second altar on the long side opposite the side entrance. This arrangement was greatly altered by the rebuilding of the seventeenth century, and the enlargement of the high altar recess about 1900. For the reconstruction, see Lewine, *op. cit.*

30. R. Wittkower, *Art Bulletin*, XIX (1937), 263.

31. D. Frey, *Bramante's St Peter-Entwurf und seine Apokryphen* (Vienna, 1915), 75.

32. Cf. E. Hubala, 'Roma Sotterranea, Andachtsstätten in Rom und ihre Bedeutung für die barocke Baukunst', *Das Münster*, XVIII (1965), 157 ff., and R. Krautheimer, 'A Christian Triumph in 1597', in *Essays in the History of Art presented to Rudolf Wittkower* (London, [1967]), 174 ff.

For the following, see also the fine survey and analysis of Roman architecture during the last decades of the Cinquecento in H. Hibbard, *Carlo Maderno and Roman Architecture 1580–1630* (London, 1971), 22–34.

33. Completed in 1585; cf. J. S. Ackerman, *The Architecture of Michelangelo* (London, 1964), II, 96.

34. See p. 99.

35. Cf. H. Hibbard, 'The Early History of Sant'Andrea della Valle', *Art Bulletin*, LXIII (1961), 305. For Porta's training and his first buildings see J. von Henneberg, 'An Early Work by Giacomo della Porta: The Oratorio del SS. Crocefisso di S. Marcello in Rome', *Art Bulletin*, LII (1970), 157 ff.

36. Cf. Wölfflin, *Renaissance und Barock*, 2nd ed. (Munich, 1907), 77 f.; H. Willich, *Vignola* (Strasbourg, 1910), 140 f.; T. H. Fokker, 'The First Baroque Church in Rome', *Art Bulletin*, XV (1933), 241 f.; G. Giovannoni, *Saggi sull' architettura del Rinascimento*, 2nd ed. (Milan, 1935), 208 ff.; Walcher Casotti, *op. cit.* (Note 13), 207 f.; Lotz, 'Vignoliana' (*op. cit.*, Note 23), 20 ff.

37. Hibbard, *op. cit.* (Note 35), 289 ff.; *idem, op. cit.* (Note 32), 25 f.

38. According to J. Wasserman, 'Giacomo della Porta's Church for the Sapienza', *Art Bulletin*, XLVI (1964), 502, probably of 1594–7. Wasserman also deals with Porta's share in the court of the Sapienza.

39. Donated by Cardinal Alessandro Farnese; reproduction in P. Letarouilly, *Édifices de Rome moderne* (Liège–Brussels, 1840–66), III, plate 339. To a contract from Cardinal Pietro Aldobrandini, Della Porta also designed for the abbey of S. Paolo alle Tre Fontane a chapel on the site of the martyrdom of St Paul.

40. For the authorship, typology, and dating of the façades of S. Atanasio and the Trinità dei Monti, cf. Giovannoni, *Saggi* (*op. cit.*), 219 ff. The old attribution of S. Atanasio to Della Porta (cf. Hibbard, *op. cit* (Note 35), 307) is questionable; M. Zocca put forward Francesco da Volterra (*Bollettino d'Arte*, XV (1935–6), 528). According to information kindly given me personally by Dr Herwarth Röttgen, Francesco da Volterra is also mentioned in the building accounts of the church. We may expect this question to be cleared up in Klaus Schwager's monograph on Della Porta. Della Porta's palazzi, among others the palazzi Maffei–Marescotti, Crescenzi–Serlupi, and Chigi in the Piazza Colonna, till now have been examined only by W. Arslan (cf. 'Forme architettoniche civili di Giacomo della Porta', *Bollettino d'Arte*, VI (1927), 508–27; see also Hibbard, *op. cit.* (Note 32), 31, and, for the Palazzo Chigi, 215). For Della Porta's work on the Villa Aldobrandini at Frascati (under construction from 1601), cf. Schwager, 'Kardinal Pietro Aldobrandinis Villa di Belvedere in Frascati', *Römisches Jahrbuch für Kunstgeschichte*, IX/X (1961/2), 291–382, and C. D'Onofrio, *La Villa Aldobrandini di Frascati* (Rome, 1963).

41. Volterra was already in Rome as 'architetto' before his time in northern Italy; his son Orazio was baptized in St Peter's on 22 May 1559 (from unpublished notes by F. Noack in the Bibliotheca Hertziana). In 1583, the Mantuan agent in Rome recommended Volterra for a post as court architect at Mantua; cf. A. Bertolotti, 'Artisti in relazione coi Gonzaga...', *Atti e Memorie Dep. di S. Patria Mod. e Parmensi*, serie III, vol. III (1885), 17. Della Porta is mentioned in the same letter as 'primo architetto di questa citta' (i.e. Rome); a document of 1593 says of Porta 'he is generally held to be the first and principal architect of Rome' (cf. H. Hibbard, *Burlington Magazine*, CIX (1967), 713, with the information that Volterra died before 20 March 1595); see also Hibbard, *op. cit.* (Note 32), 29 and *passim*.

42. Volterra was at work on the hospital buildings as early as 1582. His designs for the church, which was begun in 1592, are dated 1590. The church was vaulted and the façade completed by Carlo Maderno, who took over the building in 1595 and may have made minor adjustments in Volterra's plans. Consecration took place in 1602. Cf. W. Lotz, *Römisches Jahrbuch für Kunstgeschichte*, VII (1955), 58 ff., as corrected by Hibbard, *op. cit.* (Note 32), 27 f. and 118 ff.; see also R. Wittkower, *Art and Architecture in Italy, 1600–1750* (Pelican History of Art), 3rd ed. (Harmondsworth, 1973), 69.

43. Façade: Uffizi Disegni di Architettura 6722; plan of ground floor 6733, of the piano nobile 6732. The project for a new building near the Albergo dell'Orso in the present Via di Tor di Nona was not carried out. The site had been the property of the Gaetani since the early sixteenth century; cf. G. Gaietani, *Domus Caietana*, II (Rome, 1933), 327.

Volterra also collaborated on other enterprises of the eighties and early nineties; no systematic paper on his *œuvre* has as yet been written.

44. A short biography of Mascarino in J. Wasserman, *Ottaviano Mascarino and His Drawings in the Accademia Nazionale di S. Luca* (Rome, 1966), 1 ff. (cf. K. Schwager's review in *Zeitschrift für Kunstgeschichte*, XXIX (1968), 246 ff.). Mascarino's father, Giulio, collaborated with Vignola on a bridge in the neighbourhood of Bologna (Wasserman, *op. cit.*, 2). Vignola's son Giacinto calls Mascarino in a letter dated 4 January 1580, 'compatriota e di amicitia derivata fin dai patri nostri' (foreword to Egnatio Danti's edition of Vignola's *Due Regole di Prospettiva* (Rome, 1583)).

45. Cf. the source of 1593 mentioned in Note 41.

46. Ackerman, *op. cit.* (Note 4), 108, with a detailed enumeration of Mascarino's work in the Vatican; cf. also Wasserman, *op. cit.*, 149 ff.; also *idem*, 'The Palazzo Sisto V in the Vatican', *Journal of the Society of Architectural Historians*, XXI (1962), 26 ff.

47. For Mascarino's activities in the Quirinal, see J. Wasserman, 'The Quirinal Palace in Rome', *Art Bulletin*, XLV (1963), 205 ff., Hibbard. *op. cit.* (Note 32), 194 ff. and figure 11, and Schwager, *op. cit.* (Note 44), 253 f.; on the oval staircase see also H. Hibbard, *The Architecture of the Palazzo Borghese* (Rome, 1962), 59, note 52. Another oval staircase by Mascarino in the Belvedere Court is mentioned in Egnatio Danti's Commentary to Vignola's *Due Regole* (cf. Note 44). In his comparison of the oval Quirinal staircase with Bramante's circular staircase in the Belvedere Court, Danti remarks that the oval plan offers 'più difficoltà' than the circular one, in which 'tutte le linee vanno al punto e centro del mezzo, che nella ovale vanno a diversi punti' (*op. cit.*, 144); the criterion of 'difficoltà' is characteristic of the period. (For other oval staircases in Mascarino's designs for palazzi and villas cf. Wasserman, *op. cit.* (Note 44), *passim*.)

48. Wasserman, *ibid.*, plates 31 and 164; also Lotz, *op. cit.* (Note 25), 69 ff.

49. The first attribution to Mascarino is in P. Totti's guidebook, *Ritratto di Roma moderna* (Rome, 1638), 252; further in G. B. Baglione, *Le Vite dei pittori, scultori ed architetti* (Rome, 1642), 99; cf. Wasserman, *op. cit.* (Note 44), 191. Building began in 1591, the previous building having been destroyed by fire. The crossing, dome, and choir of the present church were not completed till about 1700. The plan published by Wasserman, figure 189, distinguishes the older from the newer parts. There is an arrangement of columns similar to that of S. Salvatore in a plan of 1585 for Sixtus V's chapel in S. Maria Maggiore; the plan was owned, but not drafted, by Mascarino (K. Schwager, *Miscellanea Bibliothecae Hertzianae* (1961), plate 248).

50. The first summary of what is known of Lunghi is that by H. Hibbard, see Appendix I, 'Biography of Martino Lunghi il Vecchio', in *The Architecture of the Palazzo Borghese* (Rome, 1962), 83–93. For Bosco Marengo see also Ackerman and Lotz, 'Vignoliana', in *op. cit.* (Note 23), 23. The design of the church, in which Pius V had his tomb erected, must have been made in Rome under the eyes of the Pope; according to a contemporary document, 'its portals, balustrades, and windows were constructed in the finest marble' and transported from Rome to Bosco Marengo by sea. The design is also attributed to the Dominican Egnatio Danti and the Genoese architect Rocco Lurago; see M. Ferrero Viale, *La Chiesa di S. Croce a Bosco Marengo* (Turin, [1959]), II.

51. Apart from the examples mentioned in Giovannoni, *Saggi* (*op. cit*), 222, cf. also Vignola's design for S. Maria in Traspontina (Ackerman and Lotz, 'Vignoliana' (*op. cit.*), figures 1–2) and S. Andrea in Via Flaminia. Palladio uses the tripartite lunette in the façade of S. Francesco della Vigna (1562), Alessi in S. Vittore Grande in Milan. For Alessi's tripartite lunettes cf. also Nancy A. Houghton Brown, *Arte Lombarda*, X (1965), 96, note 137.

52. From the seventeenth century onwards the façade and courtyard of the Palazzo Borghese have been regarded as the work of Lunghi of about 1590. H. Hibbard (cf. Note 50) has proved that the palazzo was begun by Tommaso del Giglio, a prelate in the retinue of Cardinal Alessandro Farnese. The fleur-de-lis crest of the Giglios appears in the frieze over the main portal. Hibbard was the first to connect the early building phase with Vignola, the Farnese architect *par excellence*. When Cardinal Deza acquired the palazzo in 1586, the front range was nearly finished; the only part still lacking was the roof. After the staircase had been built by the new owner, the building was ready for occupation. Work was continued in the courtyard, though it is difficult to distinguish between the older and newer parts. In 1605 the palazzo passed into the hands of the Borghese, under whom the courtyard, first planned for 5 by 5 arcades, was given its present dimensions (5 by 7 arcades) and the two-storey loggia at the rear. Deza's architect was Lunghi, who was succeeded, under the Borghese, by Flaminio Ponzio. Cf. also the reviews of Hibbard's book in *Zeitschrift für Kunstgeschichte*, XXVI (1963), 163 ff. (by C. Thoenes), *Art Bulletin*, XLV (1963), 181 ff. (by J. S. Ackerman), and *Journal of the Society of Architectural Historians*, XXIII (1964), 216 ff. (by J. Wasserman).

53. With some justification, R. Wittkower mentions the façade as a characteristic specimen of 'academic petrification' in late sixteenth-century Roman architecture in Italy (*op. cit.* (Note 42), 7; cf. *ibid.*, 12, and Hibbard, *op. cit.* (Note 50), for the development of the palazzo after its acquisition by the Borghese).

54. Fontana described and illustrated the removal of the obelisk in his book *Della Trasportatione dell'Obelisco Vaticano*, published in 1590, which also describes the buildings erected for Sixtus V. A second volume was published at Naples in 1603 under the title: *Libro Secondo in cui si ragiona di alcune fabriche fatte in Roma ed in Napoli, dal Cavalier Domenico Fontana*.

55. Thus, for instance, a wool factory was to be built in the Colosseum; in his note to the illustration of the project, Fontana remarks (in *Libro Secondo*; cf. Note 54) that Sixtus V's idea was 'to provide work for all the poor in Rome and to save them from begging in the streets'. On the ground floor 'every workman would have a workshop, and in the storey above it a free apartment of two rooms and an open loggia'.

56. During the four years and eight months of his reign Sixtus V spent more than one million ducats for building; see J. Delumeau, *Vie économique et sociale de Rome dans la seconde moitié du XVIe siècle*, II (Paris, 1959), 765; see *ibid.*, I (Paris, 1957), 331 f., for the Acqua Felice and the fountains, 504 for the Colosseum

project mentioned in the preceding Note. Cf. also the chapter 'Sisto V urbanista' in C. D'Onofrio, *Gli Obelischi di Roma*, 2nd ed. (Rome, 1967).

A traveller who revisited Rome after ten years' absence wrote: 'Everything here looks new – buildings, streets, squares, fountains, aqueducts, obelisks, and a thousand wonderful things – all the work of Sixtus V. We owe to his vigorous and noble mind a Rome which has been re-born from its own ashes' (quoted by A. Muñoz, 'Domenico Fontana architetto', *Quaderni Italo-Svizzeri*, III (Rome and Bellinzona, 1944), 39).

57. For this villa on the Esquiline, between S. Maria Maggiore and the modern railway terminus, which was destroyed in the late nineteenth century, see G. Matthiae, 'La Villa Montalto alle Terme', *Capitolium*, XIV (1939), 139 ff., and D'Onofrio, *op. cit.*, 142 ff.

58. For the memorial chapel of Sixtus V see Schwager, *op. cit.* (Note 49); see also Muñoz, *op. cit.*; G. Matthiae, 'L'Arte di Domenico Fontana', *Capitolium*, XXII (1947), 1 ff.; Wittkower, *op. cit.* (Note 42), 6 f.

59. For Maderno, see Wittkower, *op. cit.*, 7 and 69 ff., and Hibbard, *op. cit.* (Note 32).

CHAPTER 11

1. Of fundamental importance is M. Labò's article in the *Dizionario biografico degli Italiani* (Rome, 1960), II, 238 ff. Cf. also Emmina de Negri's survey of the literature in her *Galeazzo Alessi architetto a Genova* (Genoa, 1957), 111 ff. Little is known of Alessi's training; according to earlier sources he spent the years 1536 to 1542 in the households of various cardinals in Rome, and 1543 to 1548 in Perugia, where, according to Vasari (Mil, VII, 552; see also Labò, *op. cit.*, 238), he worked on the fortress of Paul III which was designed by Antonio da Sangallo and later demolished. A fairly certain early work of his is the secularized little church of S. Maria del Popolo in Perugia; its façade has the motif of a round arch on architraved columns which Alessi often employed later (illustration in Venturi, *Storia*, XI (3), figure 530). Alessi is first mentioned in Genoa in 1548.

2. The client for the villa was Luca Giustiniani. In an agreement dated 1548, the stonemasons pledge themselves to work 'iuxta voluntatem et modum' of Alessi; cf. G. Kühn, 'Galeazzo Alessi und die genuesische Architektur im 16. Jahrhundert', *Jahrbuch für Kunstwissenschaft* (1929), 151, de Negri, *op. cit.*, 60, and E. Poleggi, *Strada Nuova, una lottizzazione del Cinquecento a Genova* (Genoa, 1968), 443 ff. See also the pictorial corpus *Catalogo delle ville genovesi*, published by the Comune di Genova (1967), 41 and 415 ff.

3. From 1549 to 1570 there is documentary evidence of Alessi as architect of the church. Building began in 1552. With the exception of the dome, which was not vaulted till 1603, the interior was complete when Alessi died; the last time he was in Genoa was in 1568. The documents published by S. Varni, *Spigolature artistiche nell' archivio della basilica di Carignano* (Genoa, 1877), have been lost. For literature see Notes 1–2.

4. The height of the great dome up to the apex of the lantern corresponds to the side of the square of the ground plan.

5. The minor domes are relatively wide, in spite of their low height; the ratio of their diameter to that of the main dome is 3:4. Cf. on the other hand St Peter's (as executed) 1:4, Sangallo's model of 1539 1:3.

6. Contemporary sources certify Alessi's authorship of the Porta del Molo (with an inscription of 1553) and the octagonal drum and dome of the cathedral (under construction in 1556); further attributed to him is the Palazzo Cambiaso (originally Agostino Pallavicino; Rubens, figure 68, now Banco di Napoli), built under the direction of Bernardino da Cantone (cf. Poleggi, *op. cit.*, 96). Alessi's authorship of the villas Pallavicini delle Peschiere (first mentioned in 1560) and Scassi (under construction in 1566) has been questioned on serious grounds. Cf. on this point M. Labò, 'Studi di architettura genovese: Palazzo Carrega', in *Arte*, XXV (1922), 70ff.; *idem*, 'I Palazzi di Genova di P. P. Rubens', *Genova* (April 1939); de Negri, *op. cit.*, *passim*; *eadem*, in *Genova: Strada Nuova* (cf. Note 7), 138.

7. As early as 1568, Vasari said of the Strada Nuova that there was not in the whole of Italy a street 'more magnificent and grand, nor fuller of rich palazzi' (Vasari Mil, VII, 553). According to the travel notes of Heinrich Schickhardt, the Württemberg architect, who visited Genoa in 1599, 'The greater part of this town consists of excellently grand, very large and high houses and splendid palazzi... especially in the new streets'. In Rubens's book of engravings, published in 1622, the beginnings of which probably go back to his stay in Genoa (1607–8), all the palazzi built in the street are reproduced. For the history of the street and the individual buildings, see *Genova: Strada Nuova*, published by the Istituto di Elementi di Architettura e Rilievo dei Monumenti (Genoa, 1967), and Poleggi, *op. cit.* For the decree of 1550 see Poleggi, 403, for the sociological aspects of the street and its financial background *ibid.*, 25 ff. The wealth of the nobility derived primarily from foreign trade and extensive banking business. For this point cf. F. Chabod in *Storia di Milano*, IX (Milan, 1961), 404 ff.

8. For the chronology and documentation see Poleggi, *op. cit.*, 71–365.

9. Cf. Bernardino's letter of 1558 to the *Padri del Comune* (Poleggi, *op. cit.*, 415) in which he describes the work he has done since 1550 for the planning and tracing of the street and asks for adequate payment. His request was granted; in the pertinent document he is called *magister caput operis situum viarum* (Poleggi, *op. cit.*, 416). For Bernardino, see also Labò, *op. cit.* (Note 1), 239.

10. For these masters see the documentation in Poleggi, *op. cit.*, 443 ff.

11. Castello appears to have been active as a painter in the circle of Perino del Vaga in Rome; he died in Madrid as court painter to Philip II. For his architectural works in Genoa and his frescoes and stucco-work, cf. M. Labò, *G. B. Castello* (Biblioteca d'arte illustrata, I, 25) (Rome, 1925), 8 ff. See also Venturi, *Storia*, XI (3), 674 ff.

12. Cf. the reproduction of both buildings in R. Reinhardt, *Palast-Architektur von Oberitalien und Toscana* (Genoa and Berlin, n.d.). The Palazzo Doria Tursi, built for Nicolò Grimaldi, was acquired by the Doria in 1593 for 50,000 ducats (Poleggi, *op. cit.*, 273, with attribution to Giovanni Ponsello).

13. Cf. Labò, *op. cit.* (Note 1), 239; see also P. Torriti, *Tesori di Strada Nuova* (Genoa, 1970), 16 ff., for a rejection of Poleggi's (cf. Note 9) attribution of the street to Bernardino da Cantone.

14. 1553 is the date of Marino's first purchase of building sites. Drawings by Alessi for piers, capitals, and mouldings are mentioned in 1557 in a contract with a stonemason. Building began in 1558, and further land was purchased in 1558 and 1560. The first project provided for piers instead of the present columns on the ground floor of the courtyard. The design was changed in 1558. In December 1559 thirteen stonemasons were granted leave by the cathedral Office of Works to work on the Palazzo Marino (*Annali della Fabrica del Duomo di Milano*, IV, 35) – probably this involved the three storeys of the courtyard mentioned in 1560. Building was abandoned by Marino about 1565 for lack of funds, and after his death in 1572 the incomplete palazzo was confiscated in order to cover the debts of his estate (cf. C. Casati, 'Intorno a Tomaso de Marini', *Archivio Storico Lombardo*, XIII (1886), 622 ff.). The staircase and the façade on the Piazza della Scala are by Luca Beltrami, 1888–92. In 1943 the façades were seriously damaged by bombs, and the salone vault collapsed. Restoration was completed in 1954. See R. Gerla, *La Grande Sala detta d'Alessi in Palazzo Marino* (Milan, 1954).

The plan and elevation of the Archivio Civico, accepted in the literature as Alessi's work (cf. P. Mezzanotte, *Raccolta Bianconi, Catalogo Ragionato*, I (Milan, 1942), 79 ff. and plates XXXVI–XXXIX), in Baroni's opinion represent an initial stage of the planning, before the trapezoidal plan of the original site was 'regularized' by the new purchases (see C. Baroni, *Documenti per la storia dell'architectura a Milano nel Rinascimento e nel Barocco*, II (Rome, 1968), 398; cf. *ibid.*, 399 ff. for the building history). The same is true of the sketches of the elevation by L. Beltrami, *Archivio Storico dell'Arte*, I (1888), 146 ff.

15. The unusual planning of two courtyards is probably due to the necessity of incorporating older parts of the building. The word on three courtyard storeys, mentioned in 1558, can only refer to the Corte Nobile: plots of land acquired in the same year were probably situated in the service courtyard; cf. Baroni, *op. cit.*, 339 f. G. L. Bascapè (*I Palazzi della vecchia Milano* (Milan, 1945), 240) mentions 'older stretches of wall' which 'do not coincide with the plan [i.e. Alessi's]'. In the detailed description of the building in V. Scamozzi, *L' Idea dell'architettura universale* (Venice, 1615), part I, book III, chapter 6, he writes that there was a garden in the second court.

16. Besides Pirro Ligorio's buildings, the Palazzo Spada also belonged to the Roman examples; see J. Wasserman, *Art Bulletin*, XLIII (1961), 58 ff.

As H. Hibbard has shown, the painterly trend has to be understood as a re-evocation of the *ornata maniera* of antiquity; cf. *Stil und Überlieferung in der Kunst des Abendlandes* (Akten des 21. Internationalen Kongresses für Kunstgeschichte, Bonn 1964) (Berlin, 1967), II, 35 ff.

17. Cf. especially C. Baroni, *L'Architettura lombarda* (Milan, 1941), 120 f.

18. See G. Borlini, 'The Façade of the Certosa in Pavia', *Art Bulletin*, XLV (1963), 323 ff.

19. On 21 January 1546 the two masters were paid 100 scudi each for their drawings (A. Gatti, *La Fabbrica di S. Petronio* (Bologna, 1889), 114). The projects are illustrated in G. Zucchini, *Disegni antichi e moderni per la facciata di S. Petronio a Bologna* (Bologna, 1933), plates VI–XI.

20. First attributed to Lombardino by H. Hoffmann, 'Die Entwicklung der Architektur Mailands', *Wiener Jahrbuch für Kunstgeschichte*, IX (1934), 63 ff. In 1534 the cathedral Office of Works reduced Lombardino's salary 'quia servivit comiti Maximiliano Stampae mensibus 4'. The street fronts of the Palazzo Stampa were altered later, but the loggias of the Cinquecento court have been preserved. Their upper storey is probably the first Milanese example of arcades on architraved double columns, which means that the motif was introduced into Milan by Lombardino. The triple-tiered top to the tower also bears the mark of Lombardino's style. The curious apex, a double eagle on two tall columns, is in honour of the Emperor Charles V, whose device *Plus Ultra* appears on the columns. Massimiliano Stampa played a leading part in the occupation of Milan by Spain. Reproduction of court and tower in Mezzanotte and Bascapè, *Milano*

nell'arte e nella storia (Milan, 1948), 45 and 294.

21. Vasari Mil., VI, 497; see also P. Mezzanotte, 'S. Caterina alla Chiusa di Milano e Cristoforo Lombardi', *Palladio*, VII (1943), 23 ff., with illustration of the façade before its destruction; also Borlini (cf. Note 18), figure 15.

22. The convincing attribution of the dome (diameter *c.* 23 m., or 75 feet, height to apex *c.* 46 m., or 150 feet) to Lombardino was first made by C. Baroni, *S. Maria della Passione* (Milan, 1938); *idem, op. cit.* (Note 14), 55 ff. Vasari (Mil., VII, 544) mentions the dome as the work of Cristoforo Solari il Gobbo (d. 1527), who is often confused with Cristoforo Lombardino, though his verified works make no sense with it. The same confusion occurs in F. Malaguzzi Valeri, 'I Solari, etc.', *Italienische Forschungen*, I (Berlin, 1906), 156 ff., and in Venturi, *Storia*, XI (1), 709 f. In S. Latuada's *Guida di Milano* (Milan, 1737), I, 229, there is a note, unverified elsewhere but thoroughly probable, that the dome was erected about 1530. The attribution to Martino Bassi (b. 1542 or 1546) put forward by E. Tea cannot be supported by the style of the dome (*Atti del IV Convegno Nazionale di Storia dell'Architettura* (Milan, n.d.), 199 ff.). After 1570, an aisled nave with deep chapels was placed in front of the centrally planned church, which considerably impaired the original effect of the dome. Cf. the projects for the nave in the *Raccolta Bianconi* (see Note 14), V, fol. 15a and 15b, and the contract signed by Martino Bassi in Baroni, *op. cit.* (Note 14), 68.

23. At the end of the sixteenth century the dome was decorated with painted coffers. The original state can be seen in the drawing in the *Raccolta Bianconi*, mentioned in the preceding Note.

24. For the vestibule built in front of the church cf. p. 61. The architectural history of the nave and the dating of its magnificent tunnel-vault have not yet been elucidated. Cf. Baroni, *Documenti per la storia dell'architettura a Milano nel Rinascimento e Barocco*, I (Florence, 1940), 219 and documents 305–13; also W. Arslan in *Storia di Milano*, VIII (1957), 546 ff.; *ibid.*, 545, views of the church about 1565 with the aisles and choir finished, but the façade not yet complete.

25. Cf. W. Lotz, 'Architecture in the later 16th century', *College Art Journal*, XVII (1958), 131.

26. Cf. Baroni, *op. cit.* (Note 14), 481, for a full documentation including Giovio's letter of 15 September 1547 and the deed of sale of 27 April 1547, with a description of the existing layout. For plans and elevation see also U. Tarchi, *La Villa detta la Simonetta nel suburbio di Milano* (Monumenti Italiani, serie II, fasc. II) (Rome, 1953).

27. Cf. Vasari Mil., VI, 27 (as Domenico Giuntalocchi or Giuntalodi); C. Guasti's commentary (*ibid.*, 31 ff.) was also published separately. Giunti's Milanese *œuvre* has been collected by C. Baroni, *Archivio Storico Lombardo*, N.S. III (1938), 326 ff.; *Palladio*, II (1938), 142.; and *op. cit.* (Note 17), 121 f.; cf. also Mezzanotte and Bascapé, *op. cit.*, 47 f. and 770 ff.

28. The service wings and the gardens of the villa, which now stands in an industrial suburb, were destroyed in 1900. The main block, which suffered severely during the war, was restored not long ago.

29. The inscription submitted by Giovio for the façade is interesting: 'Ferdinandus Gonzaga ... quum ex bellicis atque civilibus curis meritam non ignobilis ocii requiem quaereret nympheum suburbani secessus honestae voluptati dedicavit.'

30. Cf. Baroni, *Archivio Storico Lombardo*, N.S. III (1938), 353 ff., and *Palladio*, II (1938), 142. A drawing of the façade (hardly by Giunti) in Milan, Archivio Civico, *Raccolta Bianconi* (cf. Note 14), VII, fol. 17A.

31. Foundation stone laid in 1549, consecrated in 1551. First attribution to Giunti by Baroni, *op. cit.* (Note 17), 122. The client, Contessa Torelli della Guastalla, was a friend of Ferrante Gonzaga.

Alessi, to whom the church was formerly attributed, is not mentioned in the documents in Milan till 1557 (cf. N. Houghton-Brown, *Arte Lombarda*, X (1965), 97, note 191, and Mezzanotte and Bascapé, *op. cit.* (Note 20), 528 f.). The attribution to Cristoforo Lombardino and Vincenzo Seregni, suggested by H. Hoffmann, *Wiener Jahrbuch für Kunstgeschichte*, IX (1934), 63 ff., is untenable for stylistic reasons. Baroni's attribution to Giunti seems convincing in view of the close connection between the client and Ferrante Gonzaga; cf. *op. cit.* (Note 14), 149.

32. For the type, see Liliana Gatti, 'Iconologia delle chiese monastiche femminili dall'alto medioevo ai sec. XVI-XVII', in *Arte Lombarda*, IX (1964), 131.

33. Cf. G. Rocco, 'Galeazzo Alessi a Milano', *IV. Convegno Nazionale di Storia dell'Architettura* (Milan, n.d.), 185.

34. Seregni's early work is difficult to trace; his later work is entirely under Alessi's influence (cf. Baroni, *op. cit.* (Note 17), 123 f.). For the Palazzo del Collegio dei Giureconsulti (1558–68) cf. Baroni, *op. cit.* (Note 14), 318 ff., and P. Mezzanotte in *Storia di Milano*, X (1957), 574 f. For the Palazzo Medici in Via Brera, begun in 1565, now demolished, cf. P. Mezzanotte, 'La Casa dei Medici di Nosiggia e il Palazzo di Pio IV in Milano', in *Rassegna d'Arte*, I (1914), 142 ff.

35. For the architectural history cf. Baroni, *op. cit.* (Note 24), 255 ff; Alessi's project: G. Rocco, 'La Facciata di S. Maria presso S. Celso a Milano', in *Palladio*, IV (1940), 123 ff.; cf. also Baroni, *op. cit.* (Note 17), 126, and Mezzanotte

in *Storia di Milano*, X (1957), 576. For the façade sculpture: E. Kris in *Mitteilungen des Kunsthistorischen Instituts Florenz*, III (1930), 201 ff. Only the lowest storey was carried out under Alessi's supervision. It corresponds to the design in all its details.

36. In May 1568 Alessi delivered drawings for the façade, choir, organ loft, and tabernacle: Baroni, *op. cit.* (Note 24), document 334; cf. also M. L. Gatti Perer, 'Martino Bassi, Il Sacro Monte di Varallo e S. Maria presso S. Celso', *Arte Lombarda*, IX, 2 (1964), 21 ff.

37. For the architectural history see Baroni, *op. cit.* (Note 14), 210 ff.; Mezzanotte and Bascapé, *op. cit.* (Note 20), 712 ff. The foundation stone of the present church was laid in 1560. The remains of the older church, which stood beside the present one, were demolished in 1576, when its relics were transferred to the new building. The late antique mausoleum which was part of the old group was at first intended to be incorporated in the new building, but was eventually demolished. The planning of the new church can be followed in Seregni's (?) drawings in the *Raccolta Bianconi*:

(1) V, fol. 1: the mausoleum as the narthex to the three-bay nave; wide octagonal dome; apses to the choir and transepts.

(2a) V, fol. 4: doubling of the mausoleum; between the twin buildings a narrow vestibule to the nave; octagonal dome and choir similar to those in (1); the transepts reduced in size. Inscribed: 'Di Vincenzo Seregni ingenere per Santo Vittore'.

(2b) V, fol. 2: copy of the above with text: 'Copia del disegno fatto per me Vincentio' (sc. Seregni).

(3) V, fol. 6: mausoleum removed, nave, transept, and chancel of same type as finished building, but with ambulatory and deep narthex instead of the sixth bay of the nave; groin-vault instead of tunnel-vault. That the church represented in the sheet is S. Vittore is proved by the staircase in the right-hand transept.

(4a) V, fol. 7 a and b: plan and elevation of present building; in front of the façade singlestoreyed portico (not executed).

(4b) Similar ground plan, but without portico, in the archives of S. Barnaba, Milan; cf. Baroni, *op. cit.* (Note 17), figure 123. Whether (4) represents the final plan or a sketch requires further investigation, like other attributions of drawings to Seregni.

38. In Italy, most medieval monks' choirs were removed in the late sixteenth century. That of S. Maria Gloriosa dei Frari in Venice is one of the few to have been preserved.

39. J. S. Ackerman has drawn attention to the importance of the Milanese churches in the liturgical reforms of the sixteenth century (lecture held at the Society of Architectural Historians, New York, unpublished). This question has never been adequately investigated. For the placing of the altar and the liturgical requirements see also S. Sinding-Larsen, 'Some Functional and Liturgical Aspects of the Centralized Church in the Italian Renaissance', in *Acta ad Archaeologiam et Artium Historiam pertinentia*, II (1965), 203 ff.

40. Sources for the building history in Baroni, *op. cit.* (Note 24), 89 ff.; cf. also N. A. Houghton Brown, 'The Church of S. Barnaba in Milan', *Arte Lombarda*, IX (1964), II, 62 ff., and X (1965), 65 ff. The planning of the new building was put in hand in 1558.

41. Two preparatory drawings in the *Raccolta Bianconi* show a dome over the crossing (cf. Houghton Brown, *op. cit.*, figures 10–11). The rectangular plan of the crossing would have required an oval dome, and it was probably to avoid the awkward oval vault that the trough-shaped vault was chosen.

42. The present high altar and its balustrade date from the late nineteenth century. The drawings in the *Raccolta Bianconi* (cf. Note 41) show the original arrangement. The façade of S. Barnaba has been altered out of recognition by rebuilding and restoration; on this cf. Houghton Brown, *op. cit.*

43. For S. Raffaelle, see G. Rocco, 'La Chiesa di S. Raffaelle a Milano', in *Rassegna d'Architettura*, XII (1940), 230 ff., and Houghton Brown, *op. cit.*, figure 33; for the work in the cathedral, G. Rocco, *Pellegrino Pellegrini e le sue opere nel duomo di Milano* (Milan, 1939), 66 ff., and Mezzanotte and Bascapé, *op. cit.* (Note 20), 184; for Varallo, A. Cavalleri-Murat in *Atti e Memorie del terzo Congresso Piemontese di Antichità ed Arte, Varallo Sesia, 1960* (Turin, 1966), 82 ff., Gatti Perer, *op. cit.* (Note 36), 21 ff., and R. Wittkower, 'Montagnes sacrées', *L'œil* (November 1959).

44. The accounts of these visits, only partially published (cf. e.g. Angelo Giuseppe Roncalli, *Gli Atti della Visita Apostolica di S. Carlo Borromeo a Bergamo nel 1575*, 4 vols. (Milan, 1936)), have so far escaped the notice of art historians.

45. *Instructionum fabricae et supellectilis ecclesiasticae libri duo* (Milan, 1577). The actual author of the book, which has a preface by the Cardinal, was his closest collaborator, Monsignore Lodovico Moneta. The latest Italian edition is that of C. Castiglioni and C. Marcora, under the title *S. Carlo Borromeo: Arte Sacra* (Milan, 1952). Also in P. Barocchi, *Trattati d'arte del Cinquecento* (Bari, 1962), III, 9 ff. For the nature and influence of the *Instructiones*, see A. Blunt, *Artistic Theory in Italy 1450–1600*, 2nd ed. (Oxford, 1962), 127 ff.

46. James Ackerman has already drawn attention to these questions; cf. Note 39.

47. Pellegrini, who occasionally used his father's Christian name Tibaldi, first worked as a painter in Rome. The frescoes in Vignola's church of S. Andrea in Via Flaminia were among his earliest works. For his career and his buildings see the literature listed by A. Peroni, 'Architetti manieristi nell'Italia settentrionale: Pellegrino Tibaldi Galeazzo Alessi', in *Bollettino del Centro Internazionale di Studi di Architettura Andrea Palladio*, IX (1967), 272 ff.

48. Pellegrini had already been active in Bologna and Ancona and on the papal fortifications in the Marches; the papal legate in the Marches at that time was Carlo Borromeo.

49. *Der Cicerone*, reprint of the first edition of 1853 (Leipzig, n.d.), 328. For the building history of the Canonica see Baroni, *op. cit.* (Note 14), 245 ff. and documents 747–82; for the Collegio Borromeo in Pavia, see Peroni, *op. cit.* (Note 47), and *idem*, in *I quattro secoli del Collegio Borromeo di Pavia* (Milan, 1961), 111 ff.

50. Sources in Baroni, *op. cit.* (Note 17), 113 ff. Interesting correspondence between the Superior of the Order and the *rettore* of the convent in Milan concerning the building in P. Pirri, *Giovanni Tristano e i primordi della architettura gesuitica* (Rome, 1955), 170 ff. In December 1567 a design by Pellegrini was sent to Rome and approved, with some slight alterations. This design provided for vaulting; the Superior had recommended a flat roof for the sake of better acoustics. At the consecration of the new building in 1579 only the nave was finished. Building resumed in the seventeenth century – the vault of the dome was begun in 1642 and closed in 1684. The apse was altered in 1723, and the façade was not finished till the nineteenth century.

The quality of the church was recognized as early as the sixteenth century. In the *Trattato dell'arte della pittura* by Lomazzo (Milan, 1585), 438, we read: 'tempio per bellezza, & vaghezza d'architettura, & d'inventione singularissima fra le fabriche moderne, uscito dal divino ingegno di Pellegrino Pellegrini'.

51. The columns are 10 m. (30 feet) in height, their bases 3.30 m. (11 feet).

52. W. Hiersche, *Pellegrino de' Pellegrini als Architekt* (Parchim, 1913), 51.

53. Cf. Baroni, *op. cit.* (Note 17), figure 157.

54. The chapels, 5 m. wide and only 2 m. deep (16 feet by 6 feet), are recessed in the outer walls.

55. On 8 April 1564 Carlo Borromeo wrote from Rome that Pellegrini had left Rome for Milan a few days before; cf. G. Rocco, *Pellegrino Pellegrini, l'architetto di S. Carlo, e le sue opere nel duomo di Milano* (Milan, 1939), 203.

56. Building began in 1577 and the main cornice was finished in 1595. The dome is by Fabio Mangone, 1617, and the present high altar is of 1759. Cf. Baroni, *op. cit.* (Note 17), 129; (Note 34), 157 ff.; Mezzanotte and Bascapé, *op. cit.* (Note 20), 297.

57. The dome of S. Sebastiano was, according to the original project, to rise as a hemisphere above the outer walls, as in the Pantheon. The present dome, buttressed above the ground floor by volutes, is smaller in diameter; cf. Baroni, *op. cit.* (Note 17), figure 158a and b, and P. Mezzanotte, in *Storia di Milano*, X, 592. For the centrally planned churches of the late sixteenth century cf. Sinding-Larsen, *op. cit.* (Note 39), 208 ff.

58. For details on this point, cf. Rocco, *op. cit.* (Note 55), and Mezzanotte and Bascapé, *op. cit.* (Note 20), 184 ff.

59. Report of the Ferrarese Ambassador; cf. A. Calderini, *La Zona monumentale di S. Lorenzo in Milano* (Milan, 1934), 38 ff., and Baroni, *op. cit.* (Note 24), 152, with the sources for the rebuilding. On the late antique building see R. Krautheimer, *Early Christian and Byzantine Architecture* (Pelican History of Art) (Harmondsworth, 1965).

60. For Bassi, see H. Hoffmann, *Wiener Jahrbuch für Kunstgeschichte*, IX (1934), 82 ff.; P. Mezzanotte, *Storia di Milano*, X (1957), 601 ff.; and M. L. Gatti Perer, *Arte Lombarda*, IX (1964), 2, 57 ff. (with F. B. Ferrari's 'Vita di Martino Bassi architetto milanese' of 1771).

61. A systematic investigation into these drawings is much to be desired; cf. Hoffmann, *op. cit.*, 80 ff.; C. Baroni, 'Due nuovi disegni per la ricostruzione del S. Lorenzo a Milano', *Palladio*, V (1941), 57 ff.; *idem*, *op. cit.* (Note 24), 145 f.; Calderari-Chierici-Cecchelli, *La Basilica di S. Lorenzo Maggiore in Milano* (Milan, [1951]), plates LXVI ff.; Mezzanotte and Bascapé, *op. cit.* (Note 20), 561 ff.

62. Cf. F. Graf Wolff Metternich, 'St Maria im Kapitol, St Peter in Rom und S. Lorenzo in Mailand', in *Vom Bauen, Bilden und Bewahren* (Festschrift Willy Weyres) (Cologne, 1964), 165 ff.

63. Cf. N. Carboneri, *Ascanio Vitozzi* (Rome, 1966); *ibid.*, 31 ff. and 143 ff. on the churches of S. Maria dei Cappuccini and SS. Trinità in Turin; 131 ff. on Vitozzi's part in the rebuilding of the Castello of Turin; 137 ff. on his design for the Piazza di Castello and the Strada Nuova, which marked the beginning of the Baroque enlargement of Turin. For the latter and Vitozzi's fortifications see also A. Scotti, *Ascanio Vitozzi ingegnere ducale a Torino* (Florence, 1969).

64. Carboneri, *op. cit.*, plates 48–102. For the derivation of these projects from Peruzzi, Serlio, Labacco, etc., see *ibid.*, 67 ff.

65. Work stopped about 1615; at that time the building had reached approximately the cornice of the ground floor. The dome was vaulted according to a changed plan of 1729–33 by Francesco Gallo; the top storeys of the campanili are nineteenth- and twentieth-century. Gallo had also modified the piers and arches below the dome. The project by Vitozzi is known from engravings. On this cf. W. Lotz, *Römisches Jahrbuch für Kunstgeschichte*, VII (1955), 85 ff.; Carboneri, *op. cit.*, 95 ff.; *idem*, *L'Architetto Francesco Gallo* (Turin, 1954), 60 and 142 ff.

66. S. Maria di Carignano, Genoa, and the designs for S. Lorenzo, Milan, being centrally planned buildings with domes and four towers, may have been the patterns used. Vitozzi's oval plan presupposes a knowledge of S. Giacomo al Corso in Rome (cf. Carboneri, *op. cit.* (Note 63), 104 ff.). For the Cistercian monastic buildings next to the church at Mondovì the Duke in 1596 received a drawing from the Cistercians of S. Pudenziana in Rome (Carboneri, *op. cit.*, III). It is quite possible that Francesco da Volterra, the architect of S. Giacomo al Corso, who during these very years was working at S. Pudenziana (cf. Lotz, *op. cit.* (Note 65), 74 f.), was consulted in the planning of the church at Mondovì. Vitozzi was twice, in 1589 and 1598, briefly in Rome; cf. Scotti, *op. cit.*, 123 and 130.

CHAPTER 12

1. For convenience, the bibliography for Palladio is given here. Only the most important works can be enumerated.

General Works

The first fully illustrated publication of Palladio's œuvre is O. Bertotti-Scamozzi, *Le Fabbriche e i disegni di Andrea Palladio* (Vicenza, 1776 and 1786). – A. Magrini's *Memorie su Andrea Palladio* (Padua, 1845) is still important for reference. – G. G. Zorzi, *I Disegni delle antichità di Andrea Palladio* (Venice, 1959); *idem*, *Le Opere pubbliche e i palazzi privati di Andrea Palladio* ([Venice], 1964); *idem*, *Le Chiese e i ponti di Andrea Palladio* ([Venice], 1966); *idem*, *Le Ville e i teatri di Andrea Palladio* ([Venice], 1968]). Indispensable documentary and illustrative sources. In years of research, the author has collected a wealth of facts from archives on Palladio's life and work. The present Notes give no detailed references to Zorzi's work. Necessary references can easily be found in the list of contents of the various volumes. – R. Pane, *Andrea Palladio*, 2nd ed. (Turin, [1961]). The first modern monograph. – J. S. Ackerman, *Palladio* (Harmondsworth, 1966). An excellent, concise introduction to Palladio's work as a whole. It also contains a survey of the literature. – N. Ivanoff, *Palladio* (Milan, 1967).

Theory and Doctrine of Proportions

R. Wittkower, *Architectural Principles in the Age of Humanism*, 3rd ed. (London, 1962). Fundamental for Palladio's principles of proportion. – E. Forssman, *Dorisch, Jonisch, Korinthisch. Studien über den Gebrauch der Säulenordnungen in der Architektur des 16.–18. Jahrhunderts* (Stockholm Studies in History of Art, V) (Stockholm, 1961). – *Idem*, *Palladios Lehrgebäude* (Stockholm Studies in History of Art, IX) (Stockholm, [1965]). An excellent review of the relations between the *Quattro Libri* and the buildings.

Villas

G. Mazzotti a.o., *Le Ville venete* (Treviso, 1954). – *Idem*, *Palladian and Other Venetian Villas* (London, 1958). – M. Muraro, *Civiltà delle ville venete* (private publication by the author, 1964). – J. S. Ackerman, *Palladio's Villas* (Institute of Fine Arts, New York University, The Annual W. W. S. Cook Lecture) (Locust Valley, N. Y., 1967). Summary catalogue of villas; sociological and economic aspects.

Single Buildings

C. Semenzato, *La Rotonda* (Vicenza, 1968); F. Barbieri, *La Basilica Palladiana* (Vicenza, 1968); W. Timofiewitsch, *La Chiesa del Redentore* (Vicenza, 1969); A. Vendetti, *La Loggia del Capitanato* (Vicenza, 1969); G. Bordignon Favero, *La Villa Emo di Fanzolo* (Vicenza, 1970); E. Bassi, *Il Convento della Carità* (Vicenza, 1971); L. Puppi, *La Villa Badoer di Fratta Polesine* (Vicenza, 1972): the first seven volumes of the *Corpus Palladianum* published by the Centro Internazionale di Studi di Architettura 'Andrea Palladio', Vicenza.

Guides

Reclam's Kunstführer, Italien, II, *Oberitalien Ost* (Stuttgart, 1965). Exhaustive description and critical appreciation of all Palladio's buildings. – F. Barbieri, R. Cevese, L. Magagnato, *Guida da Vicenza*, 2nd ed. (Vicenza, 1956).

Bibliography

W. Timofiewitsch, 'Die Palladio-Forschung in den Jahren von 1940 bis 1960', *Zeitschrift für Kunstgeschichte*, XXIII (1960), 174 ff. – G. Ferrari, 'Schede di bibliografia palladiana dal 1955', *Bollettino del Centro Internazionale di Studi di Architettura 'Andrea Palladio'*, III (1961), 163 ff. – Later volumes of the *Bollettino* contain accounts of research and bibliographical references.

2. *I Quattro Libri di Architettura di Andrea Palladio* (Venice, 1570). Countless later editions and translations. Reprint of the 1st edition, Milan, 1945.

3. Vitruvius's terminology can hardly be applied to the plans of modern secular buildings. For the efforts of the theorists, from Alberti on, to identify *entrata* (i.e. the vestibule) and *cortile* with the Vitruvian *atrium* and *peristylium*, see Forssmann, *Palladios Lehrgebäude (op. cit.)*, 63 ff.

4. Part of Palladio's great collection of architectural drawings has been preserved. Those acquired by the Earl of Burlington (now in the Royal Institute of British Architects) were part of Palladio's estate; in addition to original designs and drawings, they include sheets by Raphael and Falconetto and copies from the Codex Coner. There is as yet no catalogue of the collection. Most of the sheets are reproduced in Zorzi's four volumes. For the drawings of ancient monuments cf. also H. Spielmann, *Andrea Palladio und die Antike* (Munich and Berlin, 1966).

5. At that time Trissino was enlarging his villa at Cricoli, just outside Vicenza. The attribution of this villa to Palladio is not supported in the recent literature. Cf. Pane, *Andrea Palladio (op. cit.)*, 99 ff., and Zorzi, *Le Ville e i teatri (op. cit.)*, 221 ff.

6. For the relationship between Trissino and Palladio, see Wittkower, *Architectural Principles (op. cit.)*, 57 ff. For Palladio's connections with the nobility of Vicenza, see Barbieri, *Basilica Palladiana (op. cit.)*, 55 ff.

7. The admiration of the Pantheon and its influence on ecclesiastical architecture go hand in hand with the development and authority of that ideal of beauty. For that matter, the process was repeated in eighteenth-century classicism.

8. Cf. S. Sinding-Larsen, 'Some Functional and Iconographical Aspects of the Centralized Church in the Italian Renaissance', in *Acta ad Archaeologiam et Artium Historiam pertinentes* (Institutum Romanum Norvegiae), II (1965), 203 ff.; also Ackerman, *Palladio (op. cit.)*, 126 ff.

9. 'Of all colours, white is best suited to temples: the purity of the colour, like the purity of life, is pleasing to God' (*Quattro Libri*, IV, 2).

10. Cf. the chapter 'The Genesis of an Idea; Palladio's Church Façades', in Wittkower, *Architectural Principles (op. cit.)*, 89 ff.; also H. Lund, 'The Façade of S. Giorgio Maggiore', *Architectural Review*, CXXXIII (1963), 283 ff.

11. Cf. S. Sinding-Larsen, 'Palladio's Redentore, a Compromise in Composition', *Art Bulletin*, XLVII (1965), 419 ff., and Timofiewitsch, *La Chiesa del Redentore (op. cit.)*.

12. For sources see Sinding-Larsen, *op. cit.*, and Timofiewitsch, *op. cit.*

13. For sources and building history see Barbieri, *Basilica Palladiana (op. cit.)*.

14. Cf. Vendetti, *La Loggia del Capitanato (op. cit.)*.

15. The *Quattro Libri* also contain illustrations of Palladio's Palazzo Antonini at Udine and two designs of his for Verona. The authorship of the Palazzo Civena at Vicenza (*c.* 1540–5), confirmed by a number of original drawings, is now generally accepted. The building, 'the least assertive of Palladio's works', is not mentioned in the *Quattro Libri*; probably Palladio came to feel it too traditional.

16. The group of late façades with giant orders includes the unfinished Palazzo Porto Breganze, which is generally called the Cà del Diavolo, and has always been attributed to Palladio. First mention of the building in Vincenzo Scamozzi, *Idea della architettura universale* (Venice, 1615). There are no sources for its architectural history.

17. For the type and origin of the Venetian villa, cf. L. H. Heydenreich, 'La Villa: genesi e sviluppo fino al Palladio' (with bibliography), in *Bollettino del Centro Internazionale di Studi di Architettura Andrea Palladio*, XI (1969), 11 ff.; C. L. Frommel, *ibid.*, 47 ff.; among the other contributions to this volume, dealing with Palladio's villas, should be mentioned A. Ventura, 'Aspetti storico-economici della villa veneta', *ibid.*, 65 ff.

18. Literary references in Ackerman, *Palladio's Villas (op. cit.)*, 25, note 19; see also Ventura, *op. cit.*

19. Cf. Ackerman, *ibid.*, 13 ff.

20. For the geometry of the plan and the proportionality of the rooms, cf. especially Wittkower, *Architectural Principles (op. cit.)*, 70 f., 107 f., and 126 ff.

21. Sources and building history in Semenzato, *La Rotonda (op. cit.)*, 37 ff. C. A. Isermeyer has shown that the traditional date about 1550 is untenable. The villa was built shortly before the publication of the *Quattro Libri* ('Die Villa Rotonda von Palladio', *Zeitschrift für Kunstgeschichte*, XXX (1967), 207 ff.). The villa is first mentioned in a codicil dated 1571 to the client's will of 1569. It is not mentioned in the text of the will; cf. Semenzato, *op. cit.*, 37. For the drawing of the dome in the *Quattro Libri*, which does not tally with the one actually executed, cf. *op. cit.*, 40, note 13.

CHAPTER 13

1. As early as 1555, Palladio had applied for the commission for the Scala d'Oro, the princely staircase of the Doge's Palace, which was eventually executed by Sansovino. For his work in the Doge's Palace cf. G. Zorzi, *Le Opere pubbliche e i palazzi privati di A.P.* (Venice, 1964), 136–67 (also earlier literature).

2. Sources for the Prigioni in G. B. Lorenzi, *Monumenti per servire alla storia del Palazzo Ducale di Venezia* (Venice, 1869), documents 674–8, 741–6 (for the years 1563–73).

3. Documents for the history of planning and building in G. Zorzi, *Le Chiese e i ponti di Andrea Palladio* (Venice, 1967), 227 ff.

4. Begun *c.* 1515 by Bon, continued in 1527 by Scarpagnino, and after the latter's death in 1549 by Giangiacomo da Grigi. The staircase was erected after 1544, the façade, designed by Scarpagnino, from 1536. See P. Paoletti, *L'Architettura e la scultura del Rinascimento a Venezia* (Venice, 1893), 123 ff. and 289 ff.; for da Grigi see also G. Lorenzetti, 'Il Palazzo cinquecentesco veneziano dei Coccina-Tiepolo e il suo autore', *Rivista d'Arte*, XIV (1932), 75 ff.

The Scuola di S. Rocco was one of the five Scuole Grandi, professional associations of laymen, 'meeting on the premises of a particular monastery', who 'placed themselves under the protection of a chosen saint, and undertook to perform certain services for their own poor, sick and dead'; see B. Pullan, *Rich and Poor in Renaissance Venice. The Social Institutions of a Catholic State* (Oxford, 1971), 33 ff.

5. As early as 1522 Alessandro Leopardi had promised a model for S. Giustina which he never delivered. The foundations were laid out by the stonemason Matteo della Valle. After his death in 1532 work was continued by Andrea Moroni and after his death by Andrea della Valle (mentioned 1531–77). The building was vaulted towards the end of the Cinquecento and consecrated in 1606. Cf. G. Bresciani Alvarez in *La Basilica di S. Giustina* (Castelfranco Veneto, 1979), 121 ff.

The cathedral was begun in 1552 by Andrea della Valle and completed only in the eighteenth century; see G. Bresciani Alvarez in *Atti e Memorie Accademia Patavina di Scienze, Lettere ed Arti*, LXXVII (1964–5), part III, 605 ff.

For a project by Michelangelo cf. C. de Tolnay, 'A Forgotten Architectural Project by Michelangelo: the Choir of the Cathedral of Padua', in *Festschrift für Herbert von Einem* (Berlin, 1965), 247 ff.

A notarial document of 1552, overlooked by Tolnay, says: 'Quoniam Magister Andreas [della Valle] composuit formulam sive modellum ipsius templi aedificandi, et sic inventio modi illud fabricandi est sua...' (E. Rigoni, *L'Architetto Andrea Moroni* (Padua, 1939), 77). Michelangelo's project – which has not been preserved – was therefore not taken into consideration.

6. Cf. R. Pallucchini, 'Vincenzo Scamozzi e l'architettura veneta', *L'Arte*, XXXIX (1936), 3 ff.; F. Barbieri, *Vincenzo Scamozzi* (Vicenza and Belluno, n.d. [1952]); *idem*, *Vincenzo Scamozzi: Taccuino di viaggio da Parigi a Venezia* (Venice and Rome, n.d. [1959]), with interesting drawings of Gothic cathedrals in France. For the Procuratie Nuove see also W. Timofiewitsch, *Arte Veneta*, XVIII (1964), 147 ff. For Scamozzi's villas: C. Semenzato, 'La Rocca pisana dello Scamozzi', *Arte Veneta*, XVI (1962), 98 ff.; for his designs for Salzburg Cathedral: W. Timofiewitsch in *Festschrift Karl Oettinger* (Erlanger Forschungen, XX) (Erlangen, 1967), 411 ff.

7. History of building and sources: G. Zorzi, *Le Ville e i teatri di Andrea Palladio* (Venice, 1968), 282 ff. For Scamozzi's part in the work, L. Magagnato, 'The Genesis of the Teatro Olimpico', *Journal of the Warburg and Courtauld Institutes*, XIV (1951), 200 ff.; *idem*, *Teatri italiani del Cinquecento* (Venice, 1954), 50 ff., and *Arte Lombarda*, XI (1966), part I, 26 ff.

8. Cf. Magagnato, *Teatri italiani (op. cit.)*, 76 ff. The fortified city of Sabbioneta, the capital of his small dukedom, was planned and built by Vespasiano Gonzaga from *c.* 1550 on. For the layout of the streets cf. K. Forster, 'From "Rocca" to "Civitas": Urban Planning at Sabbioneta', *L'Arte*, N.S. II (1969), no. 5, 5 ff. According to Scamozzi's *L'Idea dell'architettura universale* (Venice, 1615), he began the theatre in 1588; it was completed in 1590; see A. Racheli, *Memorie storiche di Sabbioneta* (Casalmaggiore, 1849), 690 ff.

CHAPTER 14

1. Cf. S. Bettini, 'Note sui soggiorni veneti di Bartolommeo Ammannati', *Le Arti*, III (1940), 20 ff.; E. Vodoz, 'Studien zum architektonischen Werk des B. A.', *Mittelungen des Kunsthistorischen Instituts Florenz*, VI (1941), 1 ff.; and M. Fossi, *B. A. Architetto* (Cave dei Terreni, n.d. [1968]).

2. For analogous works in sculpture and painting, cf. for instance T. Buddensieg, 'Die Ziege Amalthea von Riccio und Falconetto', *Jahrbuch der Berliner Museen*, V (1963), 121 ff.

3. Ammannati described the Roman villa in a long letter to his Paduan patron Marco Benavides; see the text of the letter in T. Falk, 'Studien zur Topographie

und Geschichte der Villa Giulia', *Römisches Jahrbuch für Kunstgeschichte*, XIII (1971), 171 ff.

For the Villa Imperiale at Pesaro cf. A. Pinelli and O. Rossi, *Genga architetto* (Rome, n.d. [1971]), 137 ff. For Ammannati's share in the Villa Giulia see also Vodoz, *op. cit.*, 5 ff., C. H. Smyth, 'The Sunken Courts of the Villa Giulia and the Villa Imperiale', in *Essays in Memory of Karl Lehmann* (New York, 1964), 304 ff., and especially Falk, *op. cit.*, 103 ff.

4. Work had been going on on the gardens and fountains from 1550 to 1560; cf. *Diario fiorentino di Agostino Lapini*, ed. G. O. Corazzini (Florence, 1900), 107 and 127; Vodoz, *op. cit.*, 40 ff.; F. Morandini, 'Palazzo Pitti, la sua costruzione e i successivi ingrandimenti', *Commentari*, XVI (1965), 35 ff.; and Fossi, *op. cit.*, 45 ff.; see also the catalogue of the *Mostra documentaria ed iconografica di Palazzo Pitti e giardino di Boboli* (Florence, 1960).

5. The Trecento bridge was destroyed by floods in 1557; Ammannati's bridge, begun in 1558, and completed in 1570, was blown up during the retreat of the German army in 1944. It was completely restored after the war. Cf. Fossi, *op. cit.*, 70 ff., and *Michelangelo architetto*, ed. P. Portoghesi and B. Zevi (Turin, n.d. [1964]).

6. Cf. M. Walcher Casotti, *Il Vignola* (Milan, 1960), I, 46, and II, figure 77.

7. Cf. F. Kriegbaum, 'Michelangelo e il ponte S. Trinità', *Rivista d'Arte*, XXIII (1941), 137 ff., and in detail Fossi, *op. cit.*, 70 ff. It should be remembered that Ammannati was sent a clay model by Michelangelo in 1558 for the work on the staircase in the ricetto of the Laurenziana (see p. 93). He was obviously in close touch with Michelangelo at that time. For Ammannati's other palazzi in Florence and Lucca, and for his churches, cf. Vodoz, *op. cit.*, and Fossi, *op. cit.*

8. Vasari Mil., VII, 703. For the architectural history cf. U. Dorini, 'Come sorse la fabbrica degli Uffizi', *Rivista Storica degli Archivi Toscani*, V (1933), 1 ff., and R. Abbondanza, *Mostra documentaria della fabbrica degli Uffizi* (Florence, 1958).

The significance of the Uffizi for Cosimo I's building projects has been discussed by G. Kauffmann, 'Das Forum von Florenz', in *Studies in Renaissance and Baroque Art presented to Anthony Blunt* (London, 1967), 37 ff.

9. *Diario fiorentino di Agostino Lapini* (*op. cit.*, Note 4), 207. In comparison, the cost of the Gesù in Rome from 1568 to 1581 was 71,000 scudi.

10. By closing the loggia of the upper storey the effect aimed at by Vasari was forfeited. The loggia of the Palazzo Guadagni, with its projecting rafter roof in the Florentine style, shows how the original state of the Uffizi must be visualized.

11. The decoration of Vasari's dome of the Chiesa dell'Umiltà in Pistoia is, however, similar. The model was probably Michelangelo's project for S. Giovanni dei Fiorentini; cf. J. S. Ackerman, *The Architecture of Michelangelo*, I, 2nd ed. (London, 1964), figure 71b, and E. Battisti in *Quaderni dello Istituto di Storia dell'Architettura*, VI–VIII (Saggi . . . in onore del Prof. Vincenzo Fasolo) (Rome, 1961), 187, figure 3.

12. Vasari Mil., I, 131 ff.; cf. L. Bartoli, *Galleria degli Uffizi Firenze. Introduzione all'architettura. I danni di guerra e il progetto di sistemazione* (Florence, [1946]), 13 ff. Ammannati's remarks on his project for the Uffizi dated 1560, i.e. the first year of building, which represents an entirely different scheme for the ground floor and upper storey, may be a criticism of the clamping of the architrave: 'come più ragione d'architettura', i.e. correcter according to the rules of architecture. Illustration in E. Vodoz, *Mitteilungen des Kunsthistorischen Instituts, Florenz*, VI (1940/1), 67.

13. Begun in 1562, occupied in 1565; cf. M. Salmi, *Il Palazzo dei Cavalieri e la Scuola Normale Superiore a Pisa* (Bologna, 1932), 20 ff. For the church of the Order, erected by Vasari in 1565–9, cf. *op. cit.*, 37 ff.

14. For SS. Fiora e Lucilla cf. D. Viviani Fiorini, 'La Badia di Arezzo e Giorgio Vasari', *Il Vasari*, XII (1941), 74 ff.; the plan is of the same type as that of the abbey churches of S. Salvatore in Venice and S. Giustina in Padua, which belonged to the same congregation. For the Logge: D. Viviani Fiorini, 'La Costruzione delle Logge Vasariane di Arezzo', *Il Vasari*, XII (1941), 109 ff.

15. Cf. Vasari Mil., VII, 710 (S. Maria Novella) and 711 (S. Croce).

16. *Diario fiorentino di Agostino Lapini* (cf. Note 4), 152; the *Diario* also reports that the destruction of the 'ponti e cori . . . dispiacque a molti vecchi, perchè dividevano la chiesa, ove molte persone divote si ritiravano ad orare, ed erano secondo l'uso degli antichi christiani'; cf. G. Gaye, *Carteggio inedito d'artisti dei secoli XIV, XV, XVI* (Florence, 1839–40), II, 479 f.

17. At the same time the originally open loggia of the top storey was closed (cf. Note 10); see V. Giovannozzi, 'La Vita di B.B. scritta da Gherardo Silvani', *Rivista d'Arte*, XIV (1932), 509, note 3; cf. also D. Heikamp, 'Zur Geschichte der Uffizien-Tribuna, etc.', *Zeitschrift für Kunstgeschichte*, XXVI (1963), 193 ff.; idem, 'La Tribuna degli Uffizi, come era nel Cinquecento', *Antichità Viva*, III (1964),

no. 3, 11.

18. Cf. Webster Smith, 'Pratolino', *Journal of the Society of Architectural Historians*, XX (1961), 155 ff., and D. Heikamp, *Antichità Viva*, VIII (1969), no. 2, 14 ff.; for the still-standing colossal figure by Giovanni da Bologna, see W. Körte, 'Deinokrates und die barocke Phantasie', *Die Antike*, XIII (1937), 290 ff. For an important description of 1600 of the layout of water and fountains cf. W. Heyd (ed.), *Handschriften und Handzeichnungen des Heinrich Schickhardt* (Stuttgart, 1902), 188–99. According to Buontalenti's pupil Gherardo Silvani (cf. previous Note), 'this layout awakened universal admiration and it became the model for all the beautiful fountains in other countries'. Among other things, there were moving, echoing figures and hydraulic organs.

19. The development of the individual motifs can be followed in the preliminary drawings; cf. I. M. Botto, *Mostra di disegni di Bernardo Buontalenti* (Gabinetto Disegni e Stampe degli Uffizi, XXVIII) (Florence, 1968), figures 5–6 (Casino Mediceo) and figures 18–21 (Porta delle Suppliche).

20. W. and E. Paatz, *Die Kirchen von Florenz*, V (Frankfurt, 1953), 272.

21. The staircase, built in 1574, and the altar were removed in 1890–7 and incorporated in S. Stefano al Ponte. Good description in Paatz, *op. cit.*, 216 f., and also Giovannozzi, *op. cit.*, 510 f., and *Rivista d'Arte*, XV (1933), 315 f. (with illustration of the altar before its removal).

22. Cf. text and illustrations in the catalogue mentioned in Note 19.

23. Cf. Paatz, *op. cit.*, III (1952), 335 and 126–31; also L. Berti, *Architettura del Cigoli*, catalogue, Mostra del Cigoli (S. Miniato, 1959), 165 ff.

24. Dosio and Cigoli had also worked in Rome, and Dosio in Naples. For Dosio: L. Wachler, 'G.D., ein Architekt des späten Cinquecento', *Römisches Jahrbuch für Kunstgeschichte*, IV (1940), 143–251; for Cigoli, cf. Berti, *op. cit.*; for Giovanni da Bologna's architectural work, Wachler, *op. cit.*, 244 ff.; cf. also Paatz, *op. cit.*, I (1940), 105 (Cappella del Soccorso), III (1952), 10 and 18 (Giovanni da Bologna's Cappella Salviati in S. Marco), *ibid.*, 690 (Gaddi Chapel in S. Maria Novella by Dosio), I (1940), 534 (Niccolini Chapel in S. Croce).

25. Gherardo Silvani in the biography of Buontalenti quoted in Note 17. Vasari's ground floor dates from 1556–60, Buontalenti's grotto from 1583–93. The four Slaves of Michelangelo were set in place in 1585, Giovanni da Bologna's Venus Fountain in 1592. Cf. V. Giovannozzi, *Rivista d'Arte*, XIV (1932), 510, note 1; also D. Heikamp, 'La Grotta grande del giardino di Boboli', *Antichità Viva*, IV, no. 4 (1965), 27 ff.

26. This union of nature and art is described by the humanist Claudio Tolomei in 1543 as: 'l'ingegnoso artificio nuovamente ritrovato di far le fonti, il qual già si vede usato in più luoghi di Roma. Ove mescolando l'arte con la natura, non si sa discernere s'ella è opera di questa o di quella, anzi o altrui pare un natural artifizio, e ora una artifiziosa natura: in tal modo s'ingegnano in questi tempi rassembrare una fonte, che dell'istessa natura, non a caso, ma con maestrevole arte sia fatta. Alle quali opere arrecan molto d'ornamento, e bellezza queste pietre spugnose, che nascono a Tivoli, le quali essendo formate dall'acqua, ritornan come lor fatture al servizio delle acque; e molto più l'adornano con la lor varietà e vaghezza, ch'esse non avevan ricevute ornamento da loro'; see Heikamp, *op. cit.*, 43.

27. Illustrated in L. Magagnato, *Palazzo Thiene* (Vicenza, 1966), 47 ff., plates 127–34.

28. John Wood of Bath, speaking of this façade, remarks: 'This whimsical front . . . Signiore Zucchari . . . designed to exhibit in it the Samples of his threefold Profession in Theory and Practice; the first being apparent in the Door, the Windows, the Pillasters, and the other Ornaments traced and cut out of the Rock in an unfinished Manner, the second in three Pieces of Sculpture, sketch'd and cut out of the same Rock, and the third in the finished Picture . . .' (*The Origin of Building or the Plagiarism of Heathen detected* (London, 1704)); cf. R. Wittkower, *Journal of the Warburg and Courtauld Institutes*, VI (1943), 220 f., and D. Heikamp, 'Federico Zuccari a Firenze', *Paragone Arte*, N.S. XXVII (207) (1967), 9 ff.

29. According to Schickhardt's description (cf. Note 18), 195 f.

30. Believed to have been built between 1550 and 1570. For the layout, which has often been described lately, though its interpretation and authorship are not yet clear, cf. the latest account by A. Bruschi, 'Il Problema storico di Bomarzo', *Palladio*, N.S. XIII (1963), 85 ff.

31. 'Tu ch'entri qua pon mente parte a parte
e dimmi poi se tante meraviglie
sien fatte per inganno o pur per arte.'

32. For the iconography of the portal and its formal connection with Buontalenti, cf. W. Körte, *Der Palazzo Zuccari in Rom* (Leipzig, 1935), 16 f.; Heikamp, *op. cit.* (Note 28), 14; and E. Guldan, *Zeitschrift für Kunstgeschichte*, XXXII (1969), 229 ff.

Additional notes to the revised edition

p. 11   * On the problems regarding the dating of the Tempietto, see the introduction to the present edition, p. 1.

p. 13   * In fact there are two orders on each storey: Tuscan and Ionic below, and Corinthian and Composite above. See Arnaldo Bruschi, *Bramante*, ed. Peter Murray (1977), 78–82.

p. 17   * The most recent account of the Julius tomb is to be found in C. L. Frommel, 'St Peter's: The Early History', in Millon and Lampugnani, *The Renaissance from Brunelleschi to Michelangelo, op. cit.*, 399–413.

p. 28   * According to C. L. Frommel, *Der römische Palastbau der Hochrenaissance in Italien*, 3 vols (Tübingen, 1973), vol. II, 53–61, the Palazzo Vidoni-Caffarelli is probably by Lorenzetti and begun about 1524 (i.e. after Raphael's death).

p. 37   * This palace has been convincingly attributed to Raphael by Pier Nicola Pagliara, 'Due palazzi romani di Raffaello: Palazzo Alberini e Palazzo Branconio', in *Raffaello a Roma; il convegno del 1983* (Rome, 1986), 331–42.

p. 39   * The church is now accepted as a work of Raphael. See C. L. Frommel, S. Ray and M. Tafuri, *Raffaello architetto* (Milan, 1984), 143.

p. 83   * Lotz has not mentioned Sansovino's most successful Roman building, the Palazzo Gaddi. See Frommel, *Der römische Palastbau (op. cit.)*, I, 120–22, 155–56; II, 198–206.

p. 85   * The wall decoration of the vestibule was the result of its later conversion into a museum of antiquities in 1591–6. See Marilyn Perry, 'The Statuario Publico', *Saggi e Memorie di Storia dell' Arte*, VIII, 1972, 75–180.

p. 86   * The third storey was begun in 1558, and may not have been designed by him, owing to a dispute between his employers, the Procuratio de Supra, and the Mint at this time. See Deborah Howard, *Jacopo Sansovino; Architecture and Patronage in Renaissance Venice* (New Haven and London), 1987 ed., 42.

p. 88   * Because of legal difficulties the palace was not begun until after 1545. See Howard, *Jacopo Sansovino op. cit.*, 137–40.

p. 148   * Illustration [237] shows an earlier project with five arches instead of three.

p. 159   * Da Ponte's design is not indebted to Palladio to any significant degree, unlike that of his rival, Scamozzi. See Donatello Calabi and Paolo Morachiello, *Rialto: Le fabbriche e il ponte* (Turin, 1987), 219–300.

Bibliography

This is the bibliography to the first edition, however, titles regarding topics or architects mainly concerned with the period 1400–1500 have been omitted from this revised edition.

The bibliography does not aim at completeness. Encyclopedia articles and guide books have been omitted.

To a certain extent the footnotes and the bibliography supplement each other: from the latter, many references given in the footnotes (for which the index should be consulted) have been excluded; conversely, many important studies appear only in the bibliography.

In a few exceptional cases book reviews of special merit are mentioned.

Indispensable for the sources and art theory: J. Schlosser Magnino, *La Letteratura artistica* (Florence, 1956). Extremely useful also is A. Venturi's lavishly illustrated *Storia dell'arte italiana* (cf. section III, p. 192).

For headings I and II of the Bibliography additional items may be found in the bibliographies of the following volumes of *The Pelican History of Art*:

C. Seymour Jr, *Sculpture in Italy: 1400–1500* (Harmondsworth, 1966)
C. J. Freedberg, *Painting in Italy: 1500–1600* (Harmondsworth, 1971)
R. Wittkower, *Art and Architecture in Italy: 1600–1750*, 3rd ed. (Harmondsworth, 1973)

The material is arranged under the following headings:

I. SOURCES

A. *Literary Sources and Archival Documents*

BORROMEO, S. CARLO. *Instructiones Fabricae et Suppellectilis Ecclesiasticae*. Latin ed. in *Acta Ecclesiae Mediolanensis*, II and III, Milan, 1890 and 1892. Latin text with commentary by P. Barocchi in *Trattati d'arte nel Cinquecento*, III, Bari, 1962. Italian ed., as *Arte Sacra*, by C. Castiglioni and C. Marcora, Milan, 1952.

BOTTARI, M. G., and TICOZZI, S. *Raccolta di lettere sulla pittura, scultura ed architettura*. 8 vols. Milan, 1822–5.

FILANGIERI, G. *Documenti per la storia, le arti e le industrie delle provincie napoletane*, 6 vols. Naples, 1883–91.

GAYE, G. *Carteggio inedito d'artisti dei secoli XIV–XVI*. 3 vols. Florence, 1839–40.

KLEIN, R., and ZERNER, H. *Italian Art, 1500–1600. Sources and Documents*. Englewood Cliffs, N.J., 1966.

MONTAIGNE, M. E. DE. *Journal de voyage en Italie par l'Allemagne et la Suisse en 1580 et 1581*. Paris, 1957. Italian ed.: A. D'Ancona, *L'Italia alla fine del XVI secolo. Giornale di viaggio di Michel de Montaigne*. Città di Castello, 1895. English ed.: D. M. Frame (trans.), *The Complete Works of Montaigne . . .* , 861 ff. Stanford, 1958.

B. *Lives of Artists*

BAGLIONE, G. *Le vite de' pittori, scultori, architetti e intagliatori, dal pontificato di Gregorio XIII del 1572, fino a' tempi di Papa Urbano VIII nel 1642*. Rome, 1642. Facsimile ed. by V. Mariani, Rome, 1935.

SOPRANI, R., and RATTI, C. G. *Vite de' pittori, scultori, ed architetti genovesi*. 2 vols. Genoa, 1768–9; reprinted Bologna, 1969–70.

VASARI, G. *Le Vite de' più eccellenti pittori, scultori e architetti*. Florence, 1550; ed. C. Ricci, Milan–Rome, 1927. Second ed., Florence, 1568. References in the present volume are to the edition of G. Milanesi, 9 vols., Florence, 1878–81, reprinted 1906.

C. *Treatises*

ALBERTI, L. B. *L'Architettura* (De re aedificatoria libri X). Latin text, Italian trans., ed. G. Orlandi, 2 vols., Milan, 1966. English trans., ed. James Leoni, London, 1726, 1739, 1755; reprinted London, 1955.

ALGHISIDA CARPI, G., *Delle Fortificazioni*. Venice, 1570.

BARBARO, D. *De Architectura Libri Decem*. Venice, 1556. Italian trans., *I dieci libri dell'Architettura di M. Vitruvio*. Venice, 1567.

BERTANI, G. B. *Gli oscuri e difficili passi dell'opera ionica di Vitruvio*. Mantua, 1558.

CAPORALI, G. B. (ed.). *Architettura, con il suo commento et figure Vetruvio in volgar lingua raportato*. Perugia, 1536.

GATTANEO, P. *Li quattro primi libri d'Architettura*. Venice, 1554; reprinted Ridgewood, N.J., 1964. *Idem*, libri 5–8. Venice, 1567.

CESARIANO, C. *Di L. Vitruvio Pollione, De Architectura libri decem traducti de Latino in Vulgare affigurati*. Como, 1521. Reprinted as *Vitruvius De Architectura*. Munich, 1969.

CORNER, A. (Luigi Cornaro) (ed. G. Fiocco). *Frammenti di un trattato di architettura* (Atti dell' Accademia dei Lincei). Rome, 1952.

FILARETE (Antonio Averlino) (ed. A. M. Finoli and L. Grassi). *Trattato di Architettura*. 2 vols. Milan, 1972. Facsimile and English trans., ed. J. R. Spencer, *Yale Publications in the History of Art*, XVI. 2 vols. New Haven, 1965.

GIOCONDO, FRA (ed.). *M. Vitruvius per Iocundum Solitor Castigatior factus*. Venice, 1511.

LABACCO, A. *Libro appartenente all'architettura*. Rome, 1558.

LOMAZZO, G. P. *Trattato dell'arte della pittura, scultura ed architettura*. Milan, 1584.

MARTINI, Francesco di Giorgio (ed. C. Maltese). *Trattati di architettura, ingegneria e arte militare*. 2 vols. Milan, 1967.

PALLADIO, A. *Le Antichità di Roma*. Venice, 1554.

PALLADIO, A. *Li quattro libri dell'architettura*. Venice, 1570; reprinted Milan, 1952.

RUSCONI, G. A. *Dell'architettura secondo i precetti del Vitruvio*. Venice, 1590.

SERLIO, S. *Regole generali di architettura sopra le cinque maniere degli edifici*. Venice, 1537 and 1551. Books 1–5 and Libro Straordinario. Venice, 1566 and 1584.

SERLIO, S. (ed. M. Rosci). *Il Trattato di architettura di Sebastiano Serlio*. 2 vols. (Ed. of Serlio's Book Six.) Milan, 1967.

VIGNOLA, G. BAROZZI DA. *Regola delli cinque ordini di architettura*. [Rome,] 1562.

II. GENERAL HISTORY. HUMANISM AND THE REVIVAL OF THE ANTIQUE. ECONOMIC ASPECTS

The following three works are basic:

BLUNT, A. *Artistic Theory in Italy, 1450–1600*. London, 1935.

PASTOR, L. von. *Geschichte der Päpste seit dem Ausgang des Mittelalters*. Freiburg, 1885–1933. Most recent Italian ed. as *Storia dei Papi*. Rome, 1959. 3rd English ed. as *The History of the Popes from the Close of the Middle Ages*. 36 vols. London, 1950.

VOIGT, G. *Die Wiederbelebung des classischen Altertums oder das erste Jahrhundert des Humanismus*. 3rd ed. Berlin, 1893; reprinted Berlin, 1960.

BARON, H. *The Crisis of Early Italian Renaissance . . .* 2 vols. Princeton, 1955; 2nd ed., 1966.

BUCK, A. (ed.). *Zu Begriff und Problem der Renaissance* (Essays by D. Cantimori, H. W. Eppelsheimer, F. Simone, E. Mommsen, H. Baron, E. Cassirer, P. O. Kristeller, H. Weisinger, E. Garin, B. L. Ullmann, G. Weise, C. Singer, G. B. Ladner, J. Gadol). Darmstadt, 1969.

CHASTEL, A. *The Age of Humanism. Europe 1430–1530*. New York, 1964.

DELUMEAU, J. *Vie économique et sociale de Rome dans la seconde moitié du XVIe siècle*. 2 vols. Paris, 1957–9.

GARIN, E. *Scienza e vita nel Rinascimento italiano*. Bari, 1965.

JEDIN, H. *Geschichte des Konzils von Trient*. 3 vols. Freiburg, 1957–9.

JEDIN, H. 'Entstehung und Tragweite des Trienter Edikts über die Bilderverehrung', *Theologische Quartalschrift*, CXVI (1935), 143 ff. and 404 ff.

KRISTELLER, P. O. *Studies in Renaissance Thought and Letters* (Storia e Litteratura, LIV). Rome, 1956.

MÜNTZ, E. *Histoire de l'art pendant la Renaissance*. 3 vols. Paris, 1889–95.

MÜNTZ, E. *Les Arts à la cour des papes Innocent VIII, Alexandre VI, Pie III*. Paris, 1898.

III. ARCHITECTURE: GENERAL WORKS

ACKERMAN, J. S. 'Architectural Practice in the Italian Renaissance', *Journal of the Society of Architectural Historians*, XIII (1954), no. 3, 3 ff.

BAUM, J. *Baukunst und dekorative Plastik der Frührenaissance*. Stuttgart, 1920.

BENEVOLO, L. *Storia dell'architettura del Rinascimento*. 2 vols. Bari, 1968.

BONELLI, R. *Da Bramante a Michelangelo. Profilo dell'architettura del Cinquecento*. Venice, 1960.

BURCKHARDT, J. *Geschichte der Renaissance in Italien*. 1st ed. Stuttgart, 1867. As *Die Kunst der Renaissance in Italien* in *Jacob Burckhardt-Gesamtausgabe*, VI. Stuttgart, 1932.

Dizionario enciclopedico di architettura e urbanistica (diretto da P. Portoghesi). 6 vols. Rome, 1968–9.

DURM, J. *Die Baukunst der Renaissance*. Leipzig, 1914 (and later eds).

FRANKL, P. *Entwicklungsphasen der neueren Baukunst*. Leipzig, 1914. English ed. as *Principles of Architectural History: The Four Phases of Architectural Style, 1420–1900*. Cambridge, Mass., 1968.

FRANKL, P. *Die Renaissance–Architektur in Italien*. Leipzig, 1912, and later eds.

FUSCO, R. DE. *Il Codice dell'architettura*. 4th ed. Naples, 1968.

GIOVANNONI, G. *Saggi sull'architettura del Rinascimento*. 2nd ed. Milan, 1935.

LOTZ, W. 'Architecture in the Later Sixteenth Century', *College Art Journal*, XVII (1958), 129 ff.

LOWRY, B. *Renaissance Architecture* (The Great Ages of World Architecture, IV). London, 1962.

MURRAY, P. *The Architecture of the Italian Renaissance*. 2nd ed. London, 1969.

PEVSNER, N. *An Outline of European Architecture*. 6th ed. Harmondsworth, 1960.

REDTENBACHER, R. *Die Architektur der italiänischen Renaissance*. Frankfurt, 1886.

RICCI, A. *Storia dell'architettura in Italia*. 3 vols. Modena, 1857.

RICCI, C. *L'Architettura del Cinquecento in Italia*. Turin, 1923.

SALMI, M. 'Rinascimento (Il tardo Rinascimento: Architettura)', *Enciclopedia universale dell'arte*, XI (1964), columns 482–91.

SCOTT, G. *The Architecture of Humanism*. Paperback ed. London, 1961.

SEROUX D'AGINCOURT, G. B. L. G. *Storia dell'arte col mezzo di monumenti della sua decadenza nel IV secolo fino al suo risorgimento*. 7 vols. Milan, 1834–5.

TAFURI, M. *L'Architettura dell'umanesimo*. Bari, 1969.

TAFURI, M. *L'Architettura del Manierismo nel Cinquecento europeo*. Rome, 1966.

VENTURI, A. *Storia dell'arte italiana*, VIII: *Architettura del Quattrocento*, 2 parts, Milan, 1923–4; XI: *Architettura del Cinquecento*, 3 parts, Milan, 1938–40. Review by G. Giovannoni, *Palladio*, III (1938), 107 ff.

WILLICH, H., and ZUCKER, P. *Die Baukunst der Renaissance in Italien* (Handbuch der Kunstwissenschaft). Wildpark–Potsdam, 1929.

WITTKOWER, R. *Architectural Principles in the Age of Humanism*. 3rd ed. London, 1962, and New York, 1965. Italian ed. Turin, 1964. German ed. Munich, 1969.

WÖLFFLIN, H. *Renaissance und Barock*. Munich, 1888.

WÖLFFLIN, H. *Die klassische Kunst. Eine Einführung in die italienische Renaissance*. Munich, 1899.

IV. ARCHITECTURE: SPECIALIZED ASPECTS

A. *Theory and Treatises*

BURNS, H. 'Quattrocento Architecture and the Antique: Some Problems', in R. R. Bolgar (ed.), *Classical Influences on European Culture A.D. 500–1500*, 269 ff. London, 1971.

PRANDI, A. *I Trattati di architettura dal Vitruvio al secolo XVI*. Rome, 1949.

SOERGEL, G. *Untersuchungen über den theoretischen Architekturentwurf von 1450–1550 in Italien*. Cologne, 1957.

STEIN, O. *Die Architekturtheoretiker der italienischen Renaissance*. Karlsruhe, 1914.

B. *Materials, Techniques, Engineering*

AUER, J. *Die Quaderbossierung in der italienischen Renaissance*. Vienna, 1887.

HEYDENREICH, L. H. 'Il bugnato rustico nel Quattro- e nel Cinquecento', *Bollettino del Centro Internazionale di Studi d'Architettura Andrea Palladio*, II (1960), 40 f.

NOEL, P. *Technologie de la pierre de taille*. Paris, 1965.

PARSONS. W. B. *Engineers and Engineering of the Renaissance*. Baltimore, 1939.

PIERI, M. *I Marmi graniti e pietre ornamentali*. Milan, [1950].

RODOLICO, F. *Le Pietre delle città d'Italia*. Florence, 1953.

ROTH, E. *Die Rustica der italienischen Renaissance und ihre Vorgeschichte*. Vienna, 1917.

THIEM, G. U. *Toskanische Fassadendekoration in Sgraffito und Fresko 14. bis 17. Jahrhundert*. Munich, 1964.

C. *Building Types*

1. CHURCHES

LARSEN, S. SINDING. 'Some Functional and Iconographical Aspects of the Centralized Church in the Italian Renaissance', *Acta ad archaeologiam et artium historiam pertinentia*, II (1965), 203 ff.

LASPEYRES, P. *Die Kirchen der Renaissance in Mittelitalien*. Berlin and Stuttgart, 1882.

LOTZ, W. 'Notizen zum kirchlichen Zentralbau der Renaissance', *Studien zur toskanischen Kunst* (Festschrift L. H. Heydenreich), 157 ff. Munich, 1964.

LOTZ, W. 'Die ovalen Kirchenräume des Cinquecento', *Römisches Jahrbuch für Kunstgeschichte*, VII (1955), 7 ff.

STRACK, H. *Zentral- und Kuppelkirchen der Renaissance in Italien*. Berlin, 1892.

2. PALAZZI

CHIERICI, G. *Il Palazzo italiano dal secolo XI al secolo XIX*. 2nd ed. Milan, 1964.

HAUPT, A., REINHARDT, R., and RASCHDORF, O. *Palastarchitektur von Oberitalien und Toskana vom XIII, bis zum XVII. Jahrhundert*. 6 vols. Berlin, 1903–22.

3. THEATRES

MAGAGNATO, L. *Teatri italiani del Cinquecento*. Venice, 1954.

4. VILLAS AND GARDENS

DAMI, L. *Il Giardino italiano*. Milan, 1924.

FROMMEL, C. L. 'La Villa Madama e la tipologia della villa romana nel Cinquecento', *Bollettino del Centro Internazionale di Studi di Architettura Andrea Palladio*, XI (1969), 47–64.

HEYDENREICH, L. H. 'La Villa: Genesi e sviluppi fino al Palladio', *Bollettino del Centro Internazionale di Studi di Architettura Andrea Palladio*, XI (1969), 11–21. With bibliography.

MASSON, G. *Italian Villas and Palaces*. London, 1959.

MURARO, M. *Civiltà delle ville venete* (rotaprint). 1964.

PATZAK, B. *Die Renaissance- und Barockvilla in Italien. Versuch einer Entwicklungsgeschiche*. 2 vols. Leipzig, 1908 and 1913. For vol. 3 see below V.E.2, *Pesaro*.

RUPPRECHT, B. 'Villa, Zur Geschichte eines Ideals. Wandlungen des Paradiesischen zum Utopischen', *Probleme der Kunstwissenschaft*, II, 211 ff. Berlin, 1966.

RUSCONI, A. J. *Le Ville medicee*. Rome, 1938.

VENTURA, A. 'Aspetti storico-economici della villa veneta', *Bollettino del Centro Internazionale di Studi di Architettura Andrea Palladio*, XI (1969), 65–77.

D. *Town Planning and Fortifications*

ARGAN, G. C. *The Renaissance City*. New York, 1969. Reviewed by J. S. Ackerman, *Art Bulletin*, LII (1971) 115 f.

BATTISTI, E. 'Osservazioni su due manoscritti intorno all'architettura. Un album di progetti per fortificazioni in Italia nella Biblioteca Nazionale di Madrid', *Bollettino del Centro di Studi per la Storia dell'Architettura*, XIV (1959), 39–40.

BENEVOLO, L. *La Città italiana nel Rinascimento*. Milan, 1969.

BRINCKMANN, A. E. *Stadtbaukunst* (Handbuch der Kunstwissenschaft, IV). Berlin–Babelsberg, 1920.

DE LA CROIX, H. 'The Literature on Fortification in Renaissance Italy', *Technology and Culture*, VI, 1 (1963), 30–50.

DE LA CROIX, H. 'Military Architecture and the Radial City-Plan in Sixteenth Century Italy', *Art Bulletin*, XLII (1960), 263 ff.

DE LA CROIX, H. 'Palmanova, a Study in Sixteenth-Century Urbanism', *Saggi e Memorie di storia dell'arte*, V (1966), 23–41.

EDEN, W. A. 'Studies in Urban Theory: The "De Re Aedificatoria" of Leone Battista Alberti', *The Town Planning Review*, XIX (1943), 17 ff.

FORSTER, K. W. 'From "Rocca" to "Civitas". Urban Planning at Sabbioneta', *L'Arte*, V (1969), 5 ff.

GARIN, E. 'La Città Ideale', *Scienza e vita civile nel Rinascimento italiano*, 33–56. Bari, 1965.

GUTKIND, E. A. *International History of City Development*. 4 vols. London, 1964–9.

HALE, J. R. 'The Early Development of the Bastion: an Italian Chronology', in J. R. Hale and others (eds.), *Europe in the Late Middle Ages*, 466 ff. London, 1965.

HALE, J. R. 'The End of Florentine Liberty. La Fortezza da Basso', in N. Rubinstein (ed.), *Florentine Studies*, London, 1968, 501 ff.

KLEIN, R. 'L'Urbanisme utopique de Filarete à Valentin Andreae', *L'Utopie à la Renaissance*. Brussels, 1964.

LAVEDAN, P. *Histoire de l'urbanisme*. 2nd ed. 3 vols. Paris, 1959.

LILIUS, H. 'Der Pekkatori in Raahe. Studien über einen eckverschlossenen Platz und seine Gebäudetypen', *Finska Fornminnesföreningens Tidskrift*, LXV (Helsinki, 1967), 182 ff. With a useful survey of Italian city planning and building.

LOTZ, W. 'Italienische Plätze des 16. Jahrhunderts', *Jahrbuch der Max-Planck-Gesellschaft* (1968), 41–60.

MARCONI, P. 'Una Chiave per l'interpretazione dell'urbanistica rinascimentale: la cittadella come microcosmo', *Quaderni dell'Istituto di Storia dell'Architettura*, XV, fasc. 85–90 (1968), 53–94.

MORINI, M. *Atlante di storia dell'architettura*. Milan, 1963.

ROCCHI, E. *Le Fonti storiche dell'architettura militare*. Rome, 1908. Standard work.

Urbanisme et architecture, études écrites et publiées en l'honneur de Pierre Lavedan. Paris, 1954.

ZOCCA, M. 'Le Concezioni urbanistiche di Palladio', *Palladio*, X (1960), 69 ff.

ZUCKER, P. *Town and Square*. New York, 1959.

E. *Drawings*

ASHBY, T. 'Sixteenth Century Drawings of Roman Buildings Attributed to Andreas Coner', *Papers of the British School at Rome*, II (1904) and VI (1913).

BARTOLI, A. *I Monumenti antichi di Roma nei disegni degli Uffizi di Firenze*. 6 vols. Rome and Florence, 1914–22.

FERRI, P. N. *Indici e cataloghi*, III: *Disegni di architettura esistenti nella galleria degli Uffizi in Firenze*. Rome, 1885.

LOTZ, W. 'Das Raumbild in der italienischen Architekturzeichnung der Renaissance', *Mitteilungen des Kunsthistorischen Institutes in Florenz*, VII (1956), 193–226.

NACHOD, H. 'A Recently Discovered Architectural Sketchbook', *Rare Books: Notes on the History of Old Books and Manuscripts*, VIII (1955), 1–11.

WITTKOWER, R. (ed.). *Disegni de le ruine di Roma e come anticamente erano*. Milan, 1963. Cf. review by C. Thoenes, *Kunstchronik*, XVIII (1965), 10 ff.

F. *The Problem of Mannerism in Architecture*

'L'Architettura del Manierismo e il Veneto' (Papers delivered during the Ninth Corso of the Centro in 1966), *Bollettino del Centro Internazionale di Studi d'Architettura Andrea Palladio*, IX (1967), 187–416.

BATTISTI, E. 'Storia del concetto di Manierismo in architettura', *Bollettino del Centro Internazionale di Studi di Architettura Andrea Palladio*, IX (1967), 204–10.

BATTISTI, E. 'Proposte per una storia di Manierismo in architettura', *Odeo Olimpico*, VII (1968–70), 19–67.

GOMBRICH, E. 'Zum Werke Giulio Romanos', *Jahrbuch der Kunsthistorischen Sammlungen in Wien*, N.F. VIII (1934), 79 ff., and IX (1935), 121 ff.

HAGER, W. 'Zur Raumstruktur des Manierismus in der italienischen Architektur', *Festschrift Martin Wackernagel*, 112 ff. Cologne, 1958.

HOFFMANN, H. *Hochrenaissance, Manierismus, Frühbarock. Die italienische Kunst des 16. Jahrhunderts*. Zürich–Leipzig, 1938.

LOTZ, W. 'Mannerism in Architecture: Changing Aspects', *The Renaissance and Mannerism. Studies in Western Art* (Acts of the 20th International Congress of the History of Art), II (1963), 239.

MICHALSKI, E. 'Das Problem des Manierismus in der italienischen Architektur', *Zeitschrift für Kunstgeschichte*, II (1933), 88–109.

PEVSNER, N. 'The Architecture of Mannerism', in G. Grayson (ed.), *The Mint, Miscellany of Literature, Art and Criticism*, 116 ff. London, 1946.

TAFURI, M. *L'Architettura del Manierismo nel Cinquecento europeo*. Rome, 1966.

WITTKOWER, R. 'Michelangelo's Biblioteca Laurenziana', *Art Bulletin*, XVI (1934), 123 ff.

ZÜRCHER, R. *Stilprobleme der italienischen Baukunst des Cinquecento*. Basel, 1947.

V. PROVINCES AND CITIES

A. *General*

KELLER, H. *Die Kunstlandschaften Italiens*. Munich, 1960.

B. *Emilia and Romagna*

1. BOLOGNA

BERNHEIMER, R. 'Gothic Survival and Revival in Bologna', *Art Bulletin*, XLVI (1954), 263–84.

BESEGHI, U. *Le Chiese di Bologna*. Bologna, 1956.

BESEGHI, U. *Palazzi di Bologna*. Bologna, 1956.

BESEGHI, U. *Castelli e ville bolognesi*. Bologna, 1957.

COULSON, J. E. E. *Bologna, Its History, Antiquities and Art*. London, 1909.

MALAGUZZI-VALERI, F. *L'Architettura a Bologna nel Rinascimento*. Rocca S. Casciano, 1899.

RAULE, A. *Architettura bolognese*. Bologna, 1952.

SIGHINOLFI, L. *L'Architettura bentivolesca in Bologna*. Bologna, 1909.

SUPINO, J. B. *L'Arte nelle chiese di Bologna*. Bologna, 1938.

ZUCCHINI, G. *Edifici di Bologna. Repertorio bibliografico*. Rome, 1931.

2. PARMA

CRISTINELLI, G., and GREGHI, F. 'Santa Maria della Steccata a Parma', *L'Architettura*, XIV (1969), 680 ff.

C. *Liguria*

GAUTHIER, M. P. *Les plus beaux édifices de la ville de Gènes et de ses environs.* Paris, 1818.

LABÒ, M. 'Strada Nuova: più che una strada, un quartiere', *Scritti di storia dell'arte in onore di Lionello Venturi*, II, 402 ff. Rome, 1956.

NEGRI, E. DE, FERA, C., GROSSI BIANCHI, L., and POLEGGI, E. *Catalogo delle ville genovesi.* Genoa, 1967.

NEGRI, T. O. DE. *Storia di Genova.* Milan, [1968].

PARMA ARMAN, E. 'Il Palazzo del principe Andrea Doria a Fassolo in Genova', *L'Arte*, X (1970), 12–63.

POLEGGI, E. *Strada Nuova: una lottizzazione del Cinquecento.* Genoa, 1958.

D. *Lombardy*

1. GENERAL

Atti II° Convegno Nazionale Storia Architettura. Milan, 1939.

BARONI, C. *Documenti per la storia dell'architettura a Milano nel Rinascimento e nel Barocco.* Vol. I, Florence, 1940; vol. II, Rome, 1968.

BARONI, C. *L'Architettura lombarda dal Bramante al Richini: questioni di metodo.* Milan, 1941.

GRUNER, L. *Terracotta Architecture of North Italy.* London, 1867.

RICCI, C. *Geschichte der Kunst in Norditalien.* Stuttgart, 1924.

RUNGE, L. *Beiträge zur Backsteinarchitektur Italiens.* Berlin, 1897–8.

Storia di Milano (Fondazione Treccani). 16 vols. Milan, 1953 ff.

2. BERGAMO

ANGELINI, L. *Il Volto di Bergamo nei secoli.* Bergamo, 1951.

PINETTI, A. *Bergamo e le sue valli.* Brescia, 1921.

3. BRESCIA

PERONI, A. 'L'Architettura e la scultura nei secoli XV e XVI', *Storia di Brescia*, II, 620–887. Brescia, 1963.

4. MANTUA

CAMPAGNARI, A., and FERRARI, A. *Corti e dimore del contado del Mantovano.* Florence, 1969.

PACCAGNINI, G. *Il Palazzo ducale di Mantova.* Turin, 1969.

Storia di Mantova: Le Arti, II and III. Mantua, 1963.

5. MILAN

CALDERINI, A., CHIERICI, G., and CECCHELLI, C. *La Basilica di S. Lorenzo Maggiore a Milano.* Milan–Rome, 1952.

DOSSI, L. *Il S. Fedele di Milano.* Milan, 1963.

Il Duomo di Milano. Atti del Congresso Internazionale, Milano 8–12 settembre 1968 (Monografie di Arte Lombarda, Monumenti, III). Milan, 1969.

HOFFMANN, H. 'Die Entwicklung der Architektur Mailands von 1550–1650', *Wiener Jahrbuch für Kunstgeschichte*, IX (1934), 63–100.

MEZZANOTTE, P., and BASCAPÈ, G. *Milano nell'arte e nella storia.* Milan, 1948.

MEZZANOTTE, P. *Raccolta Bianconi: Catalogo ragionato*, I. Milan, 1942.

6. PAVIA

PERONI, A. 'Il Collegio Borromeo. Architettura e decorazione', *I quattro secoli del Collegio Borromeo di Pavia*, 111–61. Pavia, 1961.

7. PIACENZA

FERRARI, G. *Piacenza.* Bergamo, 1931.

GAZZOLA, P. 'Il Rinascimento a Piacenza', *Atti I° Convegno Nazionale Storia Architettura*, 245. Florence, 1936.

E. *Marche*

1. GENERAL

TERZAGHI, A. 'Indirizzi del classicismo nell'architettura del tardo Quattrocento nelle Marche', *Atti XI° Congresso Storia Architettura, Roma 1959*, 329. Rome, 1965.

2. PESARO

MARCHINI, G. 'Il Problema dell'Imperiale', *Commentari*, N.S. XXI (1970), 66 ff.

PATZAK, B. *Die Villa Imperiale in Pesaro.* Leipzig, 1908.

F. *Piedmont*

CARBONERI, N. 'Architettura', in catalogue *Mostra del Barocco piemontese.* Turin, 1963.

TAMBURINI, L. *Le Chiese di Torino dal Rinascimento al Barocco.* Turin, [1969].

G. *Rome and Lazio*

ROME

1. GENERAL

BRUHNS, L. *Die Kunst der Stadt Rom.* Vienna, 1951.

LEWINE, M. 'Roman Architectural Practice during Michelangelo's Maturity', *Stil und Überlieferung in der Kunst des Abendlandes* (Acts of the 21st International Congress for the History of Art, Bonn, 1964), 20 ff. Berlin, 1967.

MAGNUSON, T. *Studies in Roman Quattrocento Architecture.* Stockholm, 1958.

2. PLANS AND DRAWINGS

BARTOLI, A. *I Monumenti antichi di Roma nei disegni degli Uffizi di Firenze.* 6 vols. Rome, 1914–22.

EGGER, H. *Römische Veduten.* Vol. I, Vienna-Leipzig, 1911, 2nd ed., Vienna, 1932; vol. II, Vienna, 1932.

FRUTAZ, A. P. *Le Piante di Roma.* 3 vols. Rome, 1962.

HUELSEN, C. 'Das *Speculum Romanae magnificentiae* des Antonio Lafreri', *Collectanea ... Leoni S. Olschki ... sexagenario ...*, 121 ff. Munich, 1921.

HUELSEN, C., and EGGER, H. *Die römischen Skizzenbücher des Marten van Heemskerk.* 2 vols. Berlin, 1913–16.

MONGERI, G. (ed.). *Le Rovine di Roma al principio del secolo XVI; studi del Bramantino.* 2nd ed. Pisa, 1880.

WITTKOWER, R. (ed.). *Disegni de le ruine di Roma e come anticamente erono.* Milan, 1963.

3. TOPOGRAPHY AND GENERAL WORKS

GIOVANNONI, G. 'Il Quattrocento. Il Cinquecento', *Topografia e urbanistica di Roma* (Storia di Roma, XXII), 243 ff. Bologna, 1958.

GNOLI, D. *La Roma di Leone X.* Milan, 1938.

HIBBARD, H. 'Di alcune licenze rilasciate dai mastri di strade per opere di edificazione a Roma (1586–89, 1602–34)', *Bollettino d'Arte*, LII (1967), 99 ff.

LETAROUILLY, P. *Les Édifices de Rome moderne.* 3 vols. text, 3 vols. plates. Liège and Brussels, 1849–66.

ONOFRIO, C. D'. *Le Fontane di Roma.* Rome, 1957.

ONOFRIO, C. D'. *Gli Obelischi di Roma.* 2nd ed. Rome, 1967.

ONOFRIO, C. D'. *Il Tevere a Roma.* Rome, 1970.

ORBAAN, J. F. *Sixtine Rome.* London, 1910.

PASCHINI, P. 'Da Ripetta a Piazza del Popolo', *Roma.* III (1925), 211 ff.

PASTOR, L. VON. *Sisto V, creatore della nuova Roma.* Rome, 1922.

PECCHIAI, P. *Roma nel Cinquecento* (Storia di Roma, XIII). Bologna, 1948.

PONNELLE, L., and BORDET, L. *Saint Philip Neri and the Roman Society of His Times.* London, 1932.

PROIA, A., and ROMANO, P. *Roma nel Cinquecento.* 13 vols. Rome, 1933–41.

RE, E. 'Maestri di Strada', *Archivio Società Romana di Storia Patria*, XLIII (1920), 5 ff.

STEVENSON, E. *Topografia e monumenti di Roma nelle pitture a fresco di Sisto V nella Biblioteca Vaticana. Omaggio giubilare a Leone XIII.* Rome, 1887.

VALENTINI, R., and ZUCCHETTI, G. *Codice topografico della città di Roma.* 4 vols. Rome, 1940–53.

4. ST PETER'S AND THE VATICAN

ACKERMAN, J. S. *The Cortile del Belvedere* (Studi e documenti per la storia del Palazzo Apostolico Vaticano, III). Vatican City, 1954.

FREY, K. 'Zur Baugeschichte des St Peter', *Jahrbuch der Preussischen Kunstsammlungen*, XXXI (1910), XXXIII (1913).

GEYMÜLLER, H. VON. *Die ursprünglichen Entwürfe für St Peter.* 2 vols. Vienna and Paris, 1875.

GIOSEFFI, D. *La Cupola vaticana.* Trieste, 1960.

HOFMANN, T. *Die Entstehungsgeschichte des St Peter in Rom.* Zittau, 1928.

LETAROUILLY, P. *Le Vatican et la basilique de Saint-Pierre de Rome.* 2 vols. Paris, 1883.

ORBAAN, J. A. 'Zur Baugeschichte der Peters-kuppel', *Jahrbuch der Preussischen Kunstsammlungen*, XXXVIII (1917), Beiheft.

REDIGDE CAMPOS, D. *I Palazzi vaticani*. Bologna, 1967.

SIEBENHÜNER, H. 'Umrisse zur Geschichte der Ausstattung von St Peter in Rom von Paul III. bis Paul V. (1547–1606)', *Festschrift für Hans Sedlmayr*, 229 ff. Munich, 1962.

THOENES, C. 'Peterskirche', *Lexikon für Kirche und Theologie*, 2nd ed., VIII. Freiburg im Breisgau, 1957.

THOENES, C. 'Studien zur Geschichte des Peters-platzes', *Zeitschrift für Kunstgeschichte*, XXVI (1963), 97 ff.

WITTKOWER, R. *La Cupola di San Pietro di Michelangelo*. Florence, 1964.

WOLFF METTERNICH, F. Graf. 'Bramantes Chor der Peterskirche zu Rom', *Römische Quartalschrift*, LVIII (1963), 271 ff.

WOLFF METTERNICH, F. Graf. 'Le premier projet pour Saint-Pierre de Rome, Bramante et Michel-Ange', *The Renaissance and Mannerism, Studies in Western Art* (Acts of the 20th International Congress of the History of Art), II, 70 ff. Princeton, N.J., 1963.

WOLFF METTERNICH, F. Graf. 'Eine Vorstufe zu Michelangelos Sankt Peter-Fassade', *Festschrift Herbert von Einem*, 162 ff. Berlin. 1965.

WOLFF METTERNICH, F. Graf. 'Massgrundlagen des Kuppelentwurfes Bramantes für die Peterskirche in Rom', *Essays in the History of Architecture presented to Rudolf Wittkower*, 40 ff. London, 1967.

5. THE CAPITOL

LAVIN, I. 'The Campidoglio and Sixteenth-Century Stage Design', *Essays in Honor of Walter Friedlaender*, 114 ff. Locust Valley, N.Y., 1965.

PECCHIAI, P. *Il Campidoglio nel Cinquecento sulla scorta dei documenti*. Rome, 1950.

SIEBENHÜNER, H. *Das Kapitol von Rom. Idee und Gestalt*. Munich, 1954.
Review by J. S. Ackerman, *Art Bulletin*, XXXVIII (1956), 53 ff.

6. CHURCHES

PECCHIAI, P. *Il Gesù di Roma*. Rome, 1950.

RAY, S. 'La Cappella Chigi in Santa Maria del Popolo a Roma', *L'Architettura*, XIV (1969), 750 ff.

SCHWAGER, K. 'Zur Bautätigkeit Sixtus' V. an S. Maria Maggiore in Rom', *Miscellanea Bibliothecae Hertzianae*. 324. Munich, 1961.

SHEARMAN, J. 'The Chigi Chapel in S. Maria del Popolo', *Journal of the Warburg and Courtauld Institutes*, XXIV (1961), 129 ff.

SIEBENHÜNER, H. 'S. Maria degli Angeli in Rom', *Münchner Jahrbuch der bildenden Kunst*, 3rd series, VI (1955), 179 ff.

URBAN, G. 'Die Cappella Cesi in S. Maria della Pace und die Zeichnungen des Antonio da Sangallo', *Miscellanea Bibliothecae Hertzianae*, 213 ff. Munich, 1961.

7. PALACES

FROMMEL, C. L. *Die Farnesina und Peruzzis architektonisches Frühwerk*. Berlin, 1961.
Review by J. S. Ackerman, *Art Bulletin*, XLIV (1962), 243 ff.

HIBBARD, H. *The Architecture of the Palazzo Borghese*. Rome, 1962.
Review by C. Thoenes, *Zeitschrift für Kunstgeschichte*, XXVI (1963), 181 ff.

NAVENNE, F. DE. *Le Palais Farnèse et les Farnèse*. Paris, 1914.

THELEN, H. 'Der Palazzo della Sapienza in Rom', *Miscellanea Bibliothecae Hertzianae*, 302 ff. Munich, 1961.

WASSERMAN, J. 'Giacomo della Porta's Church for the Sapienza in Rome and Other Matters relating to the Palace', *Art Bulletin*, XLVI (1964), 501 ff.

WASSERMAN, J. 'Palazzo Spada', *Art Bulletin*, XLIII (1961), 58 ff.

WURM, H. *Der Palazzo Massimo alle Colonne*. Berlin, 1965.

8. VILLAS

ANDRES, G. M. 'Cardinal Giovanni Ricci: The Builder of the present Villa Medici from Montepulciano', *Atti del Quinto Convegno Internazionale del Centro di Studi Umanistici*, 283 ff. Florence, 1970.

COFFIN, D. R. 'The Plans of the Villa Madama', *Art Bulletin*, IL (1967), 111 ff.

FALK, T. 'Studien zur Topographie und Geschichte der Villa Giulia in Rom', *Römisches Jahrbuch für Kunstgeschichte*, XIII (1971), 101 ff.

GIESS, H. 'Studien zur Farnese-Villa am Palatin', *Römisches Jahrbuch für Kunstgeschichte*, XIII (1971), 179 ff.

HESS, J. 'Die päpstliche Villa bei Araceli', *Miscellanea Bibliothecae Hertzianae*, 239 ff. Munich, 1961.

HUEMER, F. 'Raphael and the Villa Madama', *Essays in Honor of Walter Friedlaender*, 92 ff. Locust Valley, N.Y., 1968.

RAY, S. 'Villa Madama a Roma', *L'Architettura*, XIV (1969), 882 ff.

LAZIO

1. BAGNAIA

ANGELIS D'OSSAT, E. (ed.). *La Villa Lante di Bagnaia*. Milan, 1961.

BRUSCHI, A. 'Bagnaia', *Quaderni dell'Istituto di Storia dell'Architettura dell'Università di Roma*, XVII (1956).

HESS, J. 'Entwürfe von Giovanni Guerra für Villa Lante in Bagnaia (1598)', *Römisches Jahrbuch für Kunstgeschichte*, XII (1969), 195 ff.

NEGRI-ARNOLDI, F. *Villa Lante in Bagnaia*. Rome, 1963.

2. CAPRAROLA

LABROT, G. *Le Palais Farnèse de Caprarola. Essai de lecture*. Paris, 1970.

3. FRASCATI

FRANCK, K. L. *Die Barockvillen in Frascati*. Munich and Berlin, 1956.
Review by H. Hibbard, *Art Bulletin*, XL (1958), 354 ff.

SCHWAGER, K. 'Kardinal Pietro Aldobrandinis Villa di Belvedere in Frascati', *Römisches Jahrbuch für Kunstgeschichte*, XIX (1961–2), 289 ff.

4. GENAZZANO

FROMMEL, C. L. 'Bramantes "Ninfeo" in Genazzano', *Römisches Jahrbuch für Kunstgeschichte*, XII (1969), 95 ff.

H. *Southern Italy*

CATALANI, L. *Le Chiese di Napoli*. 2 vols. Naples, 1845–53.

CATALANI, L. *I Palazzi di Napoli*, Naples, 1845; reprinted Naples, 1969.

PANE, R. *Architettura del Rinascimento a Napoli*. Naples, 1937.

THOENES, C. *Neapel und Umgebung*. Stuttgart, 1971.

WEISE, G. 'Chiese napoletane, anteriori al Gesù del Vignola', *Palladio*, N.S. II (1952), 148 ff.

ZANDER, G. 'A proposito di alcune chiese napoletane anteriori al Gesù di Roma', *Palladio*, N.S. III (1953), 41 ff.

I. *Tuscany*

1. GENERAL

SANPAOLESI, P. 'Architetti pre-michelangeleschi toscani', *Rivista Istituto Nazionale d'Architettura e Storia dell'Arte*, N.S. XIII/XIV (Rome, 1964/5), 269 ff.

STEGMANN, C. VON, and GEYMÜLLER, H. VON. *Die Architektur der Renaissance in Toscana*. 11 vols. Munich, 1885–1908. Abridged English ed., 2 vols., New York, c. 1924.

THIEM, G. and C. *Toskanische Fassadendekoration in Sgraffito und Fresco*. Munich, 1964.

2. FLORENCE

GINORI, L. *I Palazzi di Firenze nella storia e nell' arte*. 2 vols. Florence, 1972.

GOLDTHWAITE, R. A. 'The Florentine Palace as Domestic Architecture', *The American Historical Review*, LXXVII (1972), 977 ff.

GOLDTHWAITE, R. A. *Private Wealth in Renaissance Florence. A Study of Four Families*. Princeton, N. J., 1968.

MORANDINI, F. 'Palazzo Pitti, la sua costruzione e i successivi ingrandimenti', *Commentari*, XVI (1965), 35 ff.

PAATZ, W. and E. *Die Kirchen von Florenz*. 6 vols. Frankfurt, 1952–5.

SCHIAPARELLI, A. *La Casa fiorentina e i suoi arredi nei secoli XIV e XV*. Florence, 1908.

3. SIENA

SECCHI TARUGI, F. 'Aspetti del Manierismo nel architettura senese', *Palladio*, XVI (1966), 103 ff.

J. *Umbria*

TARCHI, U. *L'Arte nel Rinascimento nell'Umbria e nella Sabina*. Milan, 1954.

K. *Veneto*

1. VENICE

CICOGNARA, L., DIEDO, A., and SELVA, G. *Le Fabbriche e i monumenti cospicui di Venezia*. Venice, 1857.

FIOCCO, G. 'L'Ingresso del Rinascimento nel Veneto', *Atti XVIII° Congresso Internazionale Storia dell'Arte* (1955), 56 f.

FONTANA, G. *Venezia monumentale.* Venice, 1865; reprinted 1934.

HUBALA, E. *Die Baukunst der venezianischen Renaissance* (1460–1550). Habilitationsschïft (unpublished). Munich, 1958.
    This excellent work raises many stimulating points.

LORENZETTI, G. *Venezia e il suo estuario.* Venice, 1926. English ed., Rome, 1961.

OKEY, T. *The Old Venetian Palaces and Old Venetian Folk.* London, 1907.

PALLUCCHINI, R. *Storia della civiltà veneziana*, III, *La Civiltà veneziana del Quattrocento.* Florence, 1957.

PAOLETTI, P. *L'Architettura e la scultura del Rinascimento a Venezia.* 3 vols. Venice, 1893.

G. SAMONÀ (ed.). *Piazza S. Marco: L'architettura, la storia, le funzioni.* Padua, 1970.

RUSKIN, J. *The Stones of Venice.* London 1851–3.

SANSOVINO, F. *Venezia, città nobilissima.* Venice, 1581.

SELVATICO, P. *Sull'architettura e sulla scultura in Venezia dal medioevo sino ai nostri giorni.* Venice, 1847.

TEMANZA, T. *Vita dei più celebri architetti e scultori veneziani . . . nel secolo XVI.* Venice, 1778.

TRINCANATO, E. R. *Venezia Minore.* Milan, 1949.

2. VICENZA

BARBIERI, F., CEVESE, R., and MAGAGNATO, L. *Guida di Vicenza.* Vicenza, 1956.

CEVESE, R. *Ville della provincia di Vicenza.* 2 vols. Milan, 1971–2.

VI. ARCHITECTS

ALESSI

ROCCO, G. 'Giovanni Alessi a Milano', *Atti del IV Convegno Nazionale di Storia dell'Architettura*, 185 ff. Milan, 1939.

See also below: TIBALDI.

AMMANNATI

BELLI BARSALI, I. 'Ammannati', *Dizionario biografico degli Italiani*, II (1960), 798 ff.

FOSSI, M. *Bartolomeo Ammannati architetto* (Atti dell'Accademia Pontiniana). Naples, n.d.

FOSSI, M. (ed.). *La Città. Appunti per un trattato. Bartolomeo Ammannati.* Rome, 1970.

PIRRI, P. 'L'Architetto Bartolomeo Ammannati e i Gesuiti', *Archivium Hist. Soc. Jesu*, XII (1943), 5 ff.

BRAMANTE

ARGAN, G. C. 'Il Problema del Bramante'. *Rassegna Marchigiana*, XII (1934), 212 ff.

BARONI, C. *Bramante.* Bergamo, 1944.

BELTRAMI, L. *Bramante a Milano.* Milan, 1912.

Bramante tra Umanesimo e Manierismo, Mostra storico-critica, Settembre 1970.
    With catalogue of Bramante's œuvre, 213 ff., and bibliography, 219 ff., by A. Bruschi.

BRUSCHI, A. *Bramante architetto.* Bari, 1969.
    With complete bibliography.

FIOCCO, G. 'Il primo Bramante', *Critica d'Arte*, I (1935/6), 109.

FÖRSTER, O. H. *Bramante.* Vienna, 1956.

FREY, D. *Bramante-Studien*, I: *Bramantes St Peter-Entwurf und seine Apokryphen.* Vienna, 1915.

MALAGUZZI-VALERI, F. *La Corte di Lodovico il Moro*, II: *Bramante e Leonardo.* Milan, 1915.

WOLFF METTERNICH, F. Graf. 'Bramante, Skizze eines Lebensbildes', *Römische Quartalschrift*, LXIII (1968), 1 ff.

BUONTALENTI

BEMPORAD, N. 'Gli Uffizi e la scala buontalentiana', *L'Architettura*, XIV (1968), 610–19.

BOTTO, I. M. (ed.). *Mostra di disegno di Bernardo Buontalenti* (1531–1608). Gabinetto Disegni e Stampe degli Uffizi. Catalogue. Florence, 1968.

GORI-MONTANELLI, L. 'Giudizio sul Buontalenti architetto', *Quaderni dell'Istituto di Storia dell'Architettura*, XXXI-XLVIII (1961), 207 ff.

CESARIANO

KRINSKY, C. H. Introduction to reprint of Cesariano's edition of Vitruvius, *De architectura.* Munich, 1969.

CIGOLI (CARDI)

FASOLO, V. 'Un Pittore architetto: il Cigoli', *Quaderni dell'Istituto di Storia dell'Arte*, I (1952), 2 ff., and II (1953), 11 ff.

DELLA PORTA

ACKERMAN, J. S. 'Della Porta's Gesù Altar', *Essays in Honor of Walter Friedlaender*, 1 ff. Locust Valley, 1965.

ARSLAN, W. 'Forme architettoniche civili di Giacomo della Porta', *Bollettino d'Arte*, VI (1926–7), 508.

FALCONETTO

FIOCCO, G. *Alvise Cornaro, il suo tempo e le sue opere.* Venice, 1965.

WOLTERS, W. 'Tiziano Minio als Stukkator im Odeo Cornaro zu Padua', *Pantheon*, XXI (1963), 20 ff. and 222 ff.

GIOCONDO, FRA

VASARI (ed. Milanesi), *op. cit.*, V, 261, also the Bemporad Edition (Florence, 1915), with an exhaustive introduction by G. Fiocco.

FIOCCO, G. 'Fra Giocondo', *Atti dell'Accademia d'Arti, Industrie e Commercio di Verona* ser. IV, vol. XVI (Verona, 1915).

LESUEUR, P. 'Fra Giocondo en France', *Bulletin de la Société de l'Histoire de l'Art français* (1931), 115 ff.

BRENZONI, R. 'La Loggia del Consiglio di Verona e Fra Giocondo nella bibliografica veronese', *Atti dell'Accademia d'Arti, Scienze e Lettere* (1958).

Idem, Fra Giocondo (Florence, 1960).

WOLFF METTERNICH, F. Graf. 'Der Entwurf Fra Giocondo's für Sankt Peter', *Festschrift Kurt Bauch*, Munich, 1957, 155 ff.

GIULIO ROMANO

See notes to Chapter 7.

MASCARINO

GLOTON, J.-J. 'Tradition michelangesque dans l'architecture de la Contre-Reforme: le cas Mascarino', *Stil und Überlieferung in der Kunst des Abendlandes* (Acts of the 21st International Congress for the History of Art, Bonn, 1964), II, 27. Berlin, 1967.

MICHELANGELO

ACKERMAN, J. S. *The Architecture of Michelangelo.* Revised ed. 2 vols. London, 1964–6. Italian ed.: *L'Architettura di Michelangelo.* Turin, 1968.

ALKER, H. R. *Michelangelo und seine Kuppel von St Peter in Rom.* Karlsruhe, 1968.

BAROCCHI, P. (ed.). *G. Vasari: Vita di Michelangelo nelle redazioni del 1550 e del 1568.* 5 vols. Milan, 1962.

FREY, D. *Michelangelostudien.* Vienna, 1920.

LOTZ, W. 'Zu Michelangelos Kopien nach dem Codex Coner', *Stil und Überlieferung in der Kunst des Abendlandes* (Acts of the 21st International Congress for the History of Art, Bonn, 1964), II, 12 ff. Berlin, 1967.

Michelangelo artista-pensatore-scrittore. 2 vols. Novara, 1965. English ed. New York, 1965.
    With good bibliography by P. Meller, II, 597 ff.

PORTOGHESI, P. 'La Biblioteca Laurenziana e la critica michelangiolesca alla tradizione classica', *Stil und Überlieferung in der Kunst des Abendlandes* (Acts of the 21st International Congress for the History of Art, Bonn, 1964), II, 3. Berlin, 1967.

PORTOGHESI, P., and ZEVI, B. (eds.). *Michelangelo architetto.* Turin, 1964.

SCHIAVO, A. *Michelangelo architetto.* Rome, 1949.

SCHIAVO, A. *La Vita e le opere architettoniche di Michelangelo.* Rome, 1953.

THOENES, C. 'Bemerkungen zur Petersfassade Michelangelos', *Munuscula Disciplinorum, Festschrift Hans Kauffmann*, 331–41. Berlin, 1968.

TOLNAY, C. de. *The Medici Chapel.* Princeton, 1948.

TOLNAY, C. de. *Michelangelo.* Florence, 1951.

TOLNAY, C. de. 'Michelangelo architetto'. *Il Cinquecento.* Florence, 1955.

TOLNAY, C. de. 'Newly Discovered Drawings related to Michelangelo: The Scholz Scrap-book', *Stil und Überlieferung in der Kunst des Abendlandes* (Acts of the 21st International Congress for the History of Art, Bonn, 1964), II, 64. Berlin, 1967.

PALLADIO

See Chapter 12, Note 1.

PELLEGRINI *see* TIBALDI

PERUZZI

BURNS, H. 'A Peruzzi Drawing in Ferrara', *Mitteilungen des Kunsthistorischen Institutes in Florenz*, XII (1966), 245–70.

EGGER, H. 'Entwürfe Baldassare Peruzzis für den Einzug Karls V. in Rom', *Jahrbuch der Kunsthistorischen Sammlungen in Wien*, XXIII (1902), 1 ff.

FROMMEL, C. L. *Die Farnesina und Peruzzis architektonisches Frühwerk*. Berlin, 1961.

KENT. W. W. *The Life and Works of Baldassare Peruzzi*. New York, 1925.

RAPHAEL

BRIZIO, A. M. 'Raffaello', *Enciclopedia universale dell'arte*, XI, 222 ff. Venice-Rome, 1964.

GEYMÜLLER, H. von. *Raffaello Sanzio studiato come architetto*. Milan, 1884.

GOLZIO, V. *Raffaello nei documenti*. Vatican City, 1936.

HOFMANN, T. *Raffael in seiner Bedeutung als Architekt*. 4 vols. Zittau, 1904–14.

MARCHINI, G. 'Le Architetture', in A. M. Brizio (ed.), *Raffaello, L'opera. Le fonti. La fortuna*. 2 vols. Novara, 1968.

OBERHUBER, K. 'Eine unbekannte Zeichnung Raffaels [for St Peter's] in den Uffizien', *Mitteilungen des Kunsthistorischen Institutes in Florenz*, XII (1966), 225 ff.

SHEARMAN, J. 'Raphael . . . "fa il Bramante"', *Studies in Renaissance and Baroque Art presented to Anthony Blunt*, 12 ff. London and New York, 1967.

SHEARMAN, J. 'Raphael as Architect', *Journal of the Royal Society of Arts*, CXVI (1968), 388 ff.

ROMANO, G.
See GIULIO ROMANO

SANGALLO THE YOUNGER, A. DA

CLAUSSE, G. *Les San Gallo: Architectes, peintres, sculpteurs, médailleurs, XVe et XVIe siècles*. 3 vols. Paris, 1900–2.

FROMMEL, C. L. 'Antonio da Sangallos Cappella Paolina. Ein Beitrag zur Baugeschichte des Vatikanischen Palasts', *Zeitschrift für Kunstgeschichte*, XXVII (1964), 1 ff.

GIOVANNONI, G. *Antonio da Sangallo il giovane*. 2 vols. Rome, 1959.

URBAN, G. 'Die Cappella Cesi in S. Maria della Pace und die Zeichnungen des Antonio da Sangallo', *Miscellanea Bibliothecae Hertzianae*, 213 ff. Munich, 1961.

SANMICHELI

GAZZOLA, P. (ed.). *Michele Sanmicheli, Catalogo* (of exhibition, Verona, 1960). Venice, 1960.

LANGENSKIÖLD, E. *Michele Sanmicheli. The Architect of Verona*. Uppsala. 1938.

Michele Sanmicheli, Studi raccolti dall'Accademia di Agricoltura, Scienze e Lettere di Verona per la celebrazione del quarto centenario della morte. Verona. 1960.

PUPPI, L. *Michele Sanmicheli, architetto di Verona*. Padua, 1971.

RONZANI, F., and LUCIOLLI, G. *Le Fabbriche civili, ecclesiastiche e militari di Michele Sanmicheli*. Verona, 1823–30.

SANSOVINO, J.

LOTZ, W. 'Sansovinos Bibliothek von S. Marco und die Stadtbaukunst der Renaissance', *Kunst des Mittelalters in Sachsen: Festschrift Wolf Schubert*, 336 ff. Weimar, 1967.

SAMONÀ, G. (ed.). *Piazza San Marco: l'architettura, la storia, le funzioni*. Padua, 1970.

PUPPI, L. 'La Villa Garzoni ora Carraretto a Pontecasale di Jacopo Sansovino', *Bollettino del Centro Internazionale di Studi di Architettura Andrea Palladio*, XI (1969), 95 ff.

TAFURI, M. *Jacopo Sansovino e l'architettura del '500 a Venezia*. Padua, 1969. With bibliography.

SCAMOZZI

BARBIERI, F. *Vincenzo Scamozzi*. Vicenza and Belluno, 1952.

BARBIERI, F. *Vincenzo Scamozzi: Taccuino di viaggio da Parigi a Venezia*. Venice and Rome, 1959.

BARBIERI, F. 'Le Ville dello Scamozzi', *Bollettino del Centro Internazionale di Studi di Architettura Andrea Palladio*, XI (1969), 222 ff.

GALLO, R. 'Vincenzo Scamozzi e la chiesa di S. Nicolò da Tolentino a Venezia',
Atti dell' Istituto Veneto di Scienze, Lettere ed Arti, CXVII (1958/9), 103 ff.

PALLUCCHINI, R. 'Vincenzo Scamozzi e l'architettura veneta', *L'Arte*, XXXIX (1936), 3 ff.

PUPPI, L. 'Vincenzo Scamozzi trattatista nell' ambito della problematica del Manierismo', *Bollettino del Centro Internazionale di Studi di Architettura Andrea Palladio*, IX (1967), 310 ff.

PUPPI, L. 'Prospettive dell'Olimpico, documenti dell'Ambrosiana e altre cose: argomenti per una replica', *Arte Lombarda*, XI (1966), part I, 26 ff.

SEMENZATO, C. 'La Rocca pisana', *Arte Veneta*, XVI (1962), 98 ff.

TALAMINI, T. 'Le Procuratie nuove', *Piazza S. Marco. L'architettura, la storia, le funzioni*, 177 ff. Padua, 1970.

SERLIO

ARGAN, G. C. 'Sebastiano Serlio', *L'Arte*, N.S. X (1932), 183 ff.

CHASTEL, A. 'La Demeure royale au XVIe siècle et le nouveau Louvre', *Studies in Renaissance and Baroque Art presented to Anthony Blunt*, 183 ff. London and New York, 1967.

ROSCI, M. *Il Trattato di architettura di Sebastiano Serlio*. Milan, 1966.

TIMOFIEWITSCH, W. 'Ein Gutachten Sebastiano Serlios für die Scuola di S. Rocco', *Arte Veneta*, XVII (1963), 158 ff.

TIBALDI

HIERSCHE, W. *Pellegrino de' Pellegrini als Architekt*. Parchim, 1913.

PERONI, A. 'Architetti manieristi nell'Italia settentrionale: Pellegrino Tibaldi e Galeazzo Alessi', *Bollettino del Centro Internazionale di Studi di Architettura Andrea Palladio*, IX (1967), 272 ff. With bibliography.

PIGNATTI, T. 'L'Architettura del Collegio Ghislieri', *Il Collegio Ghislieri 1567–1967*, 299 ff. Milan, 1967.

TRAMELLO

GANZ, J. *Alessio Tramello*. Frauenfeld (Switzerland), 1968.

GAZZOLA, P. *Opere di A. Tramello*. Rome, 1935.

VENTURI, A. *Storia dell'arte italiana*, XI (I), 738 ff. Milan, 1938–40. For good illustrations.

VALERIANO

ENRICHETTI, M. 'L'Architetto Giuseppe Valeriano', *Archivio storico per le provincie napoletane*, XXXIX (1960), 325 ff.

PIRRI, P. *Giuseppe Valeriano S.I., architetto e pittore, 1542–1596*. Rome, 1970.

VASARI

KALLAB, W. *Vasari-Studien* (Quellenschriften für Kunstgeschichte und Kunsttechnik, N.F. XIV). Vienna, 1908.

VASARI THE YOUNGER

VASARI, G. (ed. V. Stefanelli). *La Città ideale. Piante di chiese, palazzi e ville*. Rome, 1970.

VIGNOLA

ACKERMAN, J. S., and LOTZ, W. 'Vignoliana', *Essays in Memory of Karl Lehmann*, 1 ff. Locust Valley, N. Y., 1964.

PARTRIDGE, L. W. 'Vignola and the Villa Farnese at Caprarola, part I', *Art Bulletin*, LII (1970), 81 ff.

WALCHER CASOTTI, M. *Il Vignola*. 2 vols. Trieste, 1960. Reviewed by C. Thoenes, *Kunstchronik*, XV (1962), 151 ff.

VITOZZI

CARBONERI, N. *Ascanio Vitozzi. Un architetto tra Manierismo e Barocco*. Rome, 1966.

VOLTERRA

See Chapter 10, Notes 41–3.

Select Bibliography of Books Published since 1973

Limitations of length have meant that journal articles, book reviews and unpublished theses have not been included, but further bibliographical information may be obtained from the books listed below.

GENERAL WORKS

ACKERMAN, J. S. *Distance Points: Essays in Theory and Renaissance Art and Architecture.* Cambridge, Mass. and London, 1992.

BENEVOLO, L. *The Architecture of the Renaissance*, trans. Judith Landry. 2 vol. London and Henley, 1973.

BENEDETTI, S. *Fuori dal Classicismo: Sintesi, tipologia, ragione nell'architettura del Cinquecento.* Rome, 1984.

MILLON, H. A. and MAGNANO LAMPUGNANI, V. (eds). *The Renaissance from Brunelleschi to Michelangelo: The Representation of Architecture.* London, 1994.

MURRAY, P. *Renaissance Architecture.* London, 1986; Italian translation as *L'architettura del Rinascimento.* Milan, 1978.

TAFURI, M. *Ricerca del Rinascimento: Principi, città, architetti.* Turin, 1992.

THOMSON, D. *Renaissance Architecture: Critics, Patrons, Luxury.* Manchester and New York, 1993.

THEMATIC STUDIES

Antiquity

BOBER, P. P. and RUBINSTEIN, R. *Renaissance Artists and Antique Sculpture.* London, 1986.

BORSI, F. (ed.). *Roma antica e i disegni di architettura agli Uffizi di Giovanni Antonio Dosio.* Rome, 1976.

BORSI, S. *Giuliano da Sangallo: I disegni dell'architettura e dell'antico.* Rome, 1985.

DANESI SQUARZINA, S. (ed.) *Roma centro ideale della cultura dell'Antico nei secoli XV e XVI. Da Martino V al sacco di Roma 1417–1527.* Milan, 1989.

FAGIOLO, M. (ed.). *Roma e l'antico nell'arte e nella cultura del Cinquecento.* Rome, 1985.

GÜNTHER, H. *Das Studium der antiken Architektur in der Zeichnungen der Hochrenaissance.* Tübingen, 1989.

SETTIS, S. (ed.). *Memorie dell'antico nell'arte italiana.* 3 vols. Turin, 1984–6.

Architectural Theory

CATANEO, P. and VIGNOLA, G. BAROZZI DA. *Trattati (con l'aggiunta degli scritti di architettura di Alvise Cornaro, Francesco Giorgi, Claudio Tolomei, Giangiorgio Trissino, Giorgio Vasari).* Milan, 1985.

FORSSMAN, E. *Dorico, Ionico, Corinzio nell'architettura del Rinascimento.* Rome and Bari, 1988.

GUILLAUME, J. (ed.). *Les traités d'architecture de la Renaissance* (proceedings of colloquium held at Tours, 1981). Paris, 1988.

GUILLAUME, J. (ed.). *L'emploi des ordres à la Renaissance* (proceedings of colloquium held at Tours, 1986). Paris, 1992.

HERSEY, G. *The Lost Meaning of Classical Architecture: Speculations on ornament from Vitruvius to Venturi.* Cambridge, Mass. and London, 1987.

JELMINI, A. *Sebastiano Serlio: Il trattato d'architettura.* Friborgo (Switzerland), 1986.

KRUFT, H.-W. *A History of Architectural Theory from Vitruvius to the present*, transl. Ronald Taylor, Elsie Callander and Antony Wood. London and Princeton, 1994; from *Geschichte der Architektur Theorie.* Munich, 1986.

ONIANS, J. *Bearers of Meaning: The Classical Orders in Antiquity, the Middle Ages, and the Renaissance.* Princeton, 1988.

ROSENFELD, M. N. *Sebastiano Serlio on Domestic Architecture: the 16th-century manuscript of Book VI in the Avery Library of Columbia University* (facsimile reprint, with commentary). New York, Cambridge Mass. and London, 1978.

SERLIO, S. *Architettura civile: Libri sesto, settimo e ottavo nei manoscritti di Monaco e Vienna.* ed. Francesco Paolo Fiore. Milan, 1994.

THOENES, C. (ed.). *Sebastiano Serlio* (proceedings of seminar held at Vicenza 1987). Milan, 1989.

TZONIS, A. and LEFAIVRE, L. *Classical Architecture: The Poetics of Order.* Cambridge, Mass. and London, 1986.

VITRUVIUS, *I dieci libri dell'architettura tradotti e commentati da Daniele Barbaro (1567)*, with introductory essays by Manfredo Tafuri and Manuela Morresi. Milan, 1987.

Urban History

BENEVOLO, L. *La città italiana nel Rinascimento*, revised edn. Milan, 1990.

BRAUNFELS, W. *Urban Design in Western Europe: Régime and Architecture, 900–1900*, transl. Kenneth J. Northcott. Chicago and London, 1988.

DE SETA, C. (ed.). *La città nella storia d'Italia.* Rome and Bari, many volumes, 1980 onwards. (A number of the individual volumes in this series are cited below under the specific city headings).

DE SETA, C. et al. *Imago Urbis: Dalla città reale alla città ideale.* Rome, 1986.

GUIDONI, E. and MARINO, A. *Storia dell'urbanistica: Il Cinquecento.* Bari, 1982.

KOSTOFF, S. *The City shaped: Urban Patterns and Meanings through History.* London, 1991.

KOSTOFF, S. *The City assembled: The Elements of Urban Form through History.* London, 1992.

Building and Technology

GUILLAUME, J. (ed.). *Les chantiers de la Renaissance* (proceedings of colloquium held at Tours, 1983–4). Paris, 1991.

Landscape and Cartography

COSGROVE, D. *The Palladian Landscape.* Leicester and London, 1993.

SCHULZ, J. *La cartografia tra scienza e arte: Carte e cartografi nel Rinascimento italiano.* Ferrara, 1990.

BUILDING TYPES

PEVSNER, N. *A History of Building Types.* London, 1976.

Churches

BÖSEL, R. *Jesuitenarchitektur in Italien (1540–1770). Teil I: Die Baudenkmäler der römischen und der neapolitanischen Ordensprovinz.* 2 vols. Vienna, 1985.

BRAUNFELS, W. *Monasteries of Western Europe: The Architecture of the Orders*, translated by Alastair Laing. London, 1972.

BRUSCHI, A. (ed.). *Il Tempio della Consolazione a Todi.* Milan, 1991.

COLVIN, H. *Architecture and the After-Life.* New Haven and London, 1991.

HALL, M. B. *Renovation and Counter-Reformation: Vasari and Duke Cosimo in Sta Maria Novella and Sta Croce 1565–1577.* Oxford, 1979.

JAFFÉ, I. B. and WITTKOWER, R. (eds). *Baroque Art: The Jesuit Contribution.* New York, 1972.

PATETTA, L. (ed.). *L'architettura della Compagnia di Gesù in Italia XVI–XVIII sec.* (exh. cat.). Milan, 1990.

SATZINGER, G. *Antonio da Sangallo der Ältere und die Madonna di San Biagio bei Montepulciano.* Tübingen, 1991.

Domestic Architecture

GUILLAUME, J. (ed.). *L'escalier dans l'architecture de la Renaissance* (proceedings of colloquium held at Tours, 1979). Paris, 1985.

GUILLAUME, J. (ed.). *Architecture et vie sociale à la Renaissance* (proceedings of colloquium held at Tours, 1988). Paris, 1994.

THORNTON, P. *The Italian Renaissance Interior 1400–1600.* London, 1991.

WEIL-GARRIS, K. and D'AMICO, J. F. *The Renaissance Cardinal's Ideal Palace; A Chapter from Cortesi's 'De Cardinaltu'.* Rome, 1980.

Fortifications

GURRIERI, F. and MAZZONI, P. *La Fortezza da Basso: Un monumento per la città.* Florence, 1990.

HALE, J. R. *Renaissance Fortification: Art or Engineering?* London, 1977.

LAMBERINI, D. (ed.). *L'architettura militare veneta del Cinquecento* (proceedings of seminar held at Vicenza, 1982). Milan, 1988.

PEPPER, S. and ADAMS, N. *Firearms and Fortifications: Military Architecture and Siege Warfare in Sixteenth Century Siena.* Chicago, 1986.

Villas and Gardens

ACKERMAN, J. S. *The Villa: Form and Ideology of Country Houses* (A. W. Mellon lectures in the Fine Arts, 1985). Princeton, 1990.

AZZI VISENTINI, M. *L'Orto Botanico di Padova e il giardino del Rinascimento.* Milan, 1984.

BENTMANN, R. and MÜLLER, M. *Die Villa als Herrschafts-architektur: Versuch einer kunst- und sozialgeschichtlichen Analyse.* Frankfurt, 1970. English translation by T. Spence and D. Craven, as *The Villa as Hegemonic Architecture.* New Jersey and London, 1992.

COFFIN, D. R. *The Villa in the Life of Renaissance Rome.* Princeton, 1979.

COFFIN, D. R. *Gardens and Gardening in Papal Rome.* Princeton, 1991.

FORSSMAN, E. *Visible Harmony: Palladio's Villa Foscari at Malcontenta.* Stockholm, 1973.

HOLBERTON, P. *Palladio's Villas: Life in the Renaissance Countryside.* London, 1990.

LAZZARO, C. *The Italian Renaissance Garden: From the Conventions of Planting, Design and Ornament to the Grand Gardens of Sixteenth-Century Central Italy.* New Haven and London, 1990.

KOLB LEWIS, C. *The Villa Giustinian at Roncade* (Harvard Ph.D. dissertation, 1973). New York and London, 1977.

MURARO, M. *Venetian Villas: the History and Culture.* New York, 1986.

PRINZ, W. *Schloss Chambord und die Villa Rotonda in Vicenza: Studien zur Ikonologie.* Berlin, 1980.

REGIONAL CENTRES

BOLOGNA

MILLER, N. *Renaissance Bologna.* New York, 1989.

RICCI, G. *Bologna* (volume in series *La città nell storia d'Italia*). Rome and Bari, 1980.

FLORENCE

BORSI, F. *et al. Il potere e lo spazio: La scena del principe* (exh. cat.). Florence, 1980.

FANELLI, G. *Firenze architettura e città.* 2 vols. Florence, 1973.

FANELLI, G. *Firenze* (volume in series *La città nell storia d'Italia*). Rome and Bari, 1981.

GIUSTI, M. A. *Edilizia in Toscana da XV al XVII secolo.* Florence, 1990.

GOLDTHWAITE, R. A. *The Building of Renaissance Florence: An Economic and Social History.* Baltimore and London, 1980.

GENOA

POLEGGI, E. and CEVINI, P. *Genova* (volume in series *La città nell storia d'Italia*). Rome and Bari, 1981.

MANTUA

CHAMBERS, D. and MARTINEAU, J. *Splendours of the Gonzaga* (catalogue of exhibition at Victoria & Albert Museum). London and Milan, 1982.

NAPLES

DIVENUTO, F. *Napoli sacra del XVI secolo: Repertorio delle fabbriche religiose nella cronaca del gesuita Giovan Francesco Araldo.* Naples and Rome, 1990.

DE SETA, D. *Storia della Città di Napoli dalle origini al settecento.* Rome and Bari, 1973.

DE SETA, C. *Napoli* (volume in series *La città nell storia d'Italia*). Rome and Bari, 1981.

DE SETA, C. *Napoli fra Rinascimento e Illuminismo.* Naples, 1991.

PANE, R. *Il Rinascimento nell'Italia meridionale.* Vol. 1. Milan, 1975. Vol. 2. Milan, 1977.

ROSCI, M. *Architettura meridionale del Rinascimento.* Naples, 1983.

PADUA

BELLINATI, C. and PUPPI, L. *Padova: Basiliche e Chiese.* 2 vols. Vicenza, 1975.

PUPPI, L. and UNIVERSO, M. *Padova* (volume in series *La città nell storia d'Italia*). Rome and Bari, 1982.

PUPPI, L. and ZULIANI, F. (eds). *Padova: Case e Palazzi.* Vicenza, 1977.

PARMA

ADORNI, B. *L'architettura farnesiana a Parma 1545–1630.* 2 vols. Parma, 1982.

BANZOLA, V. (ed.). *Parma: la città storica.* Parma, 1978.

DA MARETO, F. *Chiese e conventi di Parma.* Parma, 1978.

PIACENZA

PIORENTINI, E. F. *Le chiese di Piacenza.* Piacenza, 1985.

ROME

Académie de France à Rome and Ecole française de Rome, *La Villa Médicis.* 3 vols. Rome, 1991.

CHASTEL, A. *The Sack of Rome 1527* (A. W. Mellon lectures in the Fine Arts, 1977). Princeton, 1983.

CHASTEL, A. (ed.). *Le Palais Farnèse: Ecole française de Rome.* 2 vols. Rome, 1980–2.

CEEN, A. *The Quartiere de' Banchi: Urban Planning in Rome in the first half of the Cinquecento.* New York and London, 1986.

FROMMEL, C. L. *Der römische Palastbau der Hochrenaissance.* 3 vols. Tübingen, 1973.

GAMRATH, H. *Roma sancta renovata: Studi sull'urbanistica di Roma nella seconda metà del secolo XVI, con particolare riferimento al pontificato di Sisto V (1585–90).* Rome, 1987.

GUIDONI, E. *L'urbanistica di Roma tra miti e progetti.* Bari and Rome, 1990.

INSOLERA, I. *Roma* (volume in series *La città nell storia d'Italia*). Rome and Bari, 1980.

RAMSEY, P. A. (ed.). *Rome in the Renaissance: the city and the myth.* Binghamton, N.Y., 1982.

ROBERTSON, C. *Il Gran Cardinale: Alessandro Farnese, Patron of the Arts.* New Haven and London, 1992.

RUGGIERI, G. *et al. Impronte sistine: Fabbriche civili minori; Interventi nel territorio; Restauri di monumenti nell'età di Sisto V.* Rome, 1991.

SALERNO, L. SPEZZAFERRO, L. and TAFURI, M. *Via Giulia: Un'utopia urbanistica del Cinquecento.* Rome, 1973.

SPEZZAFERRO, L. and ETITTONI, M. E. *Il Campidoglio e Sisto V.* Rome, 1991.

SABBIONETA

CONFURIUS, G. *Sabbioneta, oder die schöne Kunst der Stadtgründung.* Munich and Vienna, 1984.

MICARA, L. and SCALESSE, T. *Sabbioneta.* Rome, 1979.

TURIN

COMOLI MANDRACCI, V. *Torino* (volume in series *La città nell storia d'Italia*). Rome and Bari, 1983.

PASSANTI, M. *Architettura in Piemonte da Emanuele Filiberto all'Unità d'Italia 1563–1870: Genesi e comprensione dell'opera architettonica,* ed. G. Torretta. Turin, 1990.

POLLAK, M. D. *Turin 1564–1680: Urban Design, Military Culture, and the Creation of the Absolutist Capital.* Chicago, 1991.

VENICE

BELLAVITIS, G. and ROMANELLI, G. *Venezia* (volume in series *La città nell storia d'Italia*). Rome and Bari, 1985.

CALABI, D. and MORACHIELLO, P. *Rialto: le fabbriche e il ponte 1514–1591.* Turin, 1987.

CONCINA, F. *Venezia nell'età moderna: Struttura e funzioni.* Padua, 1989.

FOSCARI, A. and TAFURI, M. *L'armonia e il conflitti: La Chiesa di San Francesco della Vigna nella Venezia del '500.* Turin, 1983.

GIANIGHIAN, G. *Dietro i palazzi: tre secoli di architettura minore a Venezia 1492–1803* (catalogue of exhibition at Scuola Grande di San Giovanni Evangelista). Venice, 1984.

GOY, R. J. *Venetian Vernacular Architecture: Traditional Housing in the Venetian Lagoon.* Cambridge, 1989.

HOWARD, D. *The Architectural History of Venice.* London, 1980; revised edn 1987.

HUBALA, E. *Venedig: Baudenkmäler und Museen* (Reclams Kunstführer Italien). Stüttgart, 1974.

HUSE, N. and WOLTERS, W. *Venedig: die Kunst der Renaissance: Architektur, Skulptur, Malerei 1460–1590.* Munich, 1986. English translation by Edward Jephcott as *The Art of Renaissance Venice: Architecture, Sculpture and Painting 1460–1590.* Chicago and London, 1990.

LIEBERMAN, R. *Renaissance Architecture in Venice 1450–1540.* London, 1982.

MCANDREW, J. *Venetian Architecture of the Early Renaissance.* Cambridge, Mass. and London, 1980.

PUPPI, L. *et al. Architettura e Utopia nella Venezia del Cinquecento* (catalogue of exhibition in the Palazzo Ducale, Venice). Milan, 1980.

SOHM, P. L. *The Scuola Grande di San Marco 1437–1550: The Architecture of a Venetian Lay Confraternity* (Ph.D. dissertation, Johns Hopkins University, 1978). New York and London, 1982.

TAFURI, M. (ed.). *'Renovatio urbis': Venezia nell'età di Andrea Gritti (1523–1538)*. Rome, 1984.

TAFURI, M. *Venezia e il Rinascimento: Religione, scienza, architettura*. Turin, 1985. English translation by Jessica Levine as *Venice and the Renaissance*. Cambridge, Mass. and London, 1989.

ARCHITECTS

ALESSI

HOUGHTON BROWN, N. A. *The Milanese Architecture of Galeazzo Alessi* (Ph.D. dissertation, Columbia University, 1978). 2 vols. New York and London, 1982.

DE NEGRI, E. *et al. Galeazzo Alessi* (exh. cat.). Genoa, 1974.

LOTZ, W. *et al. Galeazzo Alessi e l'architettura del Cinquecento* (conference proceedings, Genoa, 1974). Genoa, 1975.

BRAMANTE

Studi Bramanteschi (conference proceedings, Milan-Urbino-Rome, 1970). Rome, 1974.

BRUSCHI, A. *Bramante*. Rome and Bari, 1973 (abbreviated edition of BRUSCHI, A. *Bramante architetto*. Rome and Bari, 1969). English translation by Peter Murray. London, 1977.

Graf WOLFF METTERNICH, F. and THOENES, C. *Die frühen St. Peter-Entwürfe, 1505–1514*. Tübingen, 1987.

BUONTALENTI

FARA, A. *Buontalenti: Architettura e teatro*. Florence, 1979.

FARA, A. *Bernardo Buontalenti: L'architettura, la guerra e l'elemento geometrico*. Genoa, 1988.

FALCONETTO

PUPPI, L. *et al. Alvise Cornaro e il suo tempo* (exh. cat.). Padua, 1980.

GENGA

PINELLI, A. and ROSSI, O. *Genga architetto: aspetti della cultura urbinate del primo 500*. Rome, 1971.

FRA GIOCONDO

FONTANA, V. *Fra' Giovanni Giocondo architetto 1433–c.1515*. Vicenza, 1988.

GIULIO ROMANO

FERRARI, D. and BELLUZZI, A. *Giulio Romano: Repertorio di fonti documentarie*. 2 vols. Rome, 1992.

GOMBRICH, E. H. *et al. Giulio Romano* (catalogue of exhibition held at the Palazzo del Tè, Mantua). Milan, 1989.

VERHEYEN, E. *The Palazzo del Te in Mantua: Images of Love and Politics*. Baltimore and London, 1977.

Giulio Romano (Atti del Convegno dell' Academia Nazionale Vigiliana, Mantua, 1989). Mantua, 1991.

LIGORIO

GASTON, R. (ed.). *Pirro Ligorio: Artist and Antiquarian* (proceedings of seminar at Villa I Tatti, 1983). Milan, 1988.

SMITH, G. *The Casino of Pius IV*. Princeton, 1977.

MICHELANGELO

ARGAN, G. C. and CONTARDI, B. *Michelangelo Architect*, trans. Marion L. Grayson. London, 1993.

MILLON, H. A. and SMYTH, C. H. *Michelangelo Architect: The façade of San Lorenzo and the drum and dome of St Peter's* (exh. cat., Florence and Washington). Milan, 1988.

NOVA, A. *Michelangelo architetto*. Milan, 1984.

THIES, H. *Michelangelo: Das Kapitol*. Munich, 1982.

WALLACE, W. E. *Michelangelo at San Lorenzo: The Genius as Entrepreneur*. Cambridge, 1994.

PALLADIO

ASSUNTO, R. *La Rotonda* (Novum Corpus Palladianum). Milan, 1988.

BARBIERI, F. *Architetture palladiane: Dalla pratica del cantiere alle immagini del Trattato*. Vicenza, 1992.

BOUCHER, B. *Andrea Palladio: the architect in his time*. New York, 1994.

BURNS, H. BOUCHER, B. and FAIRBAIRN, L. *Andrea Palladio 1508–1580: The portico and the farmyard* (Arts Council exh. cat.). London, 1975.

CEVESE, R. (ed.). *Mostra del Palladio* (catalogue of exhibition at Basilica Palladiana, Vicenza). Milan, 1973.

CHASTEL, A. and CEVESE, R. (eds). *Andrea Palladio: Nuovi contributi* (proceedings of seminar held at Vicenza, 1988). Milan, 1990.

FORSSMAN, E. *The Palazzo da Porto Festa in Vicenza* (Corpus Palladianum VIII). University Park and London, 1973.

FORSTER, K. and KUBELIK, M. *Palladio: Ein Symposium*. Rome, 1980.

LEWIS, D. *The Drawings of Andrea Palladio* (exh. cat.). Washington, 1981.

PUPPI, L. *Andrea Palladio*. 2 vols. Milan, 1973.

PUPPI, L. *Palladio Drawings*, trans. Jeremy Scott. New York, 1989.

PUPPI, L. (ed.). *Andrea Palladio: Il testo, l'immagine, la città* (exh. cat.). Vicenza, 1980.

PUPPI, L. *Palladio: Corpus dei disgni al Museo Civico di Vicenza*. Milan, 1989.

TAVERNOR, R. *Palladio and Palladianism*. London, 1991.

ZAUP, G. *Andrea Palladio e la sua committenza: Denaro e architettura nella Vicenza del Cinquecento*. Rome and Reggio Calabria, 1990.

PELLEGRINI

PELLEGRINI, P. *L'architettura*, ed. G. Panizza, with introduction by A. Buratti Mazotta. Milan, 1990.

PERUZZI

FAGIOLO, M. and MADONNA, M. L. (eds). *Baldassare Peruzzi: pittura, scena, e architettura nel Cinquecento*. Rome, 1987.

WURM, H. *Baldassare Peruzzi: Architekturzeichnungen*. Tübingen, 1984.

RAPHAEL

CALVANI, A. *et al. Raffaello e l'architettura a Firenze nella prima metà del Cinquecento* (exh. cat.). Florence, 1984.

CHASTEL, A. *et al. Raffaello a Roma* (proceedings of 1983 conference). Rome, 1986.

FROMMEL, C. L. RAY, S. and TAFURI, M. *Raffaello architetto*, with section on 'Raffaello e l'antico' by H. Burns and A. Nesselrath. Milan, 1984.

JONES, R. and PENNY, N. *Raphael*, New Haven and London, 1983.

ANTONIO DA SANGALLO THE ELDER

COZZI, M. *Antonio da Sangallo il Vecchio e l'architettura del Cinquecento in Valdichiana*. Genoa, 1992.

ANTONIO DA SANGALLO THE YOUNGER

FROMMEL, C. L. and ADAMS, N. *The Architectural Drawings of Antonio da Sangallo the Younger and his Circle*, vol. I: *Fortifications, Machines, and Festival Architecture*. Cambridge, Mass. and London, 1994.

SPAGNESI, G. (ed.). *Antonio da Sangallo il Giovane: La vita e l'opera* (proceedings of XXII Congresso di Storia dell'Architettura). Rome, 1986.

SANMICHELI

PUPPI, L. *Michele Sanmicheli, architetto di Verona*. Padua, 1971.

SANSOVINO

BOUCHER, B. *The Sculpture of Jacopo Sansovino*. 2 vols. New Haven and London, 1991 (includes biography and discussion of tombs, the Loggetta, etc.).

HOWARD, D. *Jacopo Sansovino: Architecture and Patronage in Renaissance Venice*. New Haven and London, 1975; revised edn. 1987.

ROMANELLI, G. *Ca' Corner della Ca' Granda: architettura e committenza nella Venezia del Cinquecento*. Venice, 1993.

VASARI

CONFORTI, C. *Giorgio Vasari architetto*. Milan, 1994.

SATKOWSKI, L. *Giorgio Vasari: Architect and Courtier*. Princeton, 1993.

VIGNOLA

FANTINI BONVICINI, O. *Caprarola: Il Palazzo e la Villa Farnese*. Rome, 1973.

ORAZI, A. M. *Jacopo Barozzi da Vignola 1528–1550: Apprendistato di un architetto bolognese*. Rome, 1982.

Index

References to the notes are given to the page on which the note occurs, followed by the chapter number and the number of the note; thus 181 (8)⁵ indicates page 181, Chapter 8, note 5.

Photographic Acknowledgements

Paul Davies: titlepage, 14, 32, 41, 42, 49, 50, 51, 52, 61, 93, 98, 107, 114, 115, 121, 123, 155, 164, 167, 169, 170, 173, 175, 177, 231, 243, 251, 275, 276, 277; GFN: 1, 47, 61, 69, 82, 141, 156, 192, 196, 197, 199, 203, 217, 218, 221, 222, 227, 263; Soane Museum: 2; Brogi, Florence: 3, 4, 5, 55, 65A, 70, 149, 201, 212, 220, 224, 268, 271; Brügner, Rome: 6; Istituto di Storia dell'Arte, Pisa: 7; Vasari, Rome: 8, 22, 186; TCI: 9; J.S. Ackerman, *The Architecture of Michelangelo*: 10, 74; Bibliotheca Hertziana, Rome: 12, 13, 23, 35, 44, 80, 110, 138, 158, 180, 181, 182, 183, 184, 202, 209, 211; Albertina, Vienna: 15, 31, 195; Uffizi, Florence: 18, 25, 29, 163, 166; Cooper, London: 19; Kleinhempel, Hamburg: 21; Anderson, Rome: 24, 56, 64, 67, 72, 75, 81, 154, 200, 238, 257, 264; Soprintendenza, Florence: 26, 270; Paul Mellon Collection, Washington: 27, 28; Scala: 33, 86, 104, 134, 135, 146, 153; Sansaini, Rome: 37; after Gutensohn-Thuermer: 39; Fototeca Unione, Rome: 40; Gerhard Krämer: 43; P. Letarouilly, *Edifices de Rome moderne*: 45, 65B, 76, 179; Dr J. Zänker: 48; after A. Schiavo: 53; Alinari, Florence: 54, 57, 58, 66, 79, 88, 112, 125, 145, 147, 178, 207, 213, 216, 240, 249, 256A, 268, 274; C.L. Frommel, *Die Farnesina und Peruzis architektonisches Frühwerk*: 59; Nationalmuseum Stockholm: 62, 194; Metropolitan Museum of Art, New York: 73; The Metropolitan Museum of Art, New York, Dick Fund, 1941: 83, 142, 143, 144; Mella, Milan: 84, 230; Eugene Marseglia: 85; Vaghi, Parma: 87; Dr J. Ganz, Frauenfeld, Switzerland: 89, 160; after Gazzola: 90; after Fabriczy: 91; Fiorentini, Venice: 92, 94, 95, 99, 100; after Ronzani-Luciolli: 96, 97, 101, 102, 103, 105, 106, 108; W. Lotz: 109, 157; after a drawing by Giacomo della Strada in Düsseldorf: 111; Calzolari, Mantua: 113, 120, 261; Landesbildestelle Rheinland, Düsseldorf: 116; Soprintendenza, Mantua: 117; *Storia di Mantova*: 118; Osvaldo Böhm, Venice: 124, 259; G. Paolo Marton: 126, 246, 252; after Cicognara-Diedo-Selva: 127; Stegmann-Geymüller: 129, 130, 267; Bencini, Florence: 131; GEKS: 132; after Apolloni: 133; Dr Hilde Lotz: 136, 265, 266, 272, 273; Leonard von Matt, Buochs: 139; Arch. Fot. Gall. Vat.: 148, 159, 198; Dr Ohr: 150; after an engraving by Calcagni: 151; after Pagliarino: 152; W. Friedlaender, *Das Kasino Pius des Vierten*: 161; Dr Ernest Nash, Rome: 162; Private Collection: 165; Dr Carl Lamb: 172; Hönig, Frankfurt: 174; after Lewine: 185; Fotostudio Lotz, Grünwald: 187; after Soprintendenza ai Monumenti, Rome: 189; R. Moscioni, Rome: 190; after an engraving by de'Rossi: 191; Foto Marburg: 193; Massimo Marchelli: 204; Publifoto, Genoa: 205, 208; after Cassina: 210; The Trustees of the Victoria and Albert Museum, London: 214; Musei Civici, Milan: 215; Bibliotheca Ambrosiana, Milan: 219; after Houghton Brown: 222; Rotalfoto, Milan: 225; W. Hiersche, *Pellegrino di Pellegrini als Architekt*: 226; after drawings in the Bianconi Collection: 228; I. Kohte, *Die Kirche S. Lorenzo in Mailand*: 229; Pellegrino, Mondovi: 233; Museo Civico, Vicenza: 237; O. Bertotti-Scamozzi, *Le Fabbriche e i Disegni di Andrea Palladio*: 239; © Archivio Veneziano photograph: Sarah Quill: 241, 254, 256B; after *Corpus Palladianum*: 242, 245, 253; Cinecolorfoto, Vicenza: 244; Vajenti, Vicenza: 248; P. Paoletti, *La Scuola Grande di San Marco*: 255; C. Gurlitt, *Geschichte des Barockstils in Italien*: 258; Museo Civico, Padua: 262.

All the line drawings were drawn or adapted for the first edition of this book by Sheila Gibson, with the exception of the following: 16; Paul White: 74; J. S. Ackerman and Frank Krüger: 140; Gerhard Krämer: 185B.

Architecture in Italy 1500–1600

Wolfgang Lotz
Revised by Deborah Howard

This classic work presents a stimulating survey of the most exciting and innovative period in the history of architecture. Described as 'The most comprehensive and reliable introduction to Italian Renaissance architecture' by the *Times Literary Supplement*, it was first published in 1974 as the second part of a volume examining Italian architecture in the fifteenth and sixteenth centuries.

Moving between the various centres of architectural activity throughout Italy, Wolfgang Lotz discusses with authority the work of such well-known architects as Bramante, Giulio Romano, Michelangelo and Palladio. He focuses on the different schemes for St Peter's in Rome, the projects connected with the church of S. Lorenzo in Florence and the churches and villas designed by Palladio in and around Venice. And yet Lotz also goes beyond the more familiar locations, architects and buildings to conquer less well-known territories, exploring Piedmont and Vitozzi and ending with a study of *bizzarrie*.

Lotz's distinguished and highly readable text is now reissued accompanied by a wide range of beautiful illustrations and a critical introduction and updated bibliography by Deborah Howard. Dr Howard assesses Lotz's standing as an architectural historian, and surveys the developments in the discipline and the new material published since the first edition. In so doing the book is given a continuing relevance and is set to remain the standard work on Italian architecture in the Cinquecento.

Wolfgang Lotz was curator of the photograph collection of the Kunsthistorisches Institut in Florence and Deputy Director of the Zentralinstitut für Kunstgeschichte in Munich. He taught at Vasser College and at the Institute of Fine Arts, New York University. Until his retirement in 1980 he was Director of the Bibliotheca Hertziana at the Max-Planck-Institut in Rome. Professor Lotz published widely in the field of the art and architecture of the Italian Renaissance and Baroque.

Deborah Howard is a Fellow of St John's College, Cambridge and Librarian of the Faculty of Architecture and History of Art, University of Cambridge. Dr Howard has published several books on architecture including *Jacopo Sansovino: Architecture and Patronage in Renaissance Venice* (Yale University Press).